Circle 38

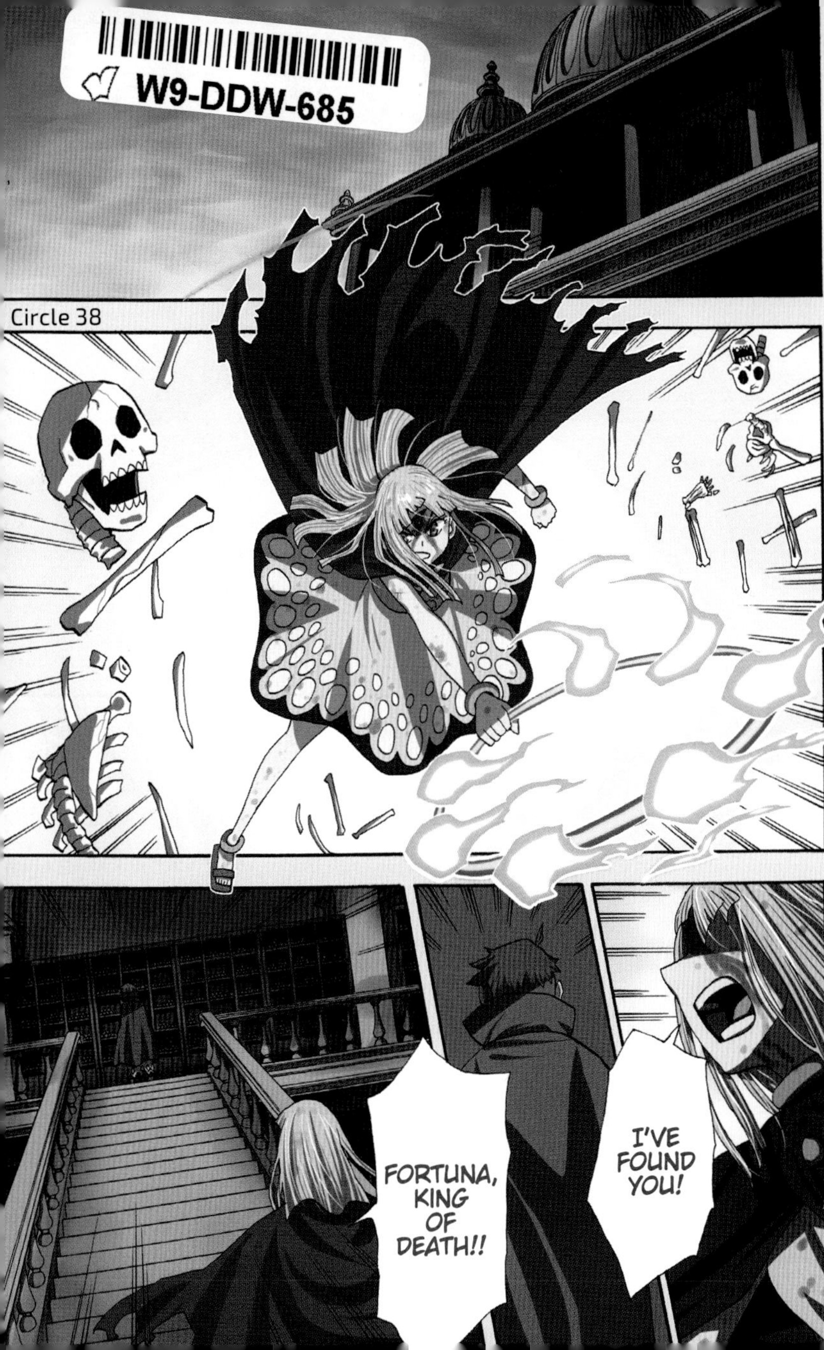
I'VE FOUND YOU!
FORTUNA, KING OF DEATH!!

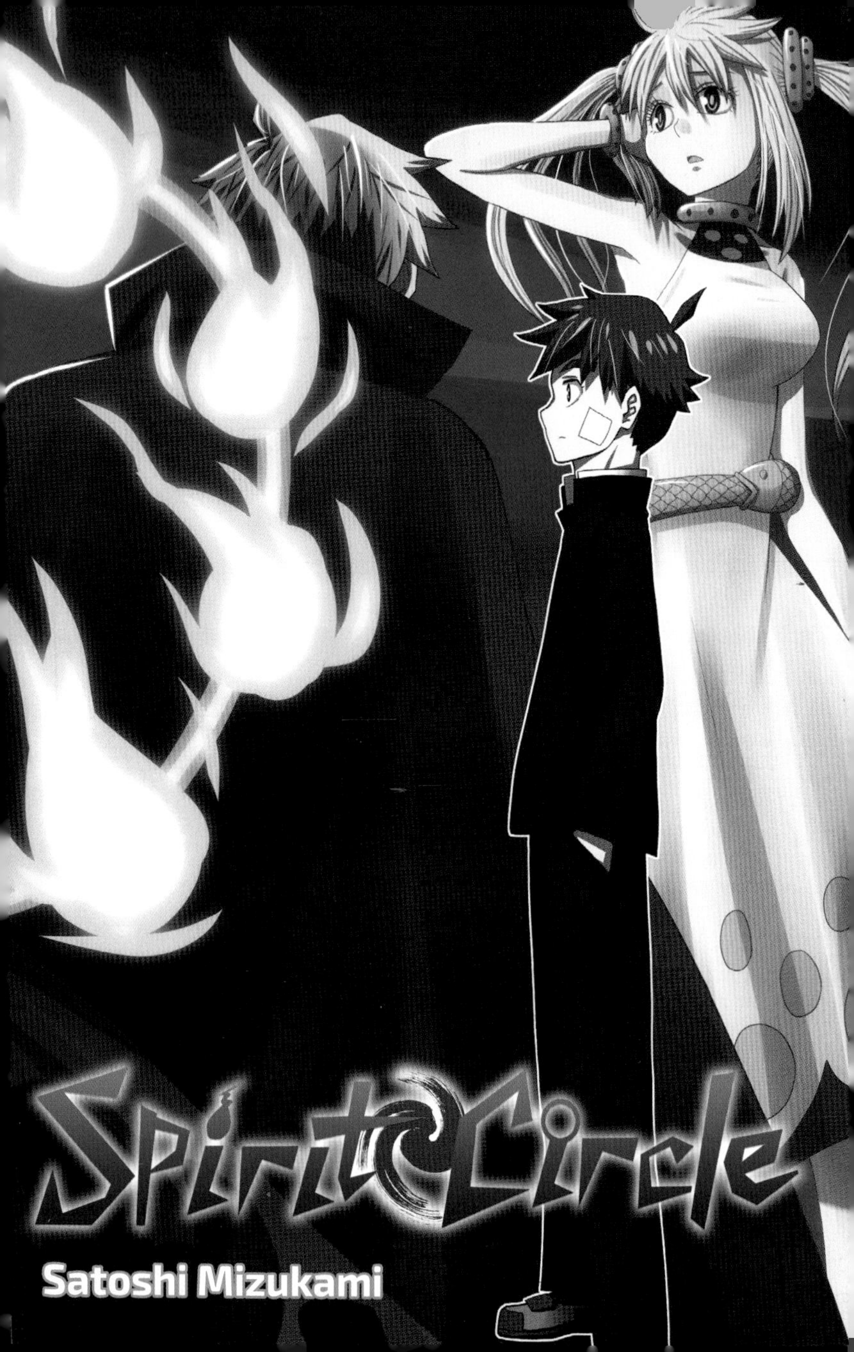
Spirit Circle
Satoshi Mizukami

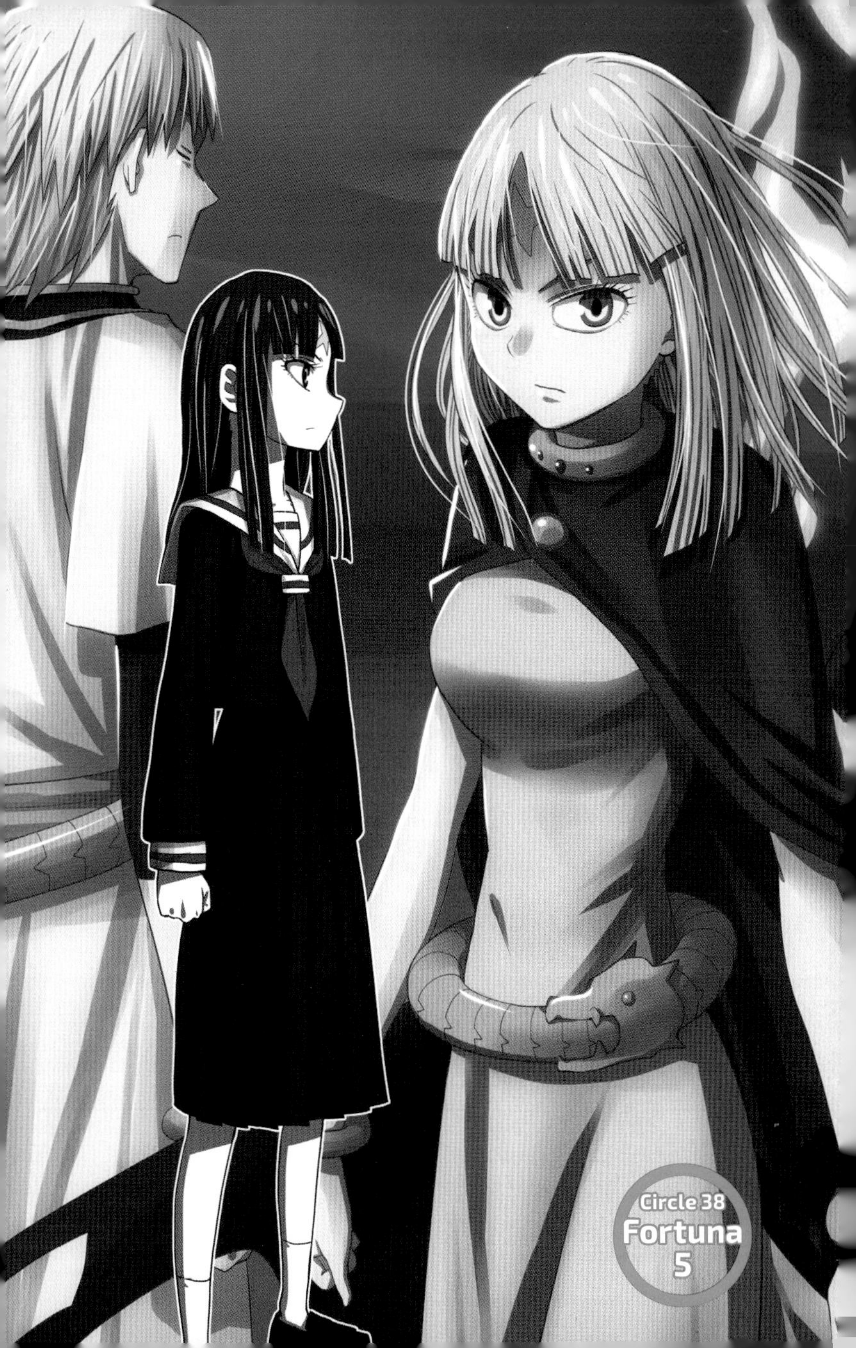
Circle 38
Fortuna
5

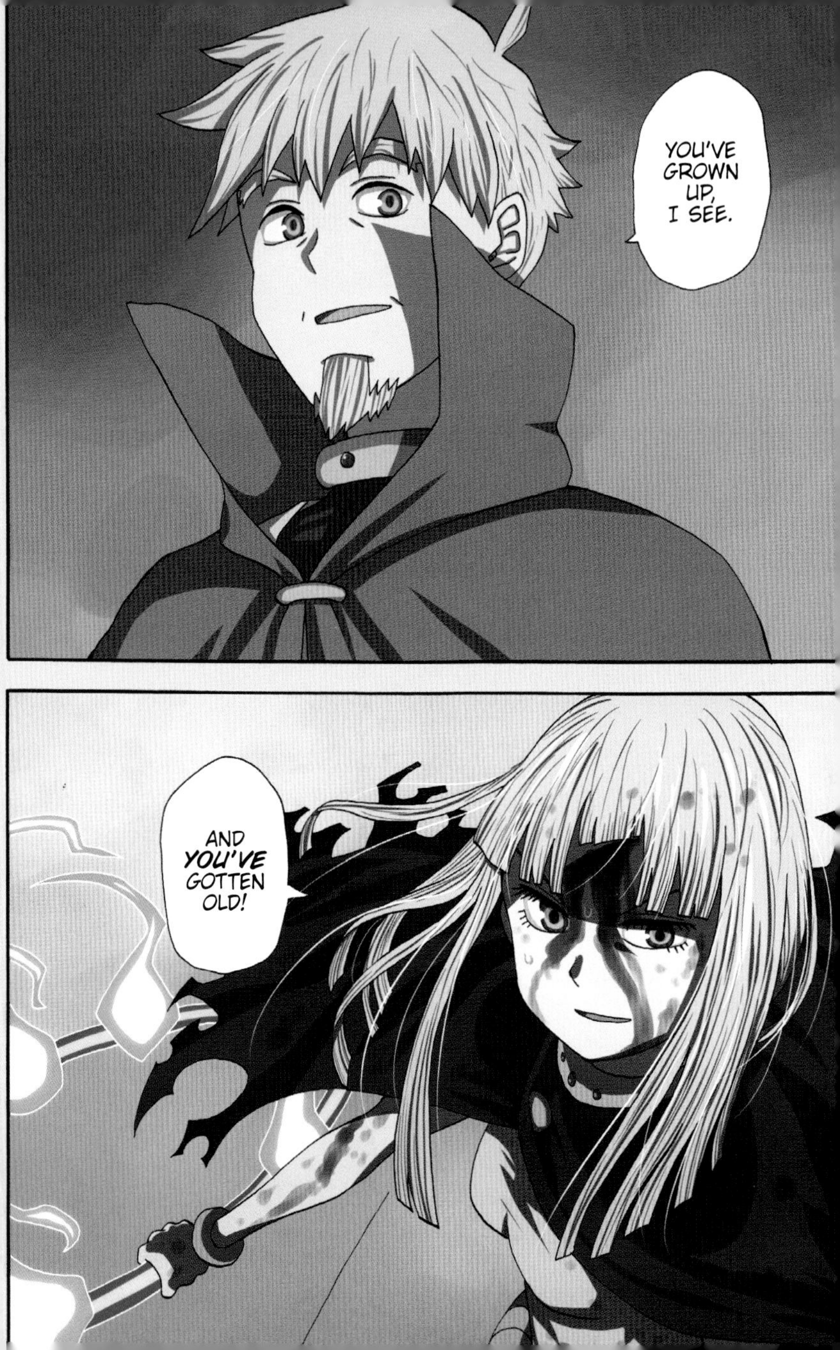
YOU'VE GROWN UP, I SEE.
AND YOU'VE GOTTEN OLD!

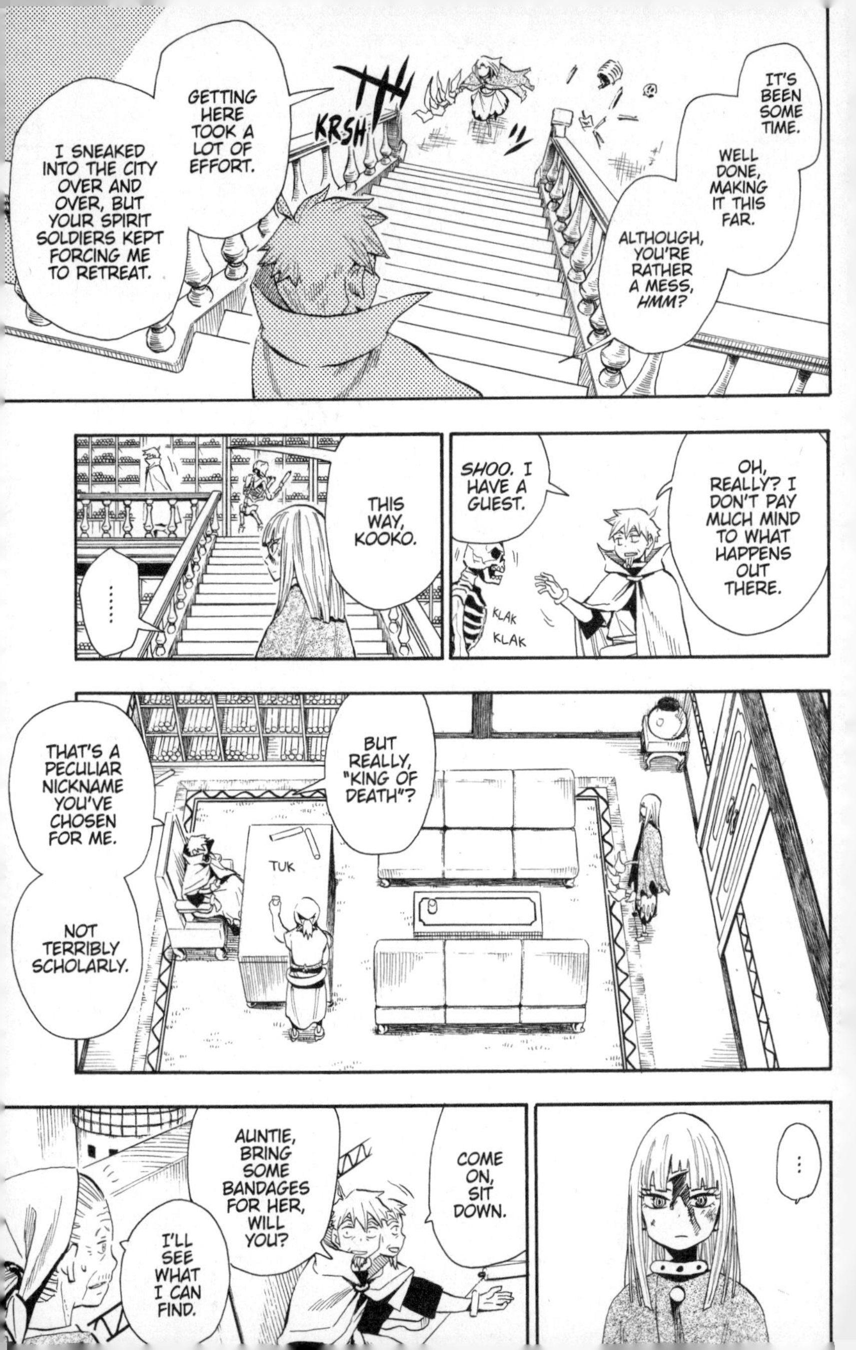
IT'S BEEN SOME TIME.
WELL DONE, MAKING IT THIS FAR.
ALTHOUGH, YOU'RE RATHER A MESS, *HMM?*
KRSH
GETTING HERE TOOK A LOT OF EFFORT.
I SNEAKED INTO THE CITY OVER AND OVER, BUT YOUR SPIRIT SOLDIERS KEPT FORCING ME TO RETREAT.
OH, REALLY? I DON'T PAY MUCH MIND TO WHAT HAPPENS OUT THERE.
SHOO. I HAVE A GUEST.
KLAK KLAK
THIS WAY, KOOKO.
......
BUT REALLY, "KING OF DEATH"?
TUK
THAT'S A PECULIAR NICKNAME YOU'VE CHOSEN FOR ME.
NOT TERRIBLY SCHOLARLY.
...
COME ON, SIT DOWN.
AUNTIE, BRING SOME BANDAGES FOR HER, WILL YOU?
I'LL SEE WHAT I CAN FIND.

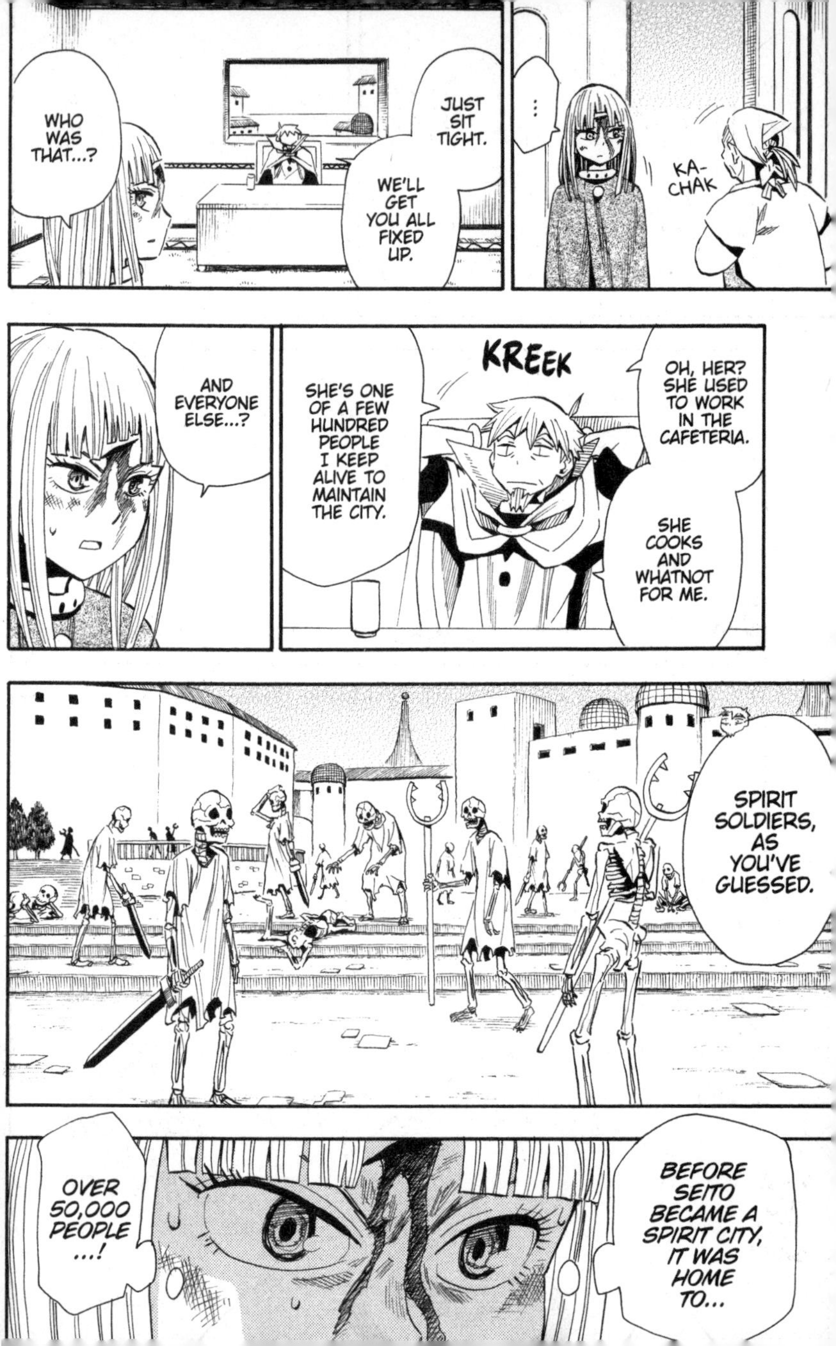
...
KA-CHAK
JUST SIT TIGHT.
WE'LL GET YOU ALL FIXED UP.
WHO WAS THAT...?
OH, HER? SHE USED TO WORK IN THE CAFETERIA.
KREEK
SHE COOKS AND WHATNOT FOR ME.
SHE'S ONE OF A FEW HUNDRED PEOPLE I KEEP ALIVE TO MAINTAIN THE CITY.
AND EVERYONE ELSE...?
SPIRIT SOLDIERS, AS YOU'VE GUESSED.
BEFORE SEITO BECAME A SPIRIT CITY, IT WAS HOME TO...
OVER 50,000 PEOPLE ...!

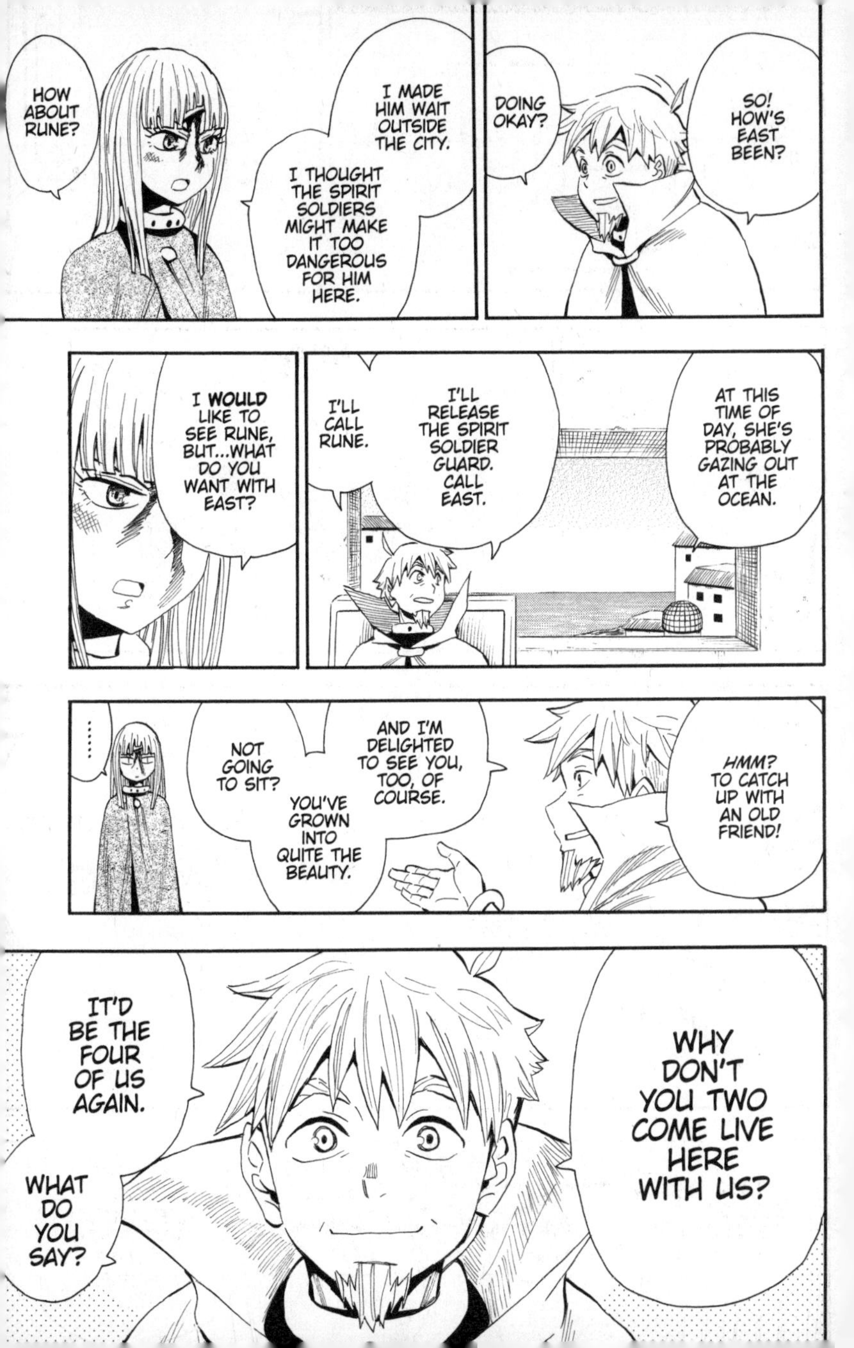
SO! HOW'S EAST BEEN?
DOING OKAY?
I MADE HIM WAIT OUTSIDE THE CITY.
I THOUGHT THE SPIRIT SOLDIERS MIGHT MAKE IT TOO DANGEROUS FOR HIM HERE.
HOW ABOUT RUNE?
AT THIS TIME OF DAY, SHE'S PROBABLY GAZING OUT AT THE OCEAN.
I'LL RELEASE THE SPIRIT SOLDIER GUARD. CALL EAST.
I'LL CALL RUNE.
I **WOULD** LIKE TO SEE RUNE, BUT...WHAT DO YOU WANT WITH EAST?
HMM? TO CATCH UP WITH AN OLD FRIEND!
AND I'M DELIGHTED TO SEE YOU, TOO, OF COURSE.
YOU'VE GROWN INTO QUITE THE BEAUTY.
NOT GOING TO SIT?
......
WHY DON'T YOU TWO COME LIVE HERE WITH US?
IT'D BE THE FOUR OF US AGAIN.
WHAT DO YOU SAY?

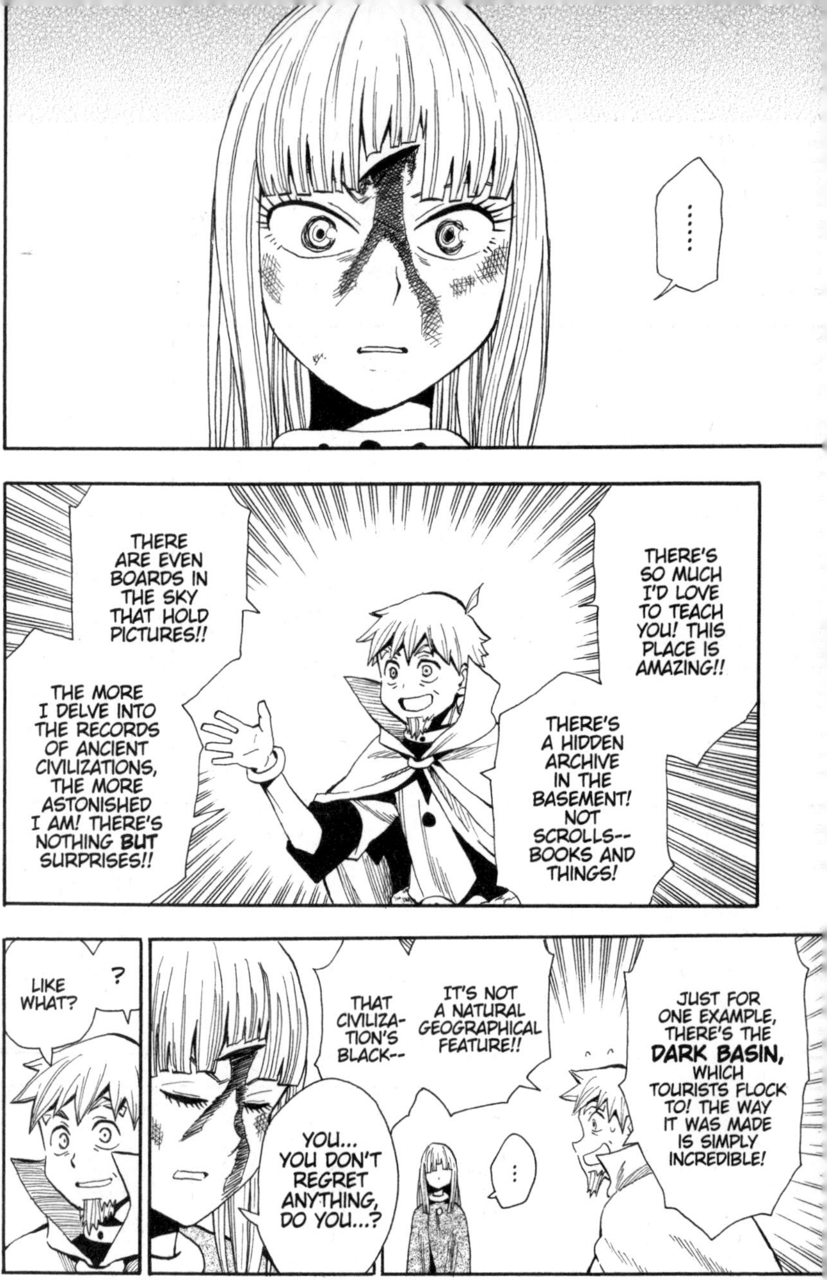
......
THERE'S SO MUCH I'D LOVE TO TEACH YOU! THIS PLACE IS AMAZING!!
THERE'S A HIDDEN ARCHIVE IN THE BASEMENT! NOT SCROLLS-- BOOKS AND THINGS!
THERE ARE EVEN BOARDS IN THE SKY THAT HOLD PICTURES!!
THE MORE I DELVE INTO THE RECORDS OF ANCIENT CIVILIZATIONS, THE MORE ASTONISHED I AM! THERE'S NOTHING **BUT** SURPRISES!!
JUST FOR ONE EXAMPLE, THERE'S THE **DARK BASIN,** WHICH TOURISTS FLOCK TO! THE WAY IT WAS MADE IS SIMPLY INCREDIBLE!
...
IT'S NOT A NATURAL GEOGRAPHICAL FEATURE!!
THAT CIVILIZA-TION'S BLACK--
YOU... YOU DON'T REGRET ANYTHING, DO YOU...?
?
LIKE WHAT?

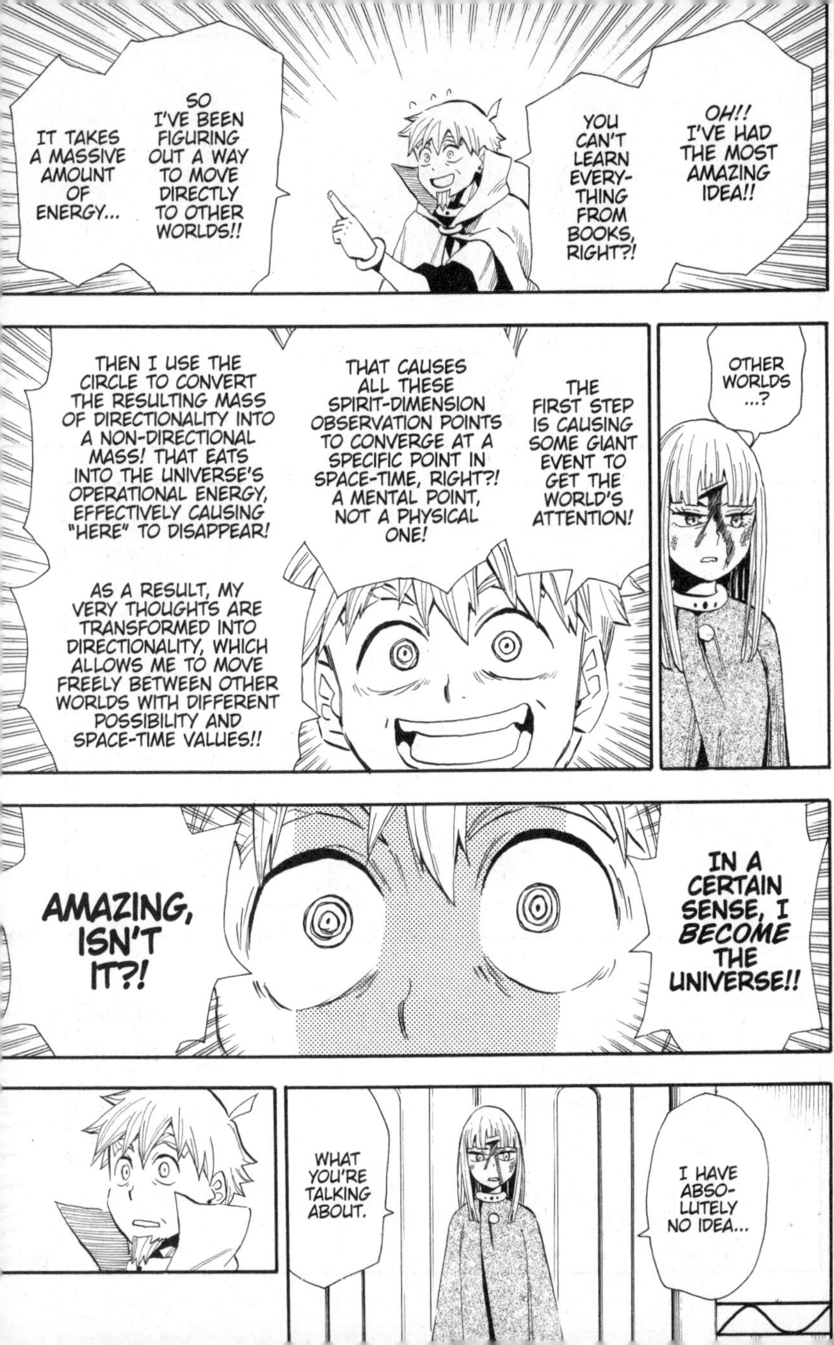
OH!! I'VE HAD THE MOST AMAZING IDEA!!
YOU CAN'T LEARN EVERY-THING FROM BOOKS, RIGHT?!
SO I'VE BEEN FIGURING OUT A WAY TO MOVE DIRECTLY TO OTHER WORLDS!!
IT TAKES A MASSIVE AMOUNT OF ENERGY...
OTHER WORLDS ...?
THE FIRST STEP IS CAUSING SOME GIANT EVENT TO GET THE WORLD'S ATTENTION!
THAT CAUSES ALL THESE SPIRIT-DIMENSION OBSERVATION POINTS TO CONVERGE AT A SPECIFIC POINT IN SPACE-TIME, RIGHT?! A MENTAL POINT, NOT A PHYSICAL ONE!
THEN I USE THE CIRCLE TO CONVERT THE RESULTING MASS OF DIRECTIONALITY INTO A NON-DIRECTIONAL MASS! THAT EATS INTO THE UNIVERSE'S OPERATIONAL ENERGY, EFFECTIVELY CAUSING "HERE" TO DISAPPEAR!
AS A RESULT, MY VERY THOUGHTS ARE TRANSFORMED INTO DIRECTIONALITY, WHICH ALLOWS ME TO MOVE FREELY BETWEEN OTHER WORLDS WITH DIFFERENT POSSIBILITY AND SPACE-TIME VALUES!!
IN A CERTAIN SENSE, I *BECOME* THE UNIVERSE!!
AMAZING, ISN'T IT?!
I HAVE ABSO-LUTELY NO IDEA...
WHAT YOU'RE TALKING ABOUT.

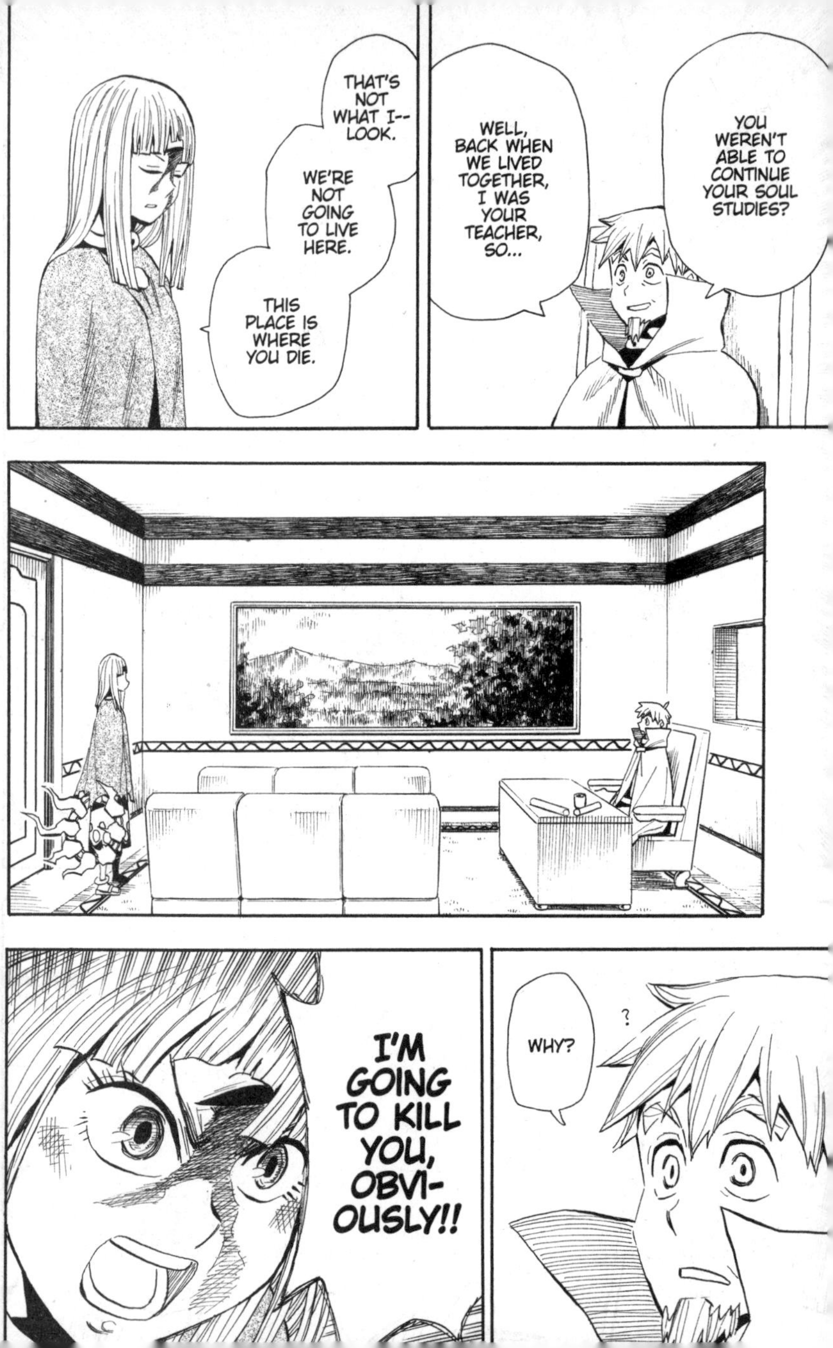
YOU WEREN'T ABLE TO CONTINUE YOUR SOUL STUDIES?
WELL, BACK WHEN WE LIVED TOGETHER, I WAS YOUR TEACHER, SO...
THAT'S NOT WHAT I-- LOOK.
WE'RE NOT GOING TO LIVE HERE.
THIS PLACE IS WHERE YOU DIE.
?
WHY?
I'M GOING TO KILL YOU, OBVI-OUSLY!!

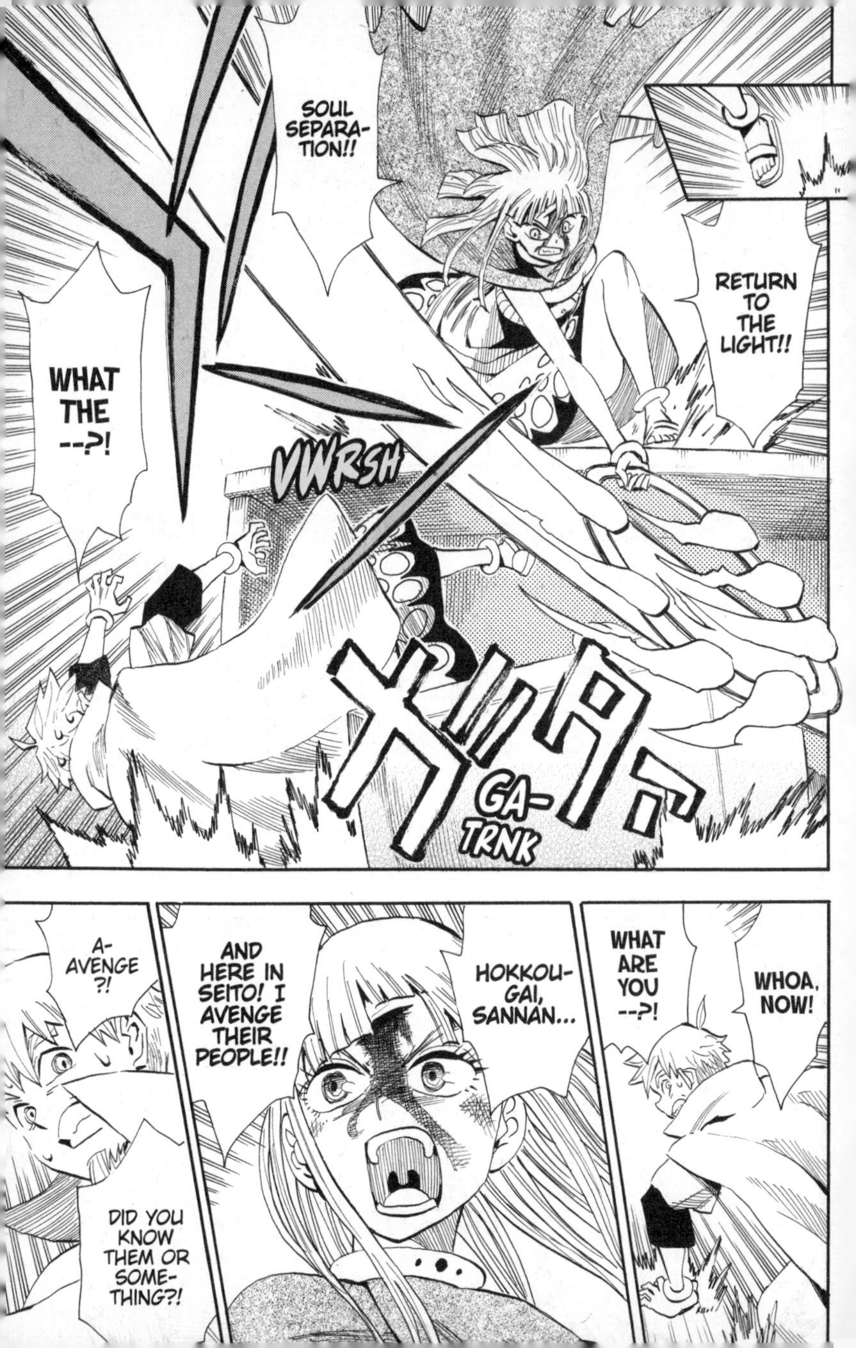
RETURN TO THE LIGHT!!
SOUL SEPARATION!!
WHAT THE --?!
VWRSH
GA-TRNK
WHOA, NOW!
WHAT ARE YOU --?!
HOKKOU-GAI, SANNAN...
AND HERE IN SEITO! I AVENGE THEIR PEOPLE!!
A-AVENGE?!
DID YOU KNOW THEM OR SOMETHING?!

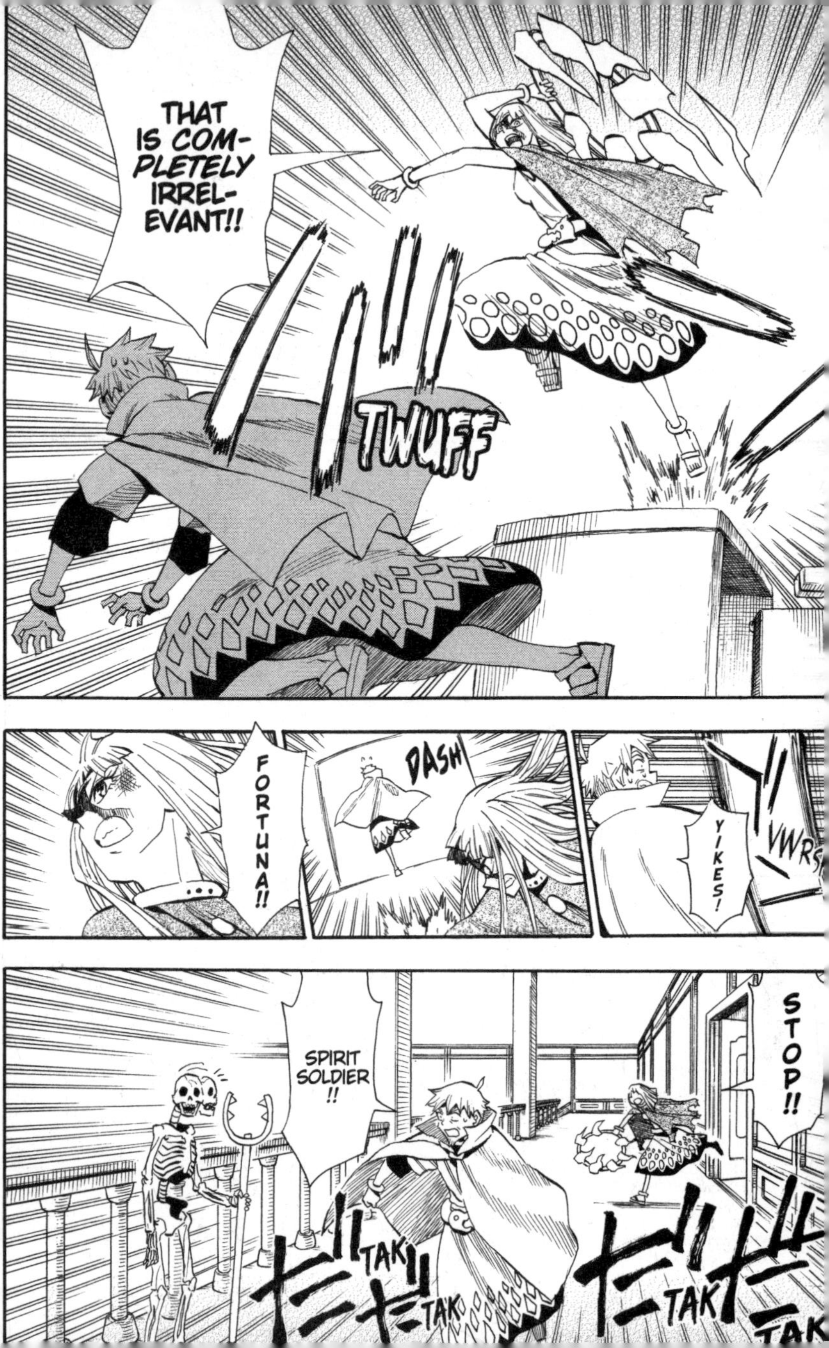
THAT IS COMPLETELY IRRELEVANT!!
TWUFF
YIKES!
VWRS
DASH
FORTUNA!!
STOP!!
SPIRIT SOLDIER!!
TAK
TAK
TAK
TAK

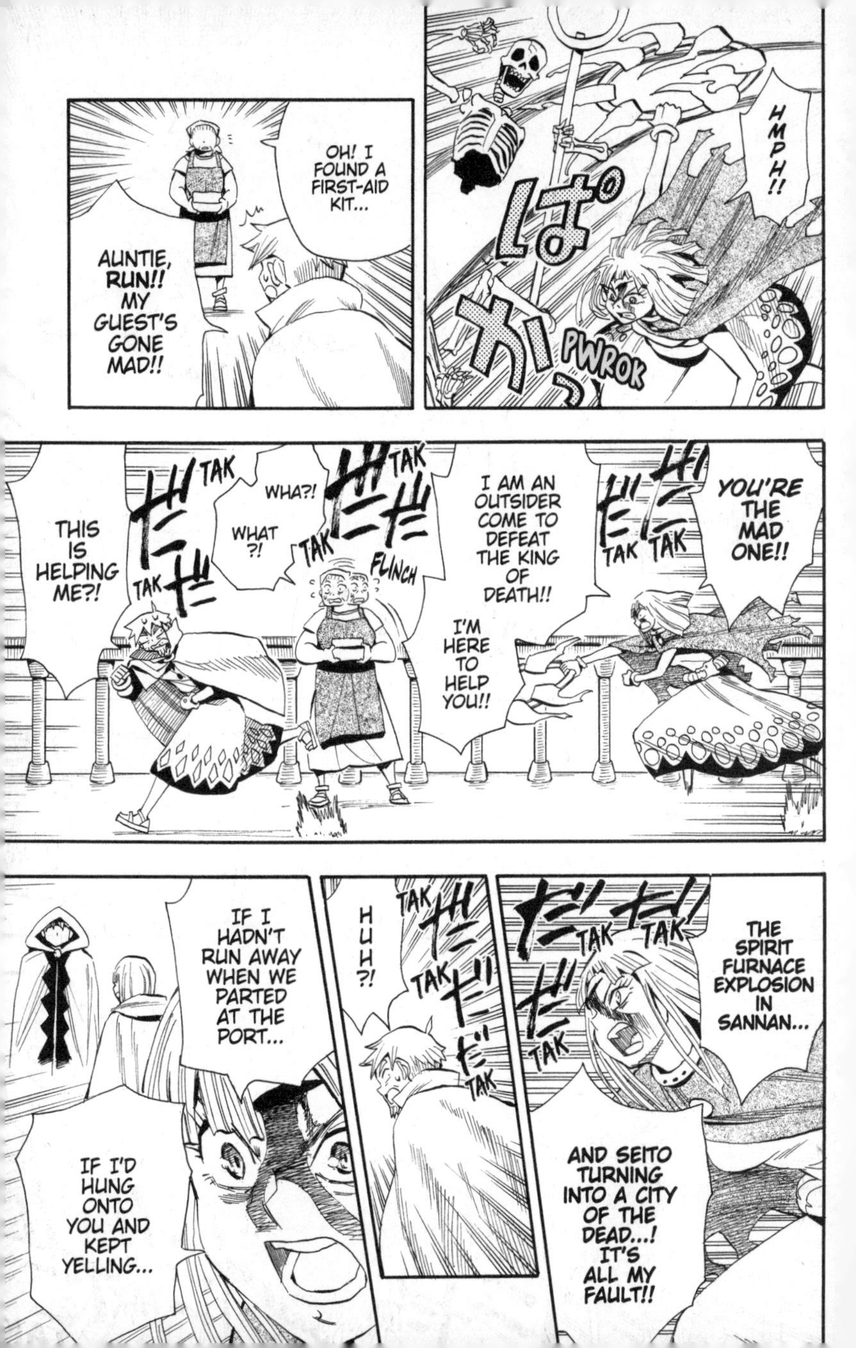
HMPH!!
ぱかっ
PWROK
OH! I FOUND A FIRST-AID KIT...
AUNTIE, RUN!! MY GUEST'S GONE MAD!!
YOU'RE THE MAD ONE!!
TAK TAK
I AM AN OUTSIDER COME TO DEFEAT THE KING OF DEATH!!
I'M HERE TO HELP YOU!!
TAK
FLINCH
TAK
WHA?!
WHAT?!
TAK
THIS IS HELPING ME?!
TAK
THE SPIRIT FURNACE EXPLOSION IN SANNAN...
TAK TAK
TAK
AND SEITO TURNING INTO A CITY OF THE DEAD...! IT'S ALL MY FAULT!!
TAK
TAK
TAK
HUH?!
IF I HADN'T RUN AWAY WHEN WE PARTED AT THE PORT...
IF I'D HUNG ONTO YOU AND KEPT YELLING...

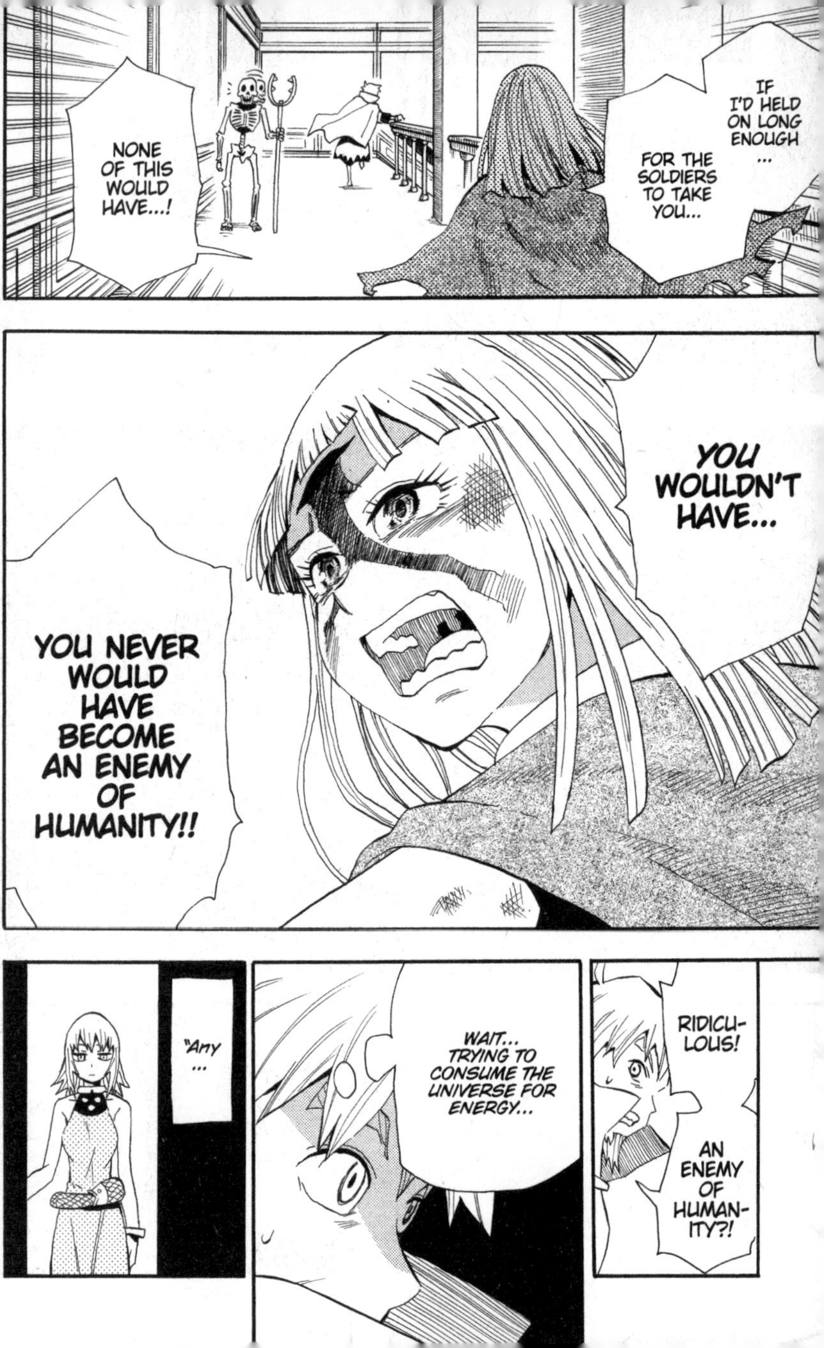
IF I'D HELD ON LONG ENOUGH ...
FOR THE SOLDIERS TO TAKE YOU...
NONE OF THIS WOULD HAVE...!
YOU WOULDN'T HAVE...
YOU NEVER WOULD HAVE BECOME AN ENEMY OF HUMANITY!!
RIDICU-LOUS!
AN ENEMY OF HUMAN-ITY?!
WAIT... TRYING TO CONSUME THE UNIVERSE FOR ENERGY...
"Any ...

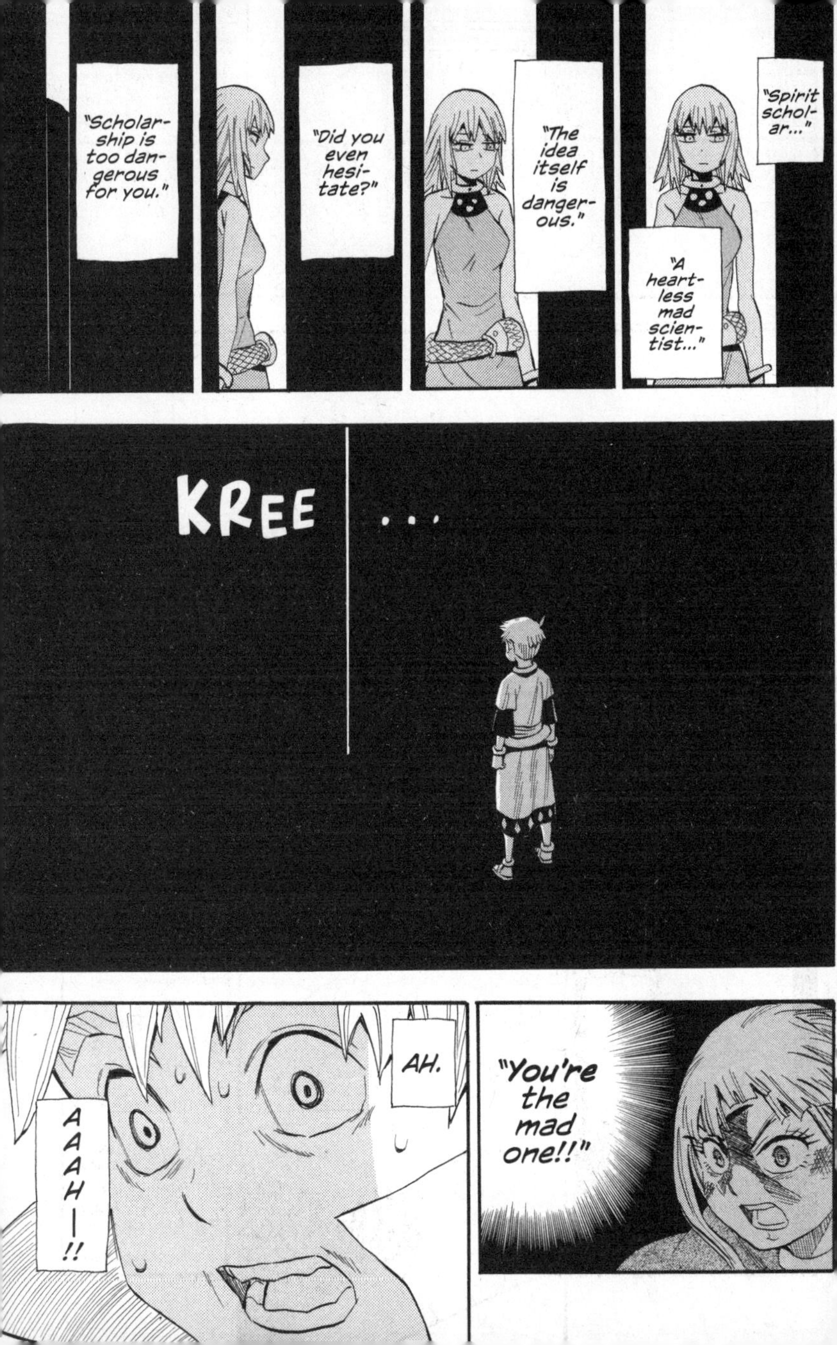
"Spirit scholar..."
"A heartless mad scientist..."
"The idea itself is dangerous."
"Did you even hesitate?"
"Scholarship is too dangerous for you."
...
KREE
"You're the mad one!!"
AH.
AAAAH—!!

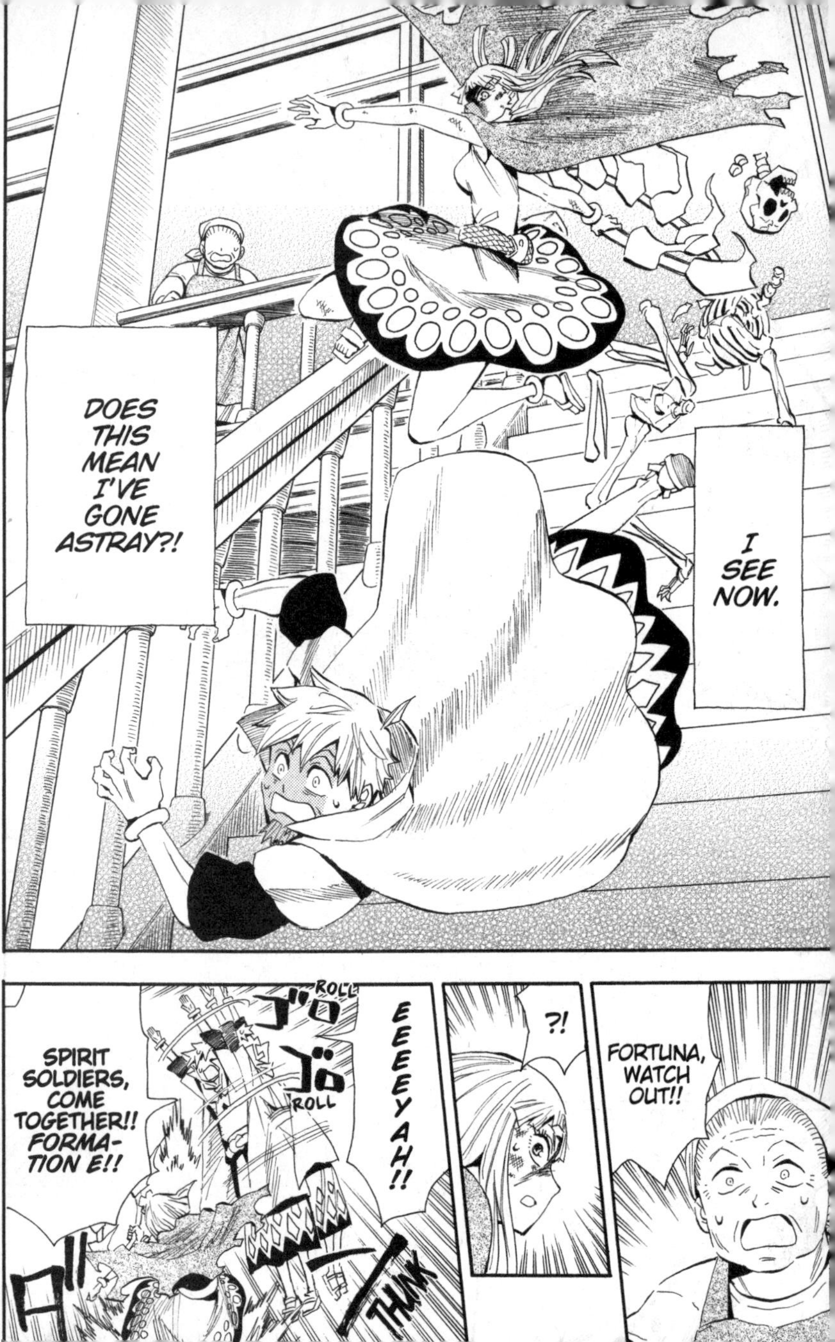
I SEE NOW.
DOES THIS MEAN I'VE GONE ASTRAY?!
FORTUNA, WATCH OUT!!
?!
EEEEYAH!!
ゴロ
ROLL
ゴロ
ROLL
SPIRIT SOLDIERS, COME TOGETHER!! FORMATION E!!
THUNK

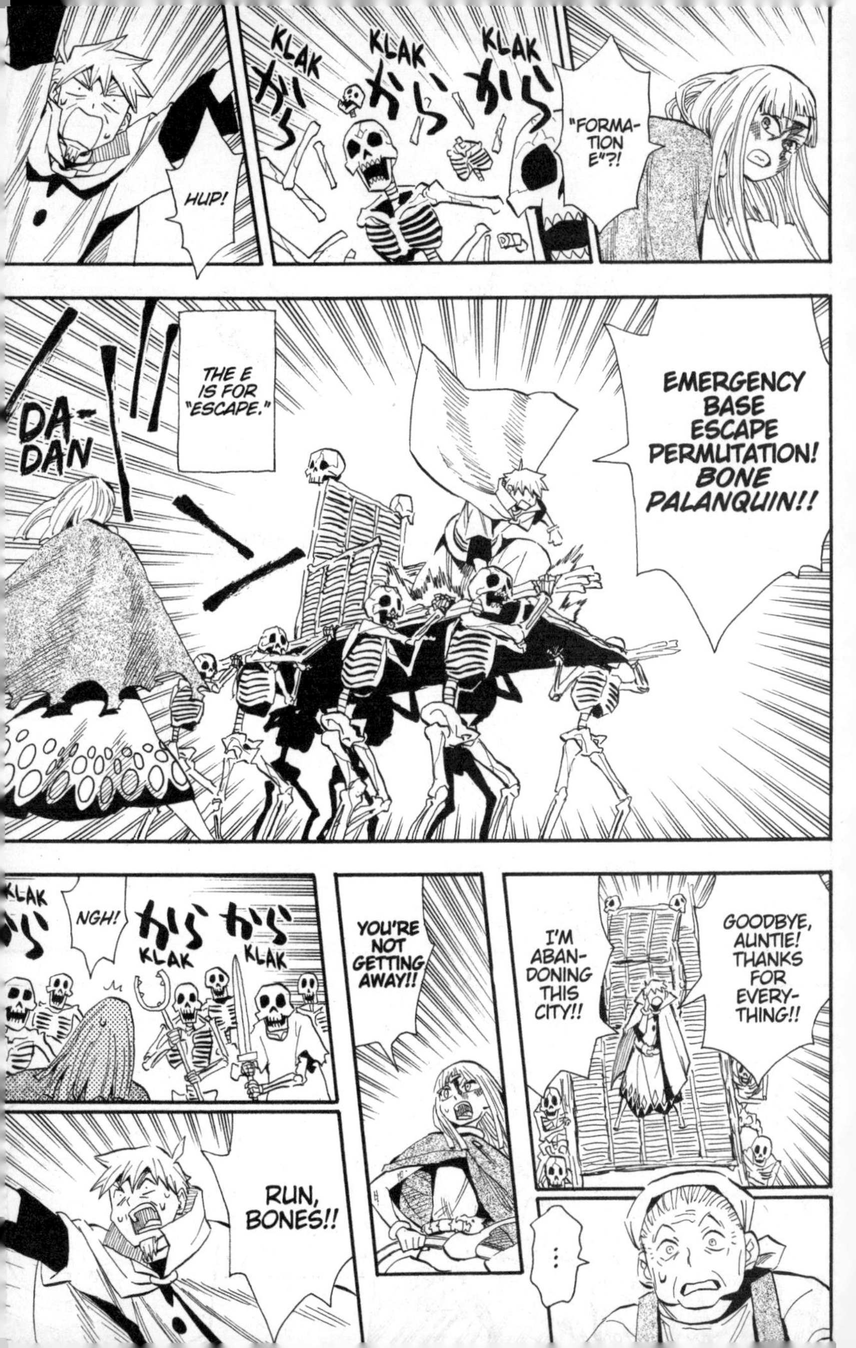
"FORMATION E"?!
KLAK
から
KLAK
から
KLAK
から
HUP!
EMERGENCY BASE ESCAPE PERMUTATION! BONE PALANQUIN!!
THE E IS FOR "ESCAPE."
DA-DAN
GOODBYE, AUNTIE! THANKS FOR EVERYTHING!!
I'M ABANDONING THIS CITY!!
...
YOU'RE NOT GETTING AWAY!!
から
KLAK
から
KLAK
NGH!
KLAK
から
RUN, BONES!!

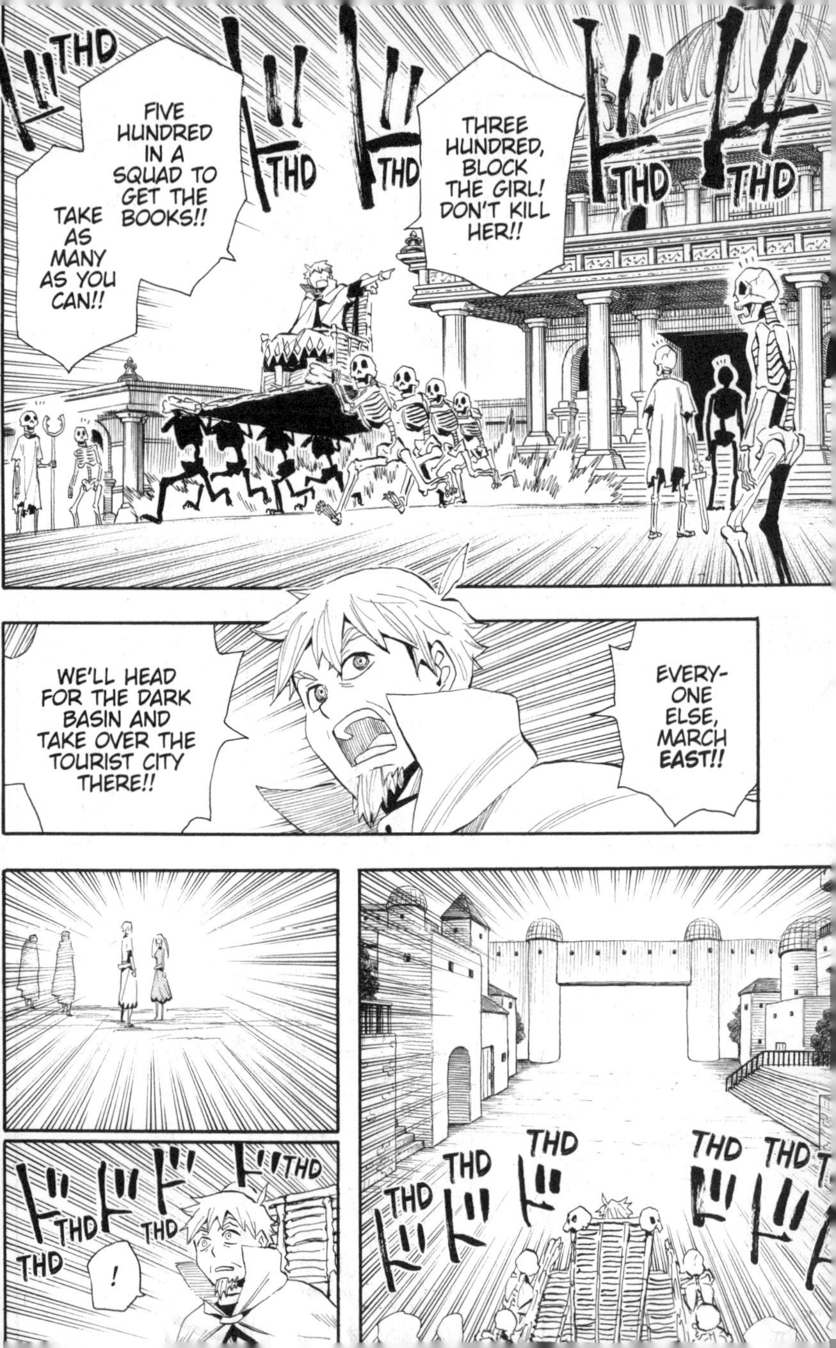
THD
THD
THREE HUNDRED, BLOCK THE GIRL! DON'T KILL HER!!
THD
THD
FIVE HUNDRED IN A SQUAD TO GET THE BOOKS!!
TAKE AS MANY AS YOU CAN!!
THD
EVERY-ONE ELSE, MARCH EAST!!
WE'LL HEAD FOR THE DARK BASIN AND TAKE OVER THE TOURIST CITY THERE!!
THD
THD
THD
THD
THD
THD
THD
THD
THD
!

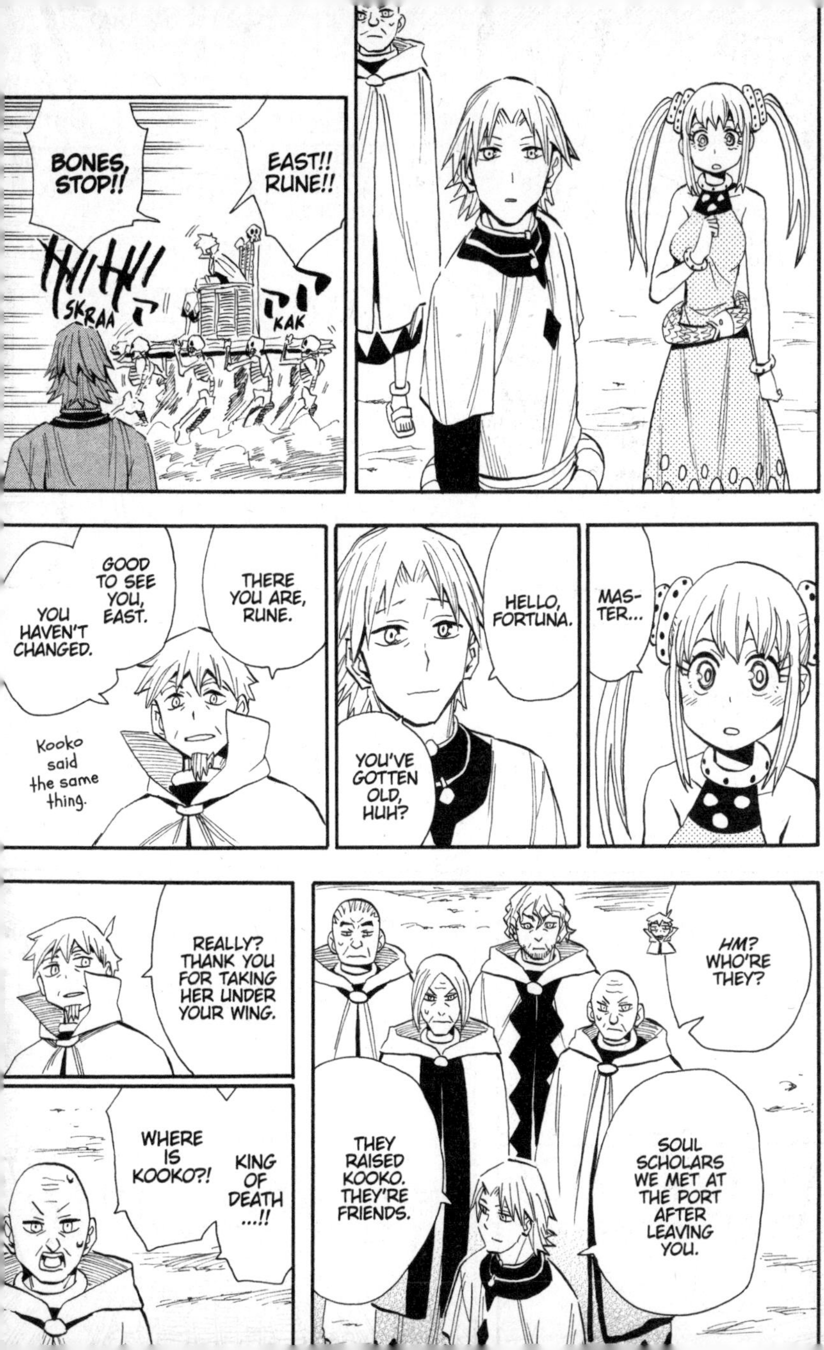
EAST!! RUNE!!
BONES, STOP!!
SKRAA
KAK
MAS-TER...
HELLO, FORTUNA.
YOU'VE GOTTEN OLD, HUH?
THERE YOU ARE, RUNE.
GOOD TO SEE YOU, EAST.
YOU HAVEN'T CHANGED.
Kooko said the same thing.
HM? WHO'RE THEY?
SOUL SCHOLARS WE MET AT THE PORT AFTER LEAVING YOU.
THEY RAISED KOOKO. THEY'RE FRIENDS.
REALLY? THANK YOU FOR TAKING HER UNDER YOUR WING.
KING OF DEATH ...!!
WHERE IS KOOKO?!

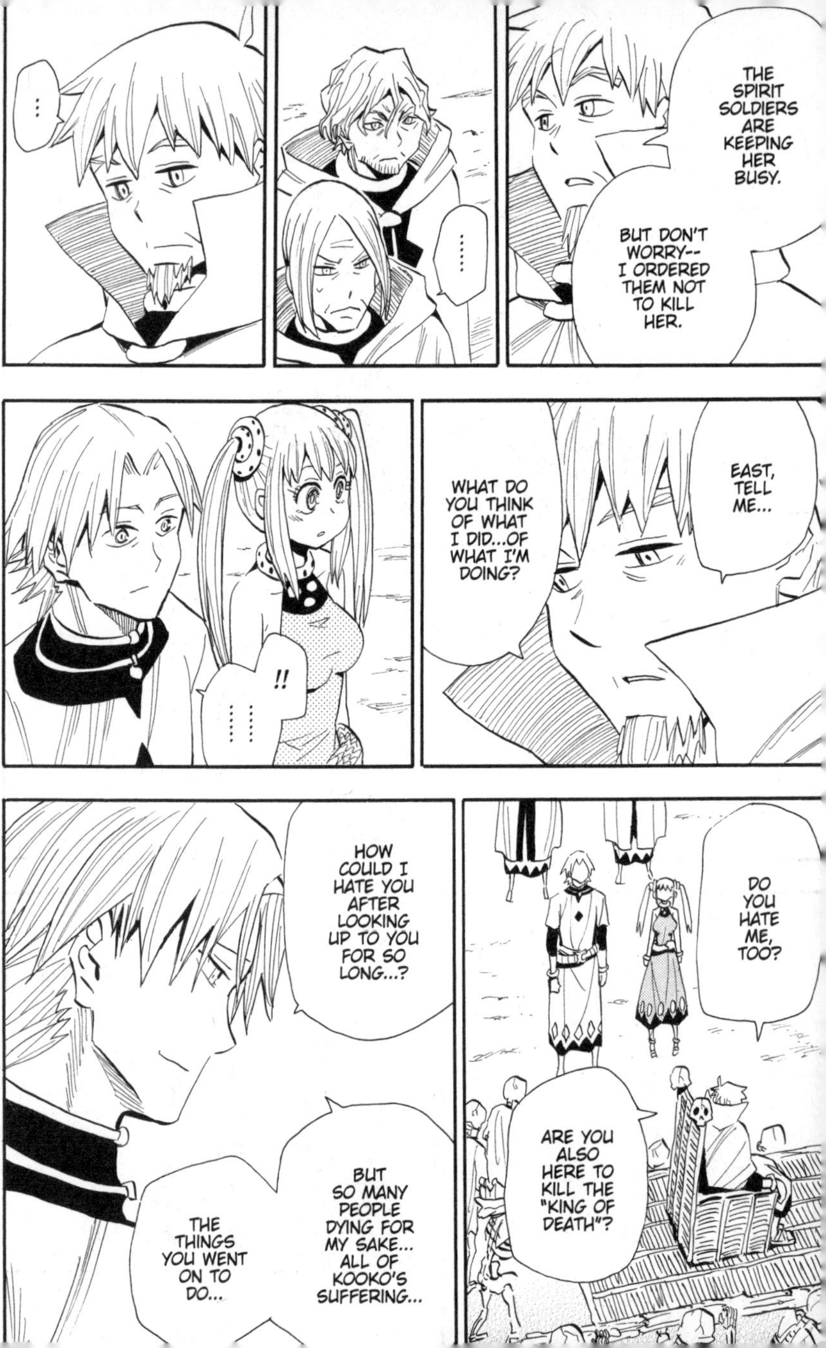
THE SPIRIT SOLDIERS ARE KEEPING HER BUSY.
BUT DON'T WORRY-- I ORDERED THEM NOT TO KILL HER.
......
...
EAST, TELL ME...
WHAT DO YOU THINK OF WHAT I DID...OF WHAT I'M DOING?
!!
......
DO YOU HATE ME, TOO?
ARE YOU ALSO HERE TO KILL THE "KING OF DEATH"?
HOW COULD I HATE YOU AFTER LOOKING UP TO YOU FOR SO LONG...?
BUT SO MANY PEOPLE DYING FOR MY SAKE... ALL OF KOOKO'S SUFFERING...
THE THINGS YOU WENT ON TO DO...

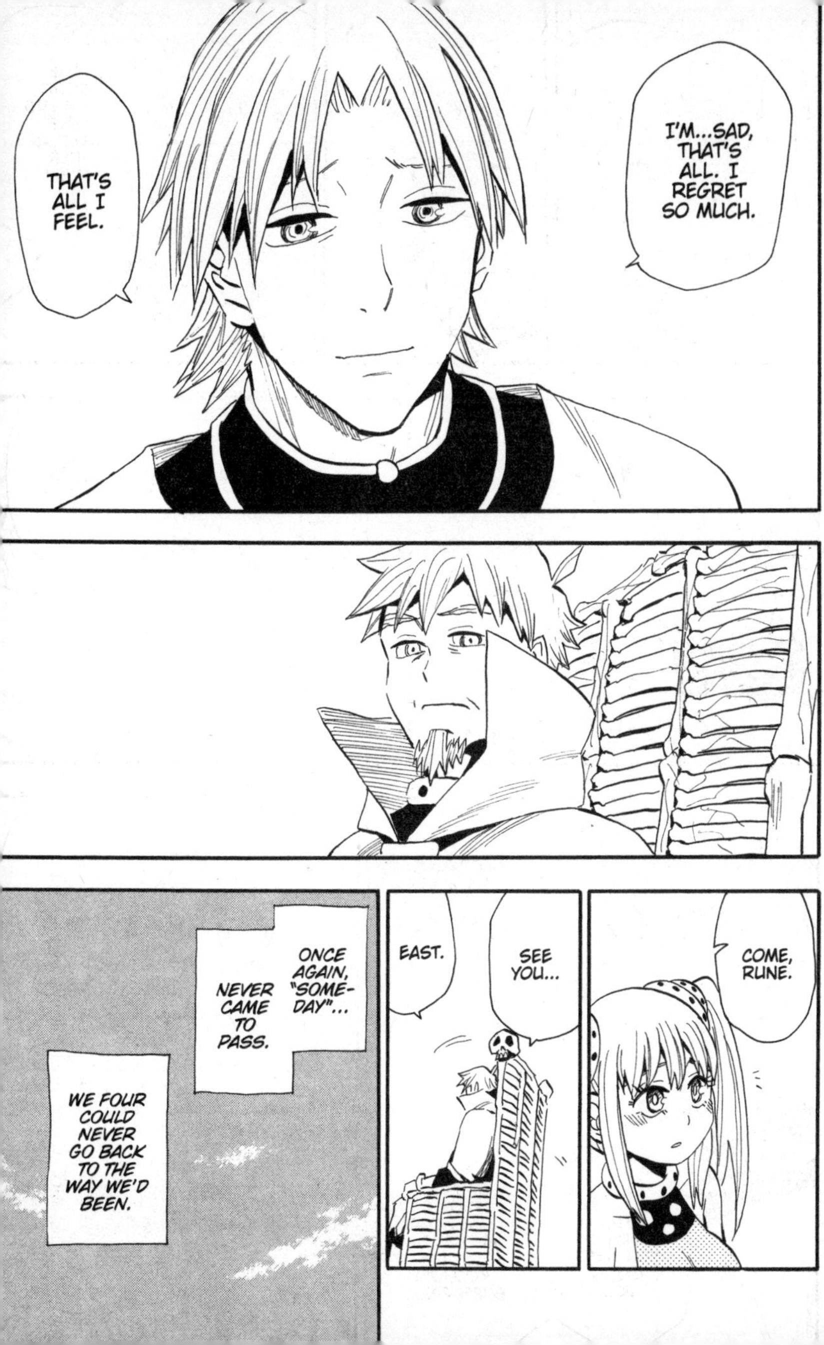
I'M...SAD, THAT'S ALL. I REGRET SO MUCH.
THAT'S ALL I FEEL.
COME, RUNE.
SEE YOU...
EAST.
ONCE AGAIN, "SOME-DAY"...
NEVER CAME TO PASS.
WE FOUR COULD NEVER GO BACK TO THE WAY WE'D BEEN.

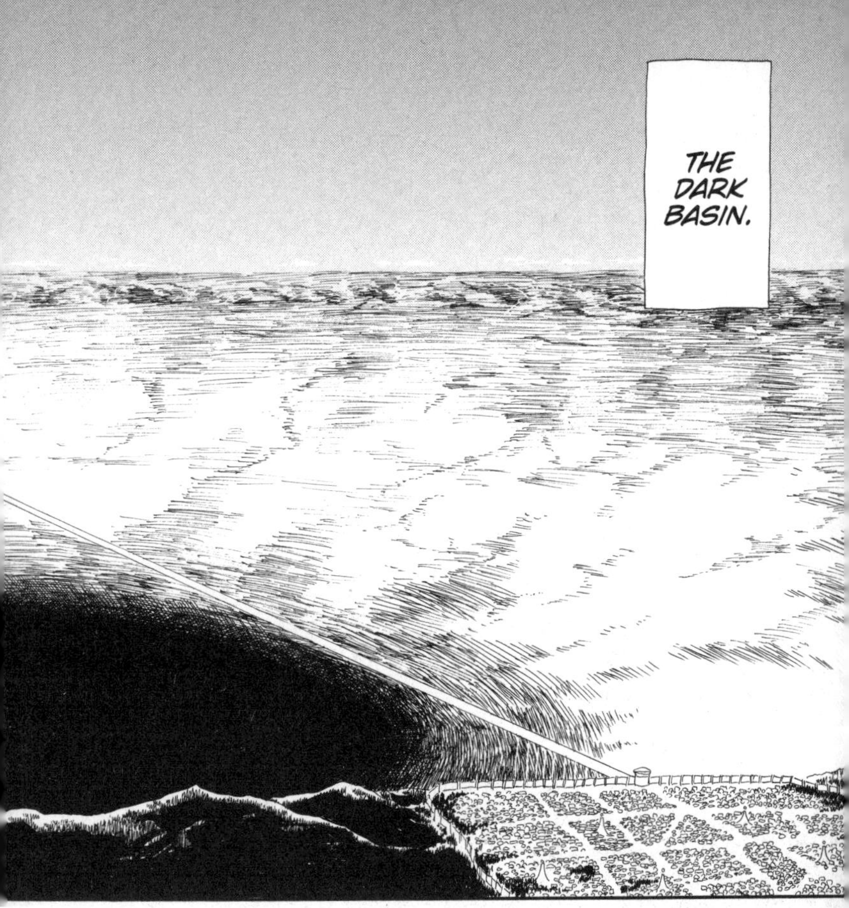
THE DARK BASIN.

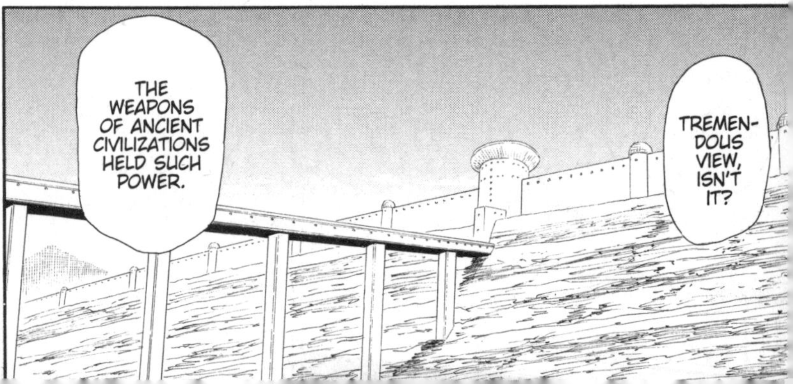
TREMEN-DOUS VIEW, ISN'T IT?
THE WEAPONS OF ANCIENT CIVILIZATIONS HELD SUCH POWER.

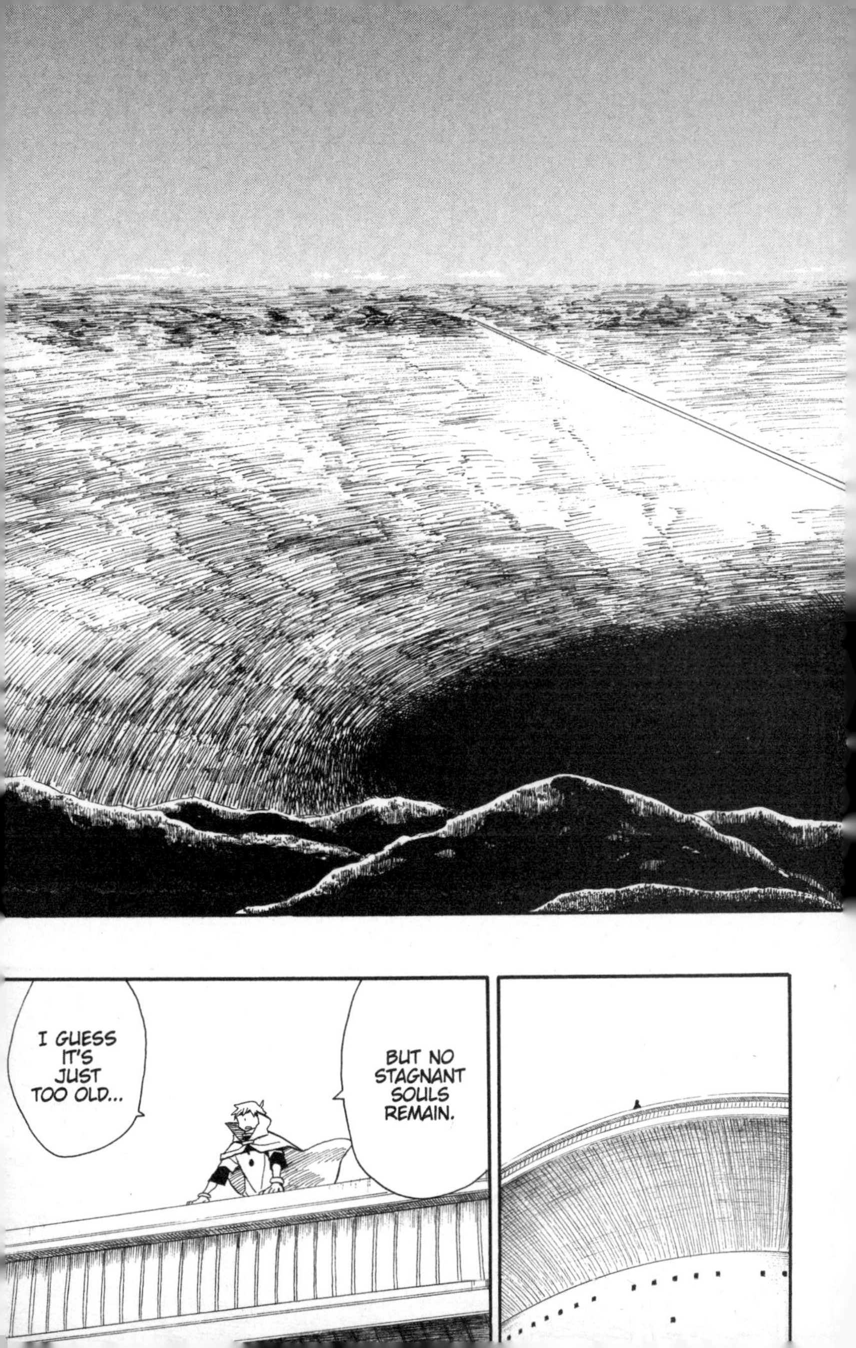
BUT NO STAGNANT SOULS REMAIN.
I GUESS IT'S JUST TOO OLD...

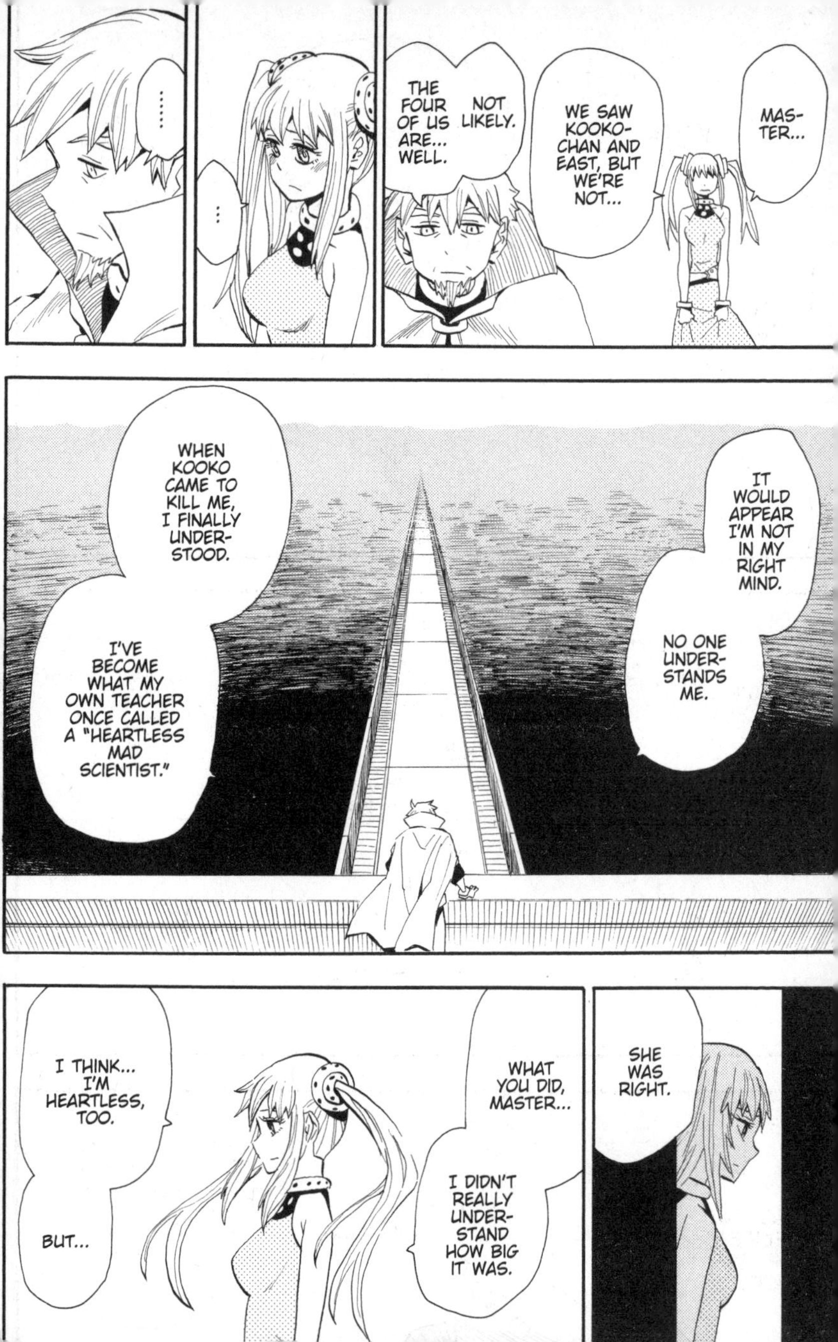

MAS-TER...
WE SAW KOOKO-CHAN AND EAST, BUT WE'RE NOT...
NOT LIKELY.
THE FOUR OF US ARE... WELL.
...
......
IT WOULD APPEAR I'M NOT IN MY RIGHT MIND.
NO ONE UNDER-STANDS ME.
WHEN KOOKO CAME TO KILL ME, I FINALLY UNDER-STOOD.
I'VE BECOME WHAT MY OWN TEACHER ONCE CALLED A "HEARTLESS MAD SCIENTIST."
SHE WAS RIGHT.
WHAT YOU DID, MASTER...
I DIDN'T REALLY UNDER-STAND HOW BIG IT WAS.
I THINK... I'M HEARTLESS, TOO.
BUT...

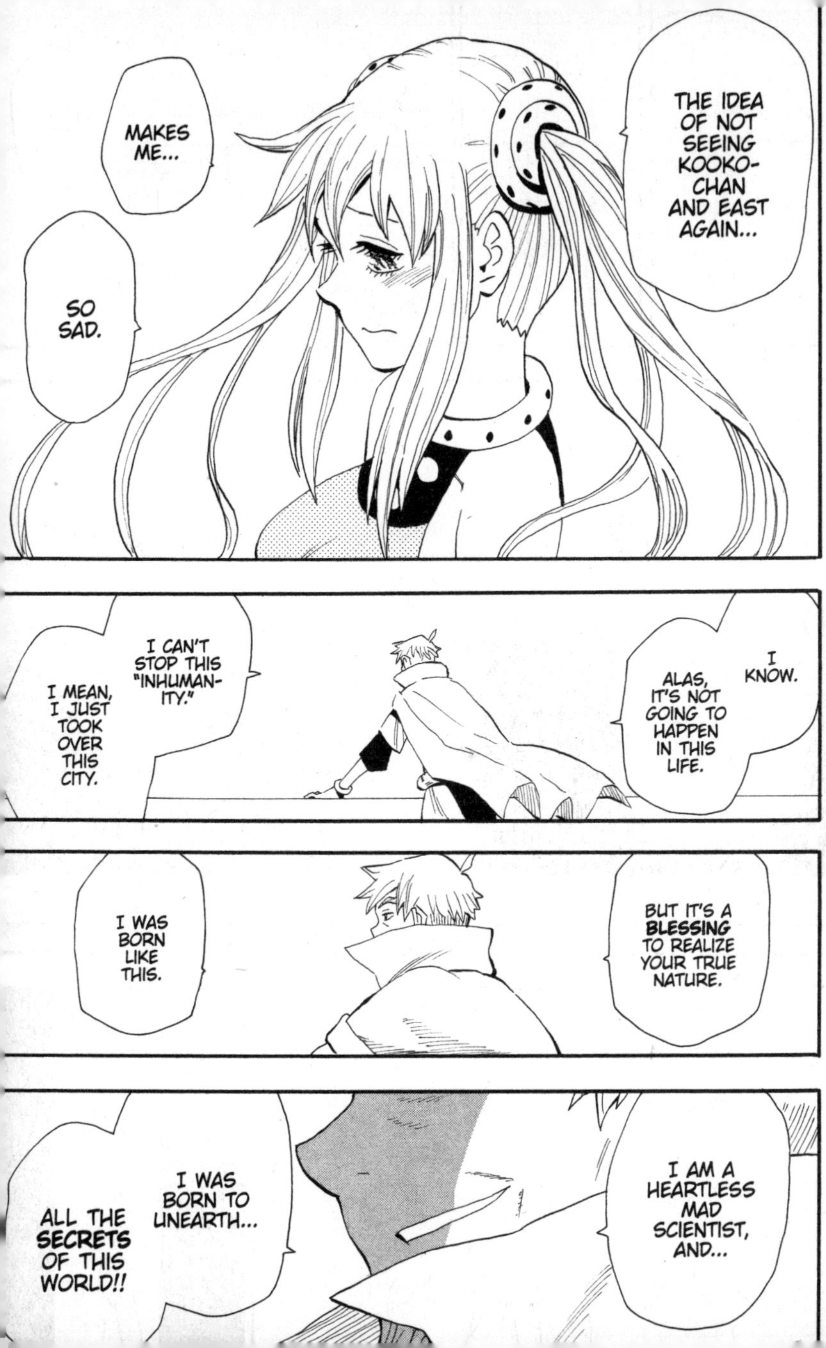
THE IDEA OF NOT SEEING KOOKO-CHAN AND EAST AGAIN...
MAKES ME...
SO SAD.
I KNOW.
ALAS, IT'S NOT GOING TO HAPPEN IN THIS LIFE.
I CAN'T STOP THIS "INHUMAN-ITY."
I MEAN, I JUST TOOK OVER THIS CITY.
BUT IT'S A **BLESSING** TO REALIZE YOUR TRUE NATURE.
I WAS BORN LIKE THIS.
I AM A HEARTLESS MAD SCIENTIST, AND...
I WAS BORN TO UNEARTH...
ALL THE **SECRETS** OF THIS WORLD!!

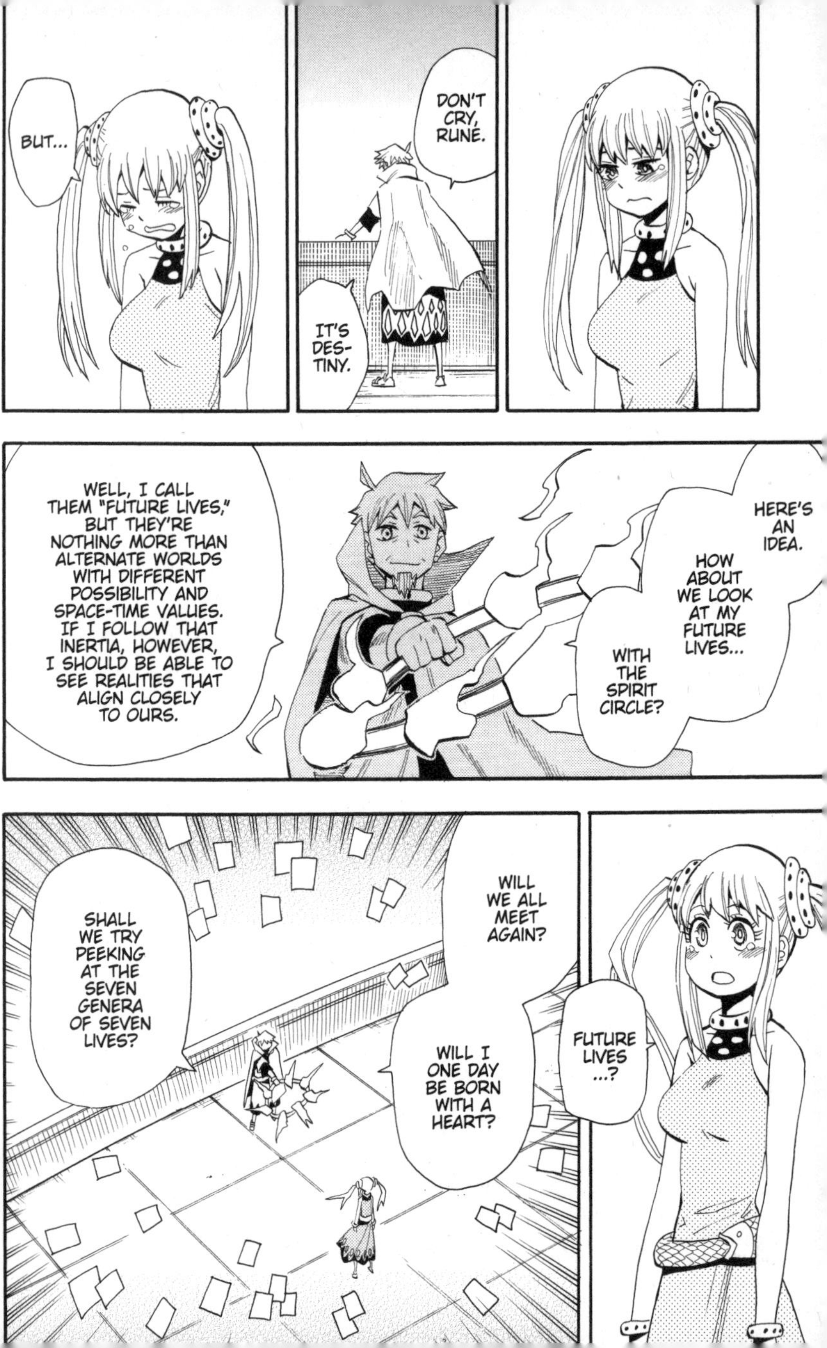
DON'T CRY, RUNE.
IT'S DES-TINY.
BUT...
HERE'S AN IDEA.
HOW ABOUT WE LOOK AT MY FUTURE LIVES...
WITH THE SPIRIT CIRCLE?
WELL, I CALL THEM "FUTURE LIVES," BUT THEY'RE NOTHING MORE THAN ALTERNATE WORLDS WITH DIFFERENT POSSIBILITY AND SPACE-TIME VALUES. IF I FOLLOW THAT INERTIA, HOWEVER, I SHOULD BE ABLE TO SEE REALITIES THAT ALIGN CLOSELY TO OURS.
FUTURE LIVES ...?
WILL WE ALL MEET AGAIN?
WILL I ONE DAY BE BORN WITH A HEART?
SHALL WE TRY PEEKING AT THE SEVEN GENERA OF SEVEN LIVES?

Spirit Circle

Spirit Circle

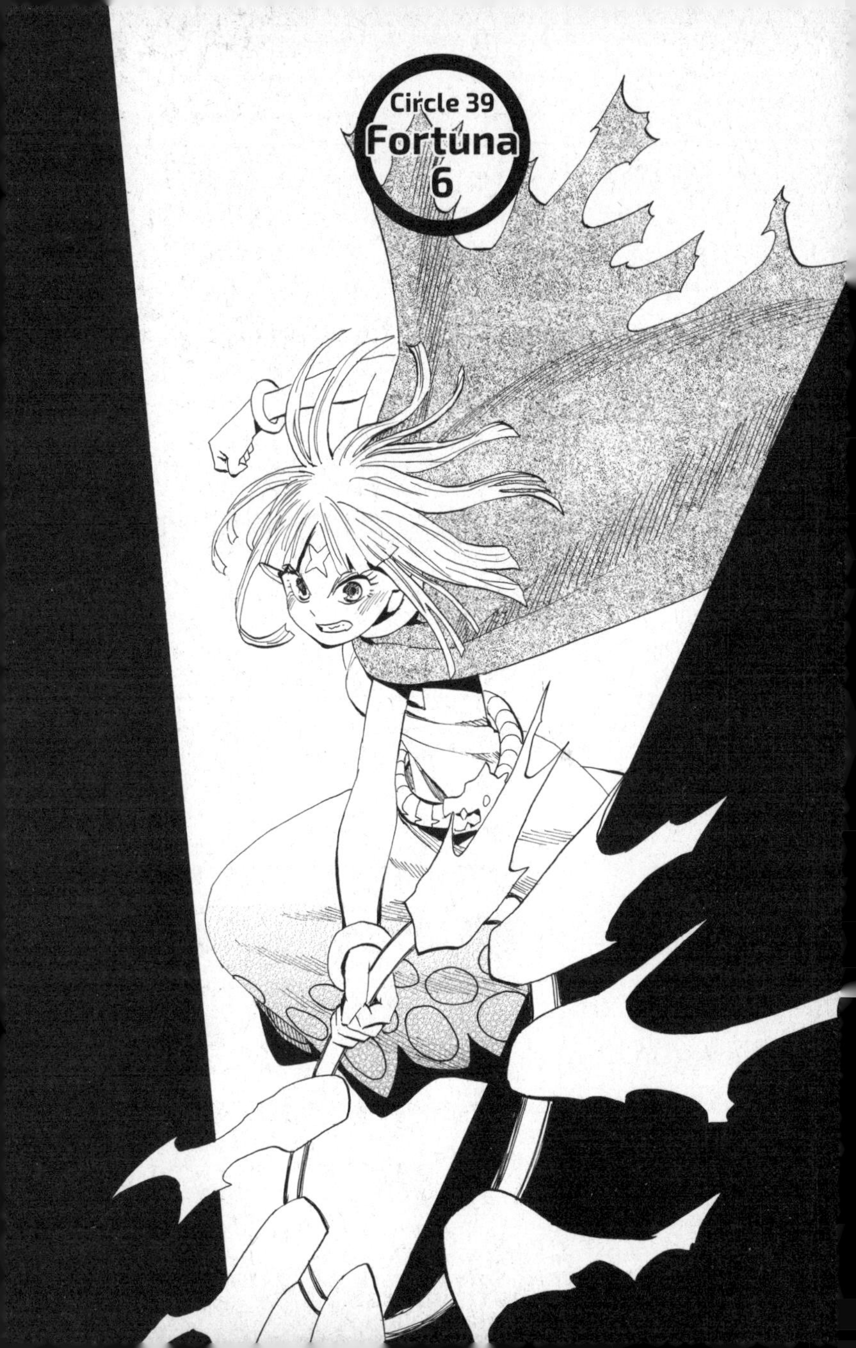
Circle 39
Fortuna
6

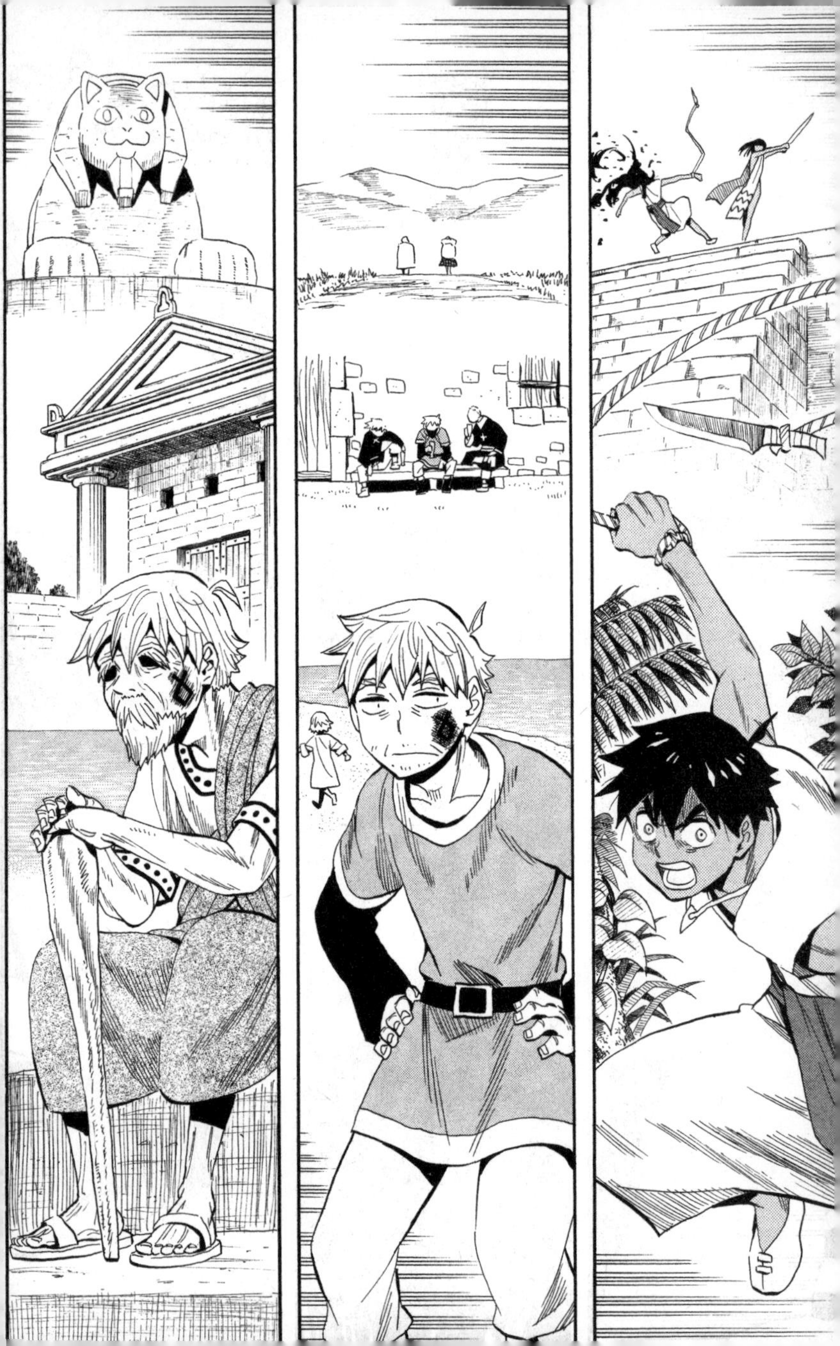

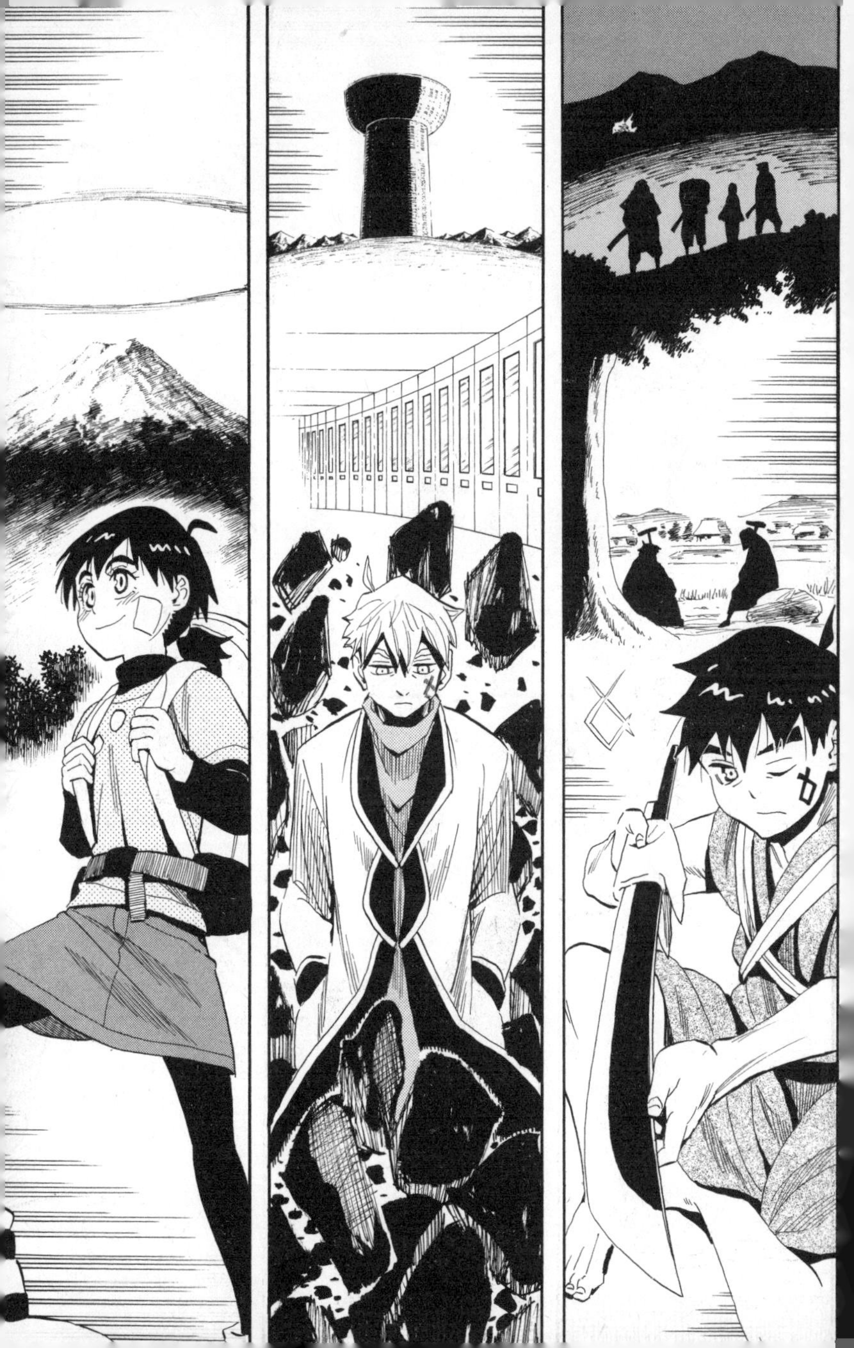

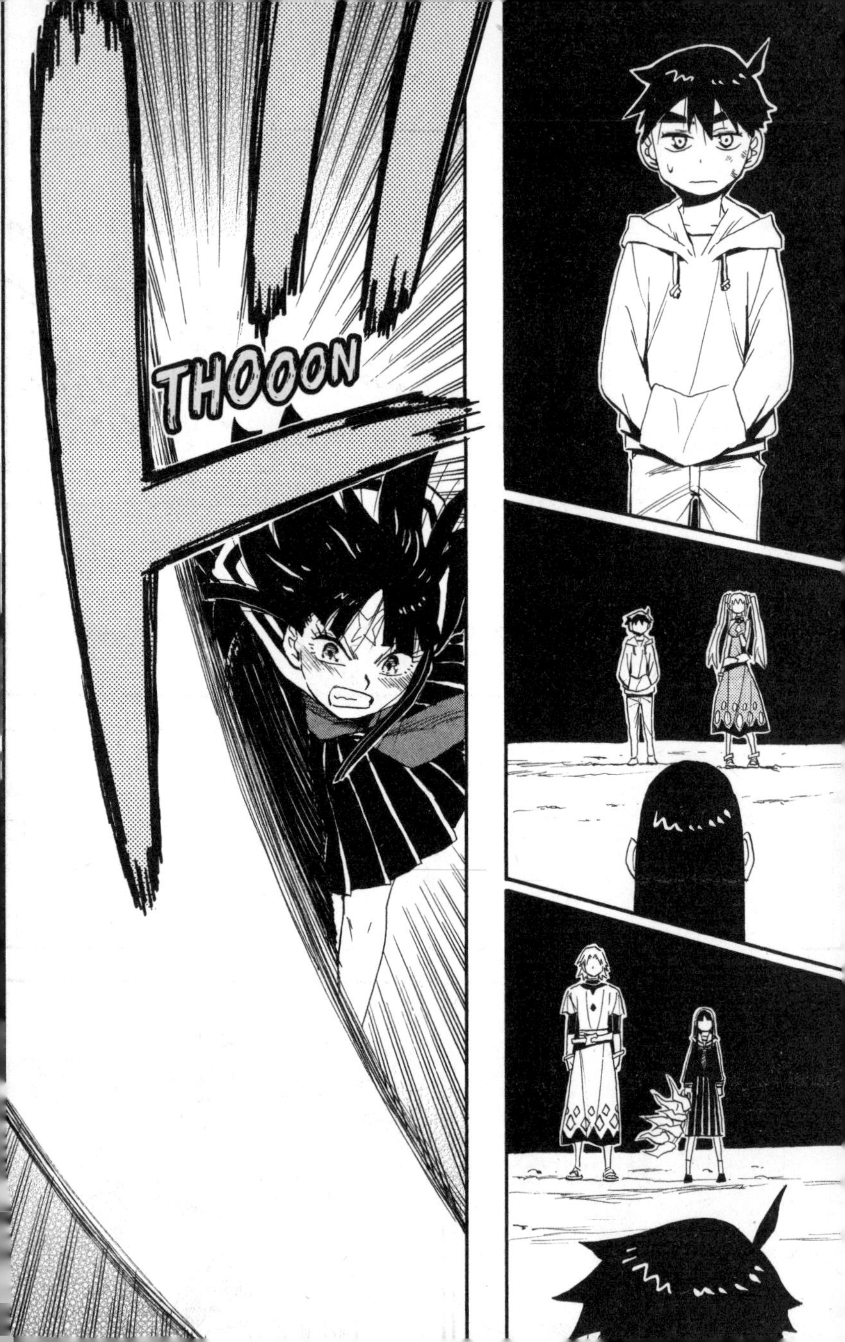
THOOON

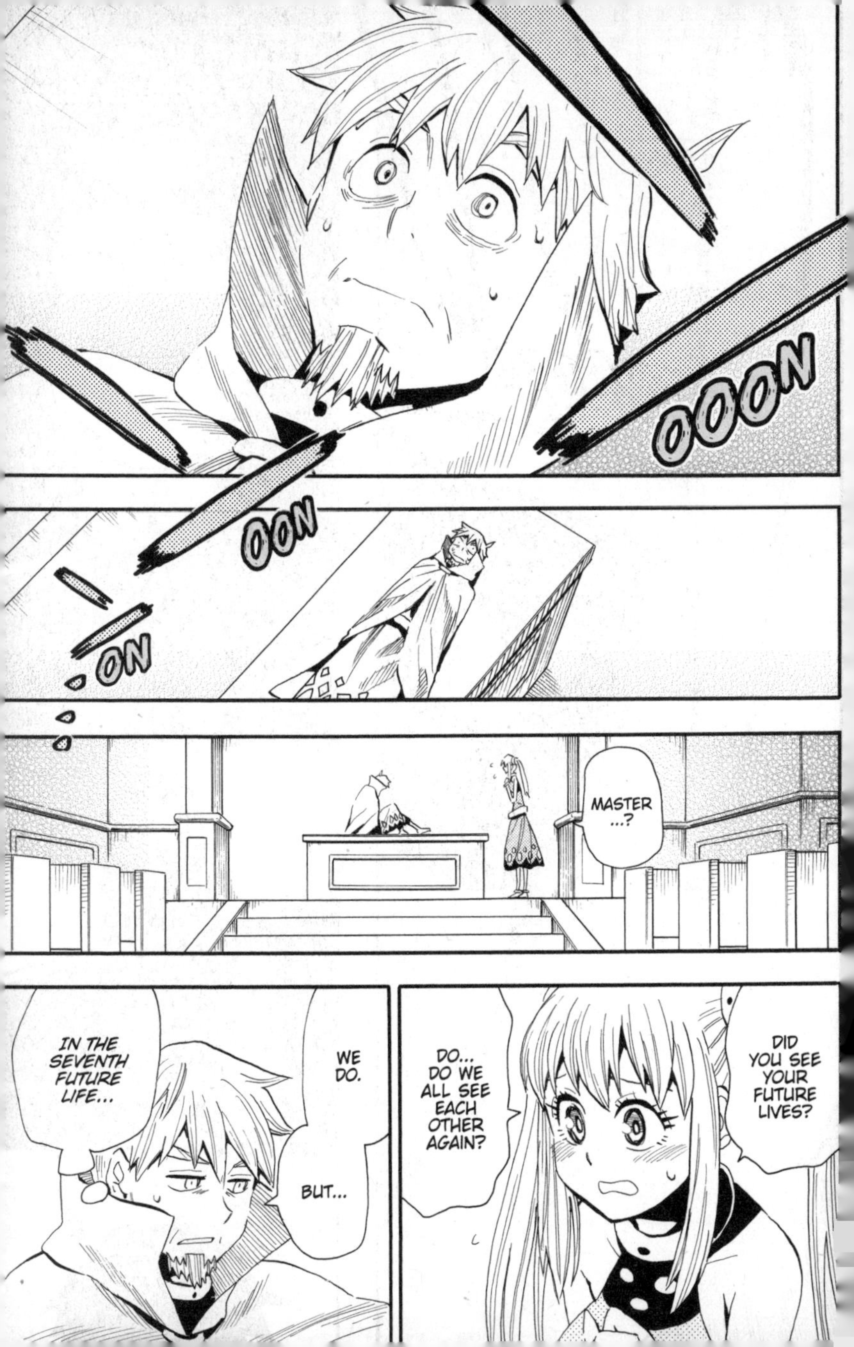
OOON
OON
ON
MASTER ...?
DID YOU SEE YOUR FUTURE LIVES?
DO... DO WE ALL SEE EACH OTHER AGAIN?
WE DO.
IN THE SEVENTH FUTURE LIFE...
BUT...

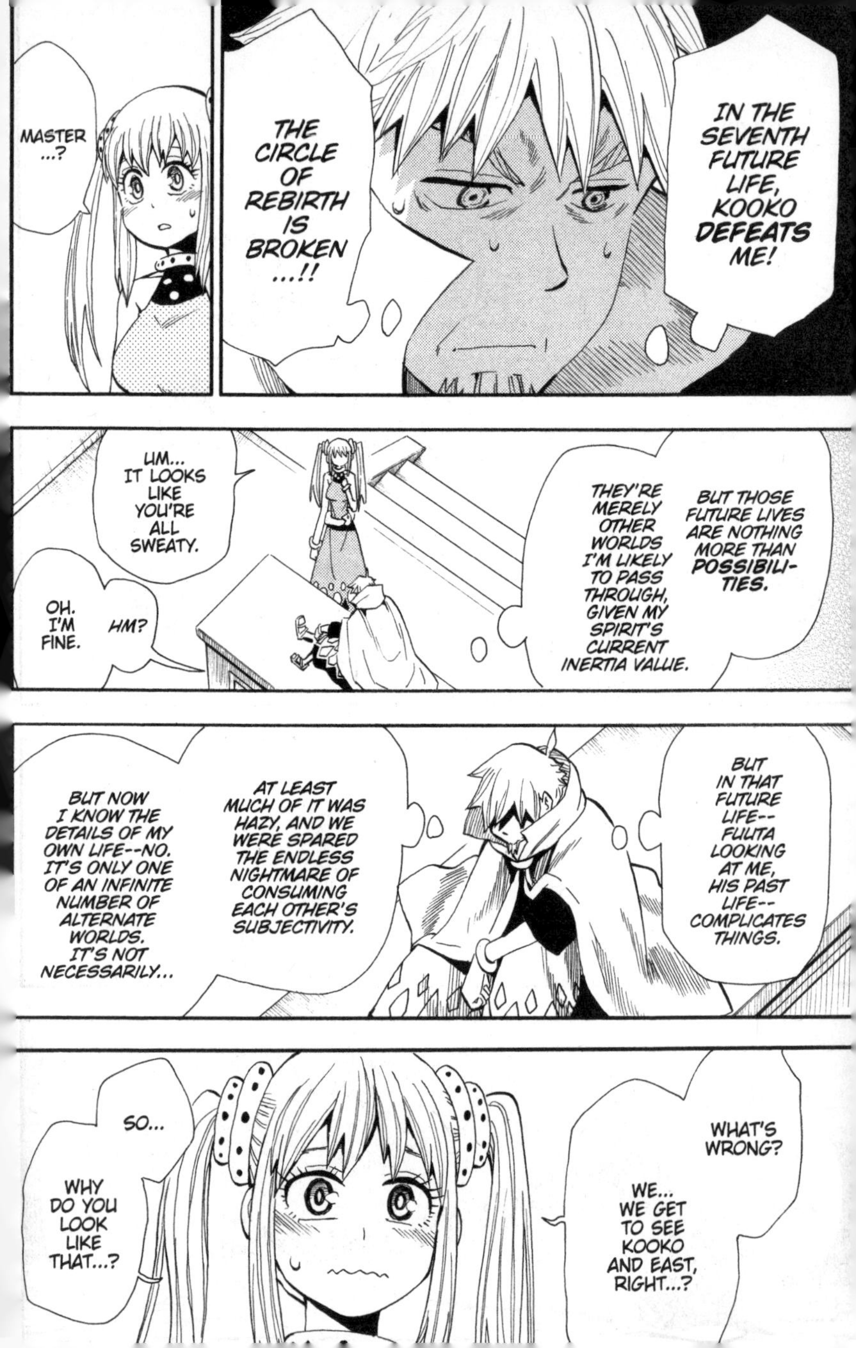
IN THE SEVENTH FUTURE LIFE, KOOKO DEFEATS ME!
THE CIRCLE OF REBIRTH IS BROKEN ...!!
MASTER ...?
BUT THOSE FUTURE LIVES ARE NOTHING MORE THAN POSSIBILITIES.
THEY'RE MERELY OTHER WORLDS I'M LIKELY TO PASS THROUGH, GIVEN MY SPIRIT'S CURRENT INERTIA VALUE.
UM... IT LOOKS LIKE YOU'RE ALL SWEATY.
HM?
OH. I'M FINE.
BUT IN THAT FUTURE LIFE-- FUUTA LOOKING AT ME, HIS PAST LIFE-- COMPLICATES THINGS.
AT LEAST MUCH OF IT WAS HAZY, AND WE WERE SPARED THE ENDLESS NIGHTMARE OF CONSUMING EACH OTHER'S SUBJECTIVITY.
BUT NOW I KNOW THE DETAILS OF MY OWN LIFE--NO. IT'S ONLY ONE OF AN INFINITE NUMBER OF ALTERNATE WORLDS. IT'S NOT NECESSARILY...
WHAT'S WRONG?
WE... WE GET TO SEE KOOKO AND EAST, RIGHT...?
SO...
WHY DO YOU LOOK LIKE THAT...?

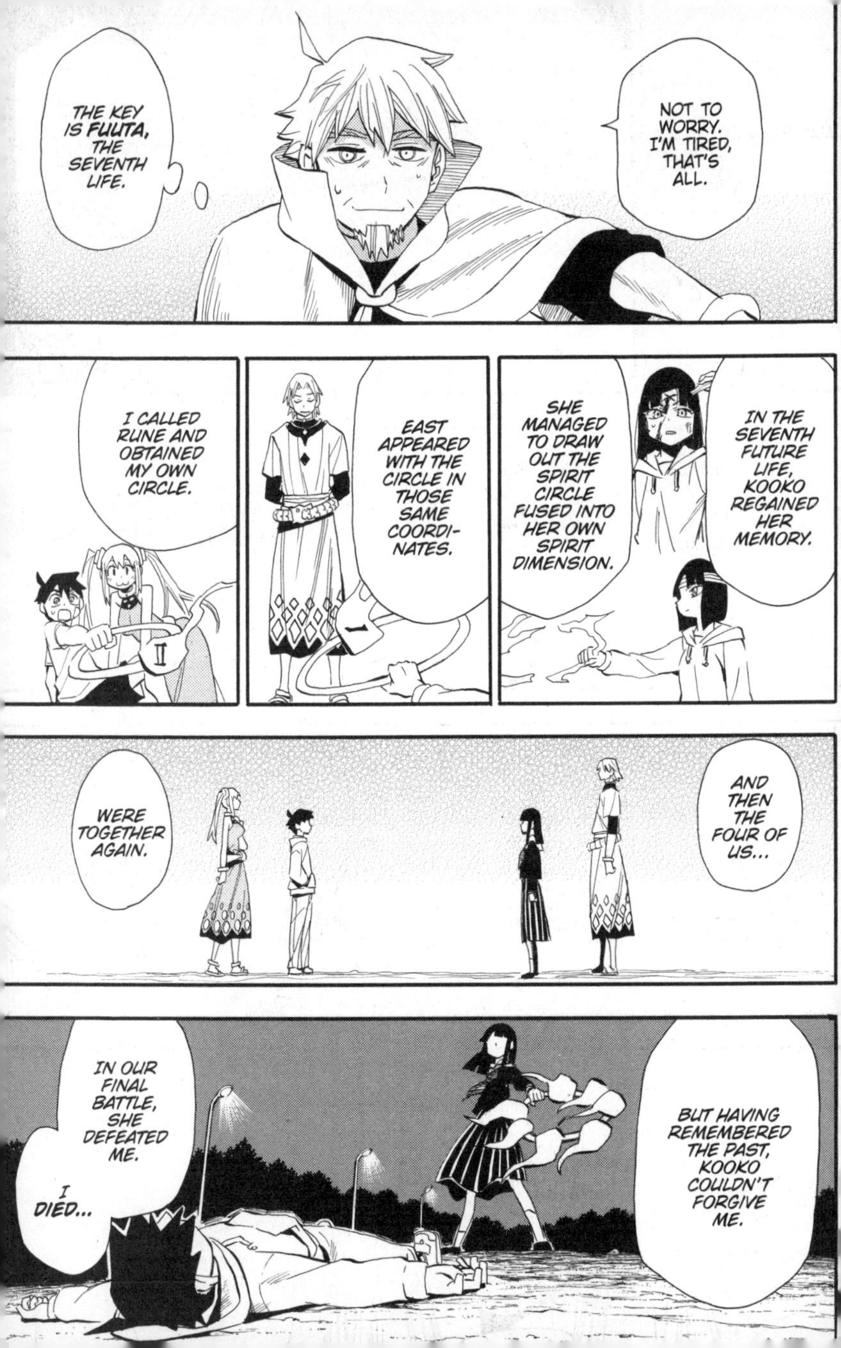
NOT TO WORRY. I'M TIRED, THAT'S ALL.
THE KEY IS **FUUTA,** THE SEVENTH LIFE.
IN THE SEVENTH FUTURE LIFE, KOOKO REGAINED HER MEMORY.
SHE MANAGED TO DRAW OUT THE SPIRIT CIRCLE FUSED INTO HER OWN SPIRIT DIMENSION.
EAST APPEARED WITH THE CIRCLE IN THOSE SAME COORDINATES.
I CALLED RUNE AND OBTAINED MY OWN CIRCLE.
AND THEN THE FOUR OF US...
WERE TOGETHER AGAIN.
BUT HAVING REMEMBERED THE PAST, KOOKO COULDN'T FORGIVE ME.
IN OUR FINAL BATTLE, SHE DEFEATED ME.
I DIED...

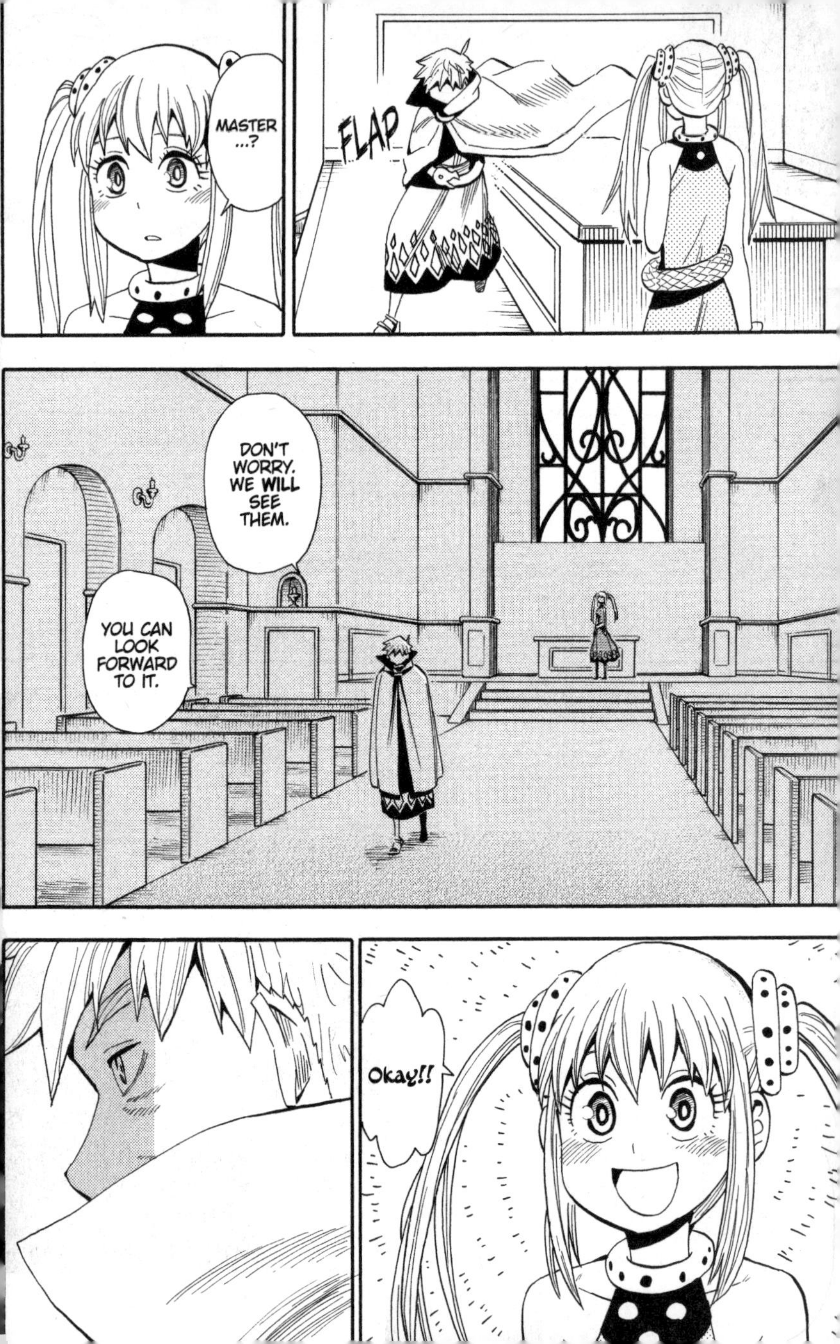
FLAP
MASTER ...?
DON'T WORRY. WE WILL SEE THEM.
YOU CAN LOOK FORWARD TO IT.
Okay!!

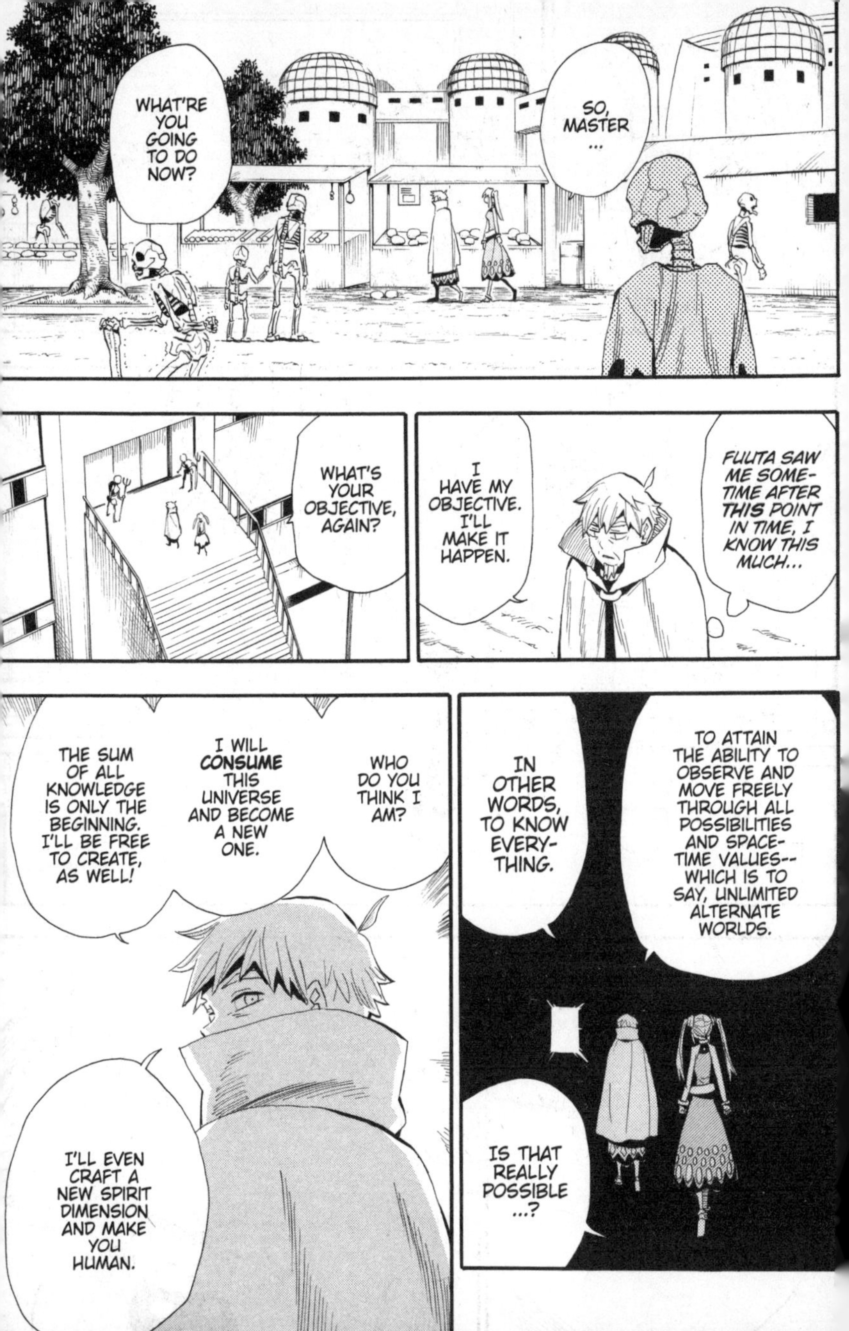
SO, MASTER ...
WHAT'RE YOU GOING TO DO NOW?
FUUTA SAW ME SOMETIME AFTER THIS POINT IN TIME, I KNOW THIS MUCH...
I HAVE MY OBJECTIVE. I'LL MAKE IT HAPPEN.
WHAT'S YOUR OBJECTIVE, AGAIN?
TO ATTAIN THE ABILITY TO OBSERVE AND MOVE FREELY THROUGH ALL POSSIBILITIES AND SPACE-TIME VALUES--WHICH IS TO SAY, UNLIMITED ALTERNATE WORLDS.
IN OTHER WORDS, TO KNOW EVERYTHING.
IS THAT REALLY POSSIBLE ...?
WHO DO YOU THINK I AM?
I WILL CONSUME THIS UNIVERSE AND BECOME A NEW ONE.
THE SUM OF ALL KNOWLEDGE IS ONLY THE BEGINNING. I'LL BE FREE TO CREATE, AS WELL!
I'LL EVEN CRAFT A NEW SPIRIT DIMENSION AND MAKE YOU HUMAN.

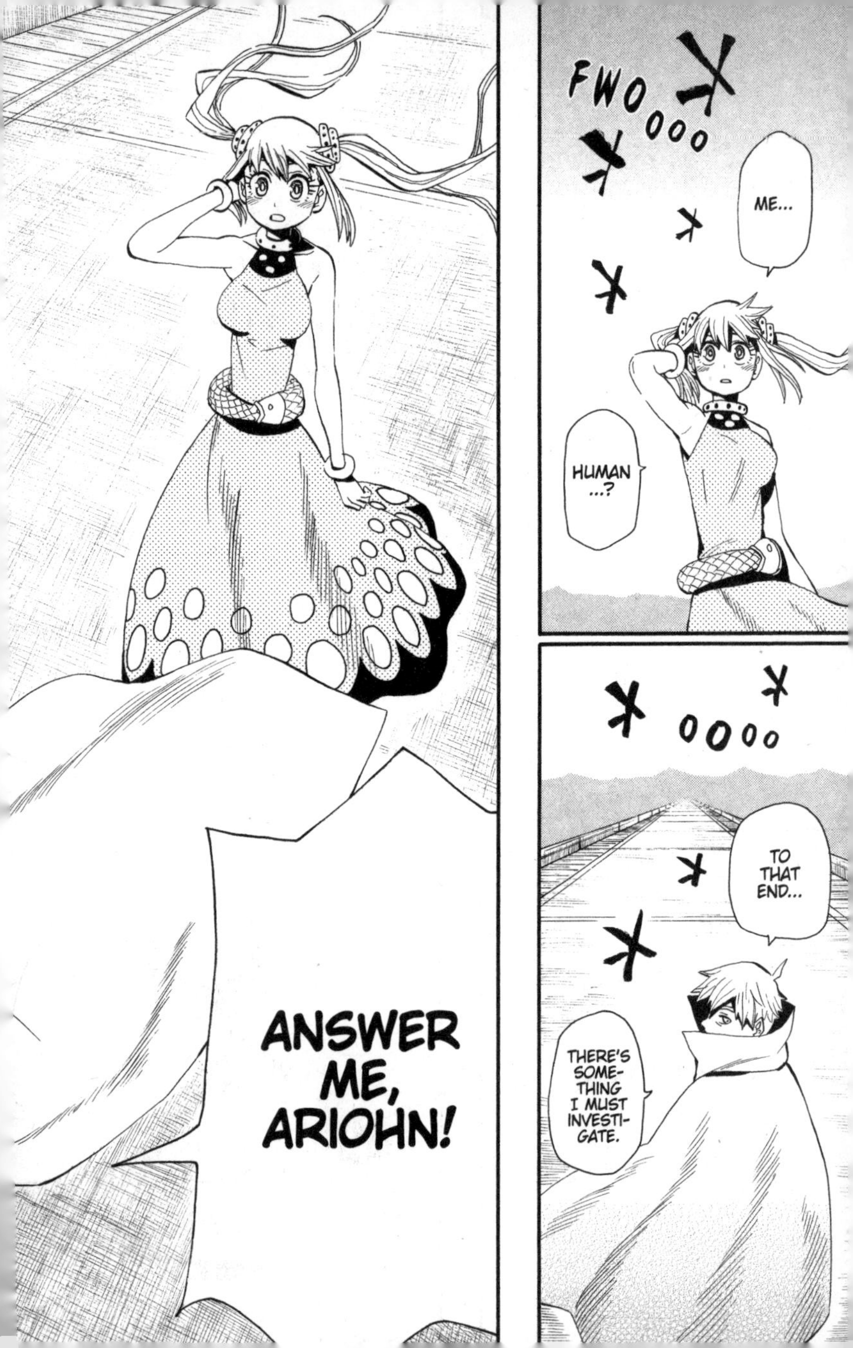
FWOOOO
ME...
HUMAN ...?
OOOO
TO THAT END...
THERE'S SOME-THING I MUST INVESTI-GATE.
ANSWER ME, ARIOHN!

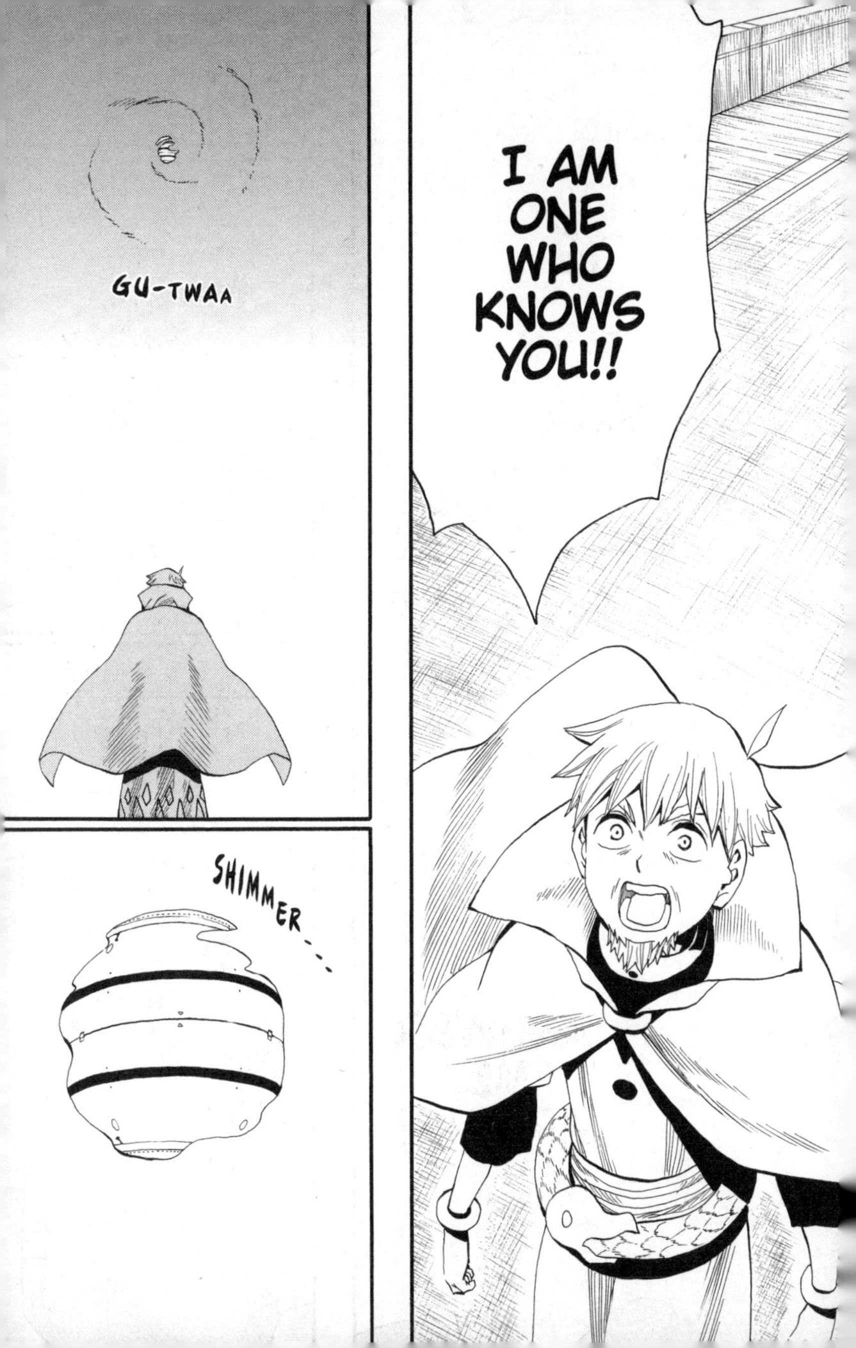
I AM ONE WHO KNOWS YOU!!
GU-TWAA
SHIMMER...

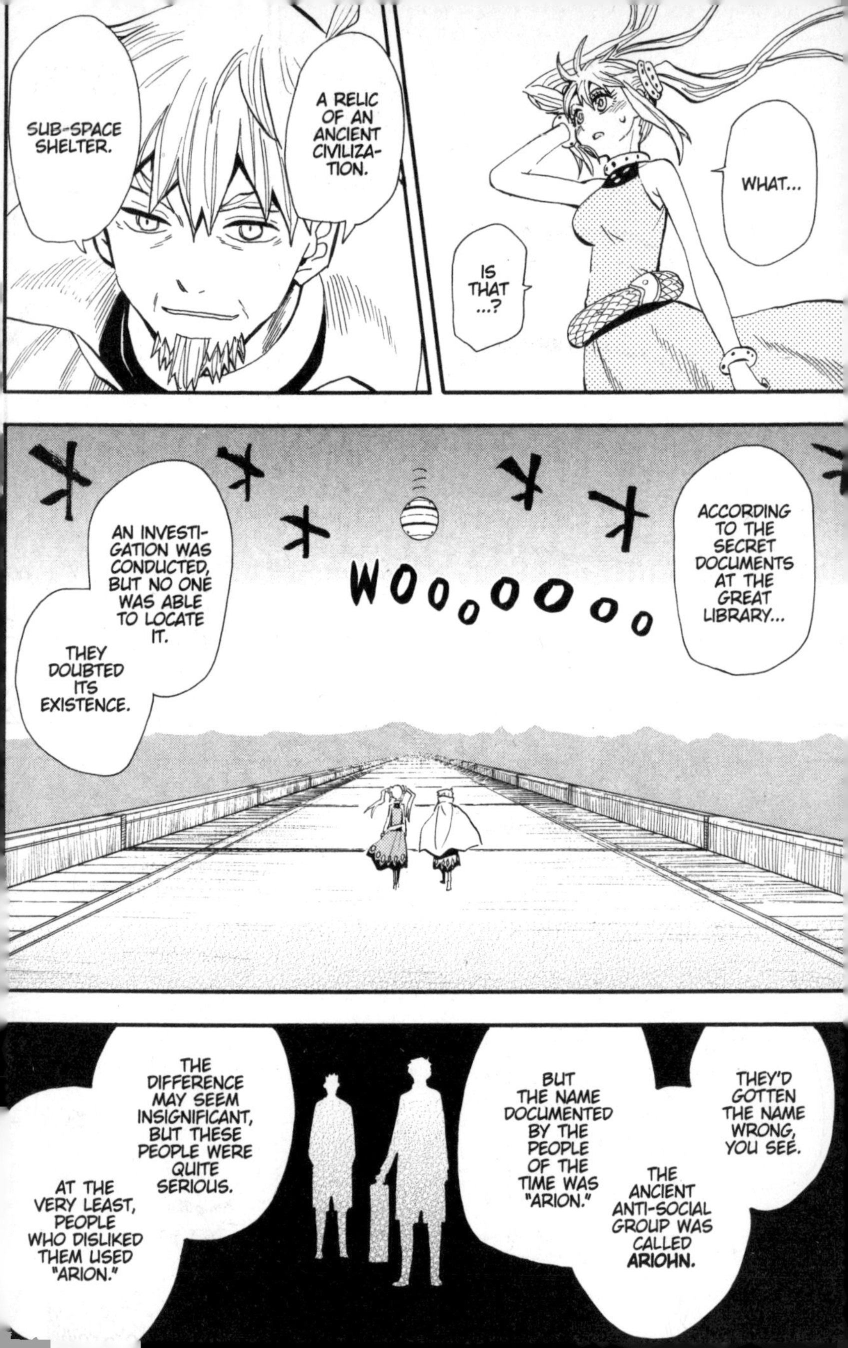
WHAT...
IS THAT ...?
A RELIC OF AN ANCIENT CIVILIZATION.
SUB-SPACE SHELTER.
ACCORDING TO THE SECRET DOCUMENTS AT THE GREAT LIBRARY...
WOOOOOOO
AN INVESTIGATION WAS CONDUCTED, BUT NO ONE WAS ABLE TO LOCATE IT.
THEY DOUBTED ITS EXISTENCE.
THEY'D GOTTEN THE NAME WRONG, YOU SEE.
THE ANCIENT ANTI-SOCIAL GROUP WAS CALLED **ARIOHN.**
BUT THE NAME DOCUMENTED BY THE PEOPLE OF THE TIME WAS "ARION."
THE DIFFERENCE MAY SEEM INSIGNIFICANT, BUT THESE PEOPLE WERE QUITE SERIOUS.
AT THE VERY LEAST, PEOPLE WHO DISLIKED THEM USED "ARION."

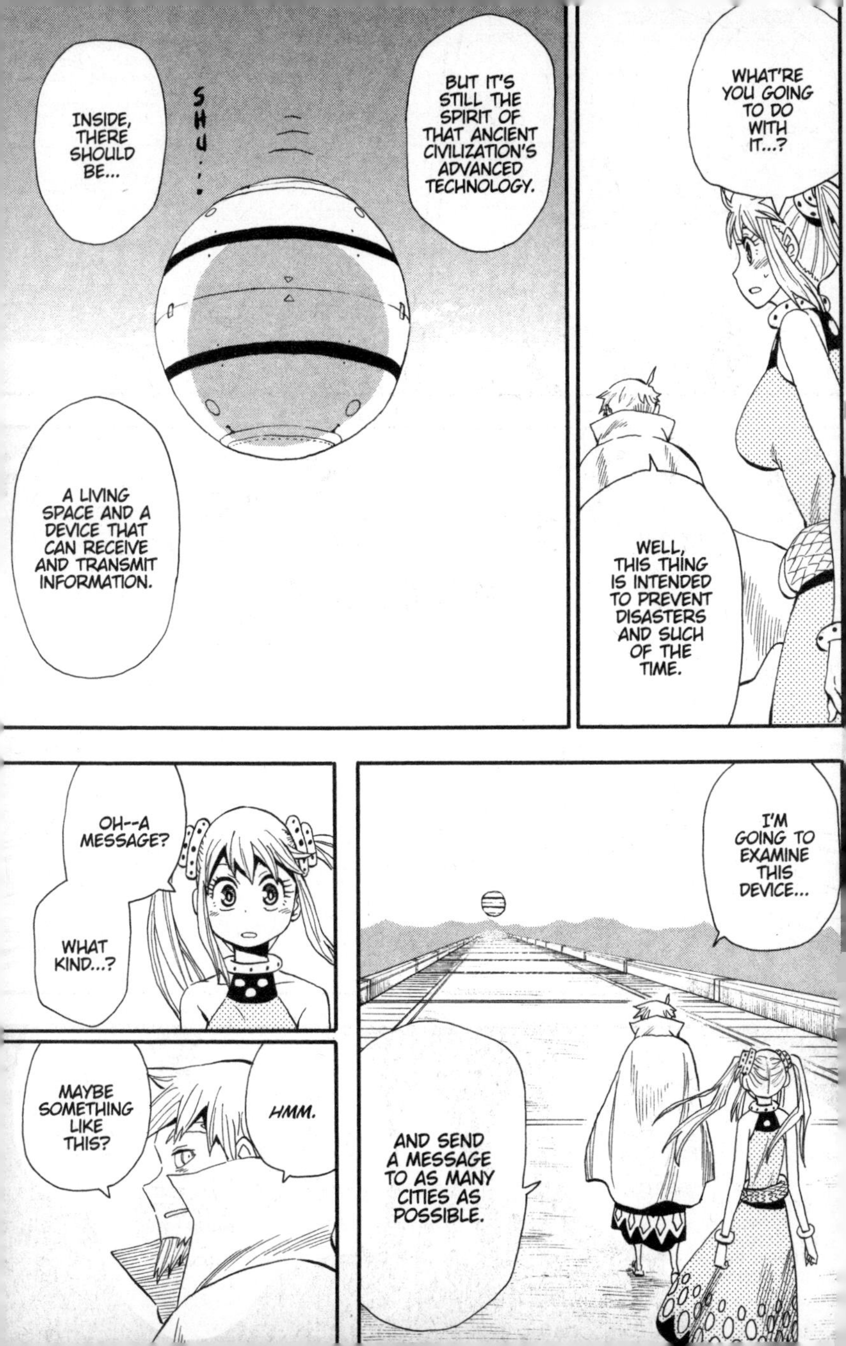
WHAT'RE YOU GOING TO DO WITH IT...?
WELL, THIS THING IS INTENDED TO PREVENT DISASTERS AND SUCH OF THE TIME.
BUT IT'S STILL THE SPIRIT OF THAT ANCIENT CIVILIZATION'S ADVANCED TECHNOLOGY.
SHU...
INSIDE, THERE SHOULD BE...
A LIVING SPACE AND A DEVICE THAT CAN RECEIVE AND TRANSMIT INFORMATION.
I'M GOING TO EXAMINE THIS DEVICE...
AND SEND A MESSAGE TO AS MANY CITIES AS POSSIBLE.
OH--A MESSAGE?
WHAT KIND...?
HMM.
MAYBE SOMETHING LIKE THIS?

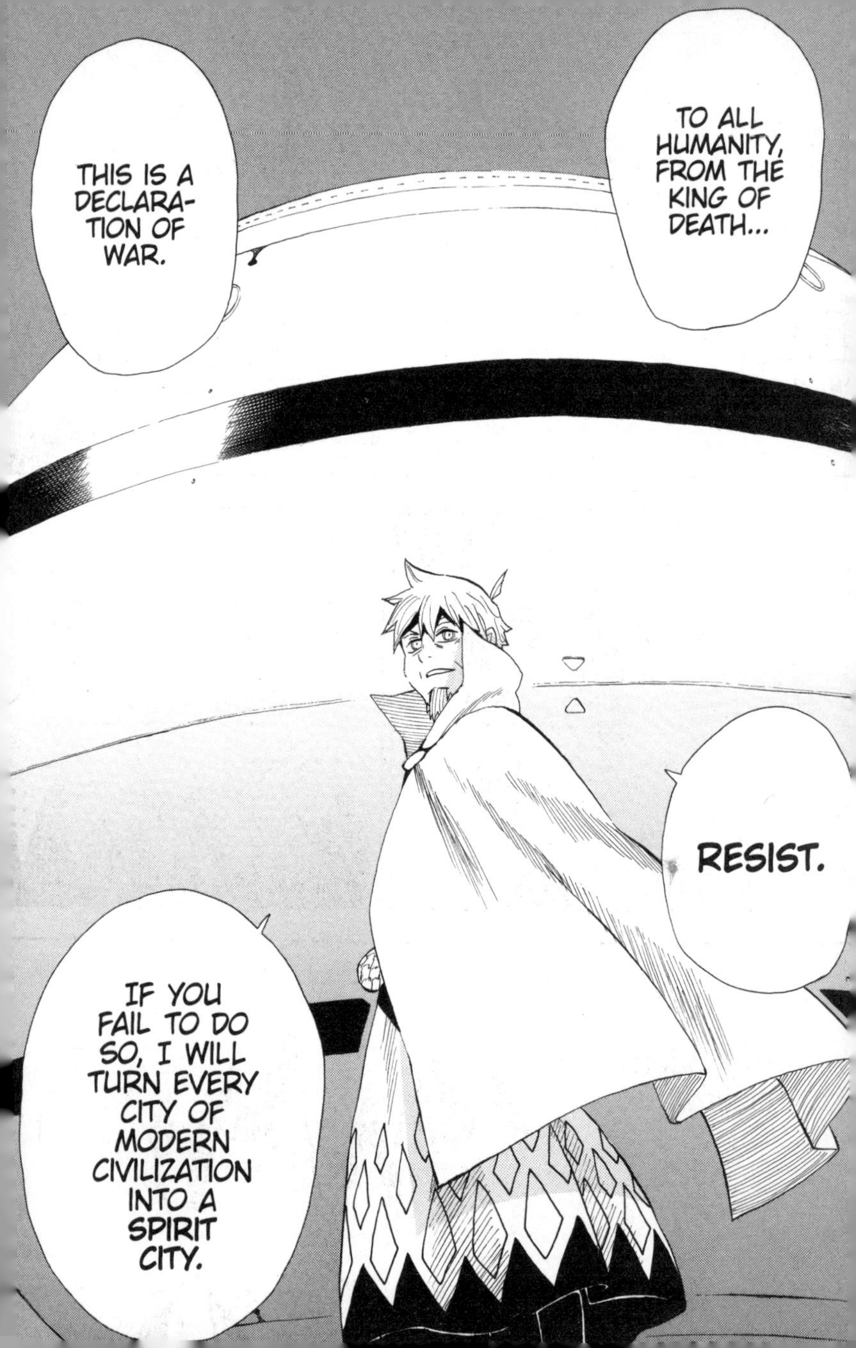
TO ALL HUMANITY, FROM THE KING OF DEATH...
THIS IS A DECLARA-TION OF WAR.
RESIST.
IF YOU FAIL TO DO SO, I WILL TURN EVERY CITY OF MODERN CIVILIZATION INTO A SPIRIT CITY.

Resist.

I will turn every city...

If you fail to do so...

of modern civilization into a spirit city.

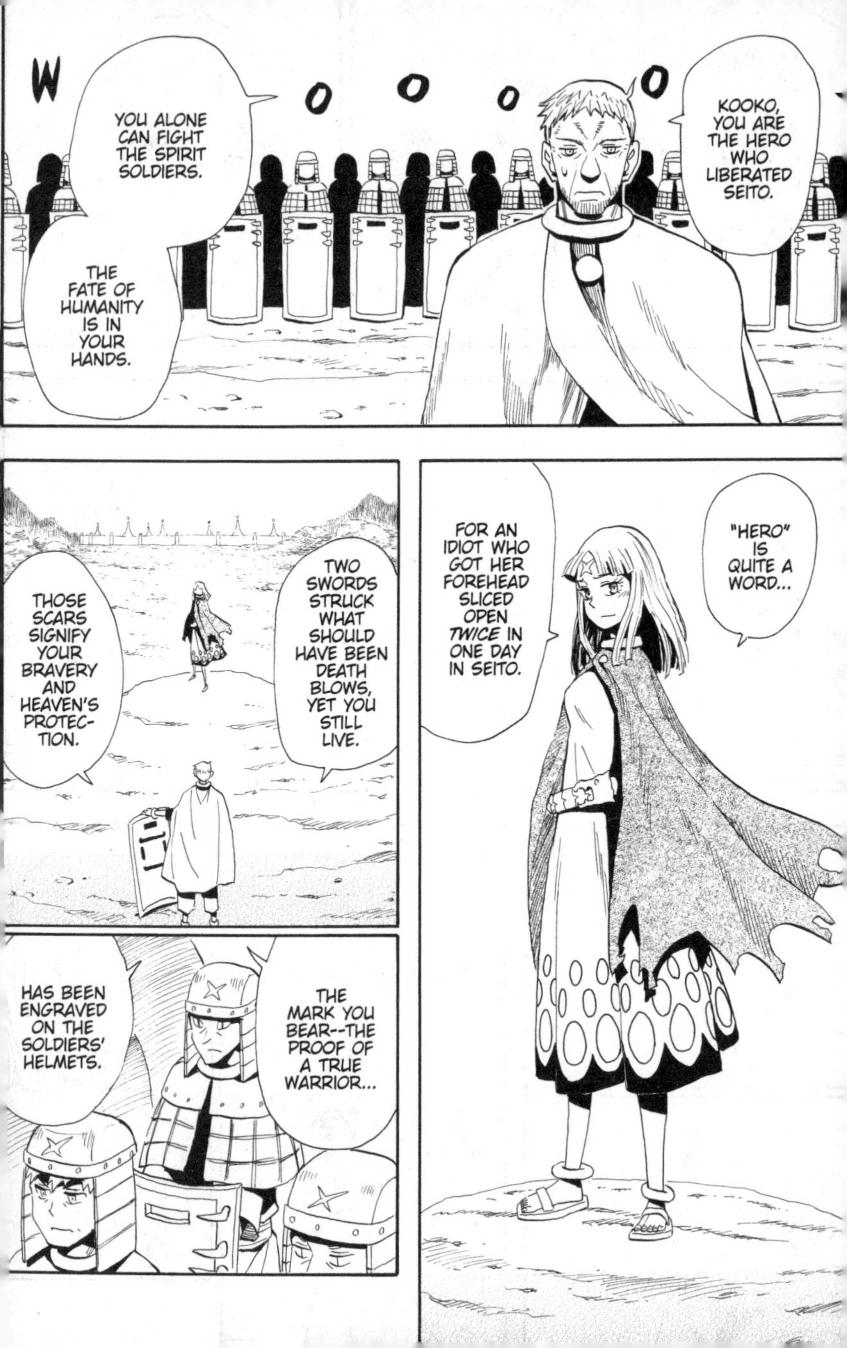
KOOKO, YOU ARE THE HERO WHO LIBERATED SEITO.
WOOOO
YOU ALONE CAN FIGHT THE SPIRIT SOLDIERS.
THE FATE OF HUMANITY IS IN YOUR HANDS.
"HERO" IS QUITE A WORD...
FOR AN IDIOT WHO GOT HER FOREHEAD SLICED OPEN *TWICE* IN ONE DAY IN SEITO.
TWO SWORDS STRUCK WHAT SHOULD HAVE BEEN DEATH BLOWS, YET YOU STILL LIVE.
THOSE SCARS SIGNIFY YOUR BRAVERY AND HEAVEN'S PROTECTION.
THE MARK YOU BEAR--THE PROOF OF A TRUE WARRIOR...
HAS BEEN ENGRAVED ON THE SOLDIERS' HELMETS.

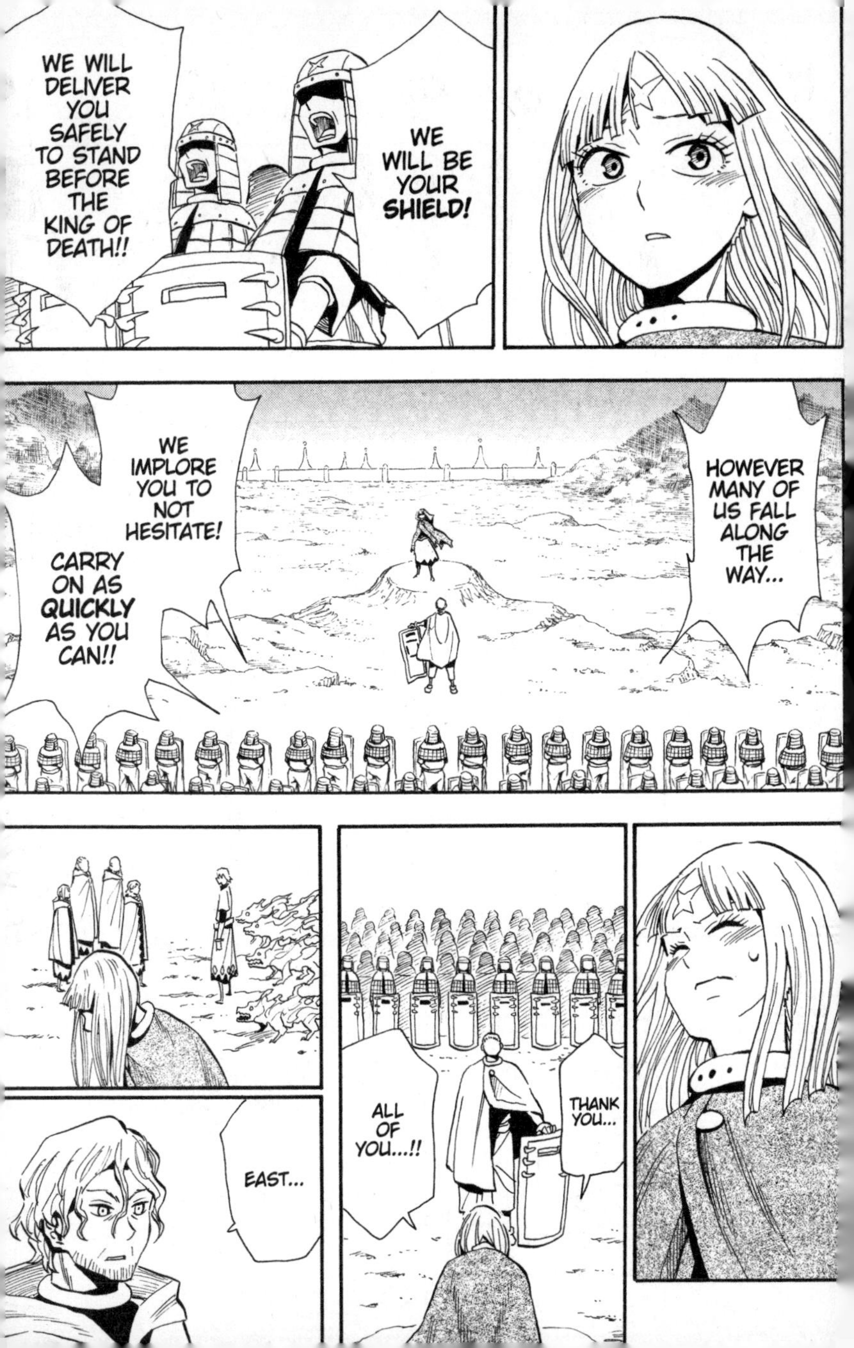
WE WILL BE YOUR SHIELD!
WE WILL DELIVER YOU SAFELY TO STAND BEFORE THE KING OF DEATH!!
HOWEVER MANY OF US FALL ALONG THE WAY...
WE IMPLORE YOU TO NOT HESITATE!
CARRY ON AS QUICKLY AS YOU CAN!!
THANK YOU...
ALL OF YOU...!!
EAST...

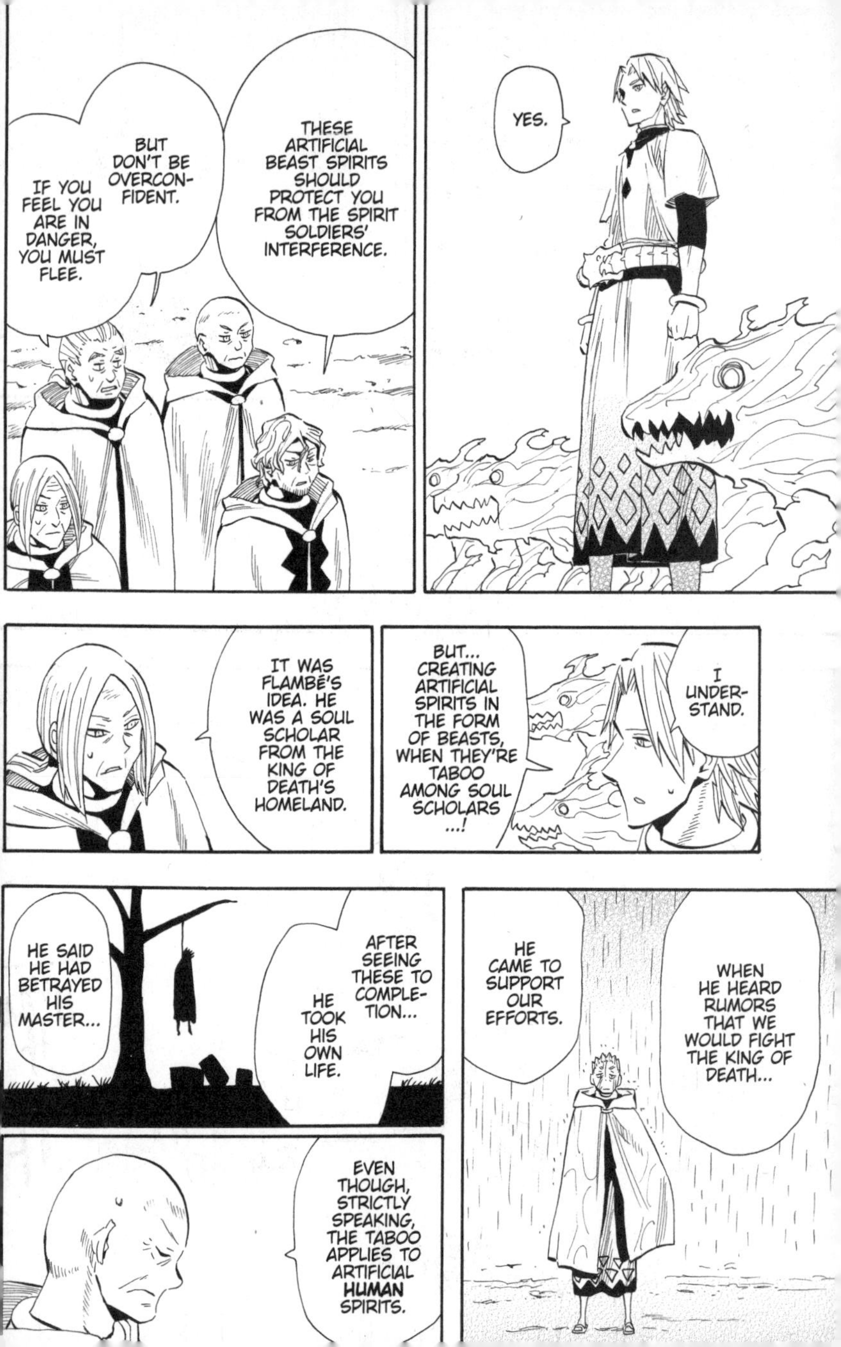
YES.
THESE ARTIFICIAL BEAST SPIRITS SHOULD PROTECT YOU FROM THE SPIRIT SOLDIERS' INTERFERENCE.
BUT DON'T BE OVERCON-FIDENT.
IF YOU FEEL YOU ARE IN DANGER, YOU MUST FLEE.
I UNDER-STAND.
BUT... CREATING ARTIFICIAL SPIRITS IN THE FORM OF BEASTS, WHEN THEY'RE TABOO AMONG SOUL SCHOLARS ...!
IT WAS FLAMBÉ'S IDEA. HE WAS A SOUL SCHOLAR FROM THE KING OF DEATH'S HOMELAND.
WHEN HE HEARD RUMORS THAT WE WOULD FIGHT THE KING OF DEATH...
HE CAME TO SUPPORT OUR EFFORTS.
AFTER SEEING THESE TO COMPLE-TION...
HE TOOK HIS OWN LIFE.
HE SAID HE HAD BETRAYED HIS MASTER...
EVEN THOUGH, STRICTLY SPEAKING, THE TABOO APPLIES TO ARTIFICIAL **HUMAN** SPIRITS.

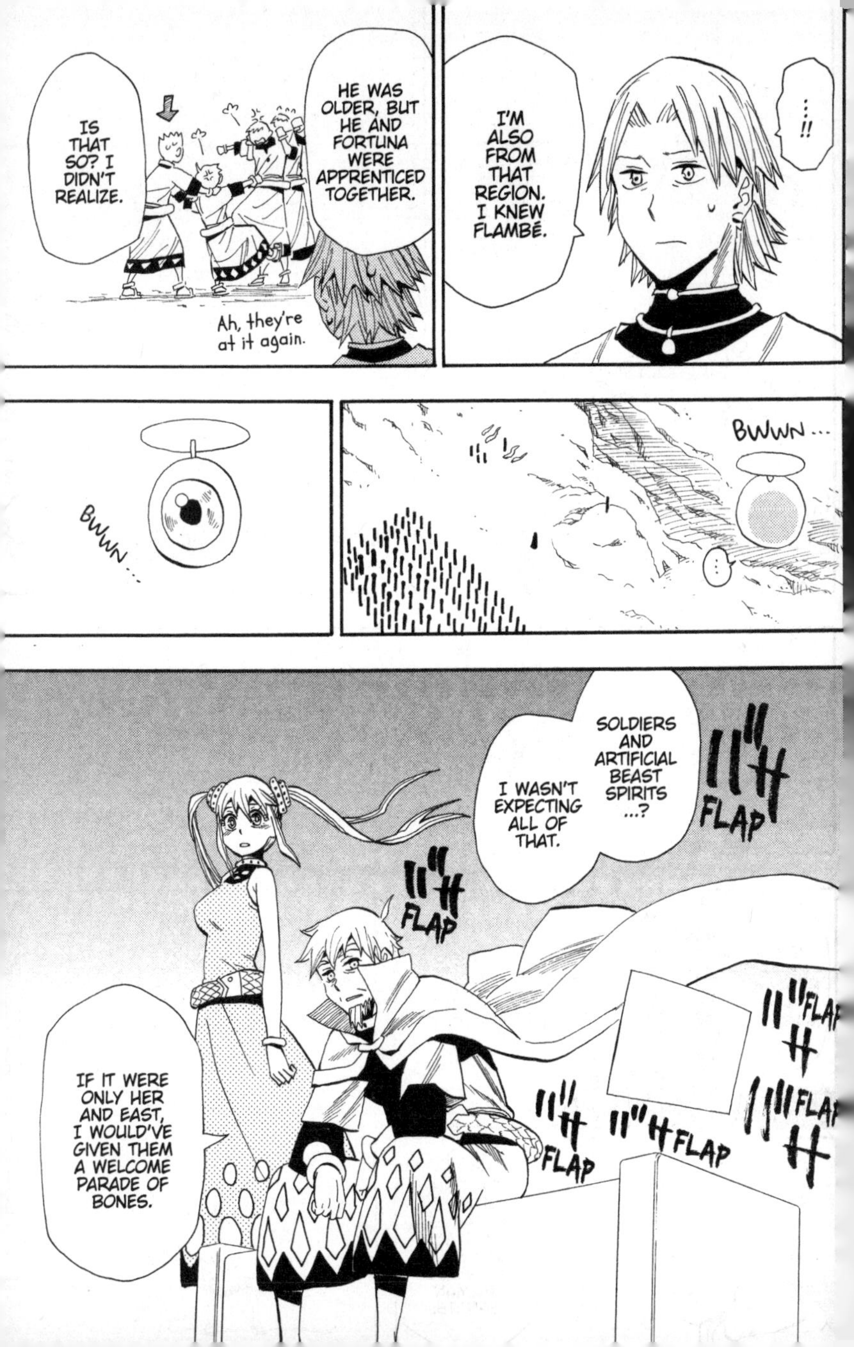
…!!
I'M ALSO FROM THAT REGION. I KNEW FLAMBÉ.
HE WAS OLDER, BUT HE AND FORTUNA WERE APPRENTICED TOGETHER.
IS THAT SO? I DIDN'T REALIZE.
Ah, they're at it again.
BWWN…
…
BWWN…
SOLDIERS AND ARTIFICIAL BEAST SPIRITS …?
I WASN'T EXPECTING ALL OF THAT.
FLAP
FLAP
FLAP
FLAP
FLAP
FLAP
IF IT WERE ONLY HER AND EAST, I WOULD'VE GIVEN THEM A WELCOME PARADE OF BONES.

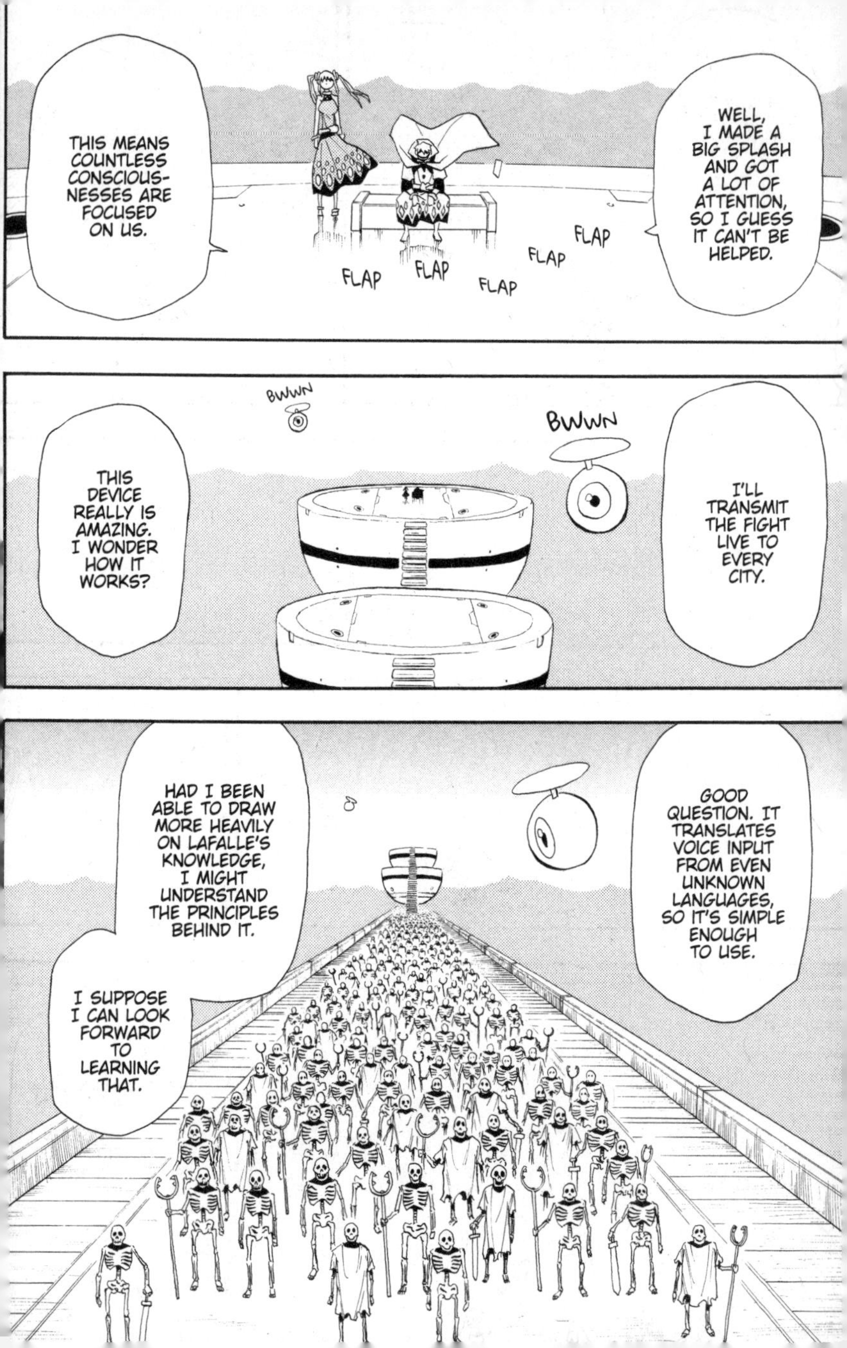
WELL, I MADE A BIG SPLASH AND GOT A LOT OF ATTENTION, SO I GUESS IT CAN'T BE HELPED.
FLAP
FLAP
FLAP
FLAP
FLAP
THIS MEANS COUNTLESS CONSCIOUS-NESSES ARE FOCUSED ON US.
BWWN
BWWN
I'LL TRANSMIT THE FIGHT LIVE TO EVERY CITY.
THIS DEVICE REALLY IS AMAZING. I WONDER HOW IT WORKS?
GOOD QUESTION. IT TRANSLATES VOICE INPUT FROM EVEN UNKNOWN LANGUAGES, SO IT'S SIMPLE ENOUGH TO USE.
HAD I BEEN ABLE TO DRAW MORE HEAVILY ON LAFALLE'S KNOWLEDGE, I MIGHT UNDERSTAND THE PRINCIPLES BEHIND IT.
I SUPPOSE I CAN LOOK FORWARD TO LEARNING THAT.

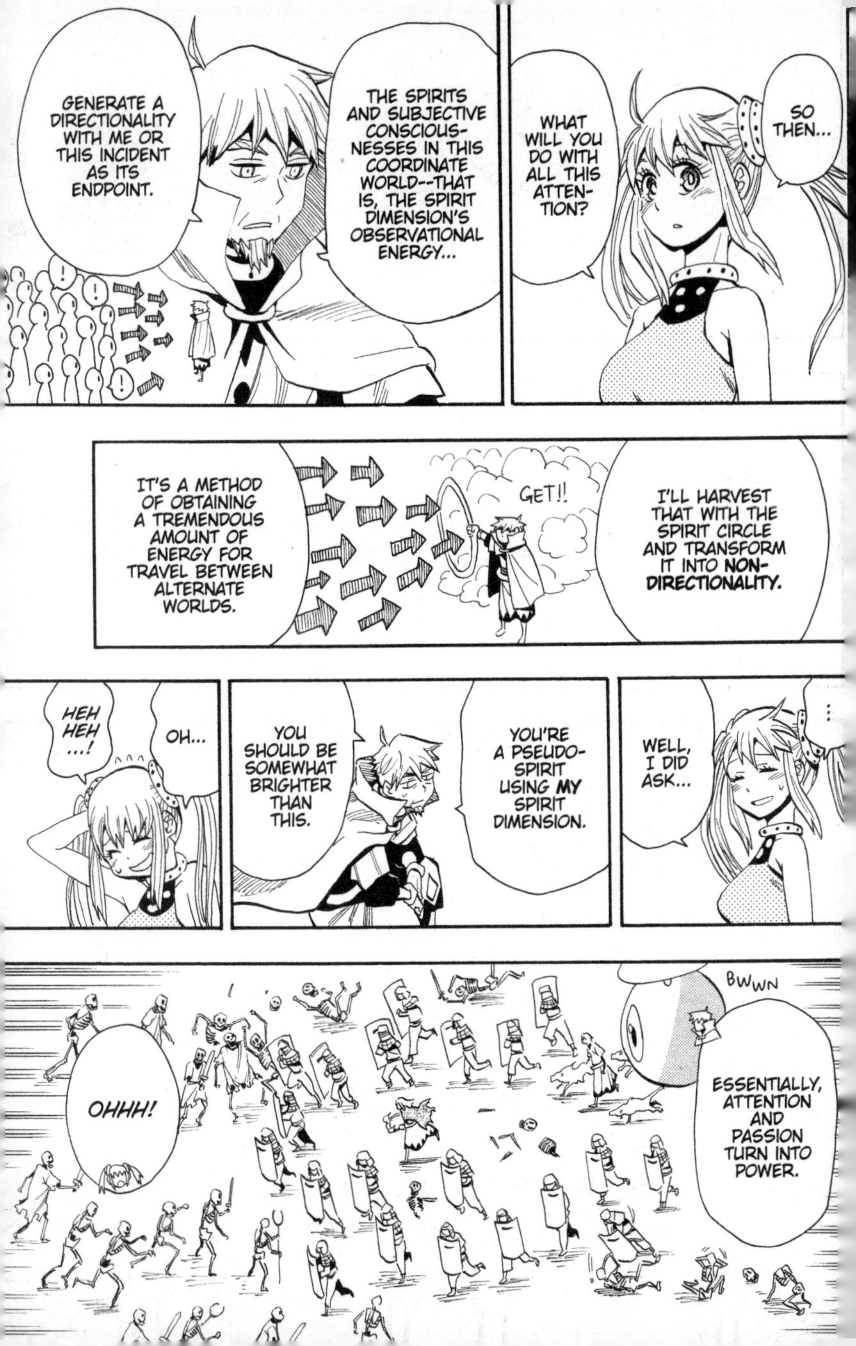
SO THEN...
WHAT WILL YOU DO WITH ALL THIS ATTEN-TION?
THE SPIRITS AND SUBJECTIVE CONSCIOUS-NESSES IN THIS COORDINATE WORLD--THAT IS, THE SPIRIT DIMENSION'S OBSERVATIONAL ENERGY...
GENERATE A DIRECTIONALITY WITH ME OR THIS INCIDENT AS ITS ENDPOINT.
!
!
!
I'LL HARVEST THAT WITH THE SPIRIT CIRCLE AND TRANSFORM IT INTO **NON-DIRECTIONALITY.**
GET!!
IT'S A METHOD OF OBTAINING A TREMENDOUS AMOUNT OF ENERGY FOR TRAVEL BETWEEN ALTERNATE WORLDS.
...
WELL, I DID ASK...
YOU'RE A PSEUDO-SPIRIT USING **MY** SPIRIT DIMENSION.
YOU SHOULD BE SOMEWHAT BRIGHTER THAN THIS.
OH...
HEH HEH ...!
BWWN
ESSENTIALLY, ATTENTION AND PASSION TURN INTO POWER.
OHHH!

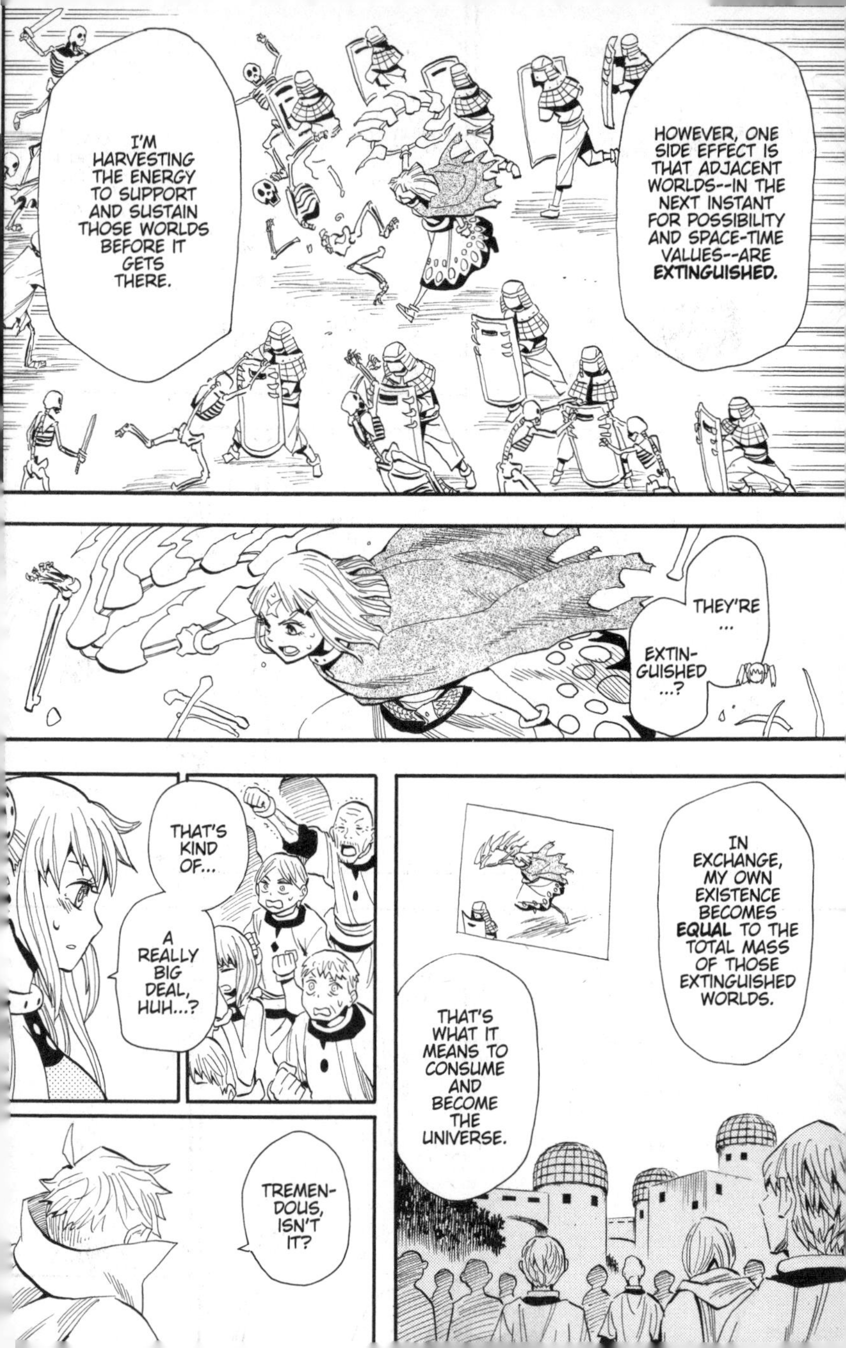
HOWEVER, ONE SIDE EFFECT IS THAT ADJACENT WORLDS--IN THE NEXT INSTANT FOR POSSIBILITY AND SPACE-TIME VALUES--ARE **EXTINGUISHED.**
I'M HARVESTING THE ENERGY TO SUPPORT AND SUSTAIN THOSE WORLDS BEFORE IT GETS THERE.
THEY'RE ...
EXTIN-GUISHED ...?
IN EXCHANGE, MY OWN EXISTENCE BECOMES **EQUAL** TO THE TOTAL MASS OF THOSE EXTINGUISHED WORLDS.
THAT'S WHAT IT MEANS TO CONSUME AND BECOME THE UNIVERSE.
THAT'S KIND OF...
A REALLY BIG DEAL, HUH...?
TREMEN-DOUS, ISN'T IT?

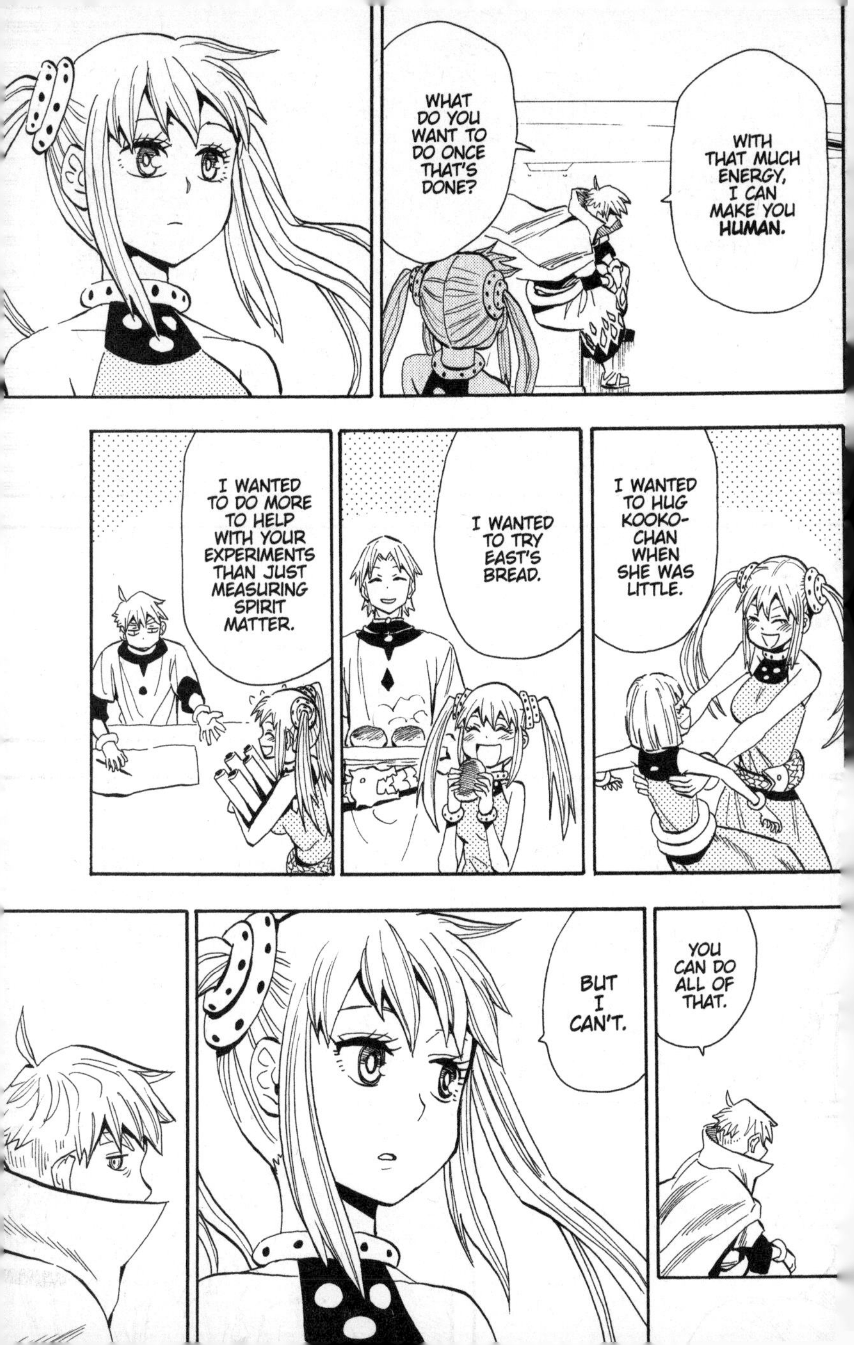
WITH THAT MUCH ENERGY, I CAN MAKE YOU HUMAN.
WHAT DO YOU WANT TO DO ONCE THAT'S DONE?
I WANTED TO HUG KOOKO-CHAN WHEN SHE WAS LITTLE.
I WANTED TO TRY EAST'S BREAD.
I WANTED TO DO MORE TO HELP WITH YOUR EXPERIMENTS THAN JUST MEASURING SPIRIT MATTER.
YOU CAN DO ALL OF THAT.
BUT I CAN'T.

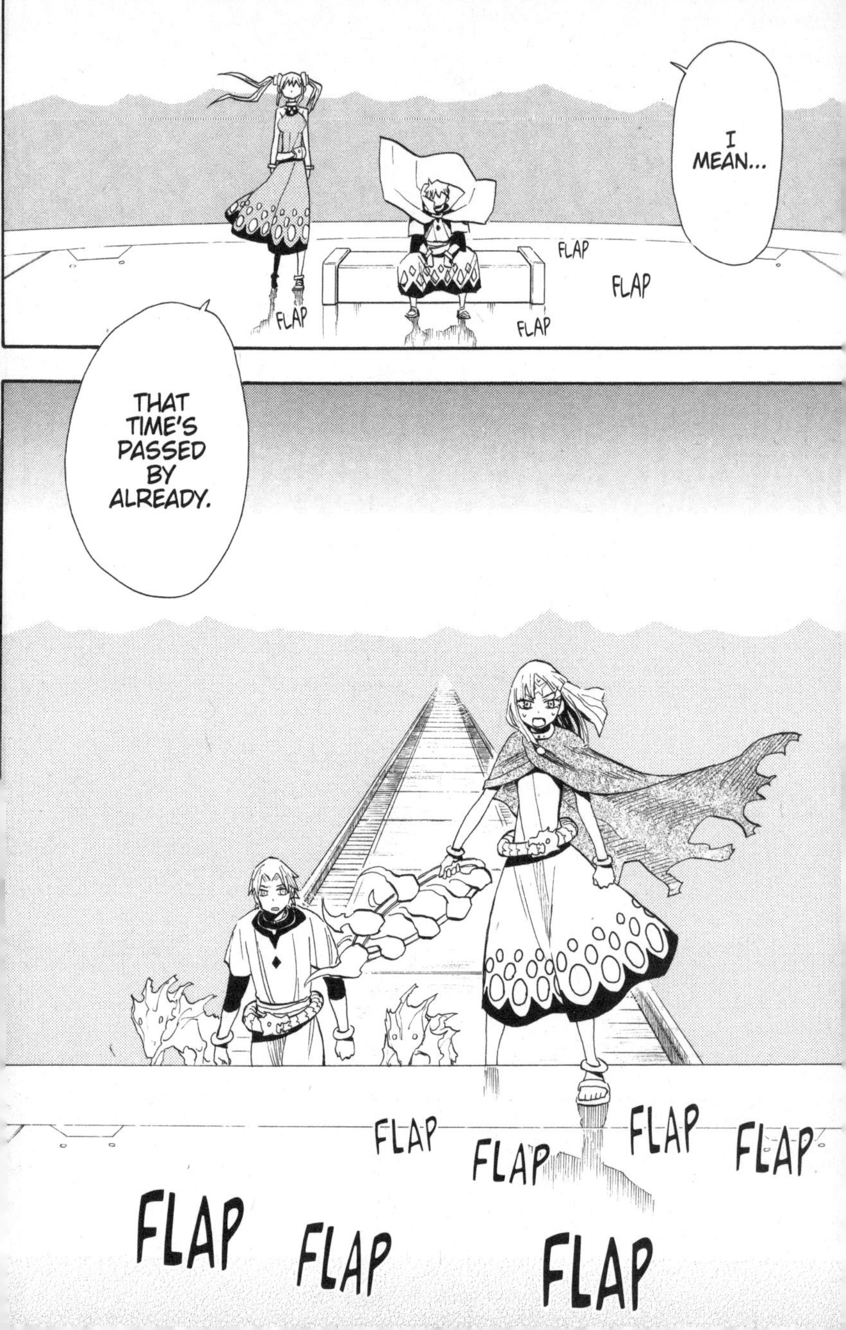
I MEAN...
FLAP
FLAP
FLAP
FLAP
THAT TIME'S PASSED BY ALREADY.
FLAP
FLAP
FLAP
FLAP
FLAP
FLAP
FLAP

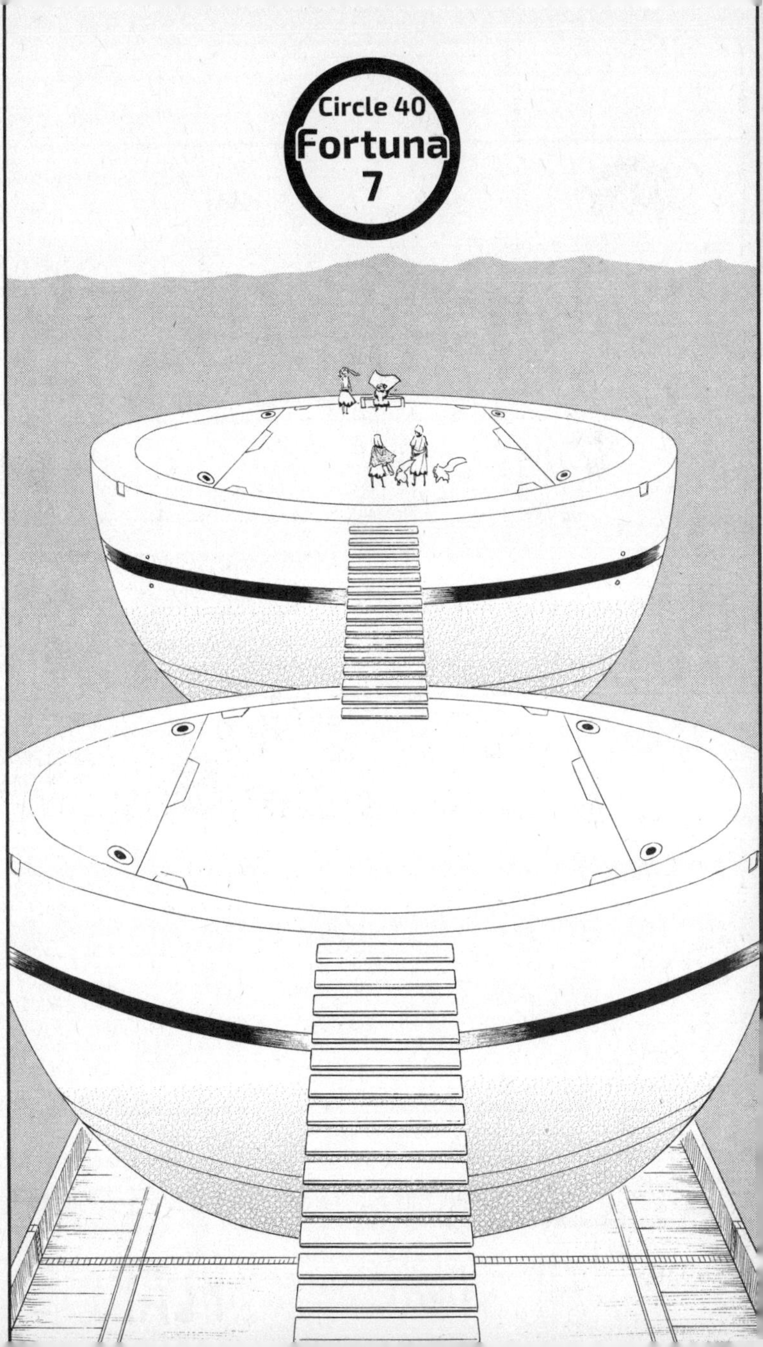
Circle 40
Fortuna
7

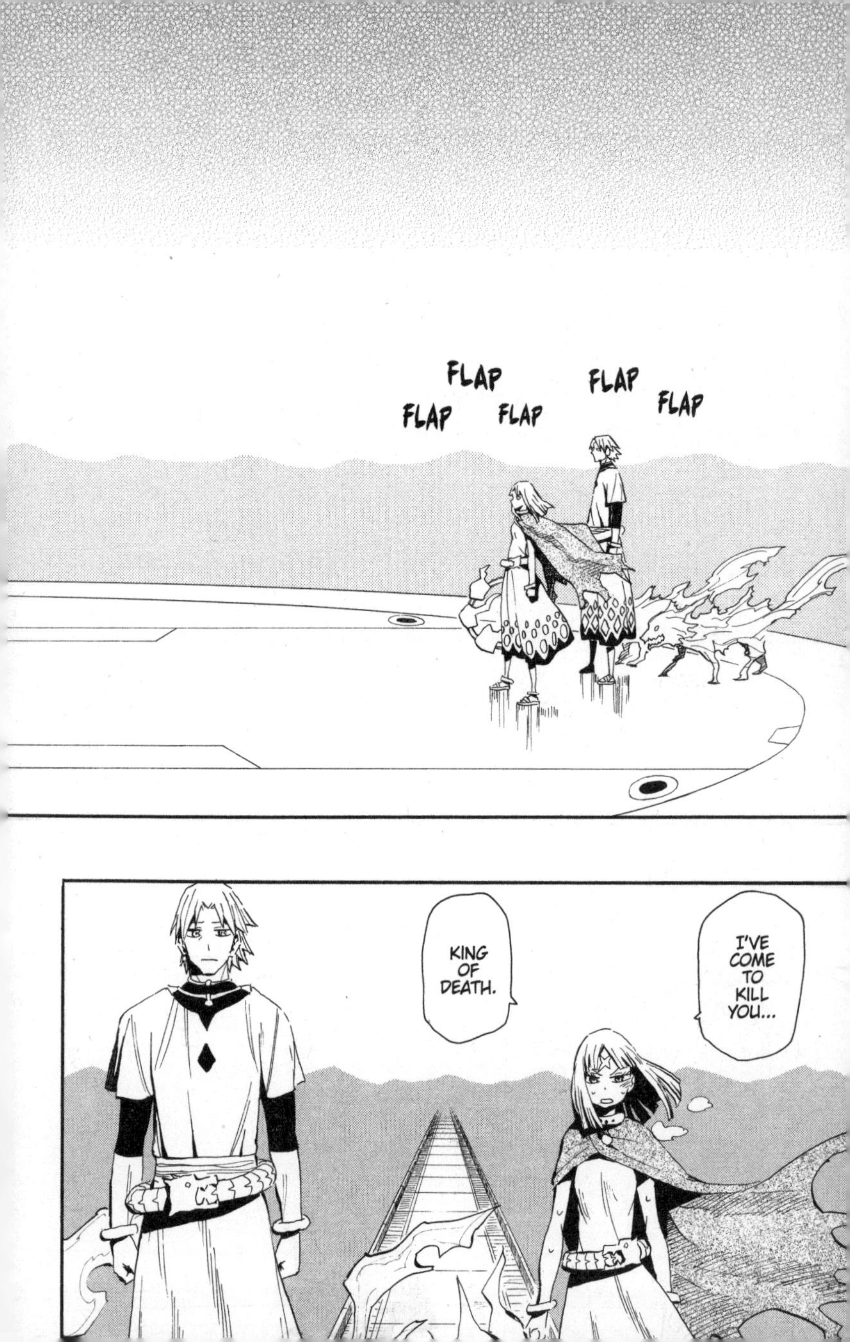
FLAP
FLAP
FLAP
FLAP
FLAP
I'VE COME TO KILL YOU...
KING OF DEATH.

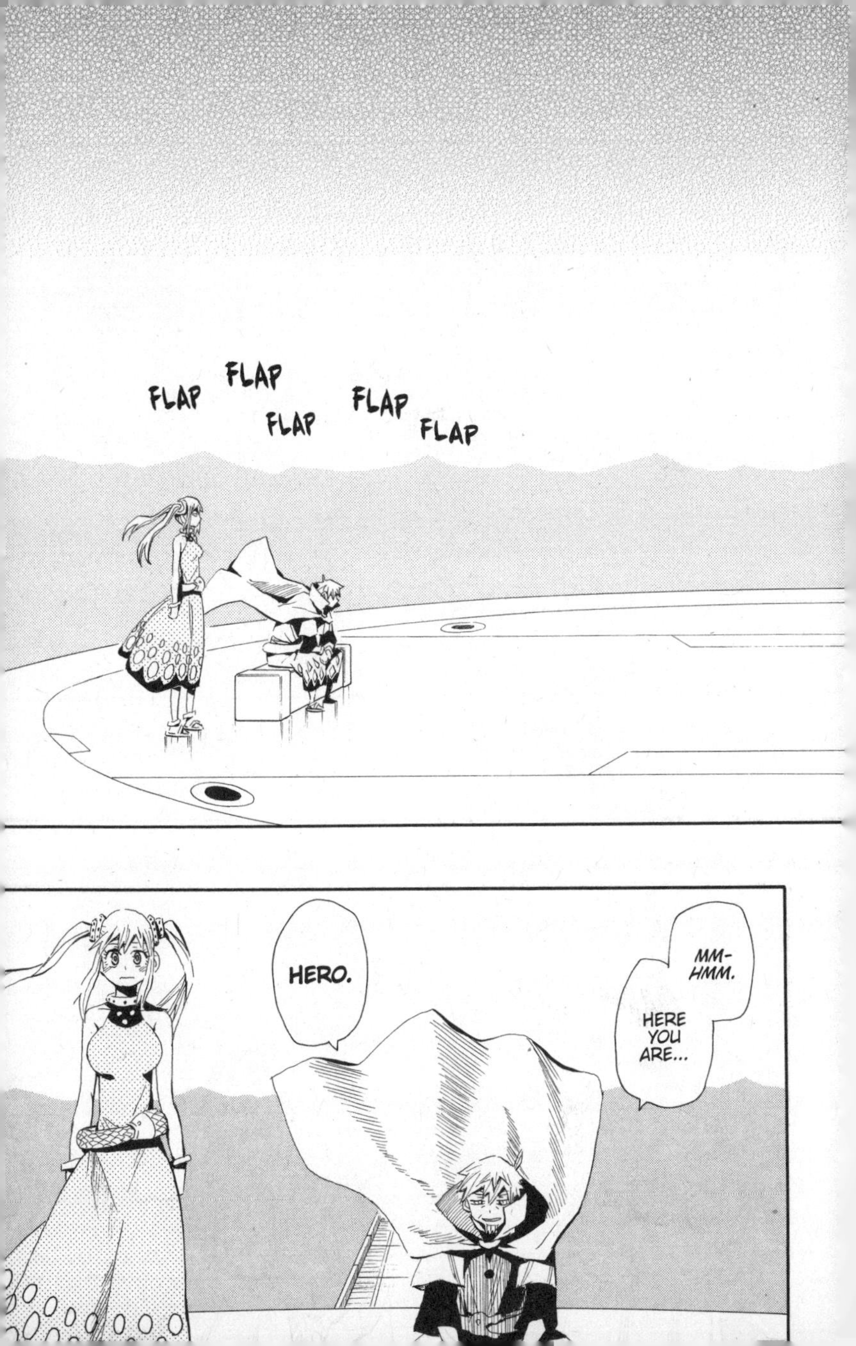
FLAP
FLAP
FLAP
FLAP
FLAP
MM-HMM.
HERE YOU ARE...
HERO.

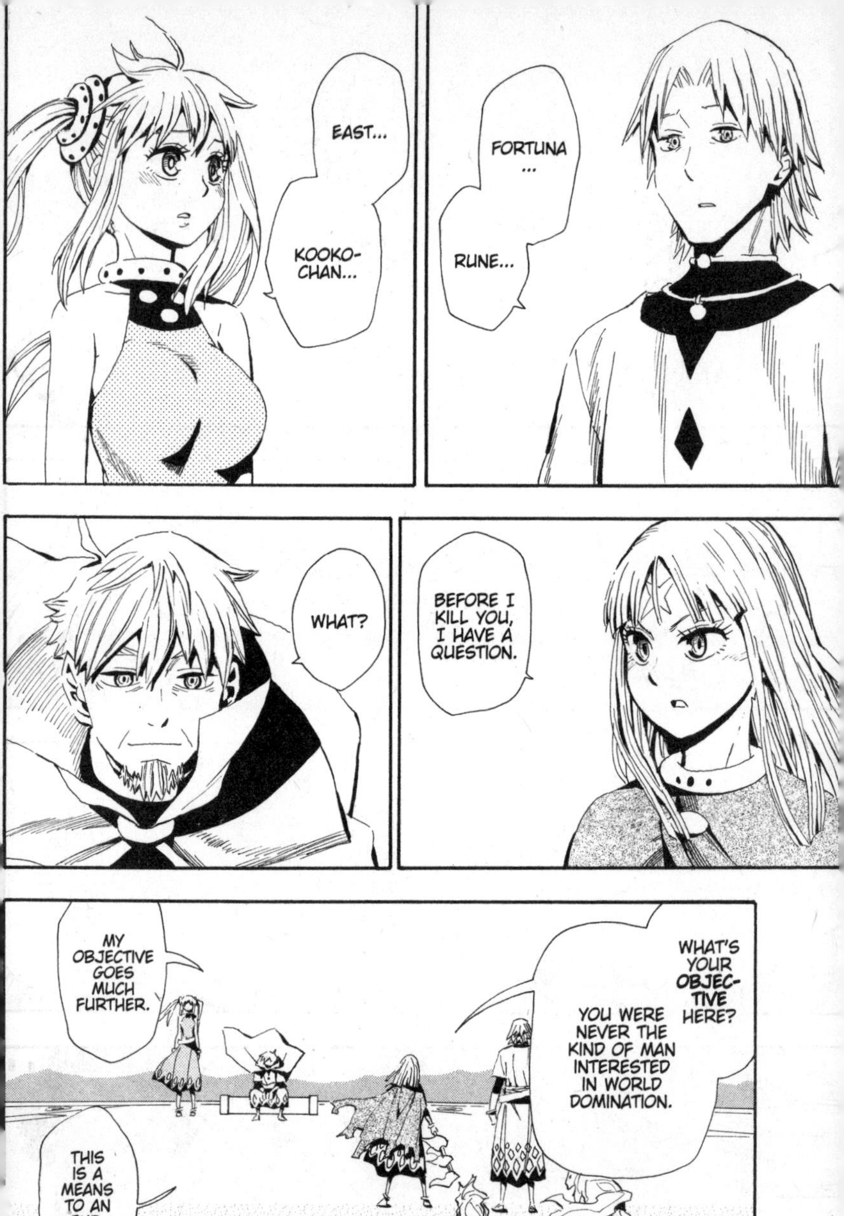

FORTUNA...
RUNE...
EAST...
KOOKO-CHAN...
BEFORE I KILL YOU, I HAVE A QUESTION.
WHAT?
WHAT'S YOUR OBJECTIVE HERE?
YOU WERE NEVER THE KIND OF MAN INTERESTED IN WORLD DOMINATION.
MY OBJECTIVE GOES MUCH FURTHER.
THIS IS A MEANS TO AN END.

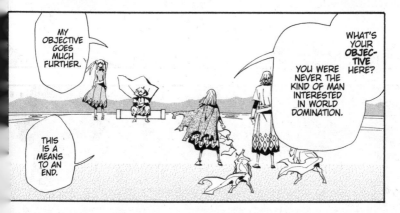

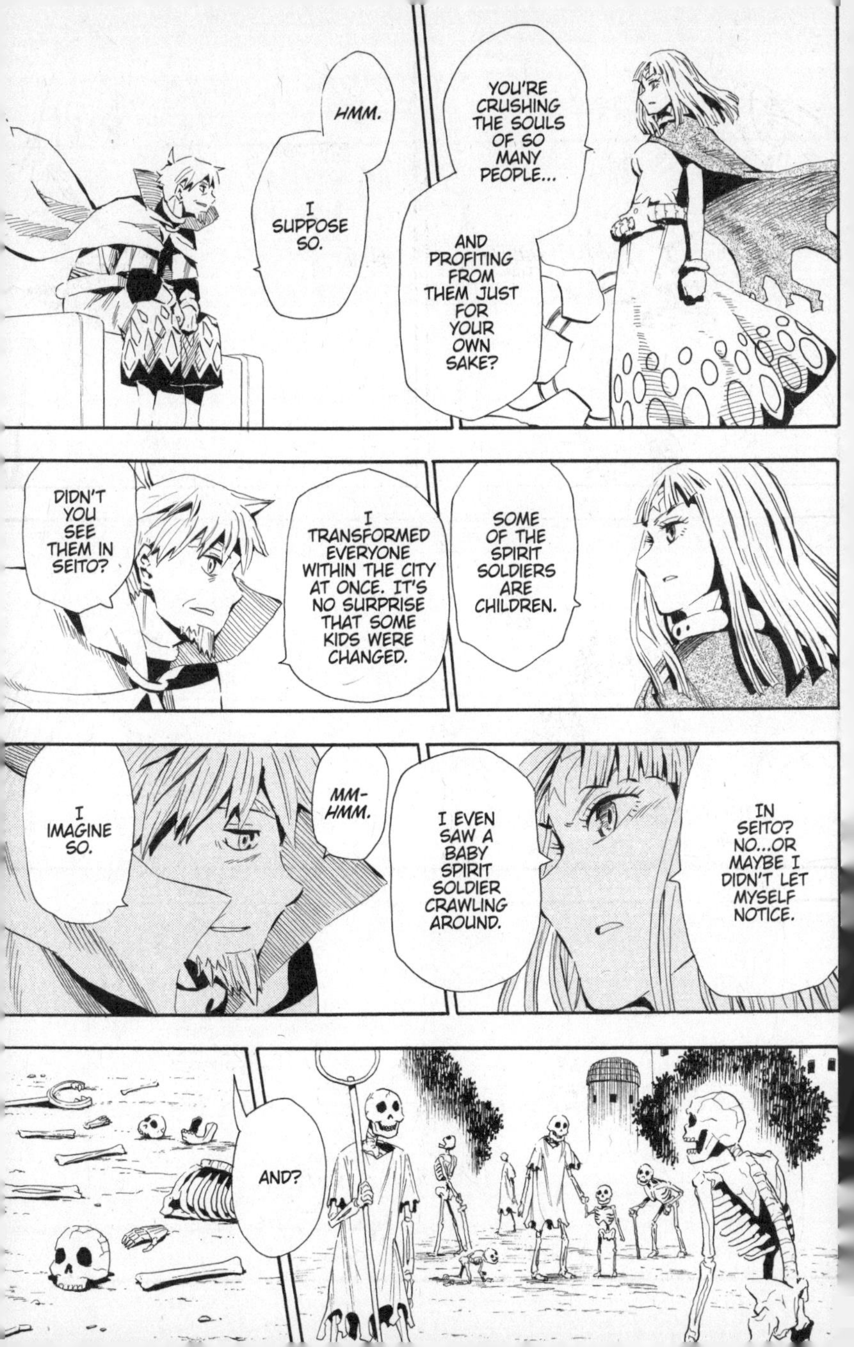
YOU'RE CRUSHING THE SOULS OF SO MANY PEOPLE...
AND PROFITING FROM THEM JUST FOR YOUR OWN SAKE?
HMM.
I SUPPOSE SO.
SOME OF THE SPIRIT SOLDIERS ARE CHILDREN.
I TRANSFORMED EVERYONE WITHIN THE CITY AT ONCE. IT'S NO SURPRISE THAT SOME KIDS WERE CHANGED.
DIDN'T YOU SEE THEM IN SEITO?
IN SEITO? NO...OR MAYBE I DIDN'T LET MYSELF NOTICE.
I EVEN SAW A BABY SPIRIT SOLDIER CRAWLING AROUND.
MM-HMM.
I IMAGINE SO.
AND?

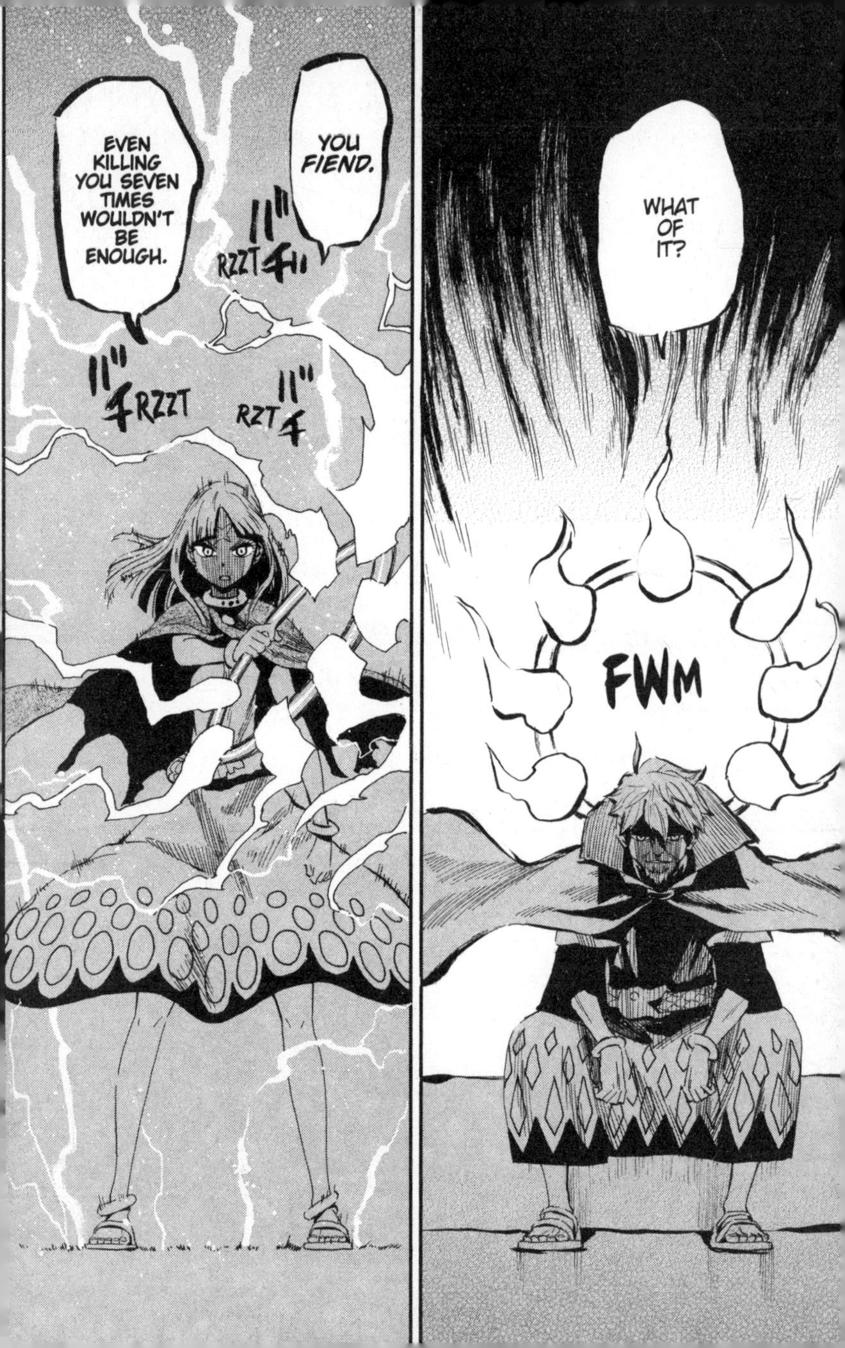
WHAT OF IT?
FWM
YOU FIEND.
EVEN KILLING YOU SEVEN TIMES WOULDN'T BE ENOUGH.
RZZT
FRZZT
RZT

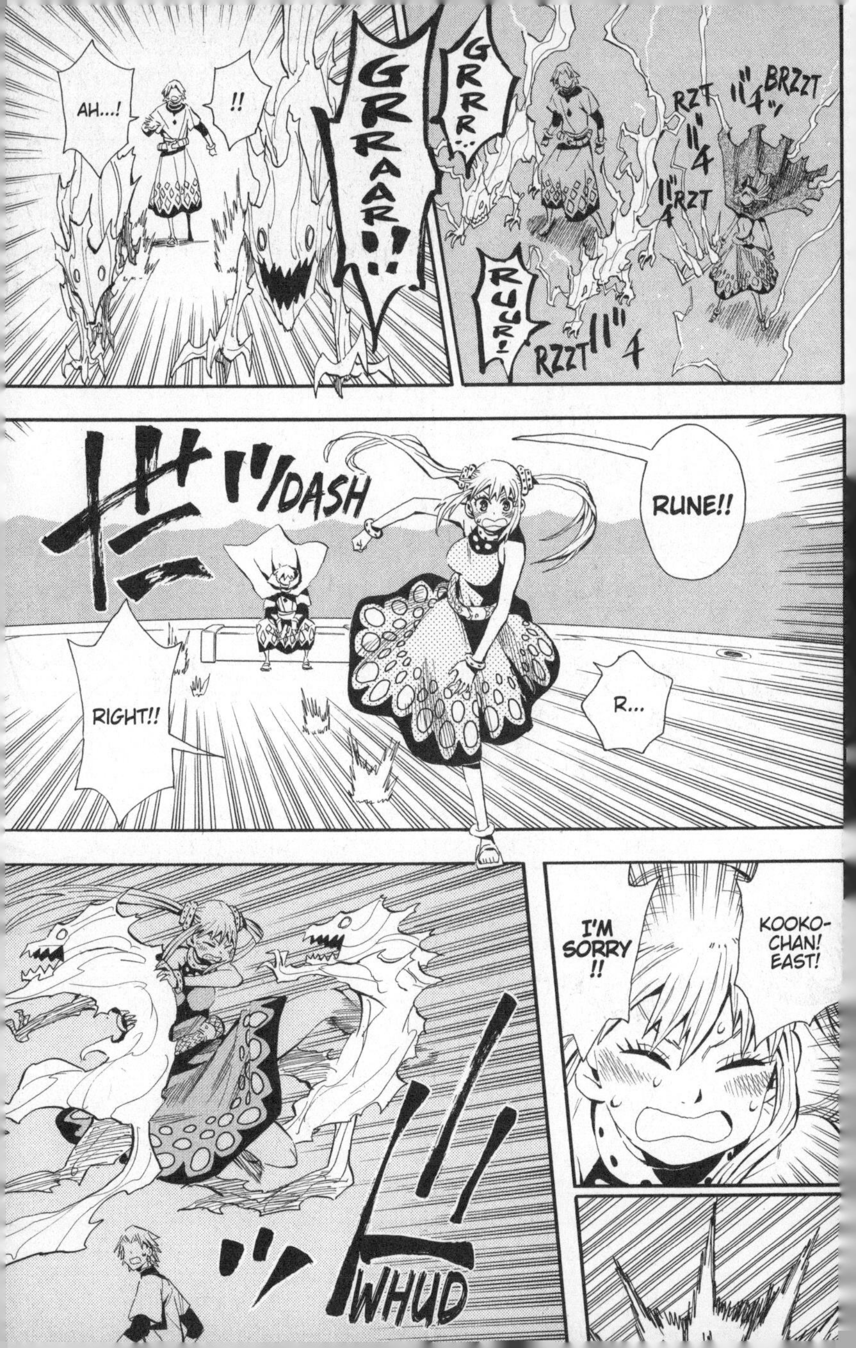
BRZZT
RZT
RZT
GRRR...
RUUR!
RZZT
GRRAAR!!
!!
AH...!
RUNE!!
R...
DASH
RIGHT!!
KOOKO-CHAN! EAST!
I'M SORRY!!
WHUD

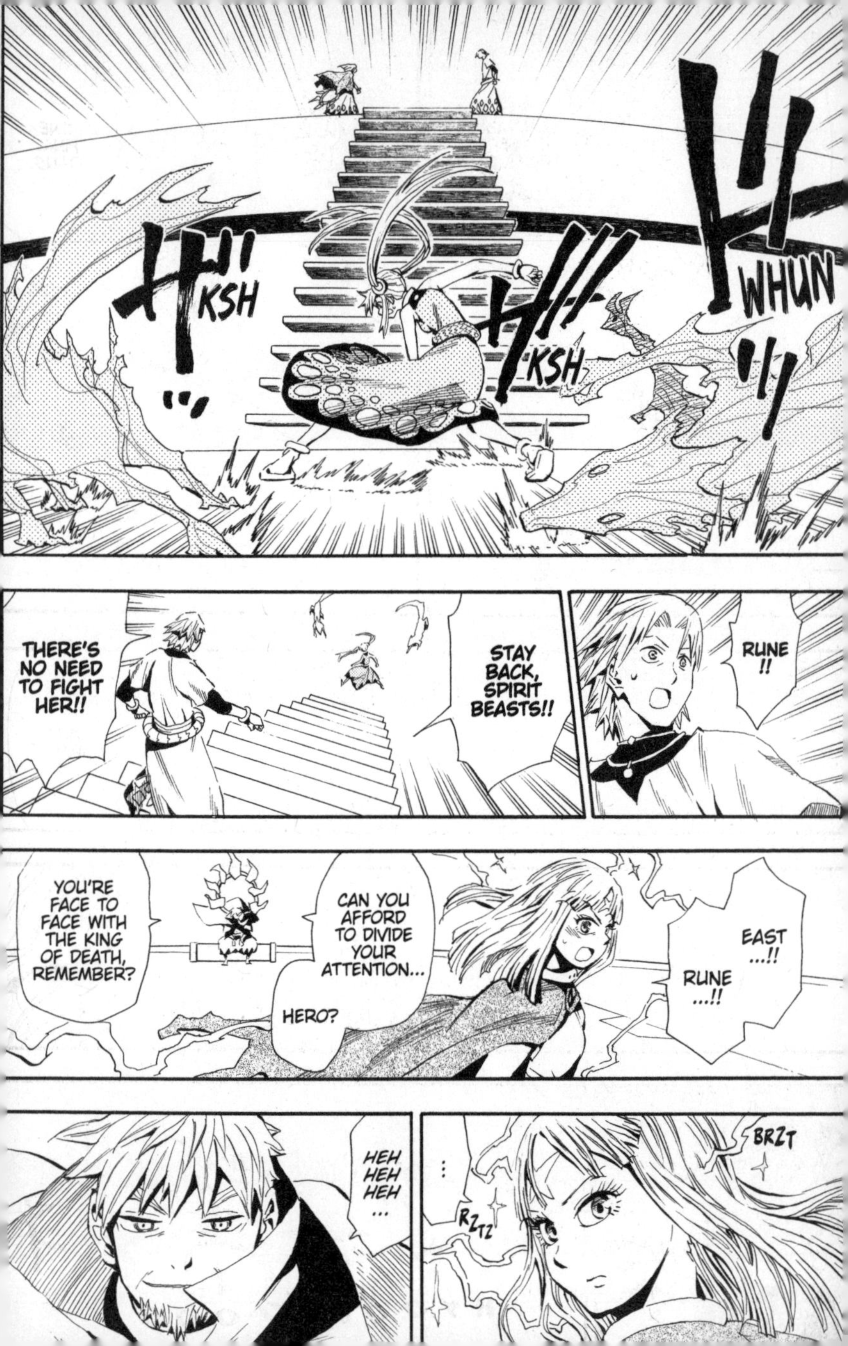
WHUN
KSH
KSH
RUNE!!
STAY BACK, SPIRIT BEASTS!!
THERE'S NO NEED TO FIGHT HER!!
EAST...!!
RUNE...!!
CAN YOU AFFORD TO DIVIDE YOUR ATTENTION...
HERO?
YOU'RE FACE TO FACE WITH THE KING OF DEATH, REMEMBER?
BRZT
RZTZ
...
HEH HEH HEH...

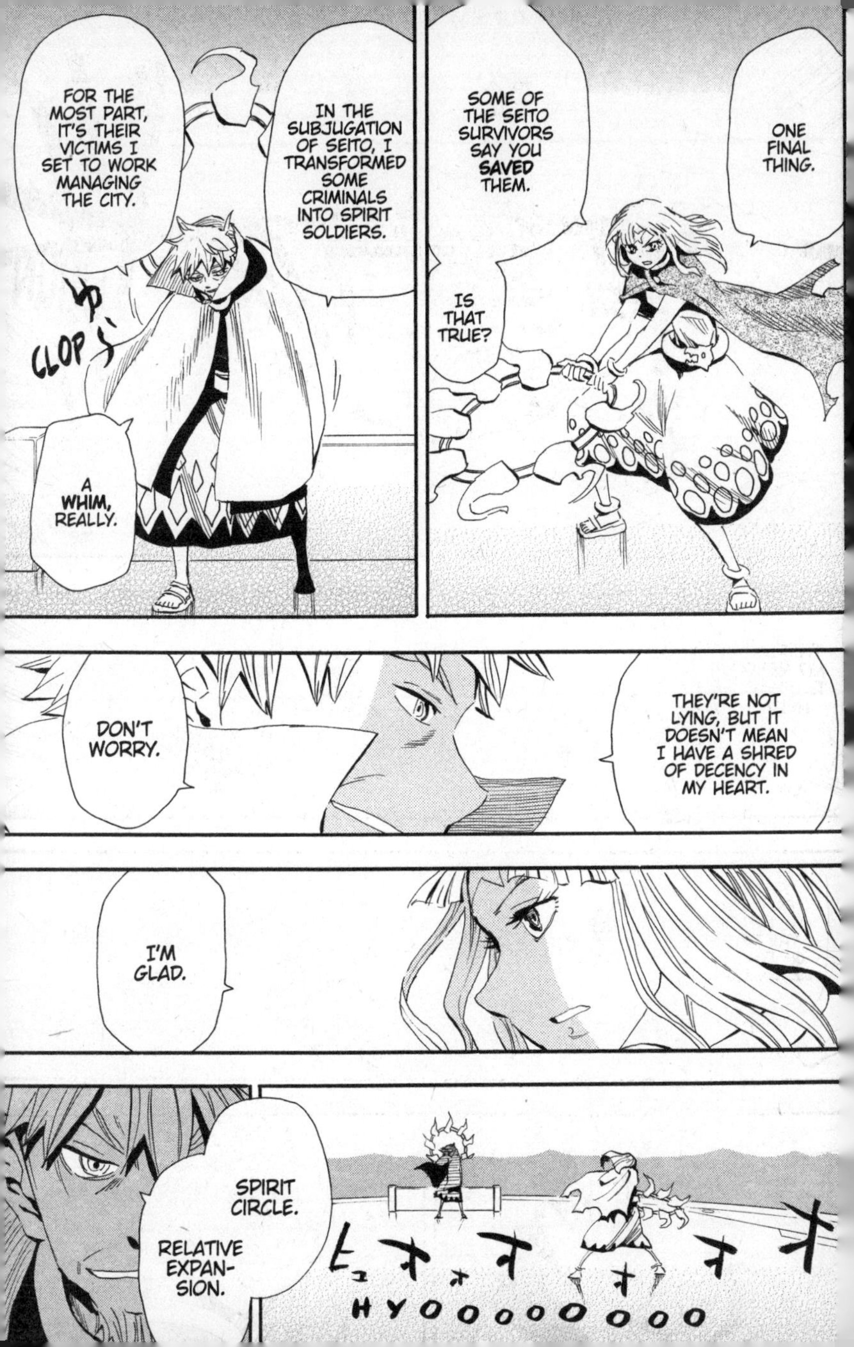
ONE FINAL THING.
SOME OF THE SEITO SURVIVORS SAY YOU SAVED THEM.
IS THAT TRUE?
IN THE SUBJUGATION OF SEITO, I TRANSFORMED SOME CRIMINALS INTO SPIRIT SOLDIERS.
FOR THE MOST PART, IT'S THEIR VICTIMS I SET TO WORK MANAGING THE CITY.
CLOP
A WHIM, REALLY.
THEY'RE NOT LYING, BUT IT DOESN'T MEAN I HAVE A SHRED OF DECENCY IN MY HEART.
DON'T WORRY.
I'M GLAD.
HYOOOOOOOOO
SPIRIT CIRCLE.
RELATIVE EXPAN-SION.

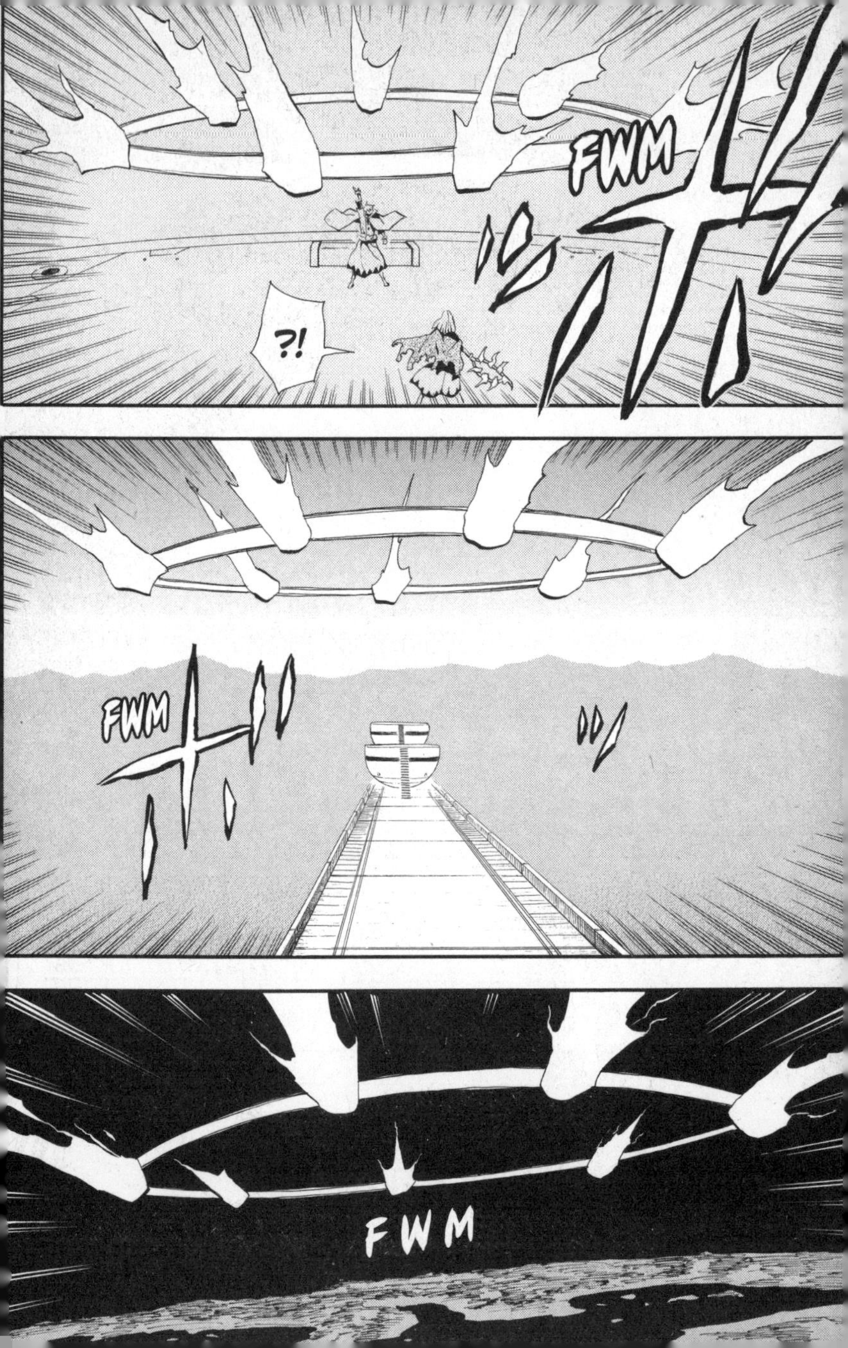
FWM
?!
FWM
FWM

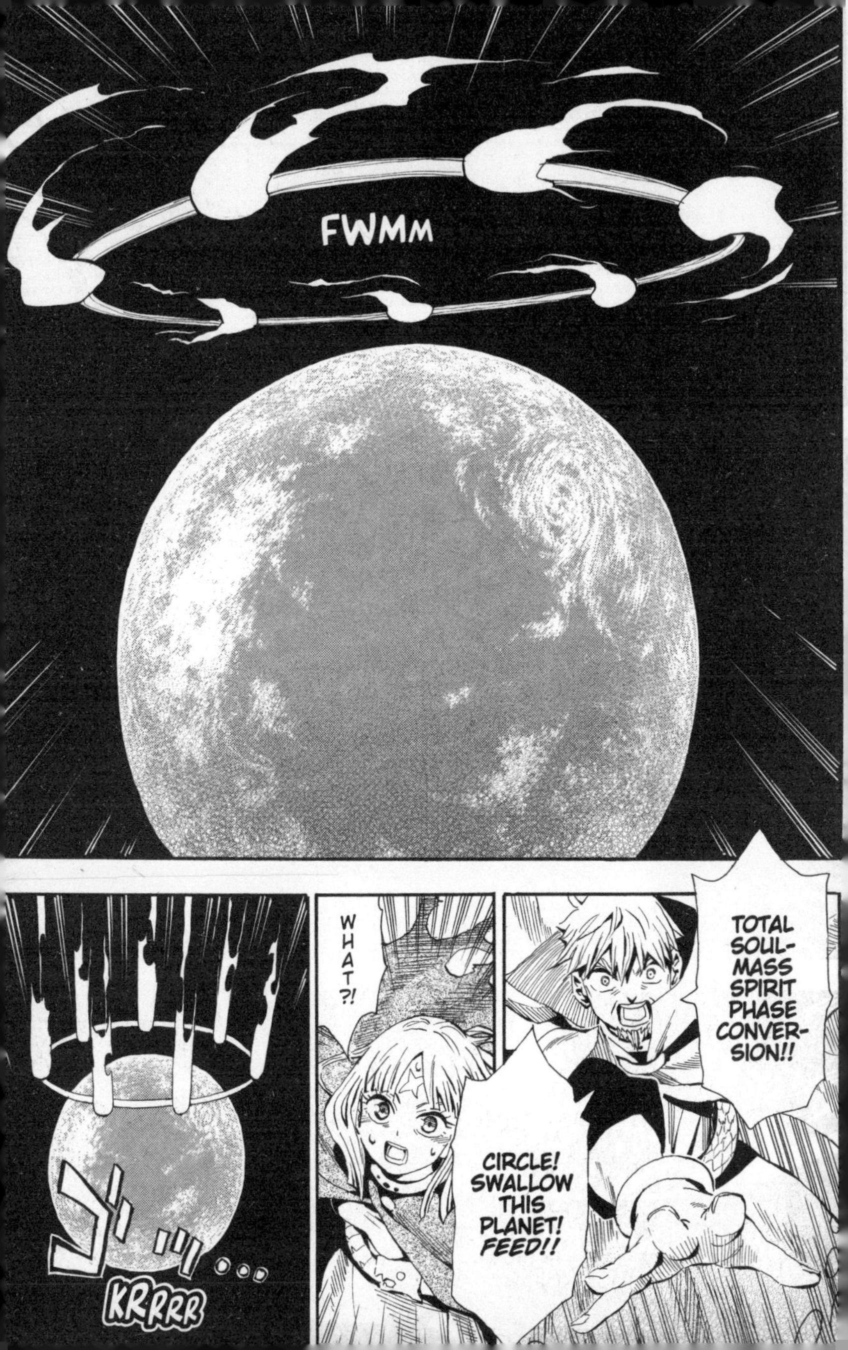
FWMm
TOTAL SOUL-MASS SPIRIT PHASE CONVERSION!!
CIRCLE! SWALLOW THIS PLANET! FEED!!
WHAT?!
KRRRR

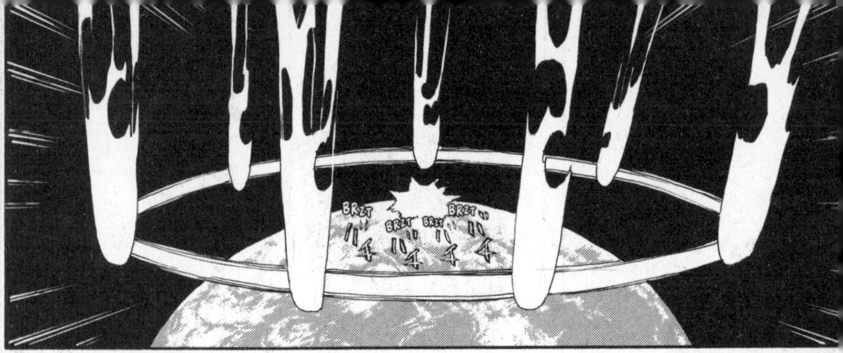
BRZT...
BRZT
BRZT
BRZT

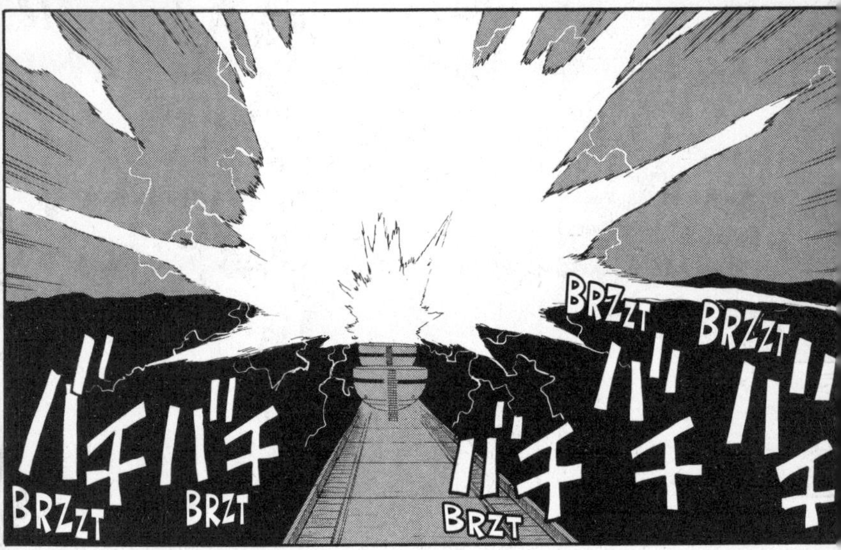
BRZZT
バチ
BRZZT
バチ
バチ
BRZT
バチバチ
BRZZT
BRZT

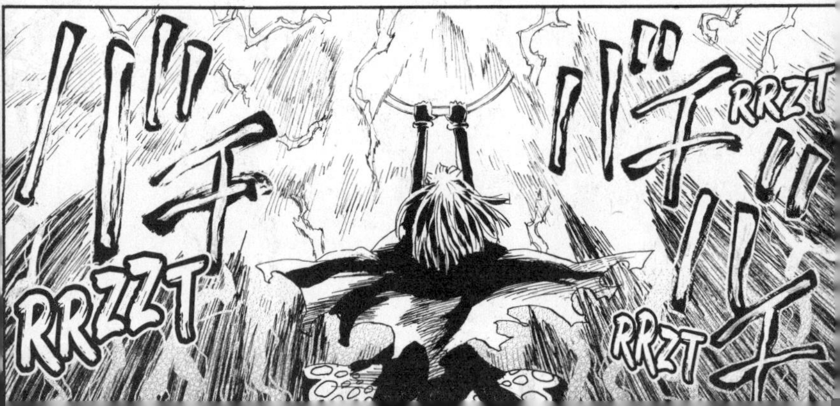
RRZT
バチィ
RRZT
バチ
RRZZZT

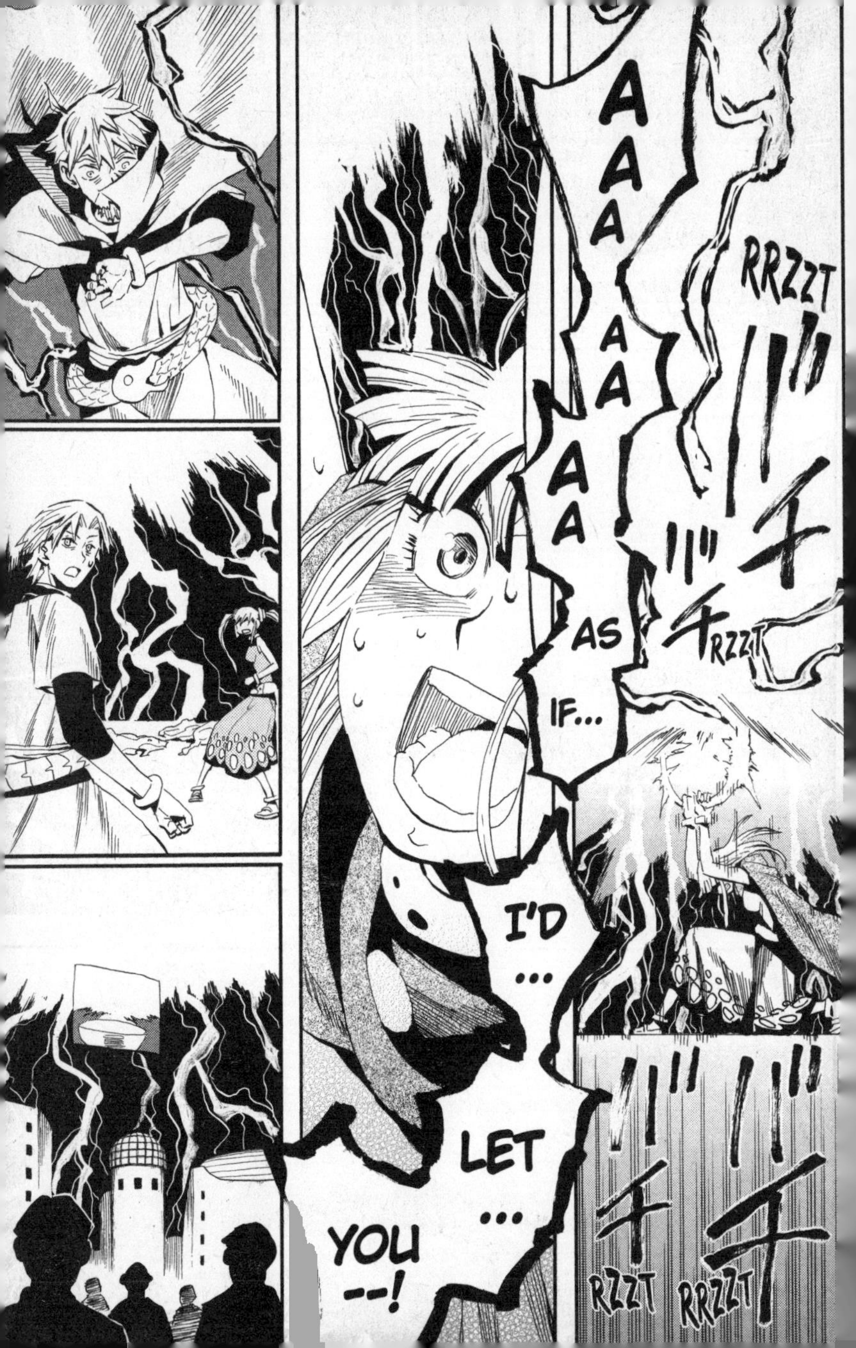
RRZZT
AAAAAAA
AS IF...
RZZZT
I'D ...
LET ...
YOU --!
RRZZZT
RZZT

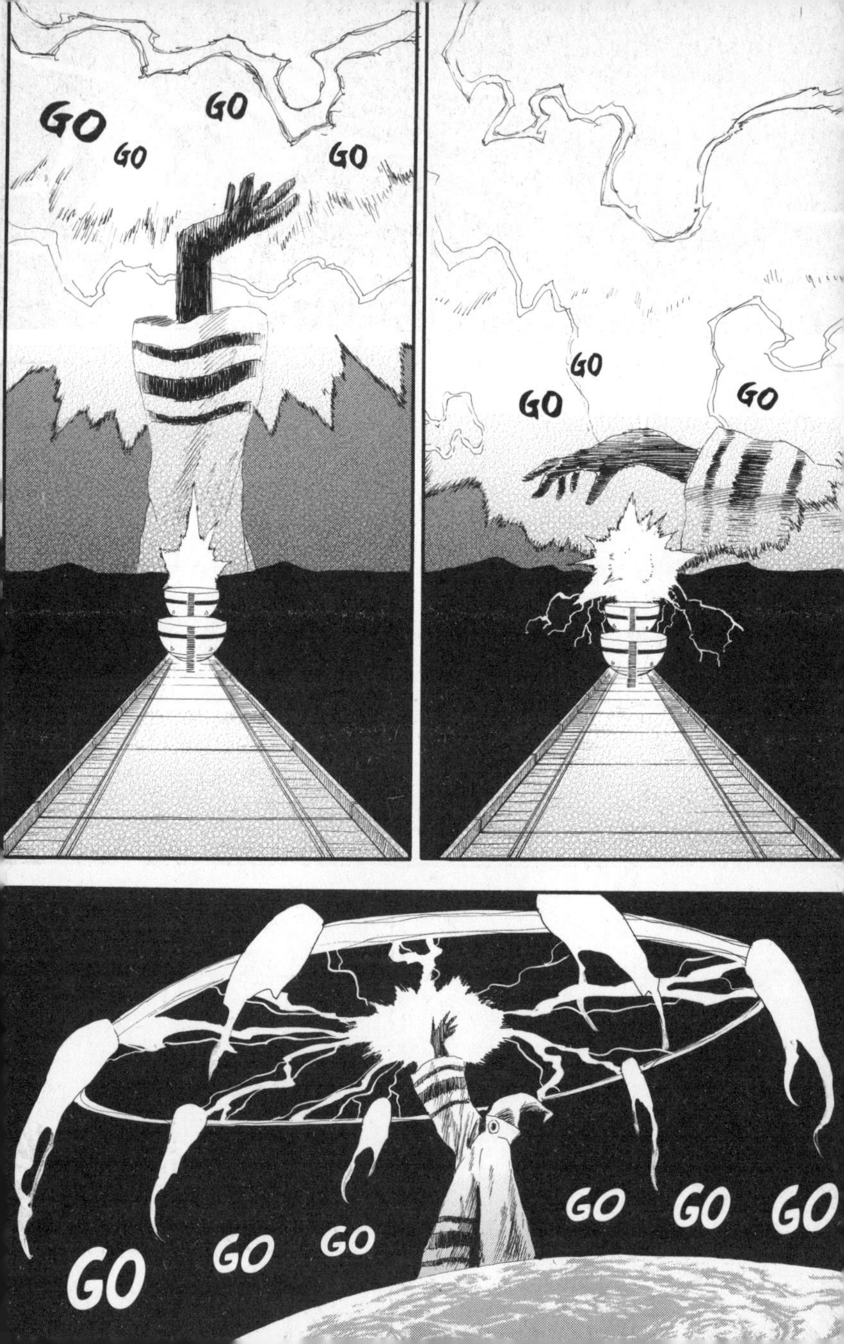
GO
GO
GO
GO
GO
GO
GO
GO
GO
GO
GO
GO
GO
GO
GO

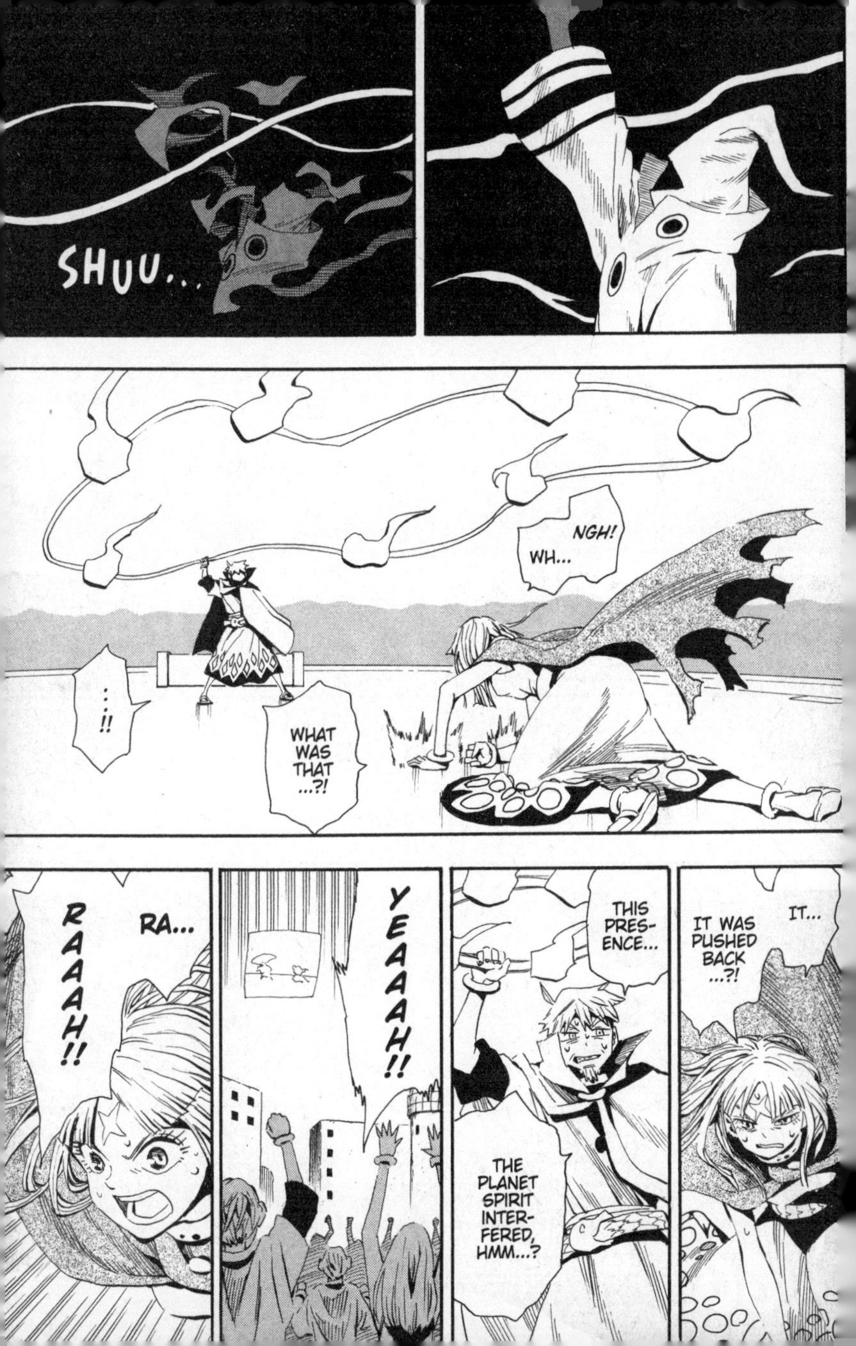
SHUU...
NGH! WH...
WHAT WAS THAT ...?!
...!!
IT... IT WAS PUSHED BACK ...?!
THIS PRESENCE...
THE PLANET SPIRIT INTERFERED, HMM...?
YEAAAAH!!
RA...
RAAAAH!!

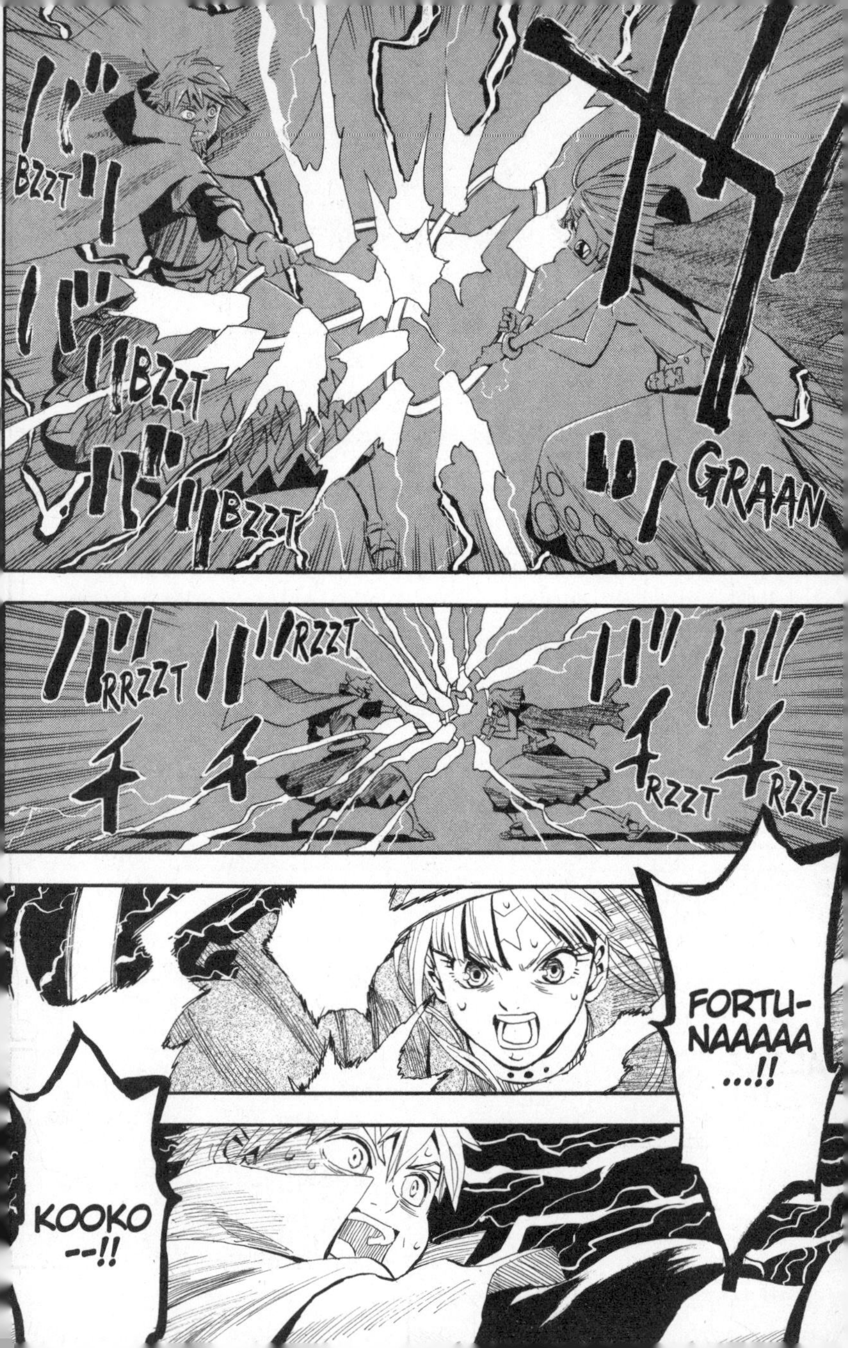
GRAAN
BZZT
BZZT
BZZT
RZZT
RZZT
RZZT
RRZZT
FORTU-NAAAAA ...!!
KOOKO --!!

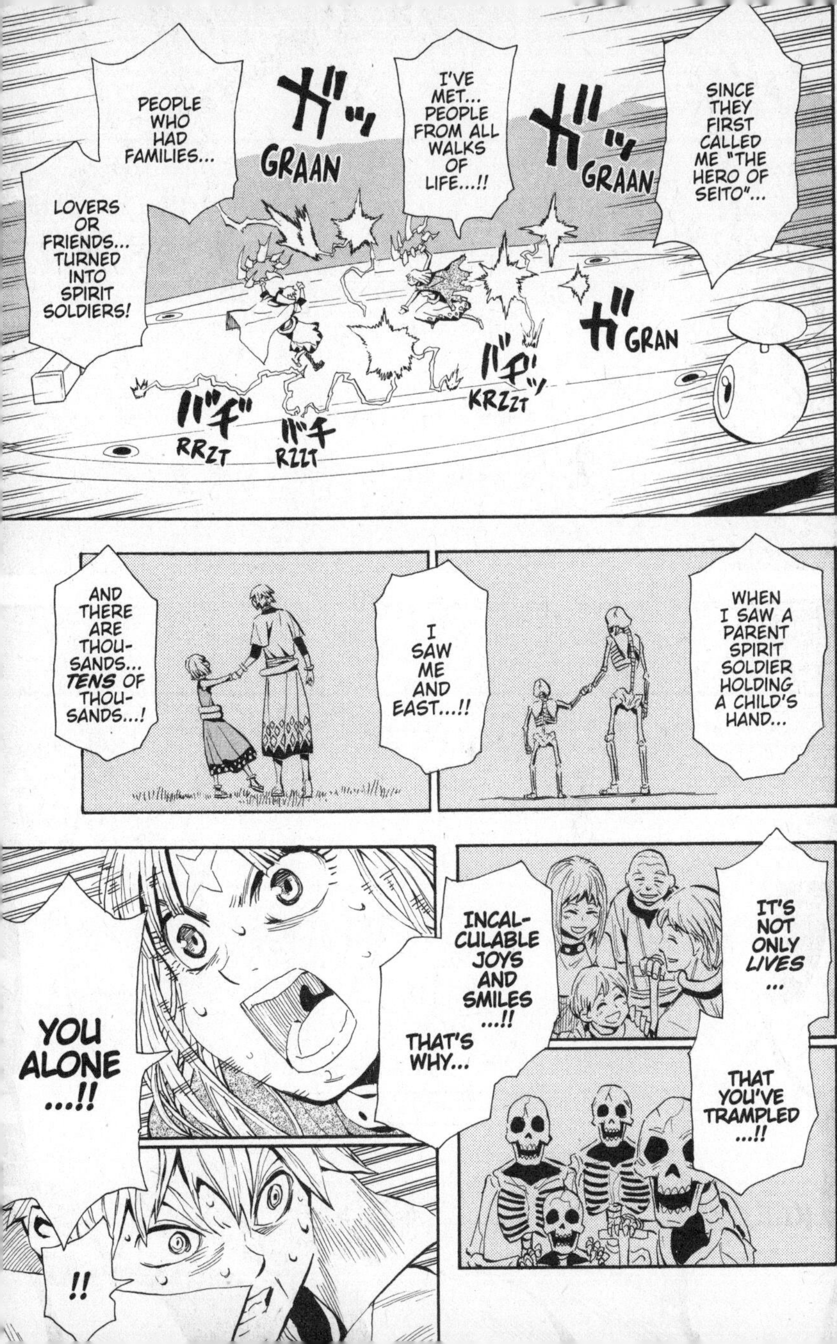
SINCE THEY FIRST CALLED ME "THE HERO OF SEITO"...
GRAAN
I'VE MET... PEOPLE FROM ALL WALKS OF LIFE...!!
GRAAN
PEOPLE WHO HAD FAMILIES...
LOVERS OR FRIENDS... TURNED INTO SPIRIT SOLDIERS!
GRAN
KRZZT
RZZT
RRZT
WHEN I SAW A PARENT SPIRIT SOLDIER HOLDING A CHILD'S HAND...
I SAW ME AND EAST...!!
AND THERE ARE THOUSANDS... *TENS* OF THOUSANDS...!
IT'S NOT ONLY *LIVES*...
THAT YOU'VE TRAMPLED...!!
INCALCULABLE JOYS AND SMILES...!!
THAT'S WHY...
YOU ALONE...!!
!!

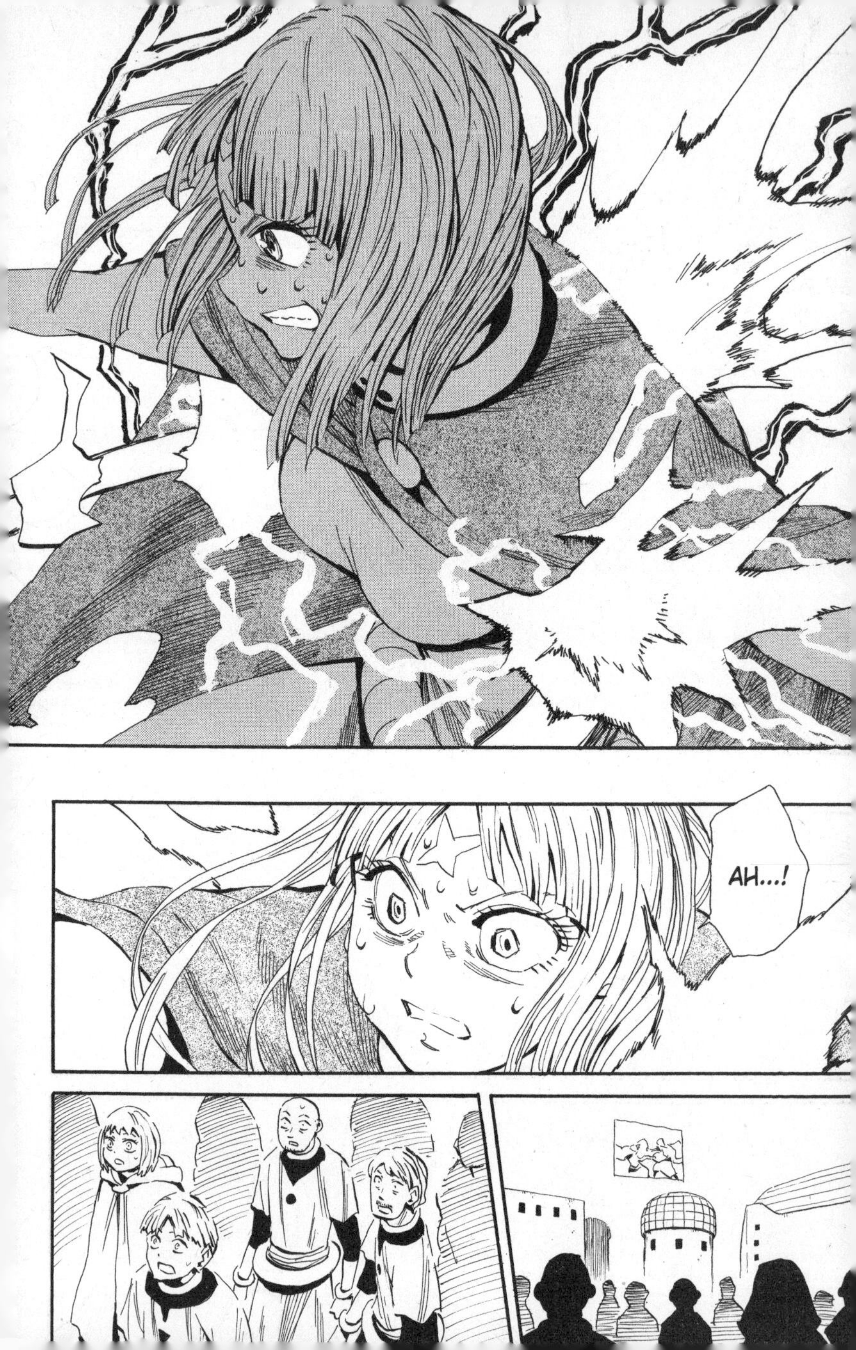
AH...!

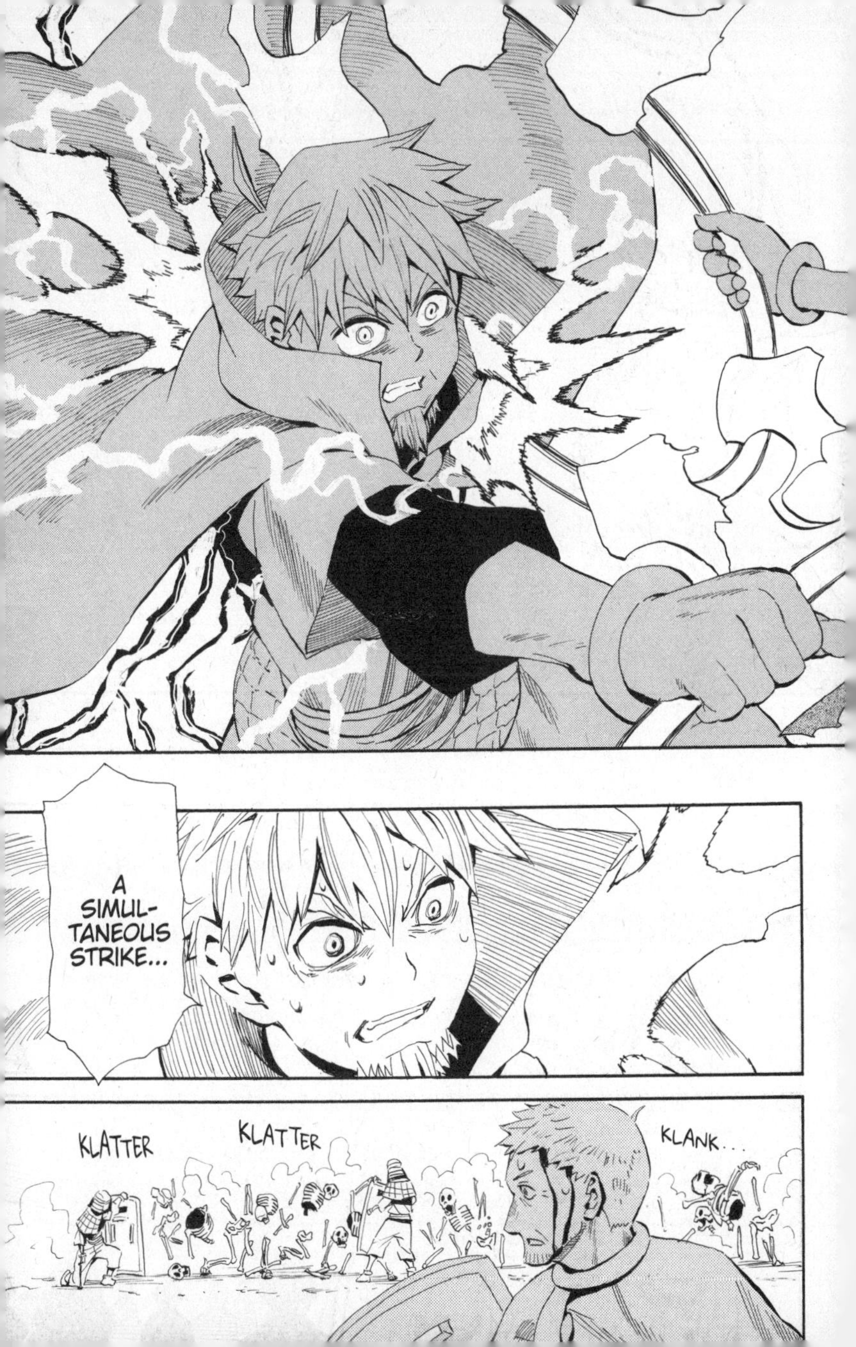
A SIMUL-TANEOUS STRIKE...
KLANK...
KLATTER
KLATTER

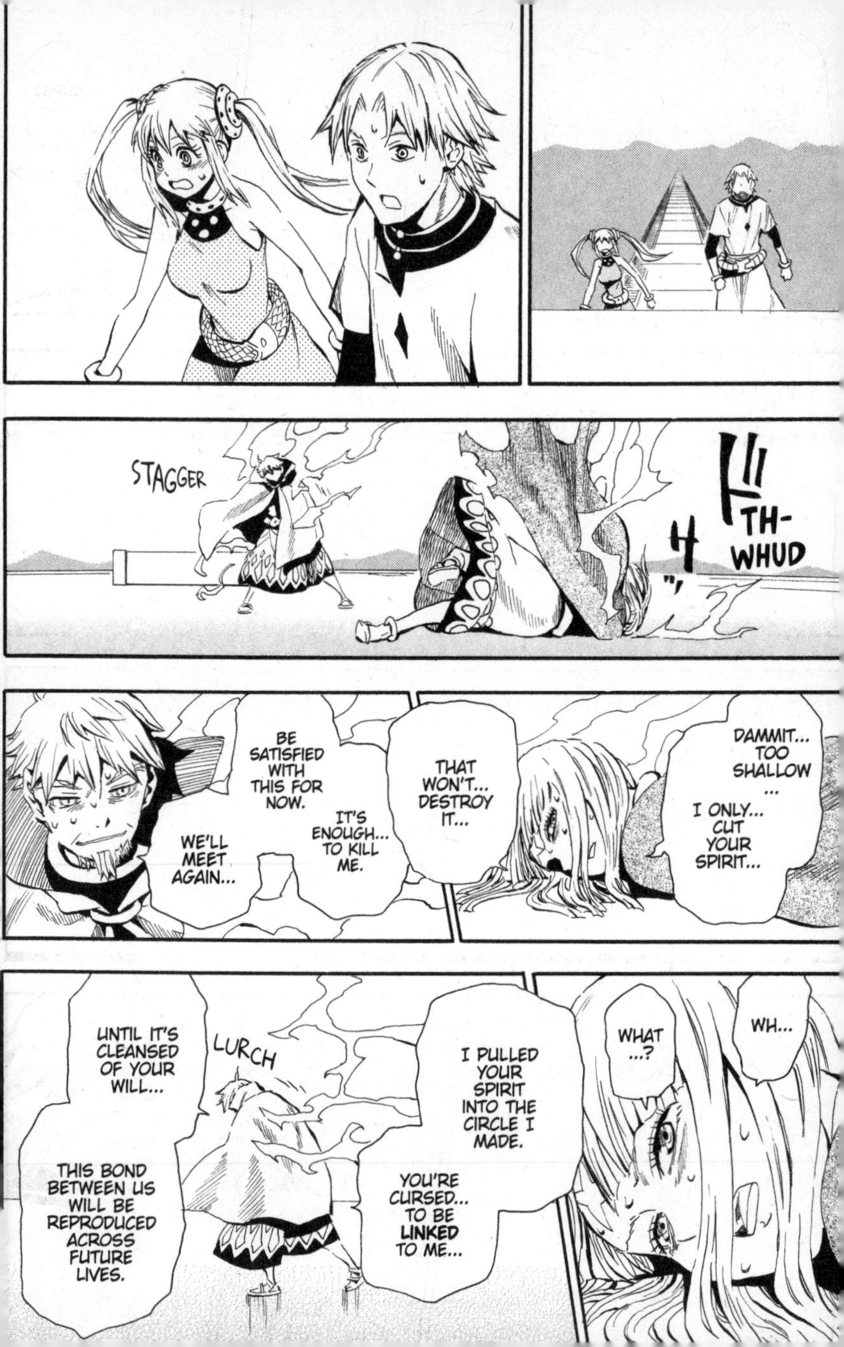
TH-WHUD
STAGGER
DAMMIT... TOO SHALLOW ...
I ONLY... CUT YOUR SPIRIT...
THAT WON'T... DESTROY IT...
IT'S ENOUGH... TO KILL ME.
BE SATISFIED WITH THIS FOR NOW.
WE'LL MEET AGAIN...
WH...
WHAT ...?
I PULLED YOUR SPIRIT INTO THE CIRCLE I MADE.
YOU'RE CURSED... TO BE LINKED TO ME...
LURCH
UNTIL IT'S CLEANSED OF YOUR WILL...
THIS BOND BETWEEN US WILL BE REPRODUCED ACROSS FUTURE LIVES.

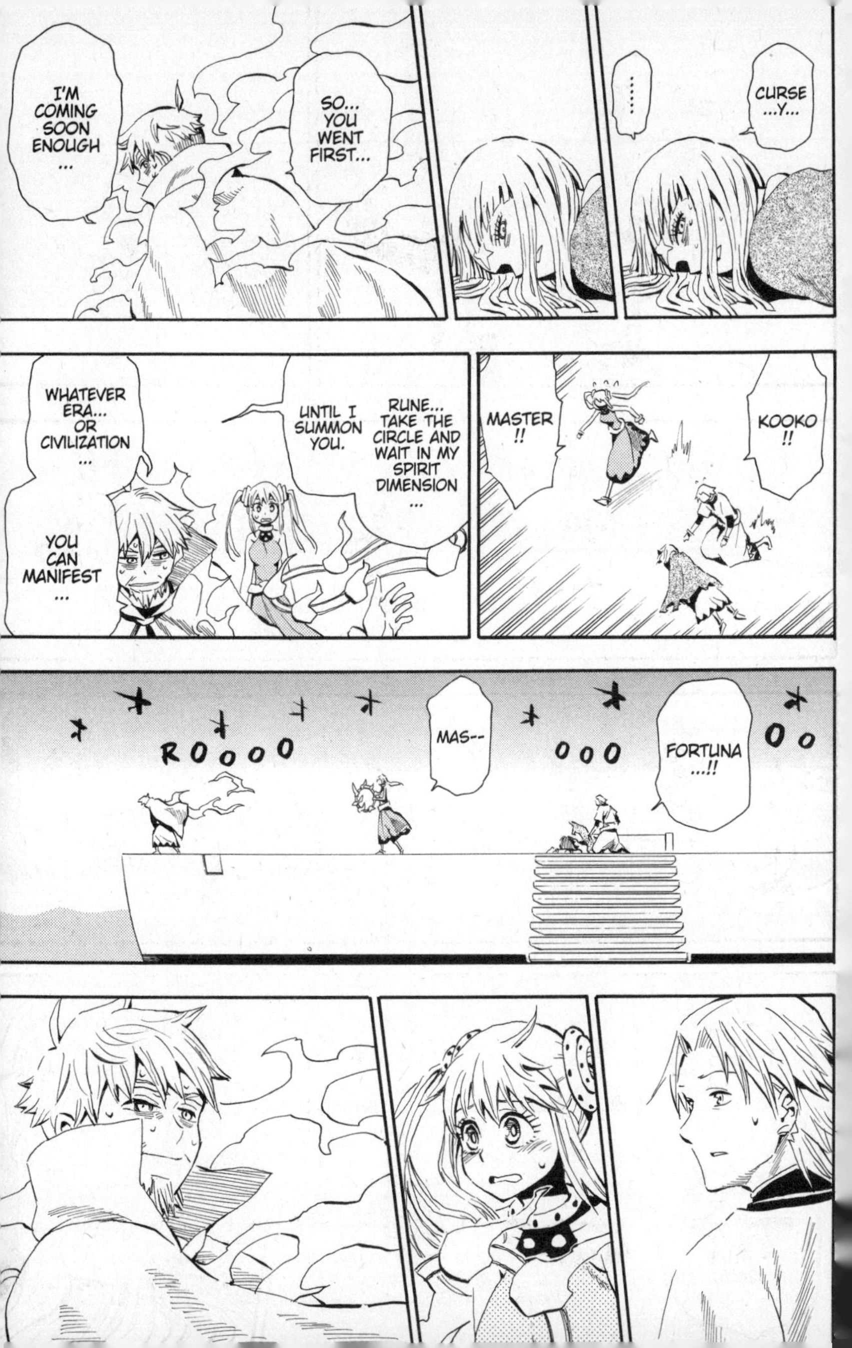
CURSE ...Y...
......
SO... YOU WENT FIRST...
I'M COMING SOON ENOUGH ...
KOOKO !!
MASTER !!
RUNE... TAKE THE CIRCLE AND WAIT IN MY SPIRIT DIMENSION ...
UNTIL I SUMMON YOU.
WHATEVER ERA... OR CIVILIZATION ...
YOU CAN MANIFEST ...
FORTUNA ...!!
MAS--
ROOOOO OOO OO

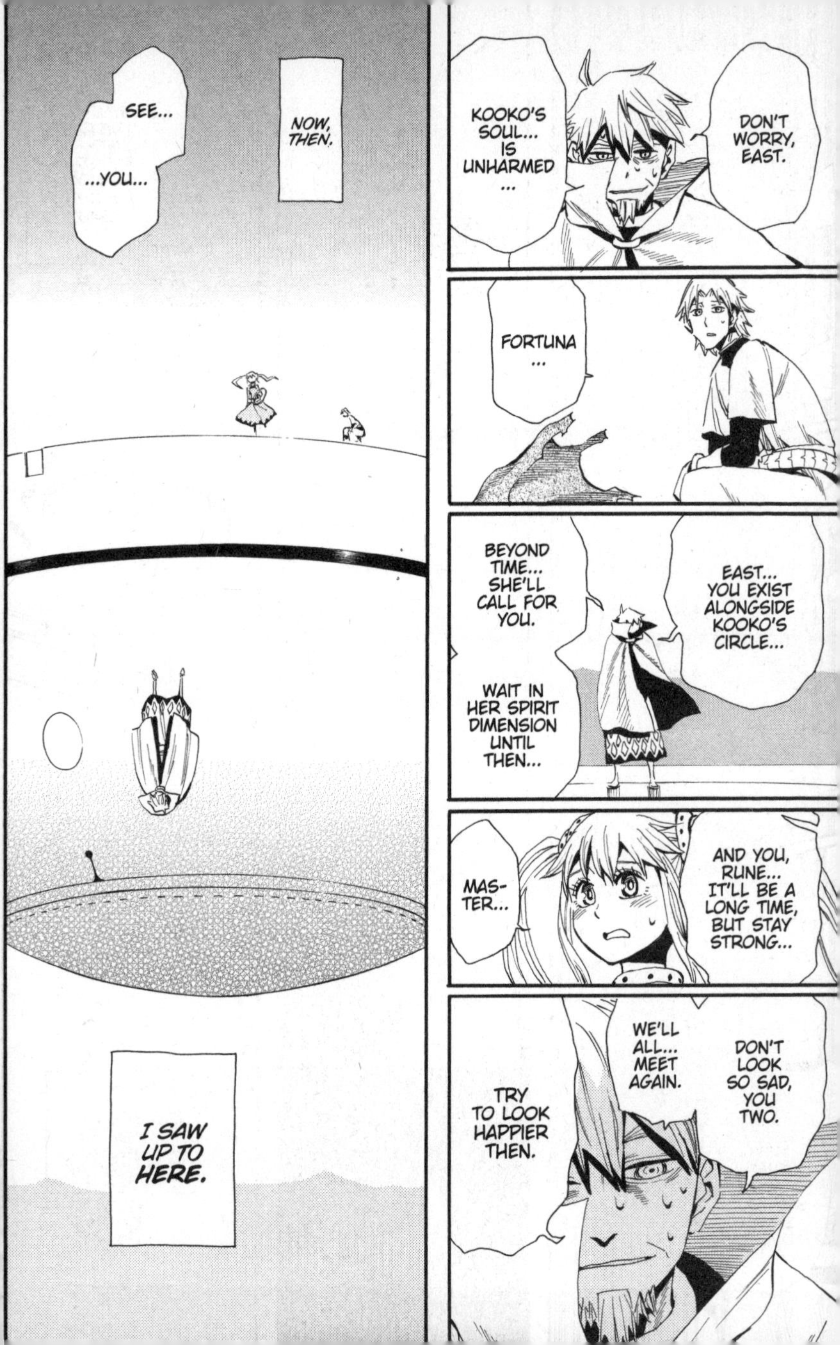
DON'T WORRY, EAST.
KOOKO'S SOUL... IS UNHARMED ...
FORTUNA ...
EAST... YOU EXIST ALONGSIDE KOOKO'S CIRCLE...
BEYOND TIME... SHE'LL CALL FOR YOU.
WAIT IN HER SPIRIT DIMENSION UNTIL THEN...
AND YOU, RUNE... IT'LL BE A LONG TIME, BUT STAY STRONG...
MAS-TER...
DON'T LOOK SO SAD, YOU TWO.
WE'LL ALL... MEET AGAIN.
TRY TO LOOK HAPPIER THEN.
NOW, THEN.
SEE...
...YOU...
I SAW UP TO HERE.

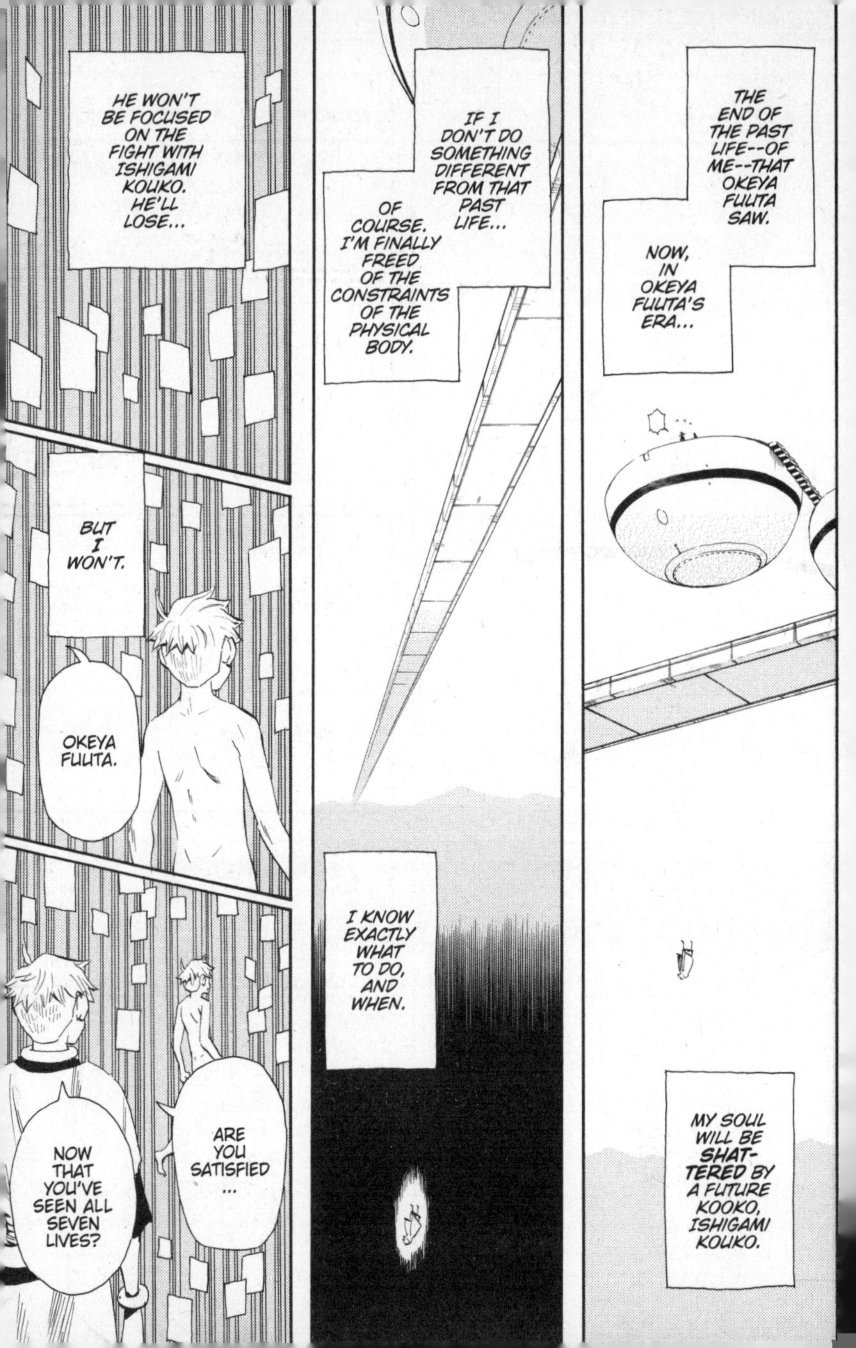
THE END OF THE PAST LIFE--OF ME--THAT OKEYA FUUTA SAW.
NOW, IN OKEYA FUUTA'S ERA...
MY SOUL WILL BE SHATTERED BY A FUTURE KOOKO, ISHIGAMI KOUKO.
IF I DON'T DO SOMETHING DIFFERENT FROM THAT PAST LIFE...
OF COURSE. I'M FINALLY FREED OF THE CONSTRAINTS OF THE PHYSICAL BODY.
I KNOW EXACTLY WHAT TO DO, AND WHEN.
HE WON'T BE FOCUSED ON THE FIGHT WITH ISHIGAMI KOUKO. HE'LL LOSE...
BUT I WON'T.
OKEYA FUUTA.
ARE YOU SATISFIED...
NOW THAT YOU'VE SEEN ALL SEVEN LIVES?

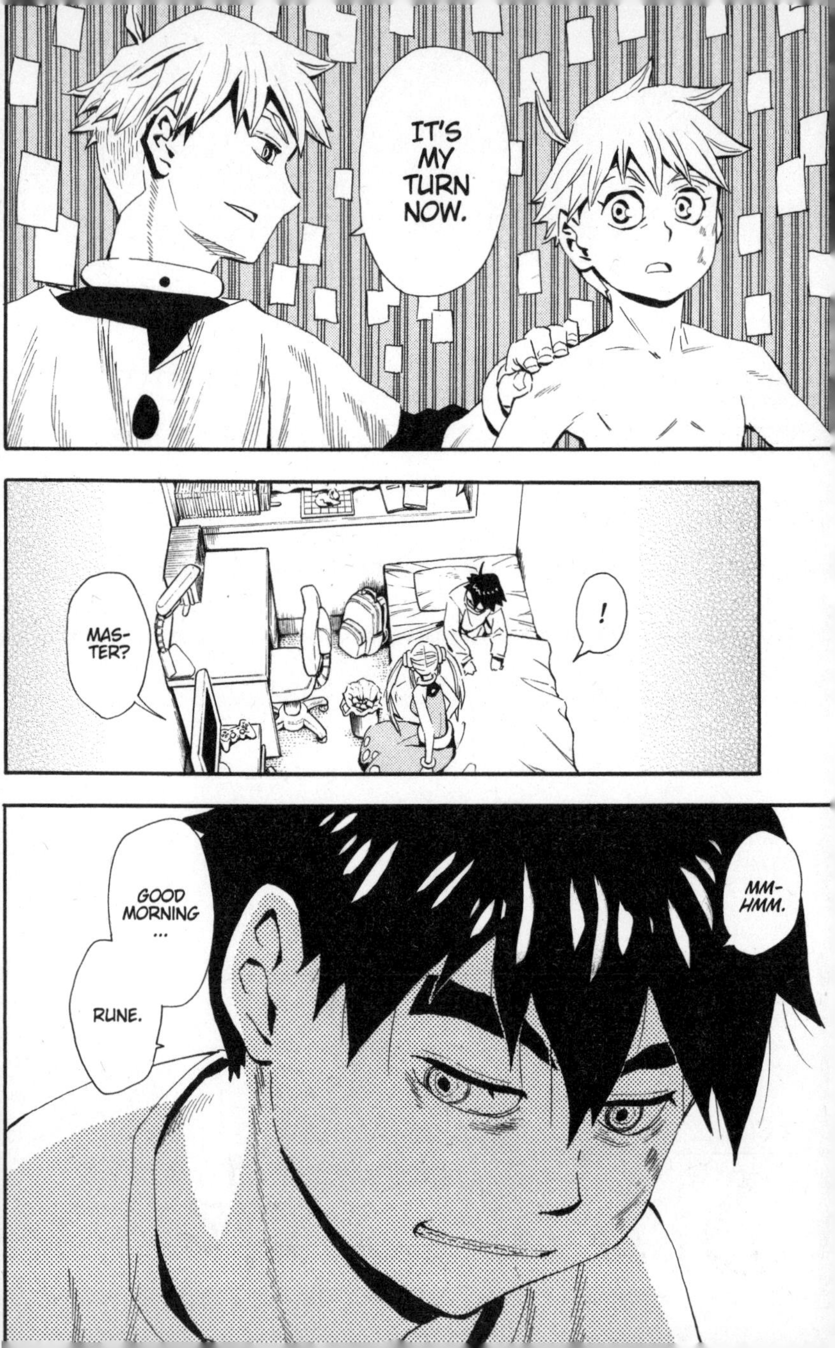
IT'S MY TURN NOW.
!
MAS-TER?
MM-HMM.
GOOD MORNING ...
RUNE.

Spirit Circle

Spirit Circle

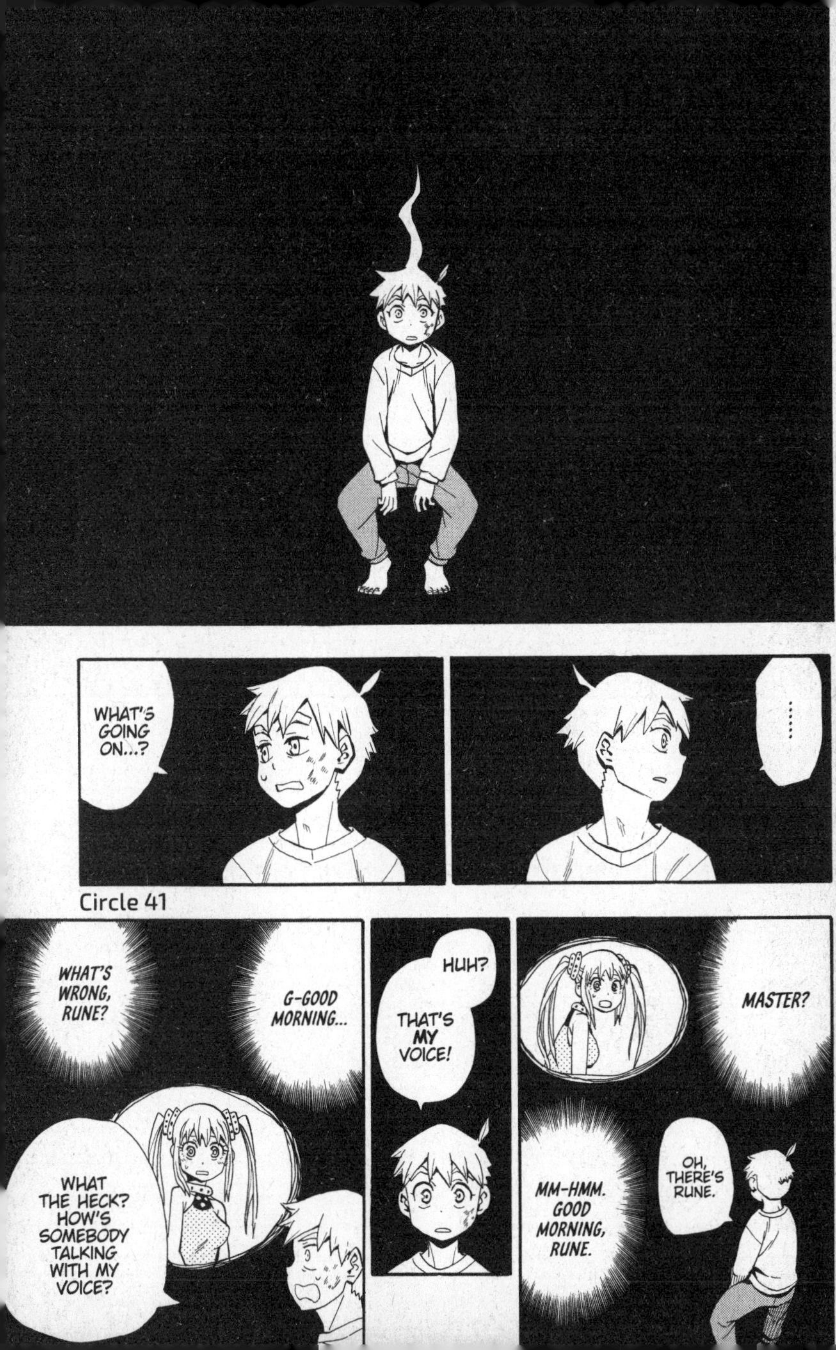
......
WHAT'S GOING ON...?
Circle 41
MASTER?
OH, THERE'S RUNE.
MM-HMM. GOOD MORNING, RUNE.
HUH?
THAT'S MY VOICE!
G-GOOD MORNING...
WHAT'S WRONG, RUNE?
WHAT THE HECK? HOW'S SOMEBODY TALKING WITH MY VOICE?

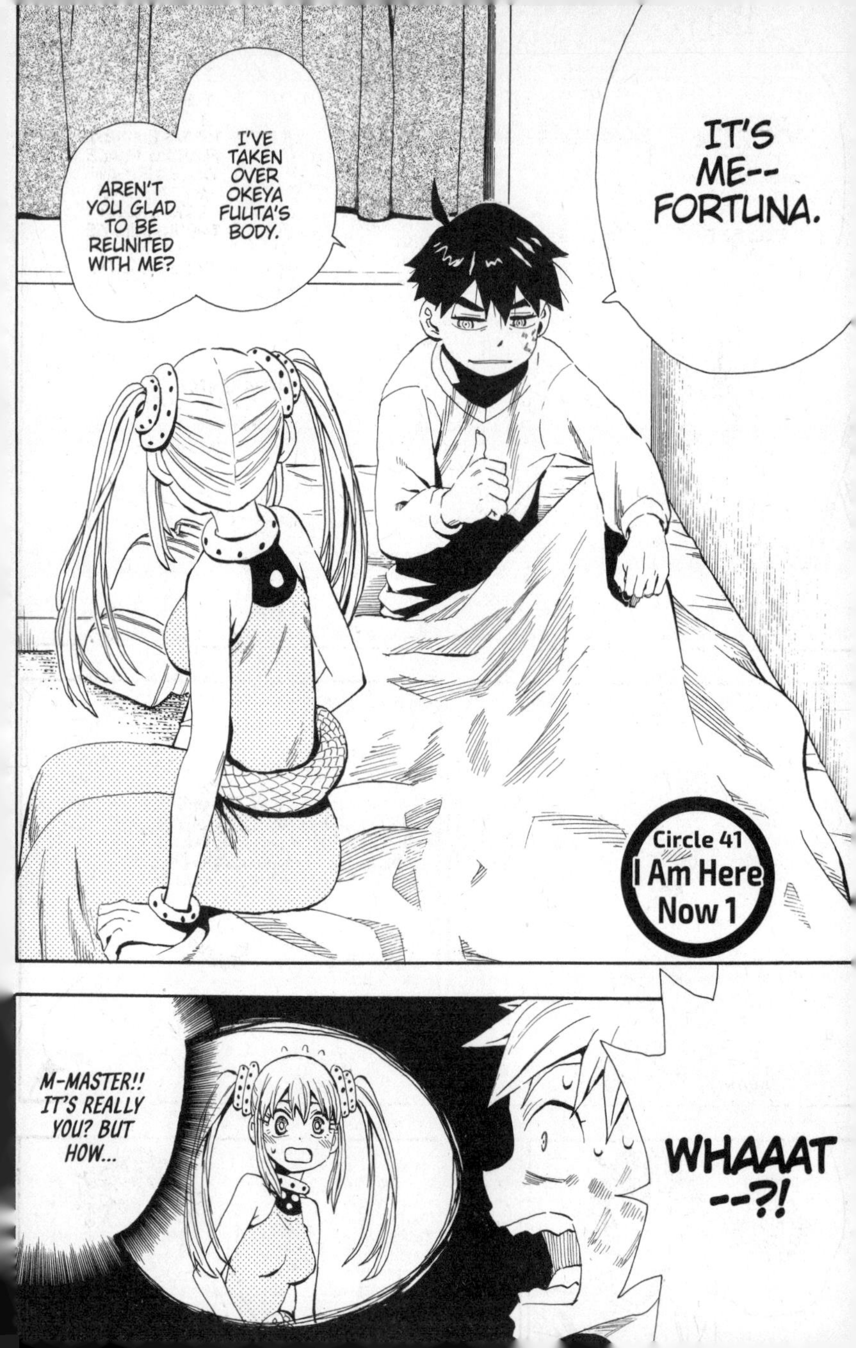
IT'S ME--FORTUNA.
I'VE TAKEN OVER OKEYA FUUTA'S BODY.
AREN'T YOU GLAD TO BE REUNITED WITH ME?
Circle 41 I Am Here Now 1
WHAAAT--?!
M-MASTER!! IT'S REALLY YOU? BUT HOW...

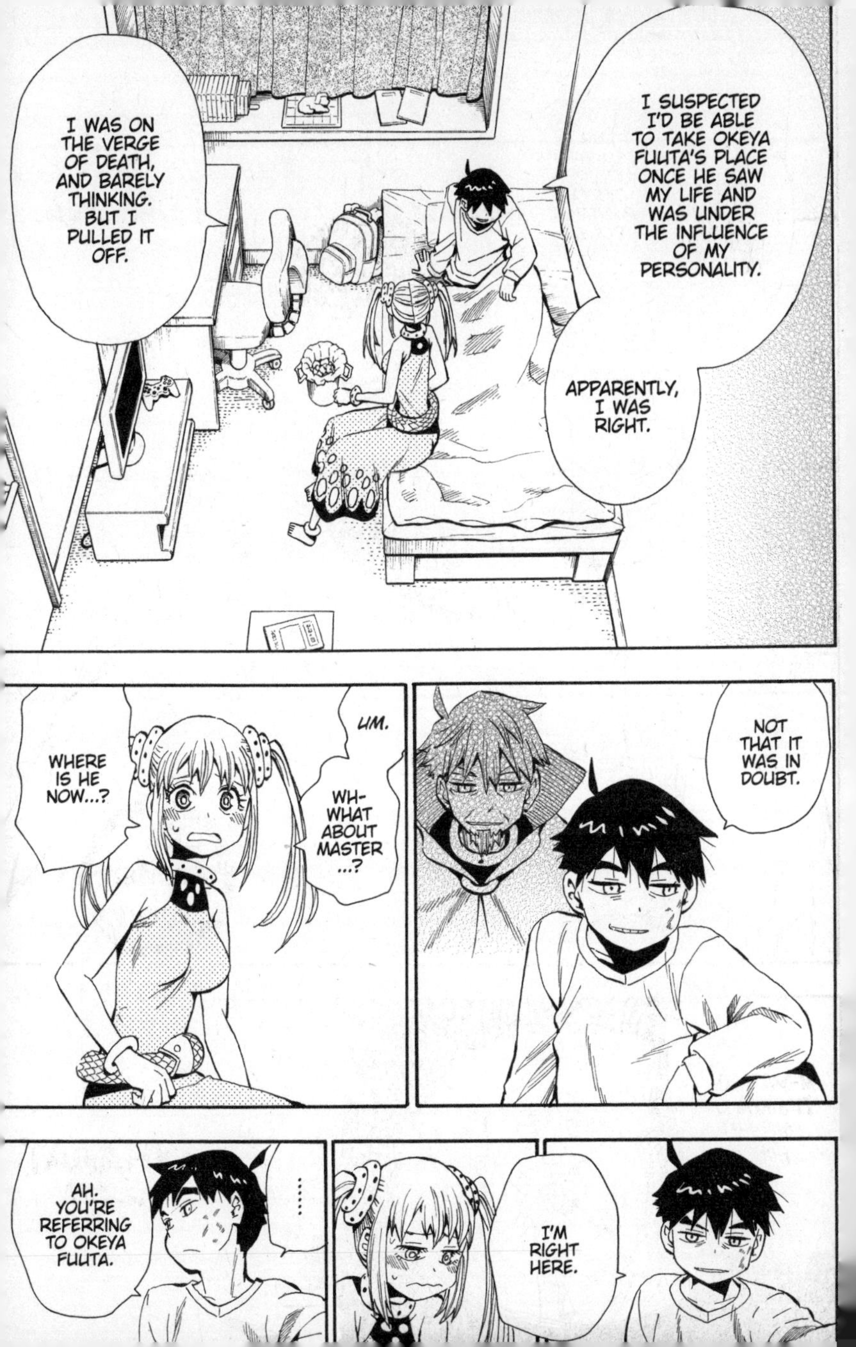
I SUSPECTED I'D BE ABLE TO TAKE OKEYA FUUTA'S PLACE ONCE HE SAW MY LIFE AND WAS UNDER THE INFLUENCE OF MY PERSONALITY.
APPARENTLY, I WAS RIGHT.
I WAS ON THE VERGE OF DEATH, AND BARELY THINKING. BUT I PULLED IT OFF.
NOT THAT IT WAS IN DOUBT.
UM.
WH-WHAT ABOUT MASTER ...?
WHERE IS HE NOW...?
I'M RIGHT HERE.
......
AH. YOU'RE REFERRING TO OKEYA FUUTA.

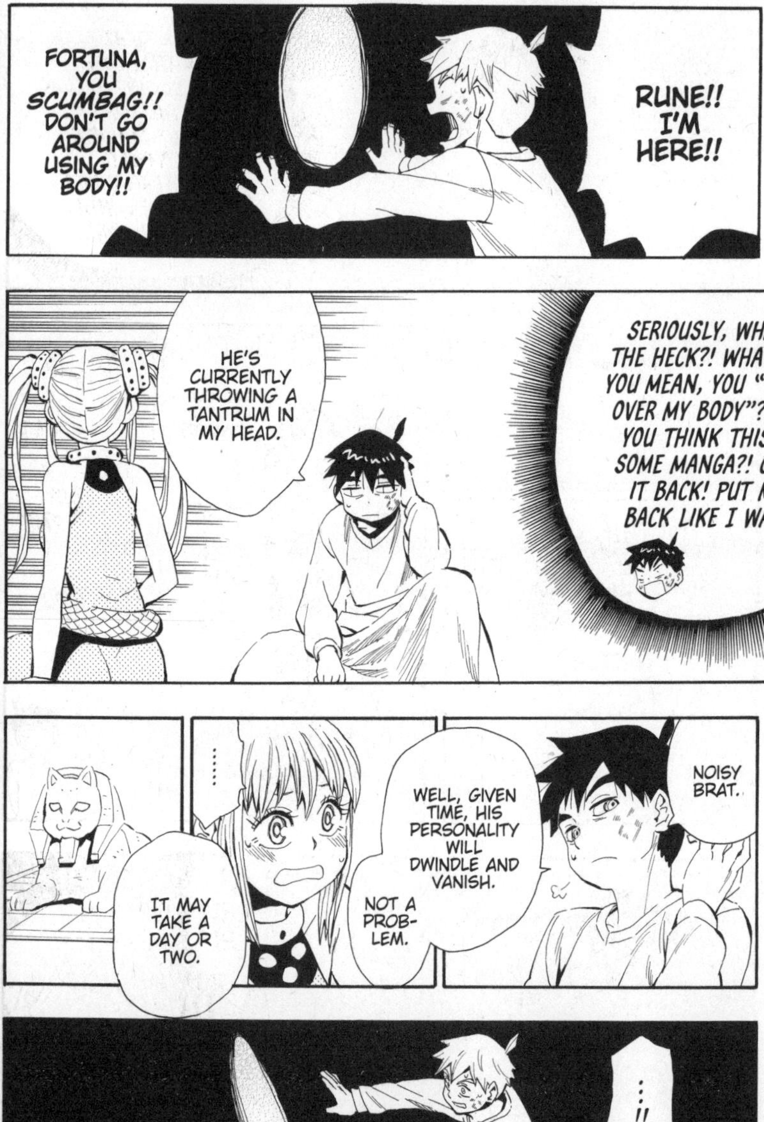
RUNE!! I'M HERE!!
FORTUNA, YOU SCUMBAG!! DON'T GO AROUND USING MY BODY!!
SERIOUSLY, WHAT THE HECK?! WHAT DO YOU MEAN, YOU "TOOK OVER MY BODY"?! DO YOU THINK THIS IS SOME MANGA?! GIVE IT BACK! PUT ME BACK LIKE I WAS!
HE'S CURRENTLY THROWING A TANTRUM IN MY HEAD.
NOISY BRAT.
WELL, GIVEN TIME, HIS PERSONALITY WILL DWINDLE AND VANISH.
......
NOT A PROB-LEM.
IT MAY TAKE A DAY OR TWO.
...!!

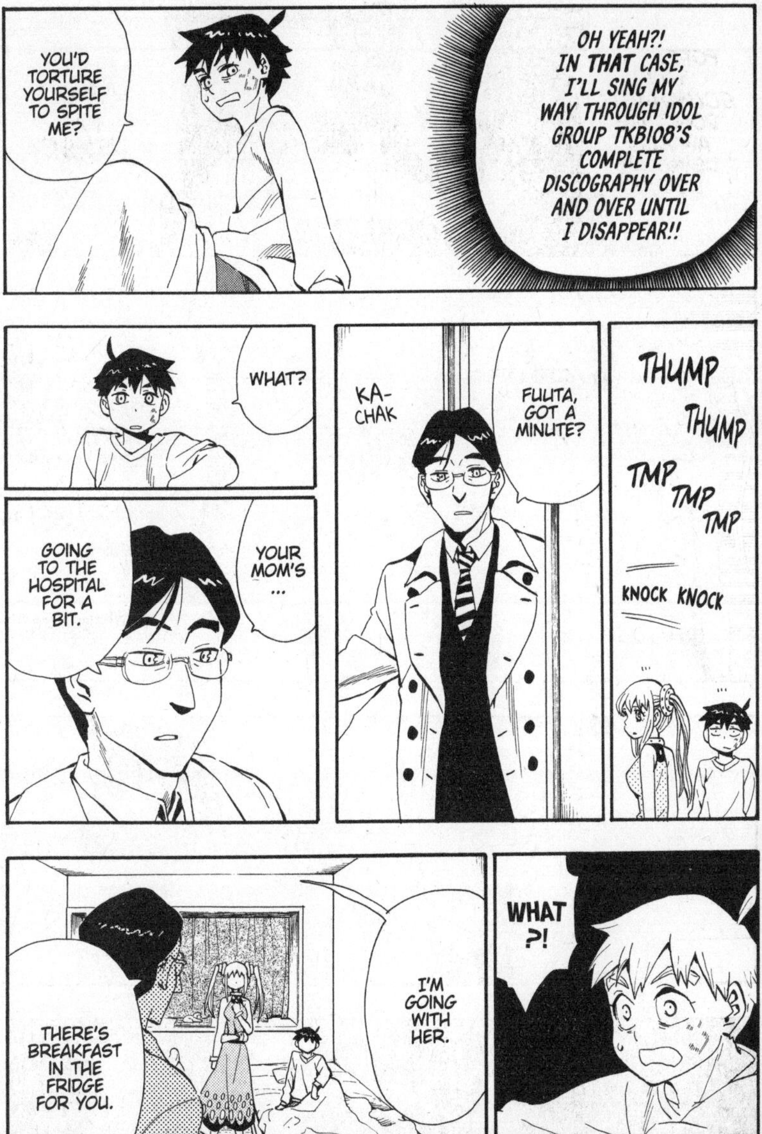
OH YEAH?! IN THAT CASE, I'LL SING MY WAY THROUGH IDOL GROUP TKB108'S COMPLETE DISCOGRAPHY OVER AND OVER UNTIL I DISAPPEAR!!
YOU'D TORTURE YOURSELF TO SPITE ME?
THUMP
THUMP
TMP
TMP
TMP
KNOCK KNOCK
...
...
FUUTA, GOT A MINUTE?
KA-CHAK
WHAT?
YOUR MOM'S ...
GOING TO THE HOSPITAL FOR A BIT.
WHAT ?!
I'M GOING WITH HER.
THERE'S BREAKFAST IN THE FRIDGE FOR YOU.

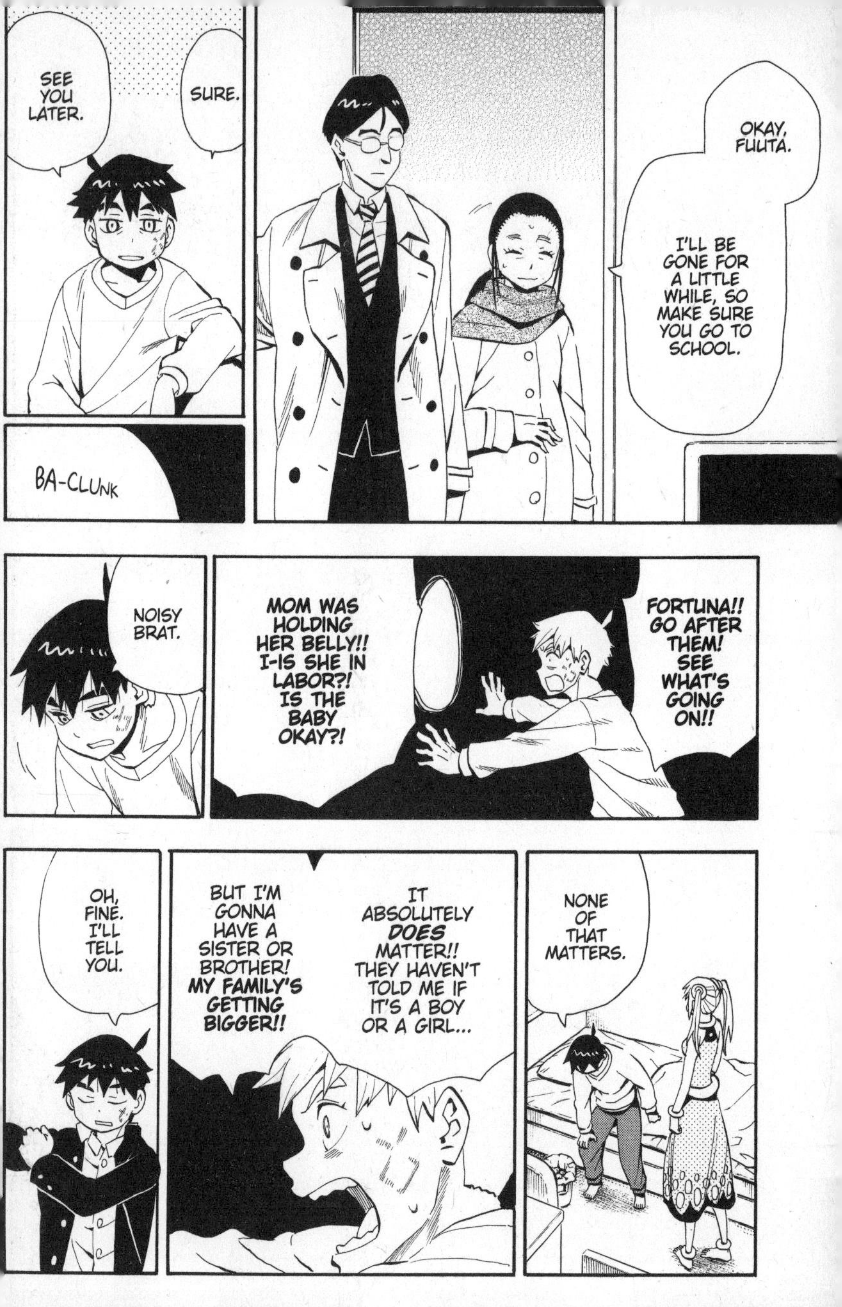
OKAY, FUUTA.
I'LL BE GONE FOR A LITTLE WHILE, SO MAKE SURE YOU GO TO SCHOOL.
SURE.
SEE YOU LATER.
BA-CLUNK
FORTUNA!! GO AFTER THEM! SEE WHAT'S GOING ON!!
MOM WAS HOLDING HER BELLY!! I-IS SHE IN LABOR?! IS THE BABY OKAY?!
NOISY BRAT.
NONE OF THAT MATTERS.
IT ABSOLUTELY **DOES** MATTER!! THEY HAVEN'T TOLD ME IF IT'S A BOY OR A GIRL...
BUT I'M GONNA HAVE A SISTER OR BROTHER! **MY FAMILY'S GETTING BIGGER!!**
OH, FINE. I'LL TELL YOU.

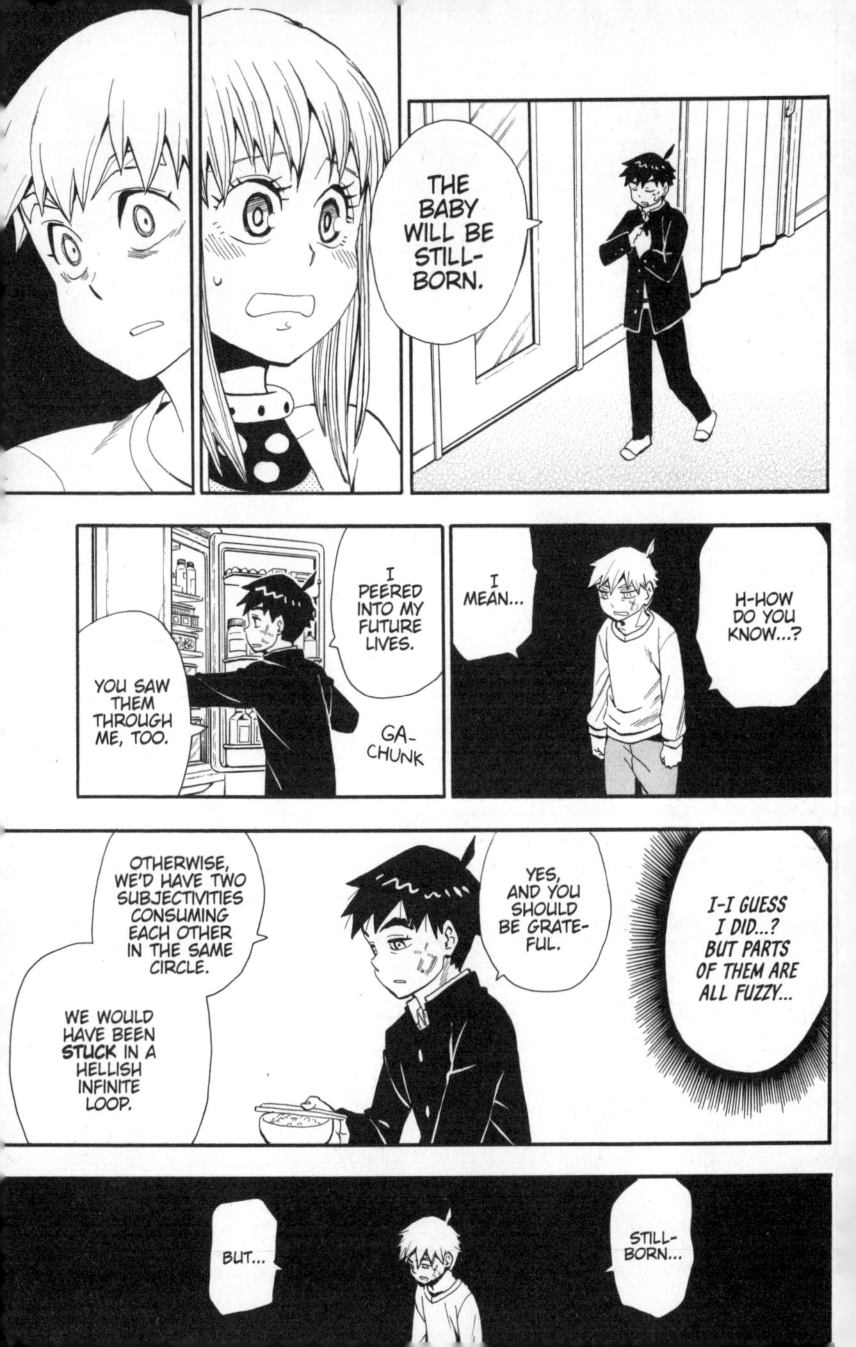
THE BABY WILL BE STILL-BORN.
H-HOW DO YOU KNOW...?
I MEAN...
I PEERED INTO MY FUTURE LIVES.
GA-CHUNK
YOU SAW THEM THROUGH ME, TOO.
I-I GUESS I DID...? BUT PARTS OF THEM ARE ALL FUZZY...
YES, AND YOU SHOULD BE GRATE-FUL.
OTHERWISE, WE'D HAVE TWO SUBJECTIVITIES CONSUMING EACH OTHER IN THE SAME CIRCLE.
WE WOULD HAVE BEEN STUCK IN A HELLISH INFINITE LOOP.
STILL-BORN...
BUT...

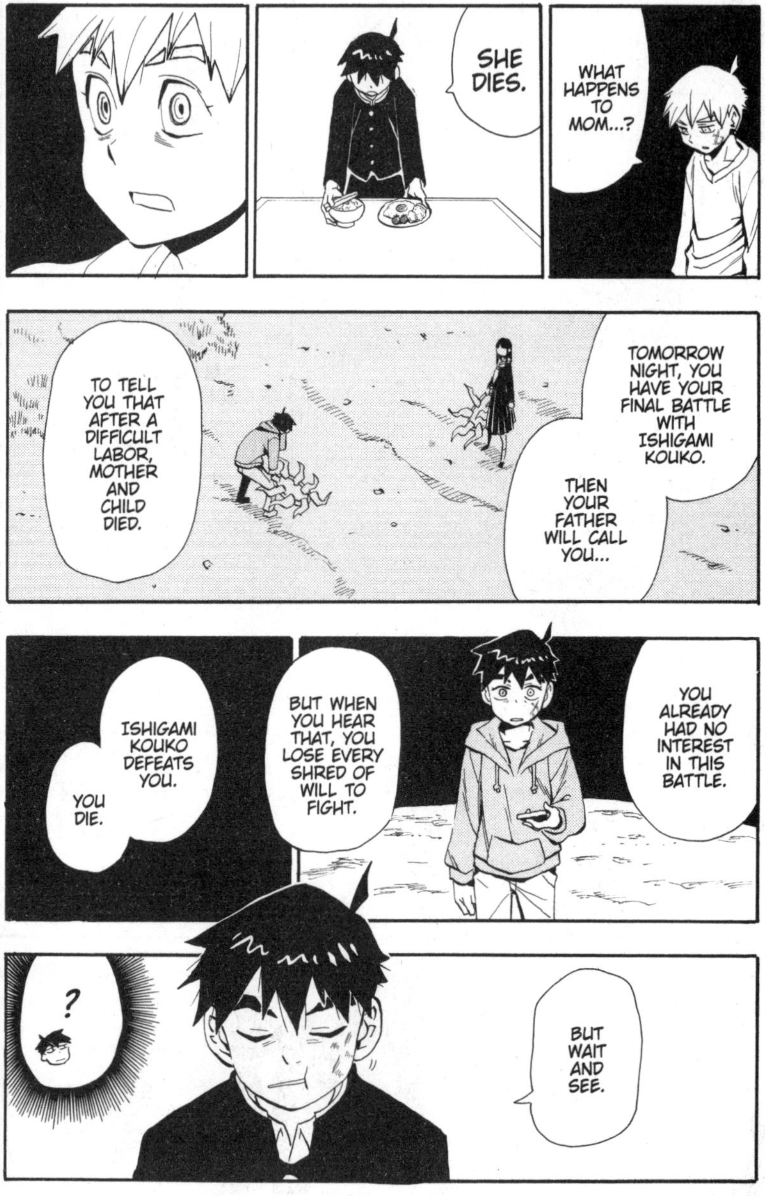
WHAT HAPPENS TO MOM...?
SHE DIES.
TOMORROW NIGHT, YOU HAVE YOUR FINAL BATTLE WITH ISHIGAMI KOUKO.
THEN YOUR FATHER WILL CALL YOU...
TO TELL YOU THAT AFTER A DIFFICULT LABOR, MOTHER AND CHILD DIED.
YOU ALREADY HAD NO INTEREST IN THIS BATTLE.
BUT WHEN YOU HEAR THAT, YOU LOSE EVERY SHRED OF WILL TO FIGHT.
ISHIGAMI KOUKO DEFEATS YOU.
YOU DIE.
BUT WAIT AND SEE.
?

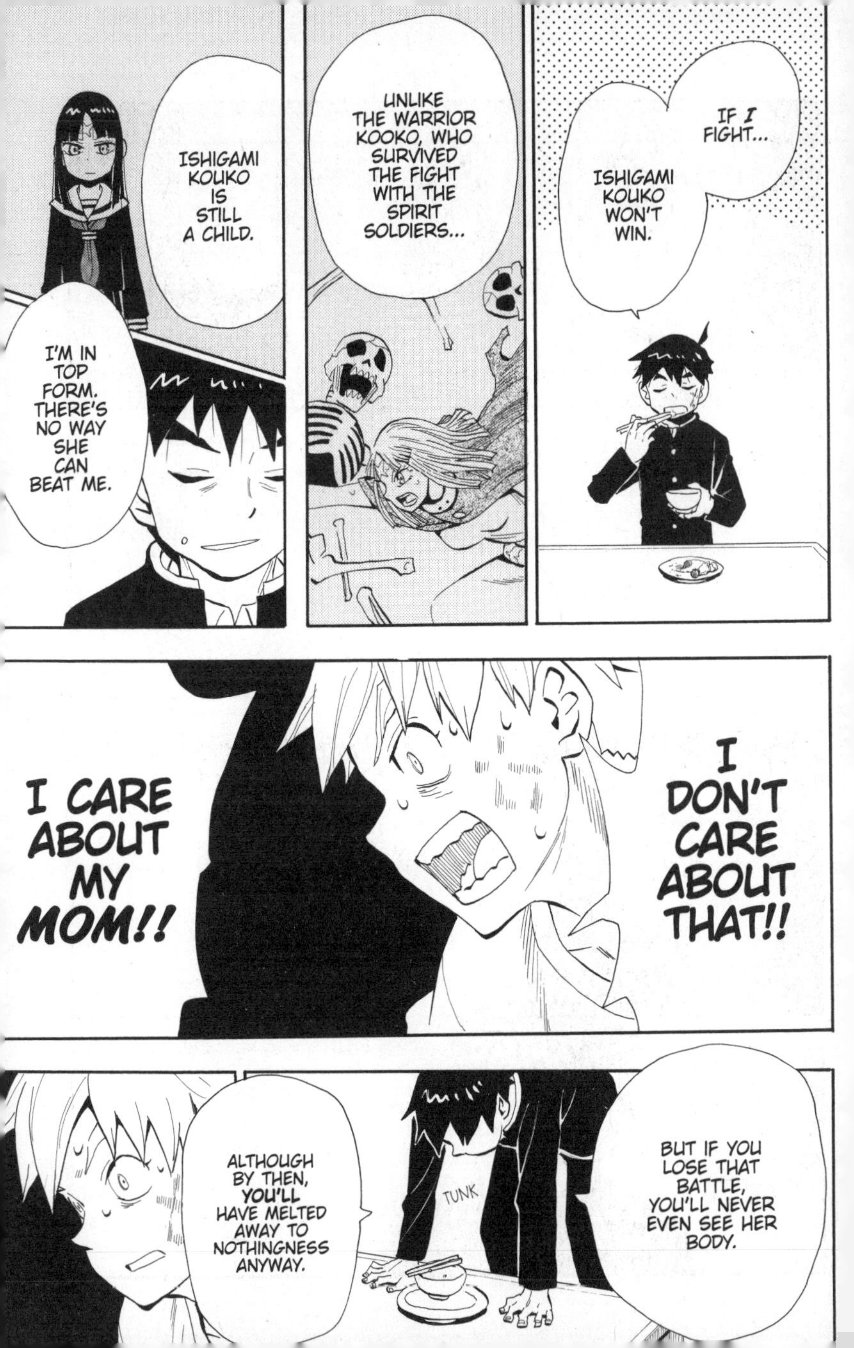
IF I FIGHT...
ISHIGAMI KOUKO WON'T WIN.
UNLIKE THE WARRIOR KOOKO, WHO SURVIVED THE FIGHT WITH THE SPIRIT SOLDIERS...
ISHIGAMI KOUKO IS STILL A CHILD.
I'M IN TOP FORM. THERE'S NO WAY SHE CAN BEAT ME.
I DON'T CARE ABOUT THAT!!
I CARE ABOUT MY MOM!!
BUT IF YOU LOSE THAT BATTLE, YOU'LL NEVER EVEN SEE HER BODY.
TUNK
ALTHOUGH BY THEN, YOU'LL HAVE MELTED AWAY TO NOTHINGNESS ANYWAY.

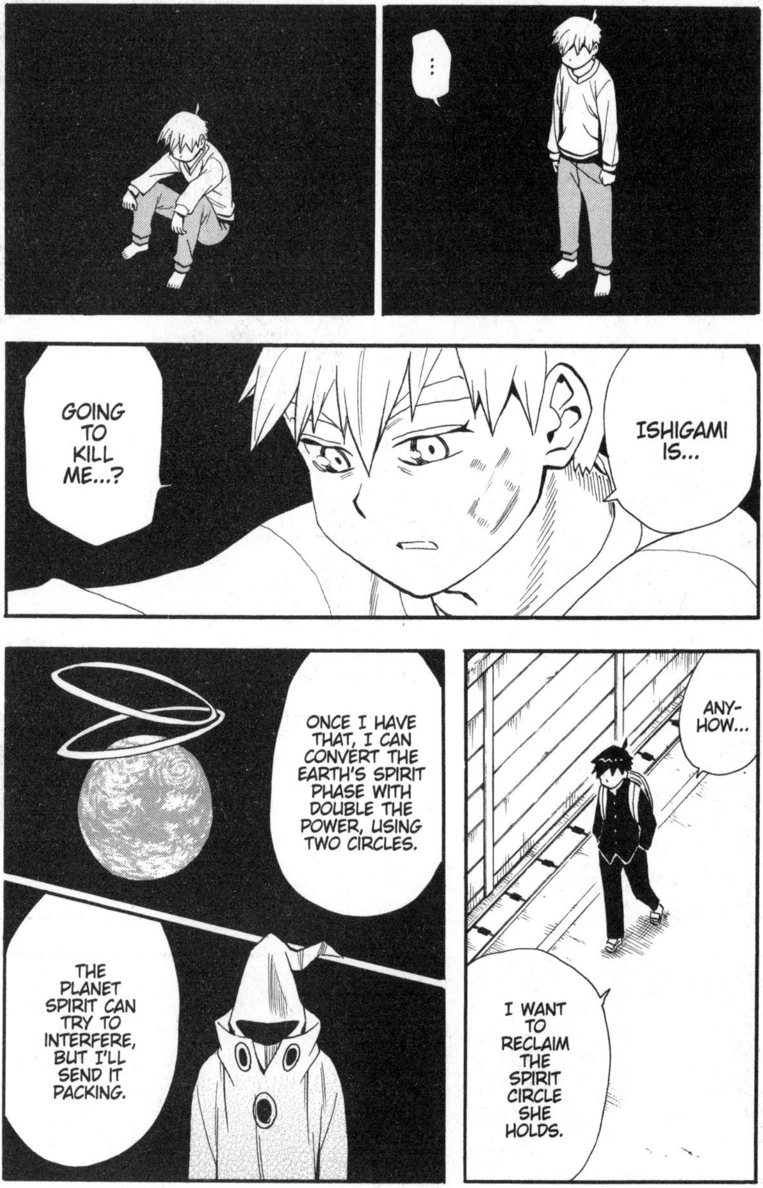
...
ISHIGAMI IS...
GOING TO KILL ME...?
ANY-HOW...
I WANT TO RECLAIM THE SPIRIT CIRCLE SHE HOLDS.
ONCE I HAVE THAT, I CAN CONVERT THE EARTH'S SPIRIT PHASE WITH DOUBLE THE POWER, USING TWO CIRCLES.
THE PLANET SPIRIT CAN TRY TO INTERFERE, BUT I'LL SEND IT PACKING.

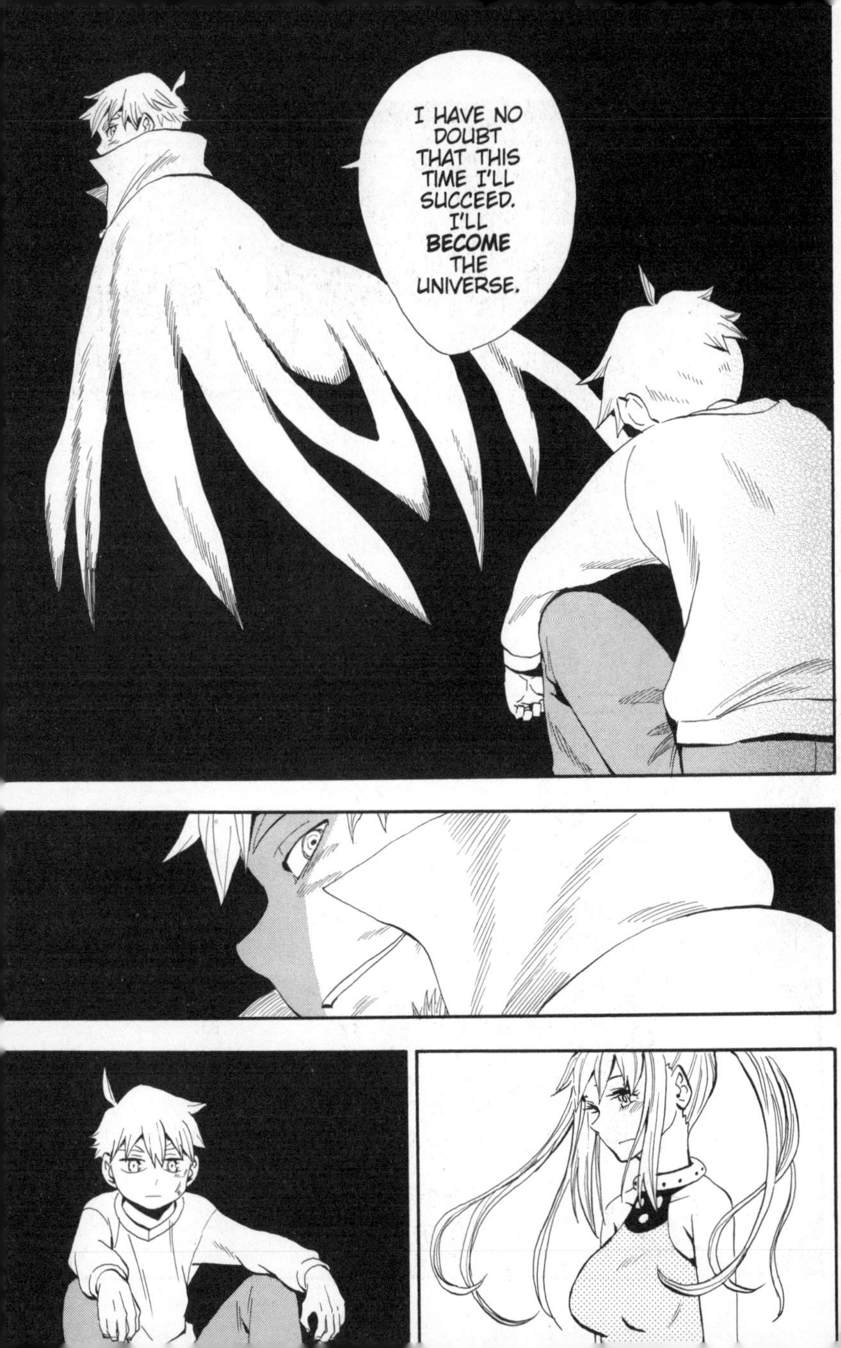
I HAVE NO DOUBT THAT THIS TIME I'LL SUCCEED. I'LL BECOME THE UNIVERSE.

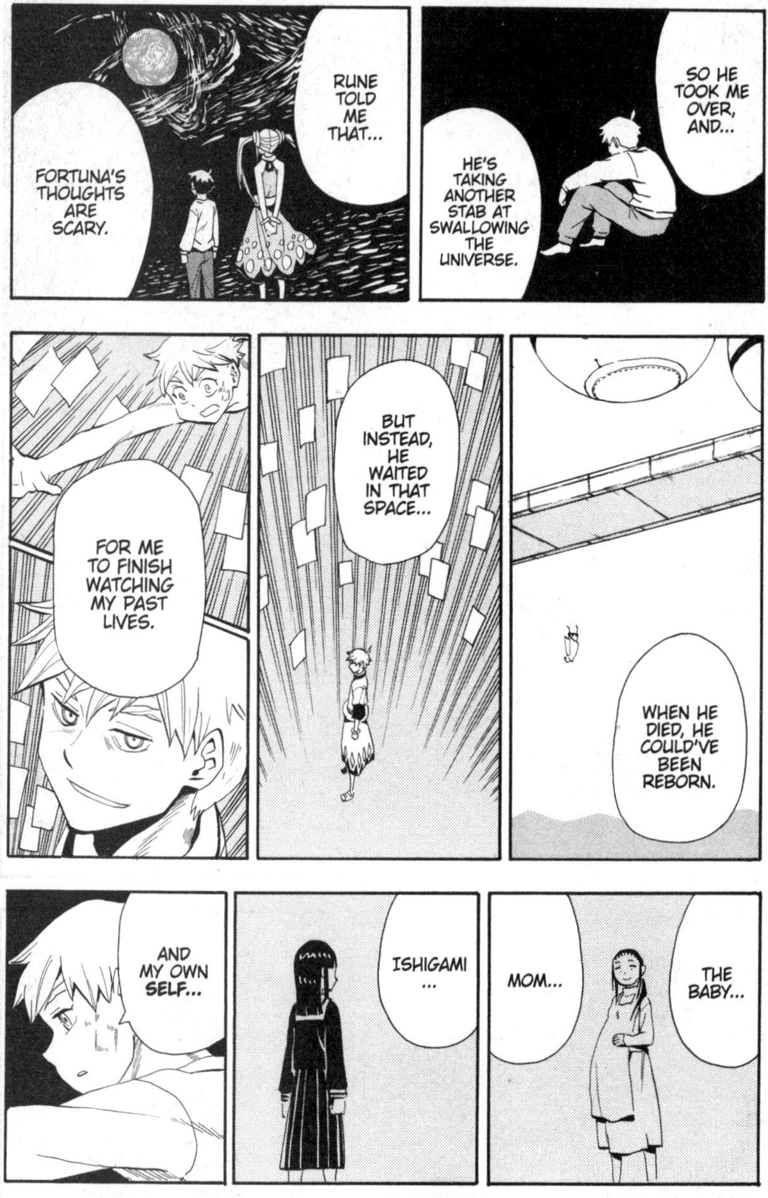
SO HE TOOK ME OVER, AND...
HE'S TAKING ANOTHER STAB AT SWALLOWING THE UNIVERSE.
RUNE TOLD ME THAT...
FORTUNA'S THOUGHTS ARE SCARY.
WHEN HE DIED, HE COULD'VE BEEN REBORN.
BUT INSTEAD, HE WAITED IN THAT SPACE...
FOR ME TO FINISH WATCHING MY PAST LIVES.
THE BABY...
MOM...
ISHIGAMI ...
AND MY OWN SELF...

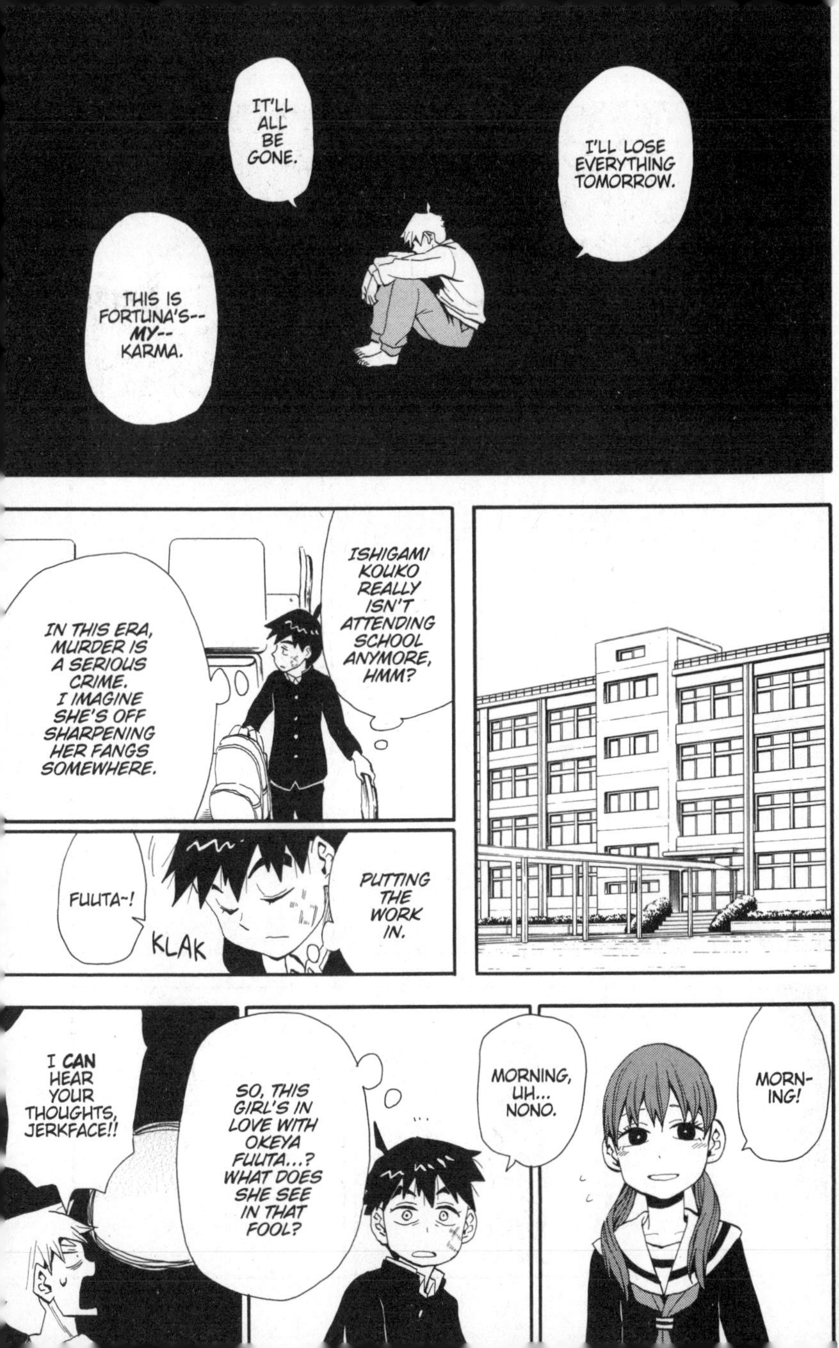
I'LL LOSE EVERYTHING TOMORROW.
IT'LL ALL BE GONE.
THIS IS FORTUNA'S-- MY-- KARMA.
ISHIGAMI KOUKO REALLY ISN'T ATTENDING SCHOOL ANYMORE, HMM?
IN THIS ERA, MURDER IS A SERIOUS CRIME. I IMAGINE SHE'S OFF SHARPENING HER FANGS SOMEWHERE.
PUTTING THE WORK IN.
KLAK
FUUTA~!
MORN-ING!
MORNING, UH... NONO.
...
SO, THIS GIRL'S IN LOVE WITH OKEYA FUUTA...? WHAT DOES SHE SEE IN THAT FOOL?
I CAN HEAR YOUR THOUGHTS, JERKFACE!!

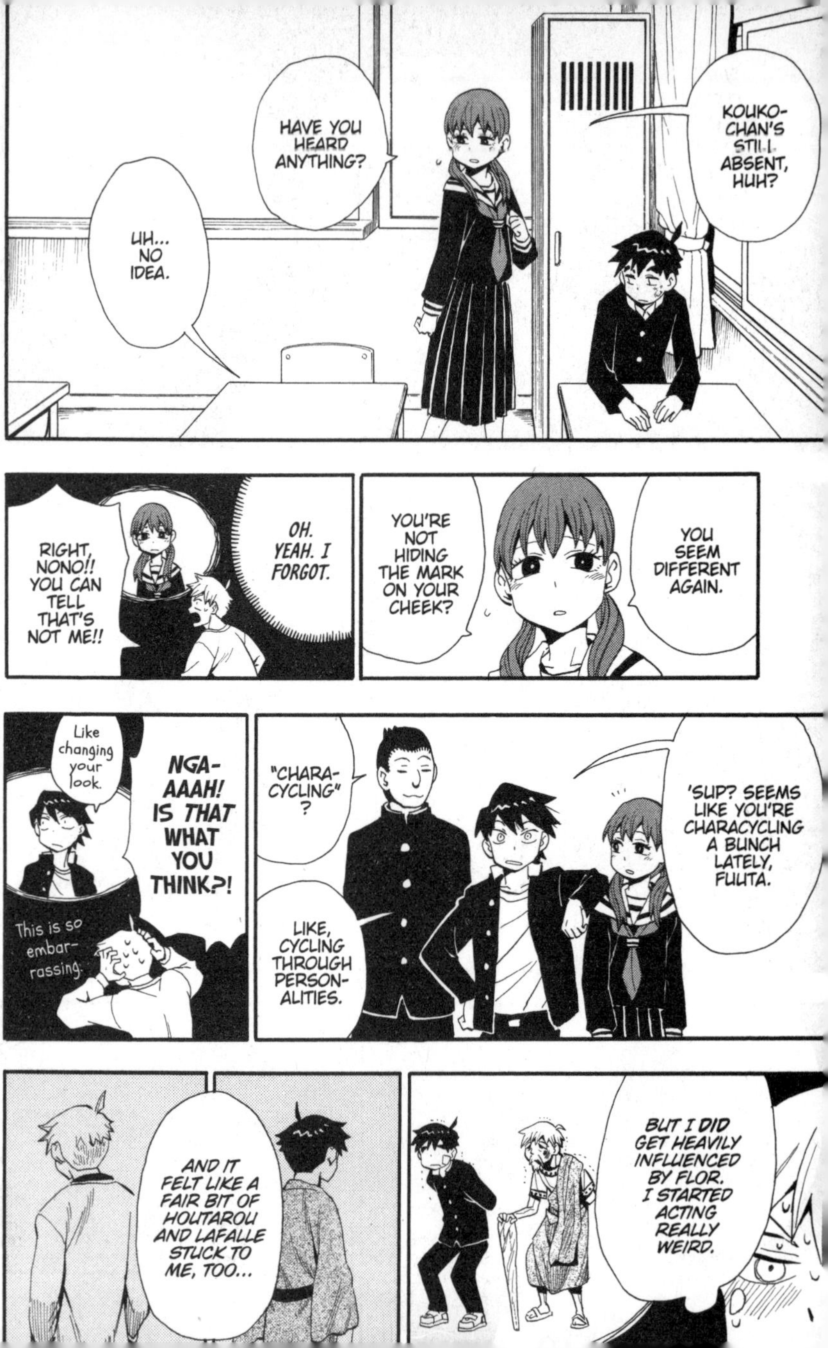
KOUKO-CHAN'S STILL ABSENT, HUH?
HAVE YOU HEARD ANYTHING?
UH... NO IDEA.
YOU SEEM DIFFERENT AGAIN.
YOU'RE NOT HIDING THE MARK ON YOUR CHEEK?
OH. YEAH. I FORGOT.
RIGHT, NONO!! YOU CAN TELL THAT'S NOT ME!!
'SUP? SEEMS LIKE YOU'RE CHARACYCLING A BUNCH LATELY, FUUTA.
"CHARA-CYCLING"?
LIKE, CYCLING THROUGH PERSONALITIES.
Like changing your look.
NGA-AAAH! IS THAT WHAT YOU THINK?!
This is so embarrassing.
BUT I DID GET HEAVILY INFLUENCED BY FLOR. I STARTED ACTING REALLY WEIRD.
AND IT FELT LIKE A FAIR BIT OF HOUTAROU AND LAFALLE STUCK TO ME, TOO...

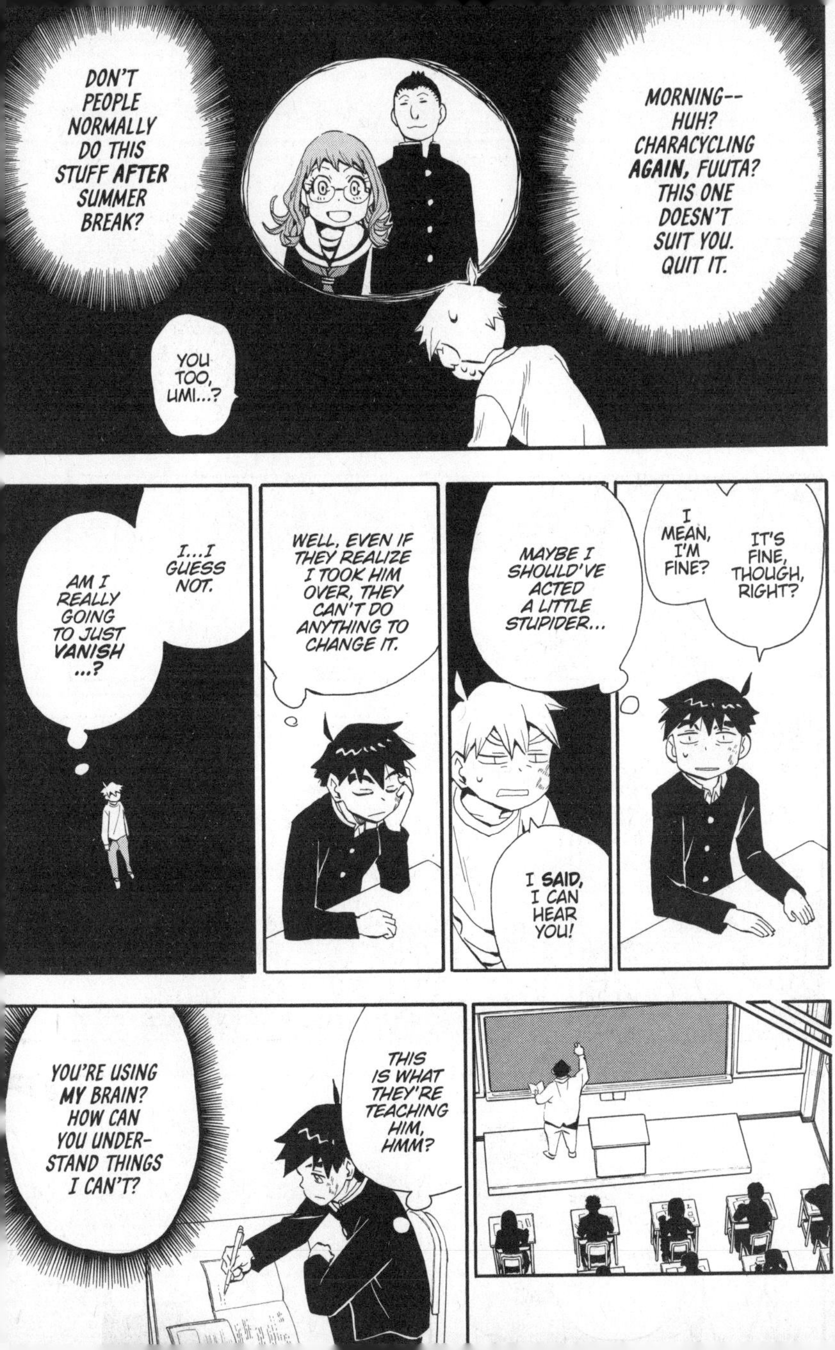
MORNING-- HUH? CHARACYCLING AGAIN, FUUTA? THIS ONE DOESN'T SUIT YOU. QUIT IT.
DON'T PEOPLE NORMALLY DO THIS STUFF AFTER SUMMER BREAK?
YOU TOO, UMI...?
IT'S FINE, THOUGH, RIGHT?
I MEAN, I'M FINE?
MAYBE I SHOULD'VE ACTED A LITTLE STUPIDER...
I SAID, I CAN HEAR YOU!
WELL, EVEN IF THEY REALIZE I TOOK HIM OVER, THEY CAN'T DO ANYTHING TO CHANGE IT.
I...I GUESS NOT.
AM I REALLY GOING TO JUST VANISH ...?
THIS IS WHAT THEY'RE TEACHING HIM, HMM?
YOU'RE USING MY BRAIN? HOW CAN YOU UNDER-STAND THINGS I CAN'T?

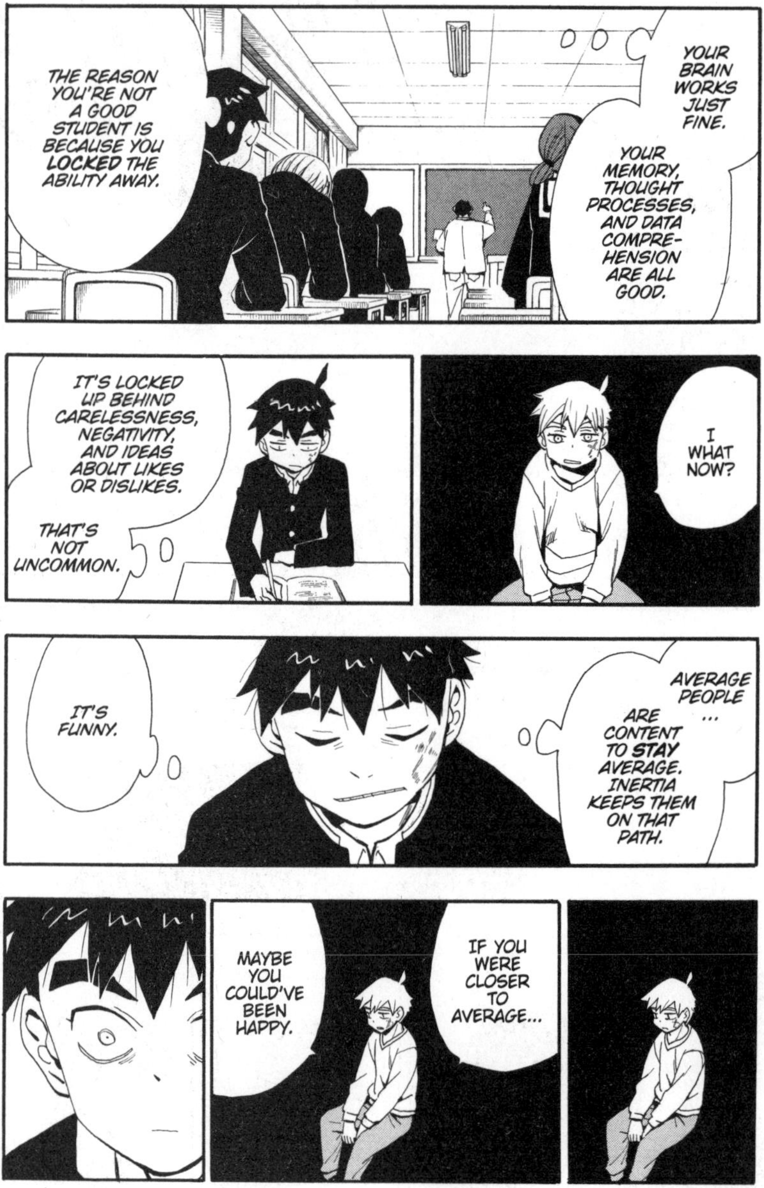
YOUR BRAIN WORKS JUST FINE.
YOUR MEMORY, THOUGHT PROCESSES, AND DATA COMPRE-HENSION ARE ALL GOOD.
THE REASON YOU'RE NOT A GOOD STUDENT IS BECAUSE YOU **LOCKED** THE ABILITY AWAY.
I WHAT NOW?
IT'S LOCKED UP BEHIND CARELESSNESS, NEGATIVITY, AND IDEAS ABOUT LIKES OR DISLIKES.
THAT'S NOT UNCOMMON.
AVERAGE PEOPLE ... ARE CONTENT TO **STAY** AVERAGE. INERTIA KEEPS THEM ON THAT PATH.
IT'S FUNNY.
IF YOU WERE CLOSER TO AVERAGE...
MAYBE YOU COULD'VE BEEN HAPPY.

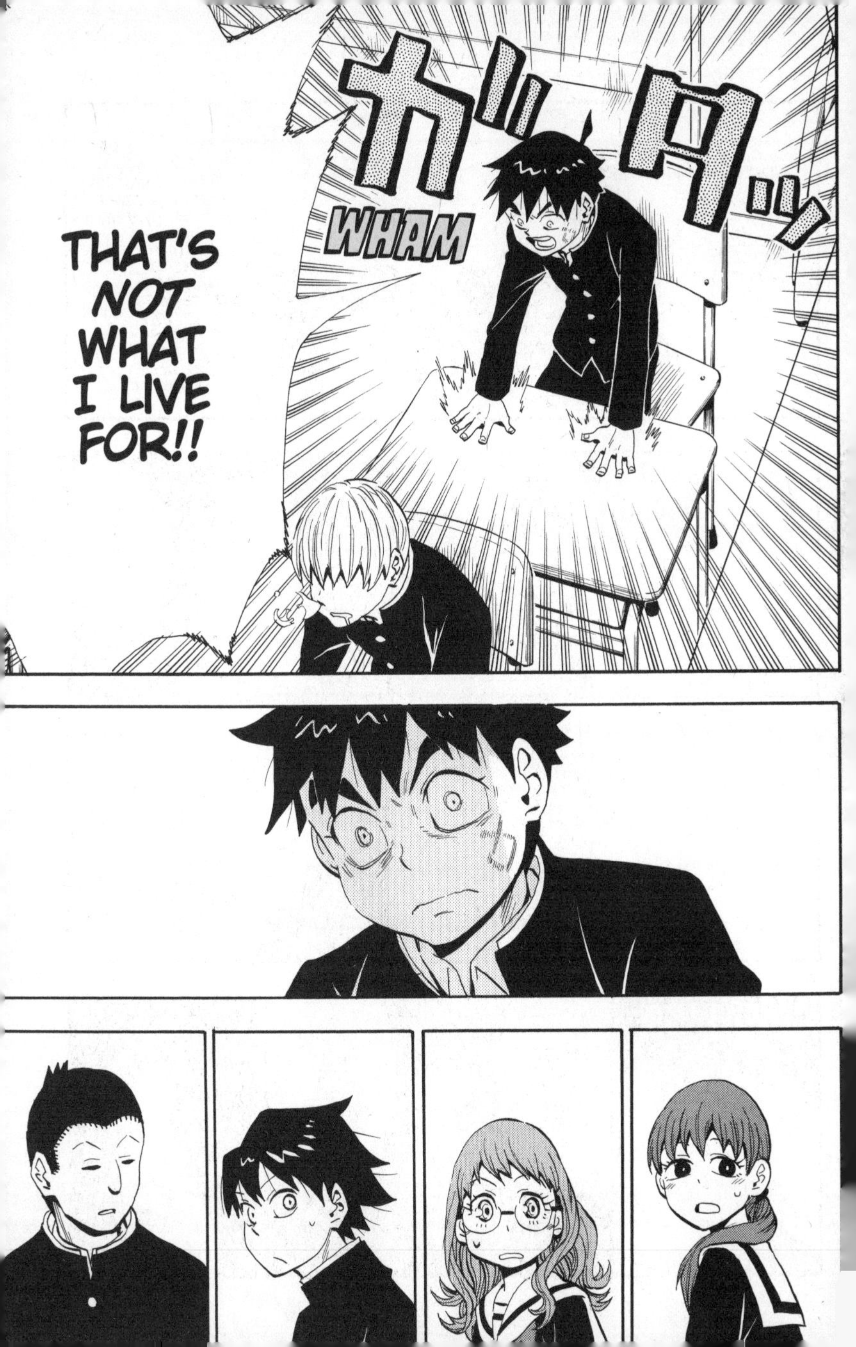

ガタッ
WHAM
THAT'S NOT WHAT I LIVE FOR!!

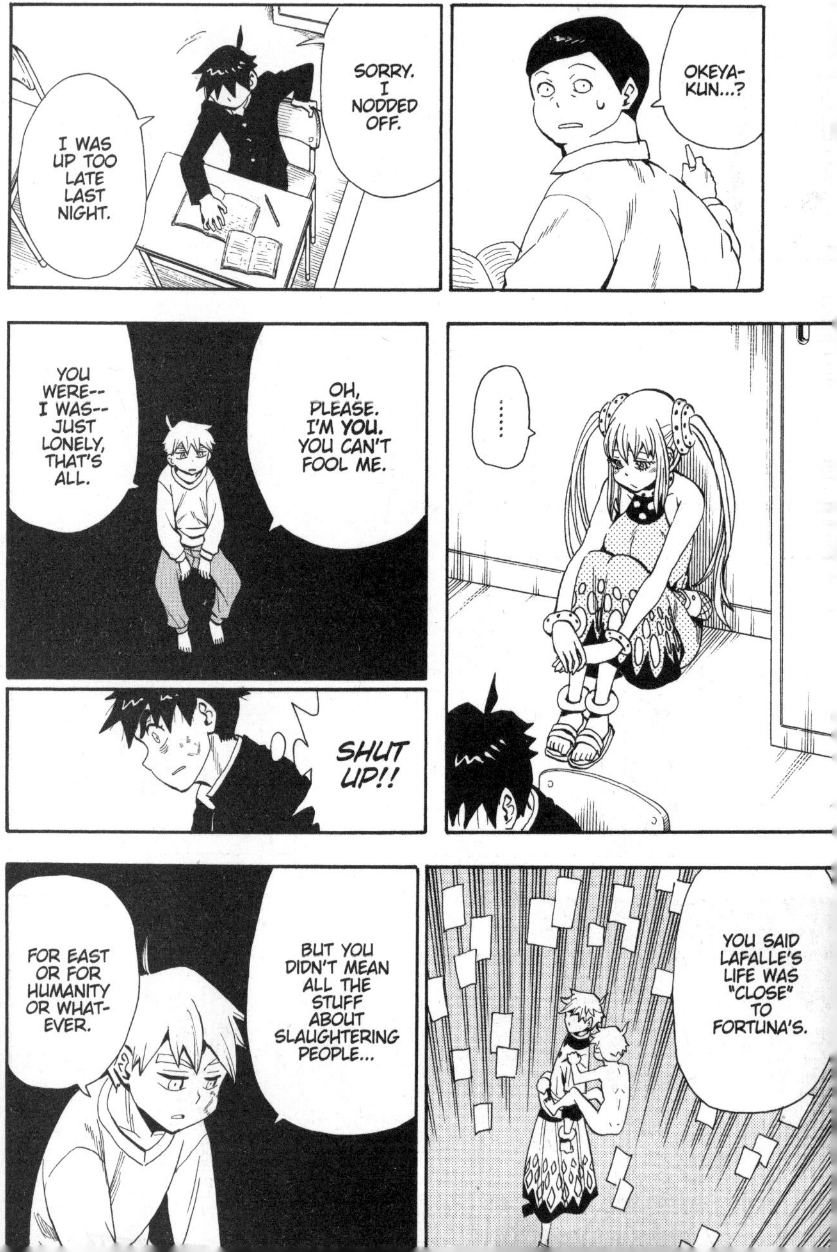
OKEYA-KUN...?
SORRY. I NODDED OFF.
I WAS UP TOO LATE LAST NIGHT.
......
OH, PLEASE. I'M YOU. YOU CAN'T FOOL ME.
YOU WERE-- I WAS-- JUST LONELY, THAT'S ALL.
SHUT UP!!
YOU SAID LAFALLE'S LIFE WAS "CLOSE" TO FORTUNA'S.
BUT YOU DIDN'T MEAN ALL THE STUFF ABOUT SLAUGHTERING PEOPLE...
FOR EAST OR FOR HUMANITY OR WHATEVER.

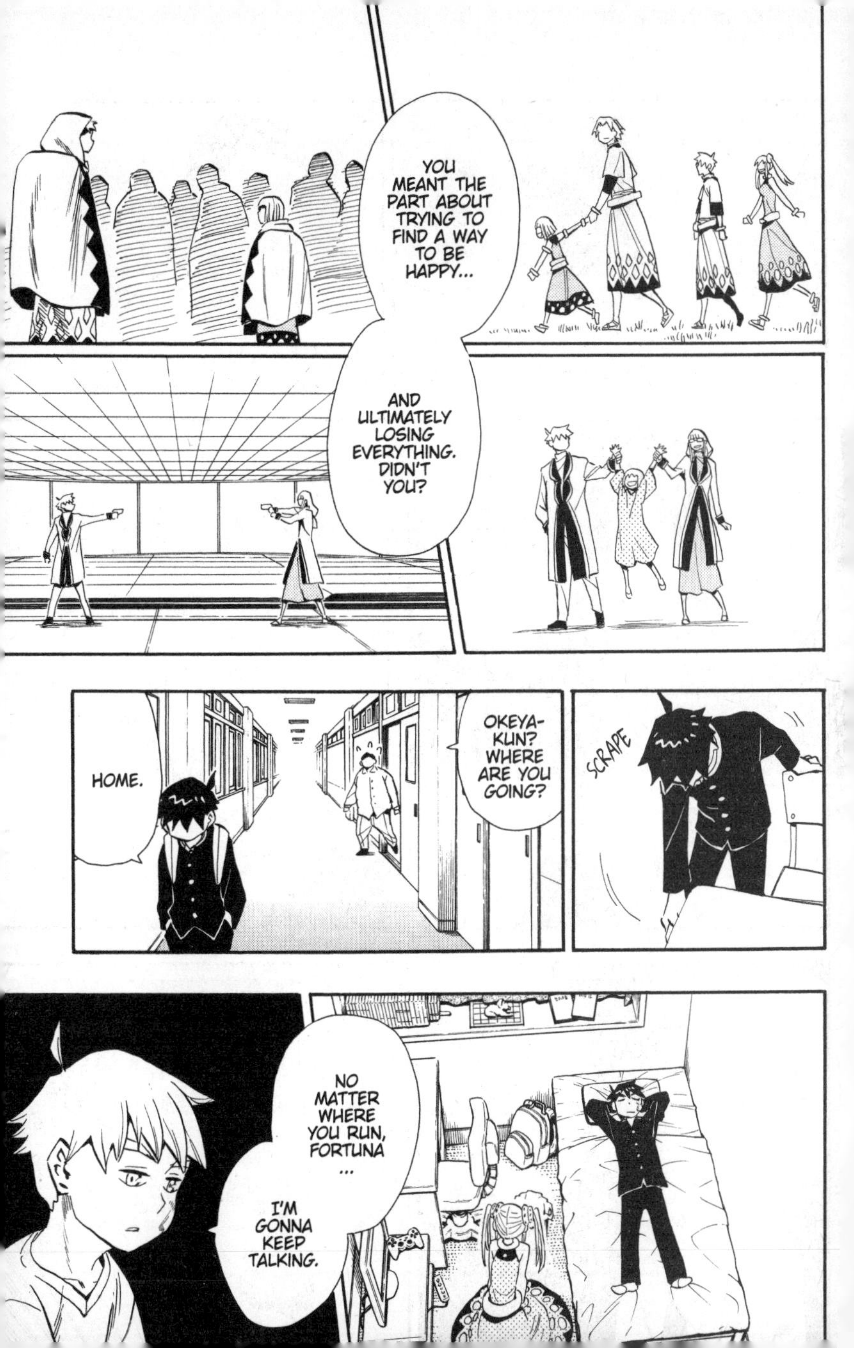
YOU MEANT THE PART ABOUT TRYING TO FIND A WAY TO BE HAPPY...
AND ULTIMATELY LOSING EVERYTHING. DIDN'T YOU?
SCRAPE
OKEYA-KUN? WHERE ARE YOU GOING?
HOME.
NO MATTER WHERE YOU RUN, FORTUNA...
I'M GONNA KEEP TALKING.

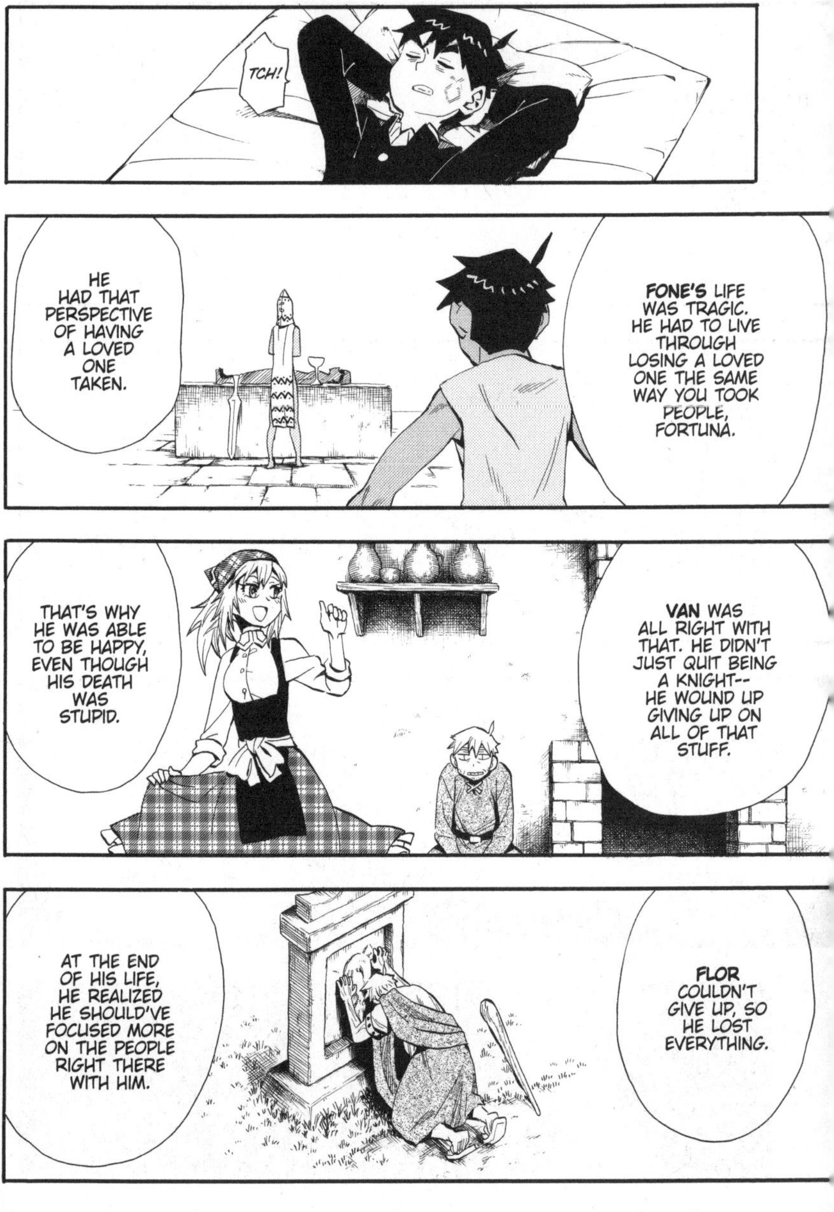
TCH!
FONE'S LIFE WAS TRAGIC. HE HAD TO LIVE THROUGH LOSING A LOVED ONE THE SAME WAY YOU TOOK PEOPLE, FORTUNA.
HE HAD THAT PERSPECTIVE OF HAVING A LOVED ONE TAKEN.
VAN WAS ALL RIGHT WITH THAT. HE DIDN'T JUST QUIT BEING A KNIGHT-- HE WOUND UP GIVING UP ON ALL OF THAT STUFF.
THAT'S WHY HE WAS ABLE TO BE HAPPY, EVEN THOUGH HIS DEATH WAS STUPID.
FLOR COULDN'T GIVE UP, SO HE LOST EVERYTHING.
AT THE END OF HIS LIFE, HE REALIZED HE SHOULD'VE FOCUSED MORE ON THE PEOPLE RIGHT THERE WITH HIM.

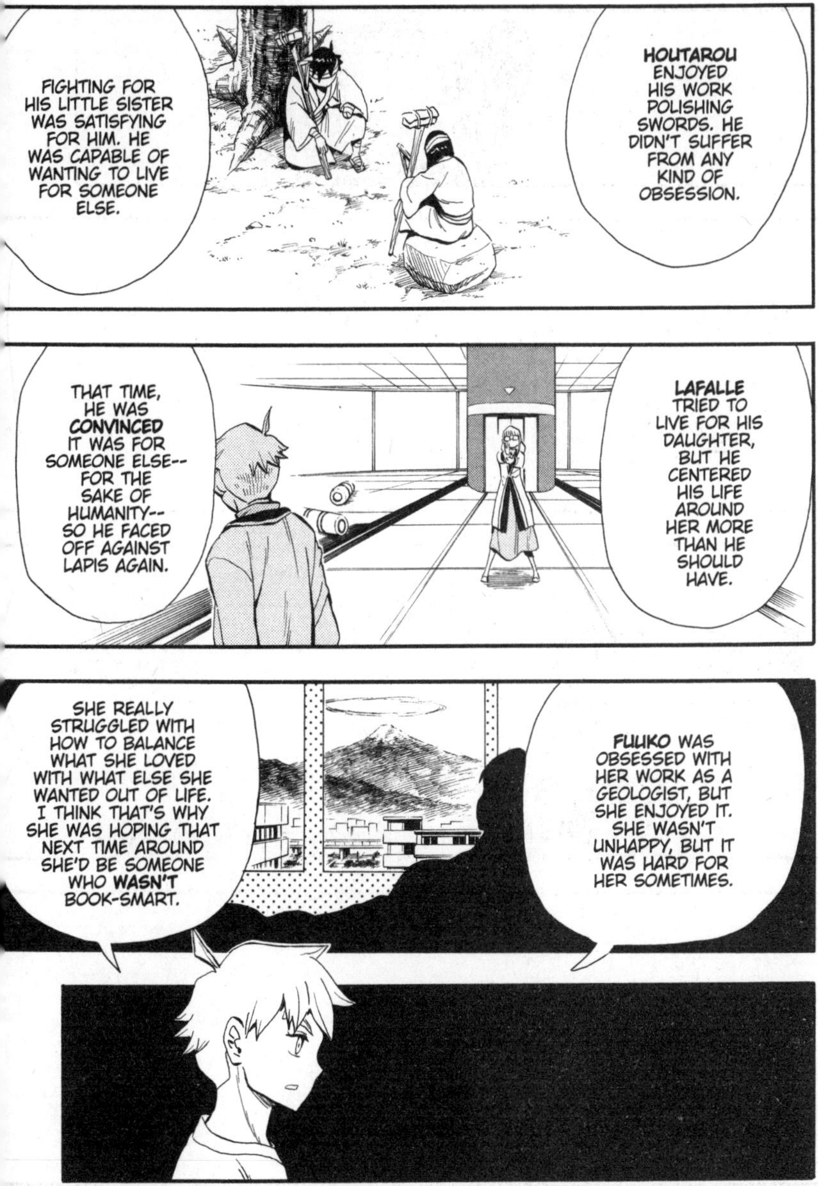
HOUTAROU ENJOYED HIS WORK POLISHING SWORDS. HE DIDN'T SUFFER FROM ANY KIND OF OBSESSION.
FIGHTING FOR HIS LITTLE SISTER WAS SATISFYING FOR HIM. HE WAS CAPABLE OF WANTING TO LIVE FOR SOMEONE ELSE.
LAFALLE TRIED TO LIVE FOR HIS DAUGHTER, BUT HE CENTERED HIS LIFE AROUND HER MORE THAN HE SHOULD HAVE.
THAT TIME, HE WAS CONVINCED IT WAS FOR SOMEONE ELSE-- FOR THE SAKE OF HUMANITY-- SO HE FACED OFF AGAINST LAPIS AGAIN.
FUUKO WAS OBSESSED WITH HER WORK AS A GEOLOGIST, BUT SHE ENJOYED IT. SHE WASN'T UNHAPPY, BUT IT WAS HARD FOR HER SOMETIMES.
SHE REALLY STRUGGLED WITH HOW TO BALANCE WHAT SHE LOVED WITH WHAT ELSE SHE WANTED OUT OF LIFE. I THINK THAT'S WHY SHE WAS HOPING THAT NEXT TIME AROUND SHE'D BE SOMEONE WHO WASN'T BOOK-SMART.

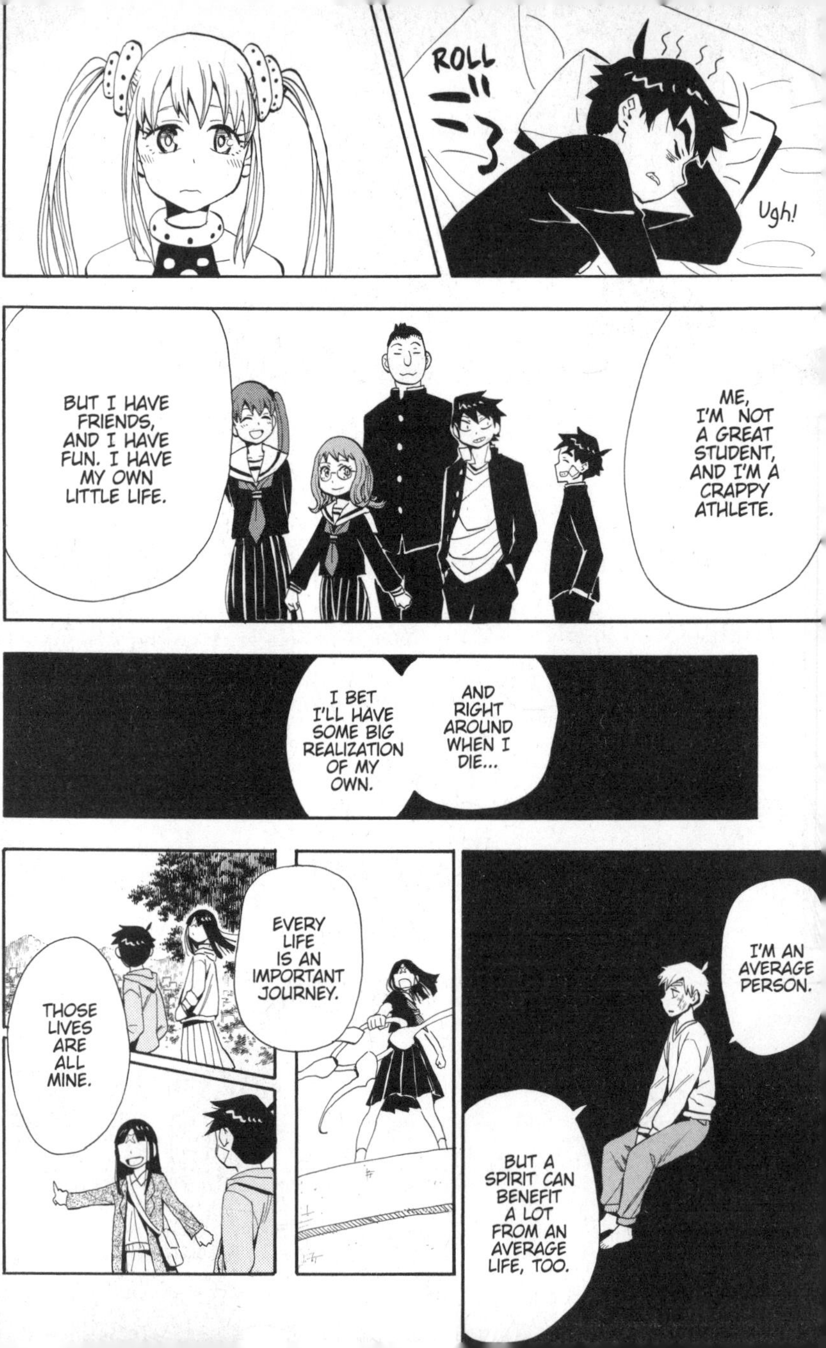
ROLL
Ugh!
ME, I'M NOT A GREAT STUDENT, AND I'M A CRAPPY ATHLETE.
BUT I HAVE FRIENDS, AND I HAVE FUN. I HAVE MY OWN LITTLE LIFE.
AND RIGHT AROUND WHEN I DIE...
I BET I'LL HAVE SOME BIG REALIZATION OF MY OWN.
I'M AN AVERAGE PERSON.
BUT A SPIRIT CAN BENEFIT A LOT FROM AN AVERAGE LIFE, TOO.
EVERY LIFE IS AN IMPORTANT JOURNEY.
THOSE LIVES ARE ALL MINE.

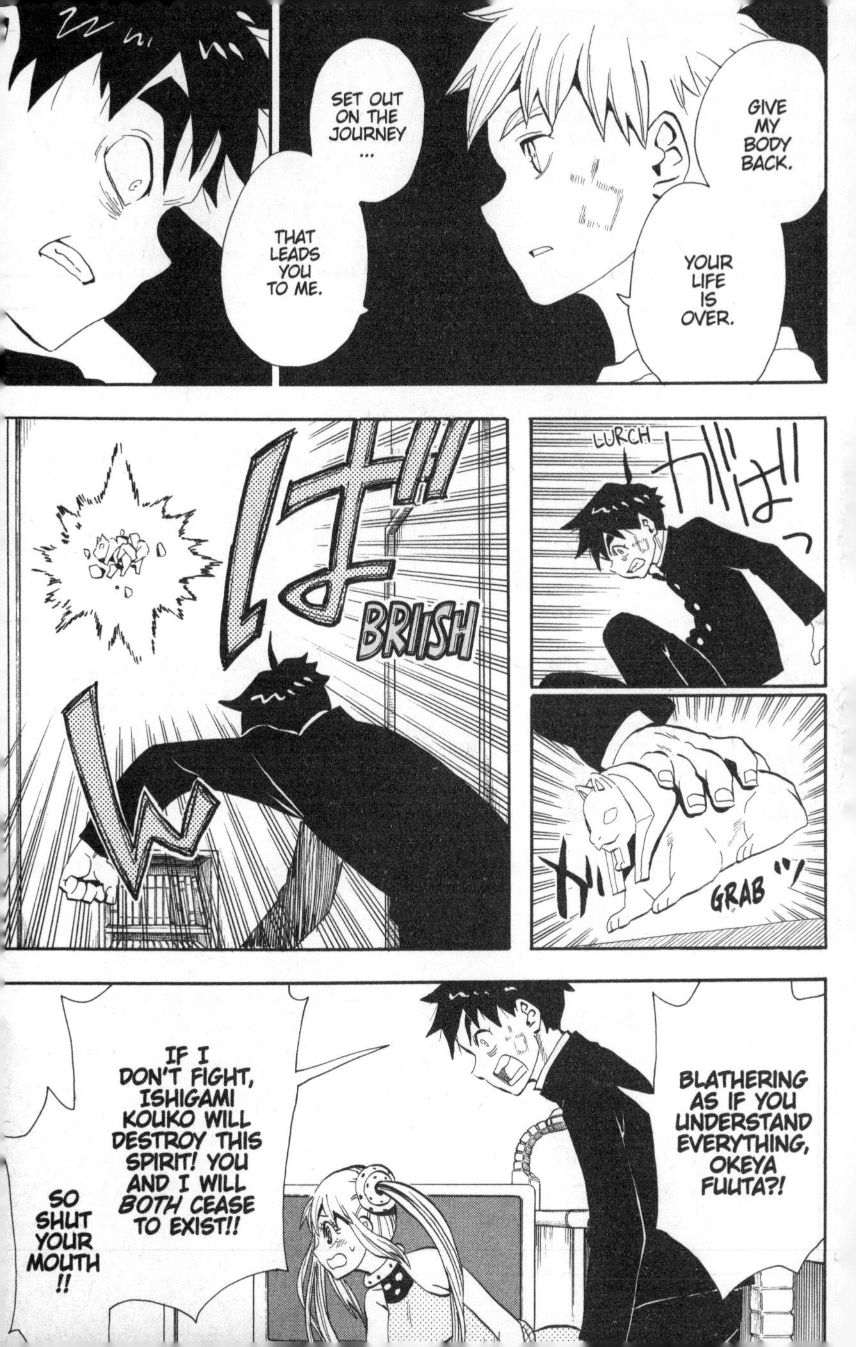
GIVE MY BODY BACK.
YOUR LIFE IS OVER.
SET OUT ON THE JOURNEY ...
THAT LEADS YOU TO ME.
LURCH
がばっ
GRAB
BRISH
BLATHERING AS IF YOU UNDERSTAND EVERYTHING, OKEYA FUUTA?!
IF I DON'T FIGHT, ISHIGAMI KOUKO WILL DESTROY THIS SPIRIT! YOU AND I WILL *BOTH* CEASE TO EXIST!!
SO SHUT YOUR MOUTH!!

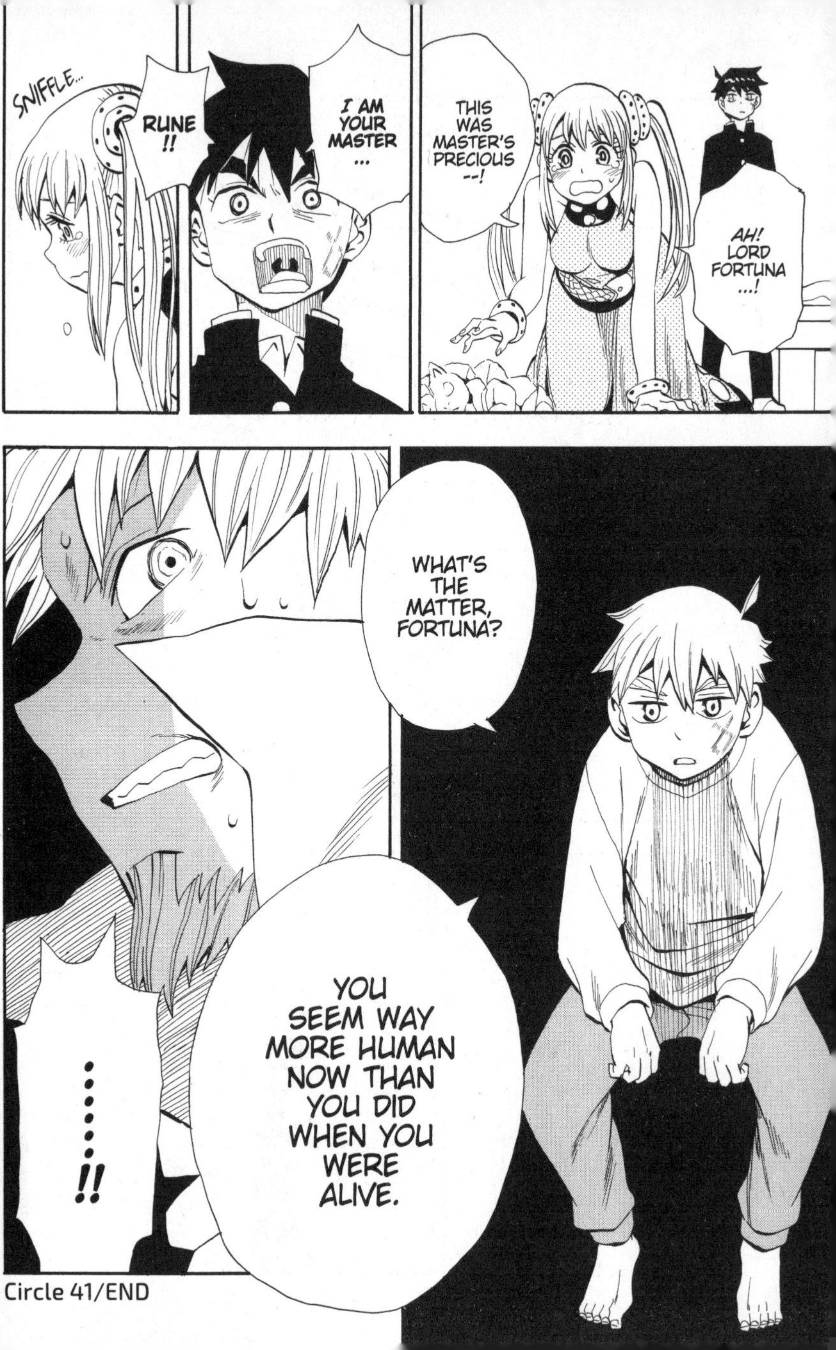
AH! LORD FORTUNA ...!
THIS WAS MASTER'S PRECIOUS --!
I AM YOUR MASTER ...
RUNE !!
SNIFFLE...
WHAT'S THE MATTER, FORTUNA?
YOU SEEM WAY MORE HUMAN NOW THAN YOU DID WHEN YOU WERE ALIVE.
......!!

Circle 41/END

Circle 42

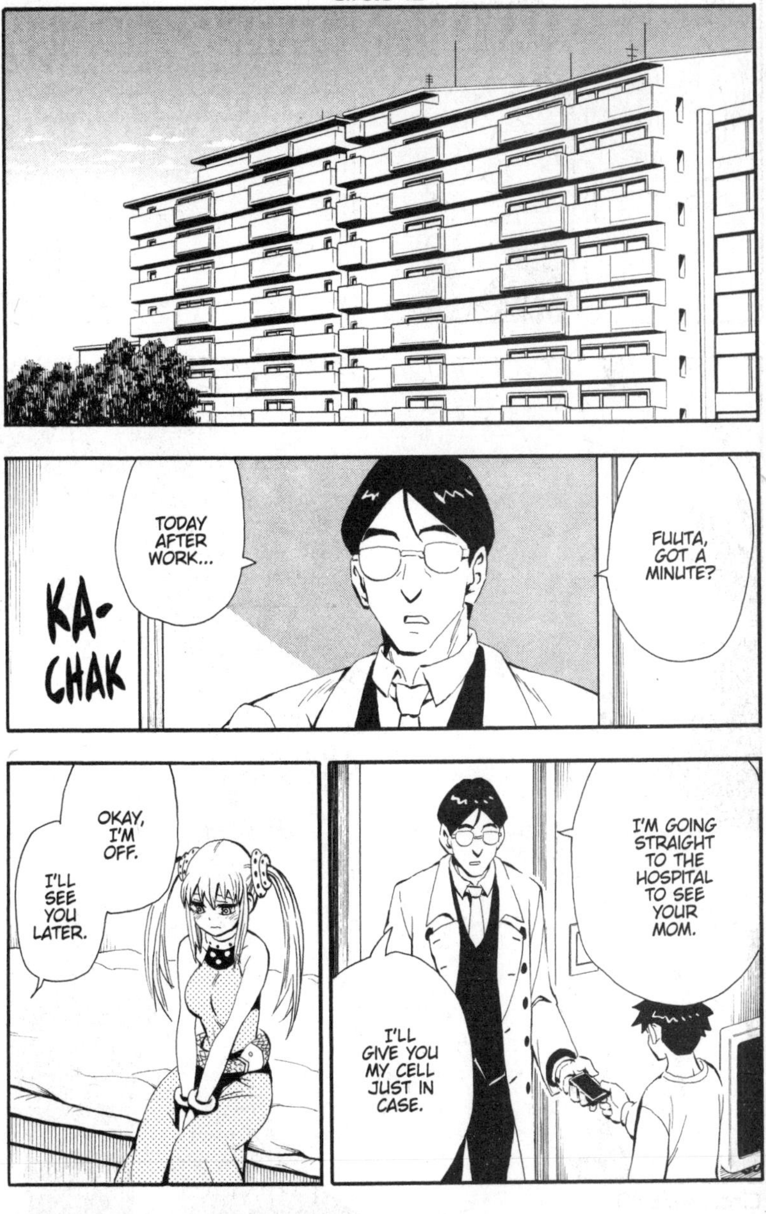
FUUTA, GOT A MINUTE?
TODAY AFTER WORK...
KA-CHAK
I'M GOING STRAIGHT TO THE HOSPITAL TO SEE YOUR MOM.
I'LL GIVE YOU MY CELL JUST IN CASE.
OKAY, I'M OFF.
I'LL SEE YOU LATER.

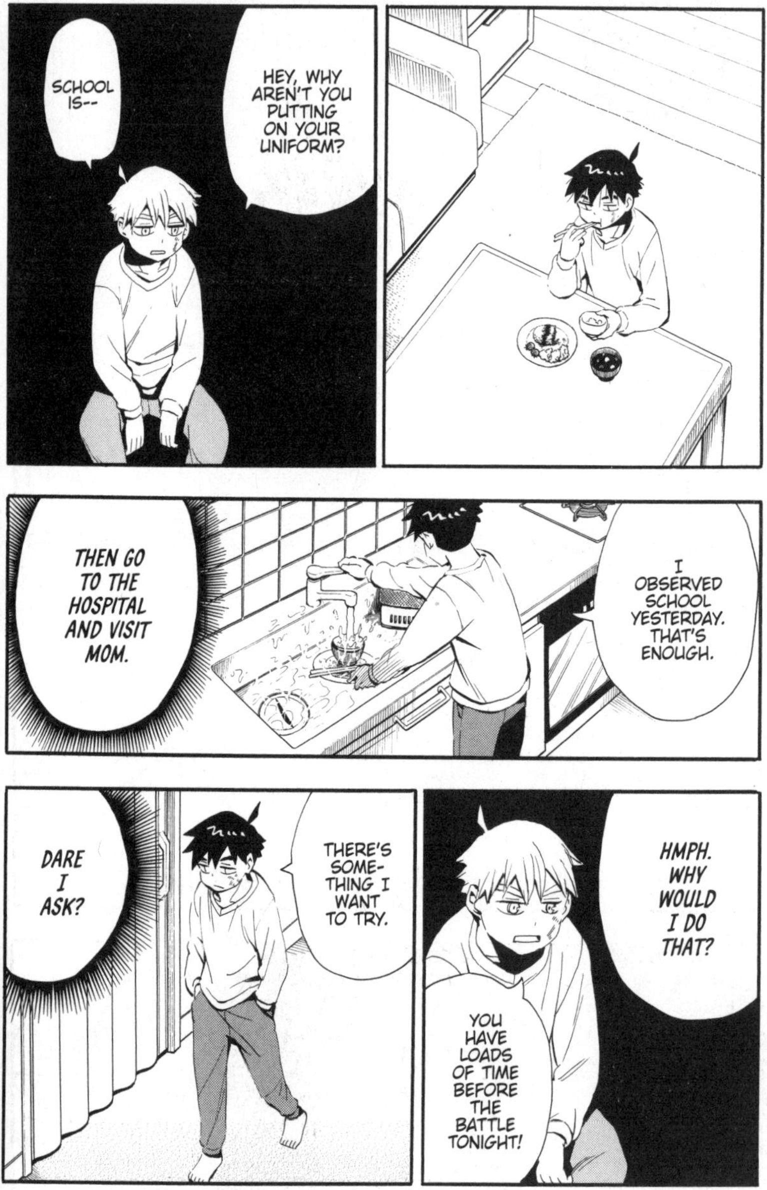
HEY, WHY AREN'T YOU PUTTING ON YOUR UNIFORM?
SCHOOL IS--
I OBSERVED SCHOOL YESTERDAY. THAT'S ENOUGH.
THEN GO TO THE HOSPITAL AND VISIT MOM.
HMPH. WHY WOULD I DO THAT?
YOU HAVE LOADS OF TIME BEFORE THE BATTLE TONIGHT!
THERE'S SOME-THING I WANT TO TRY.
DARE I ASK?

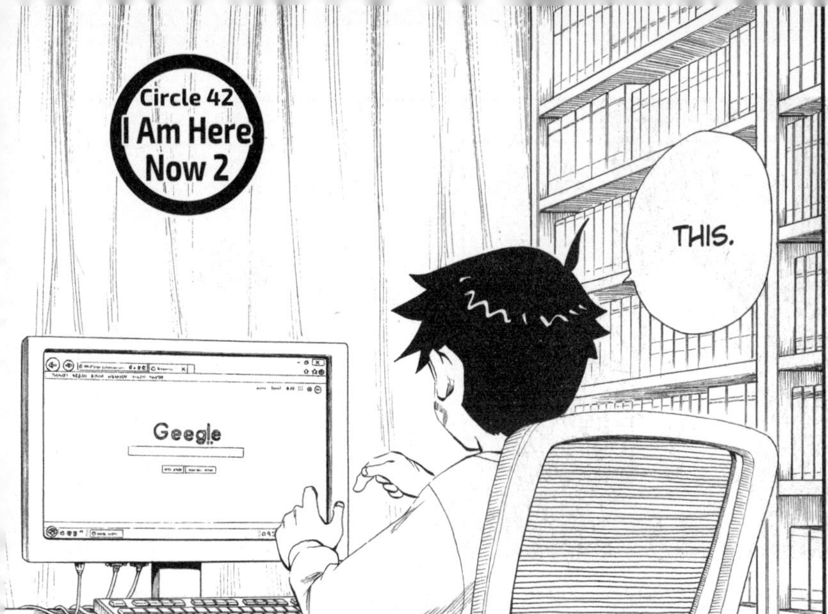
THIS.
Circle 42
I Am Here Now 2
Geegle

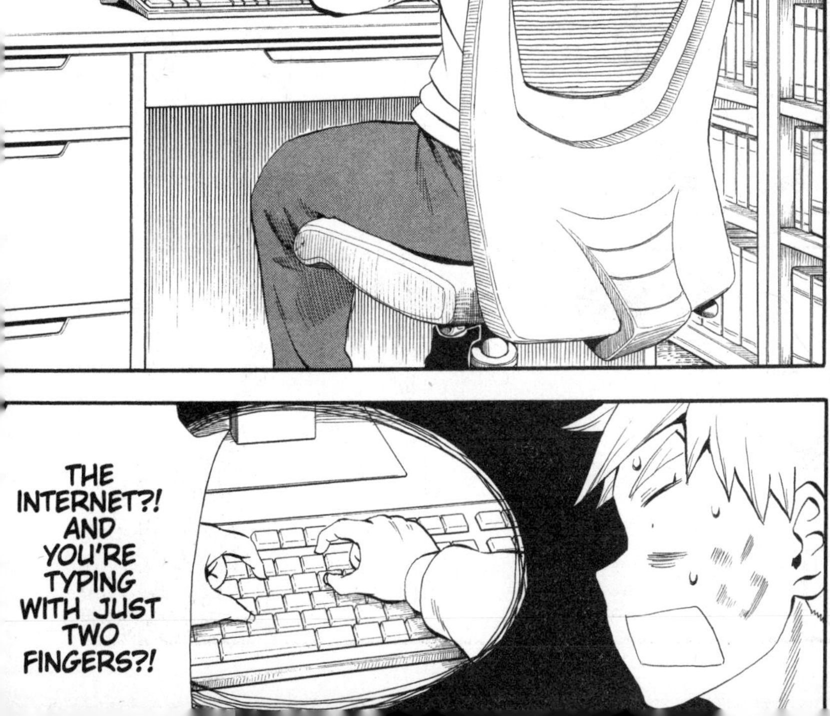
THE INTERNET?! AND YOU'RE TYPING WITH JUST TWO FINGERS?!

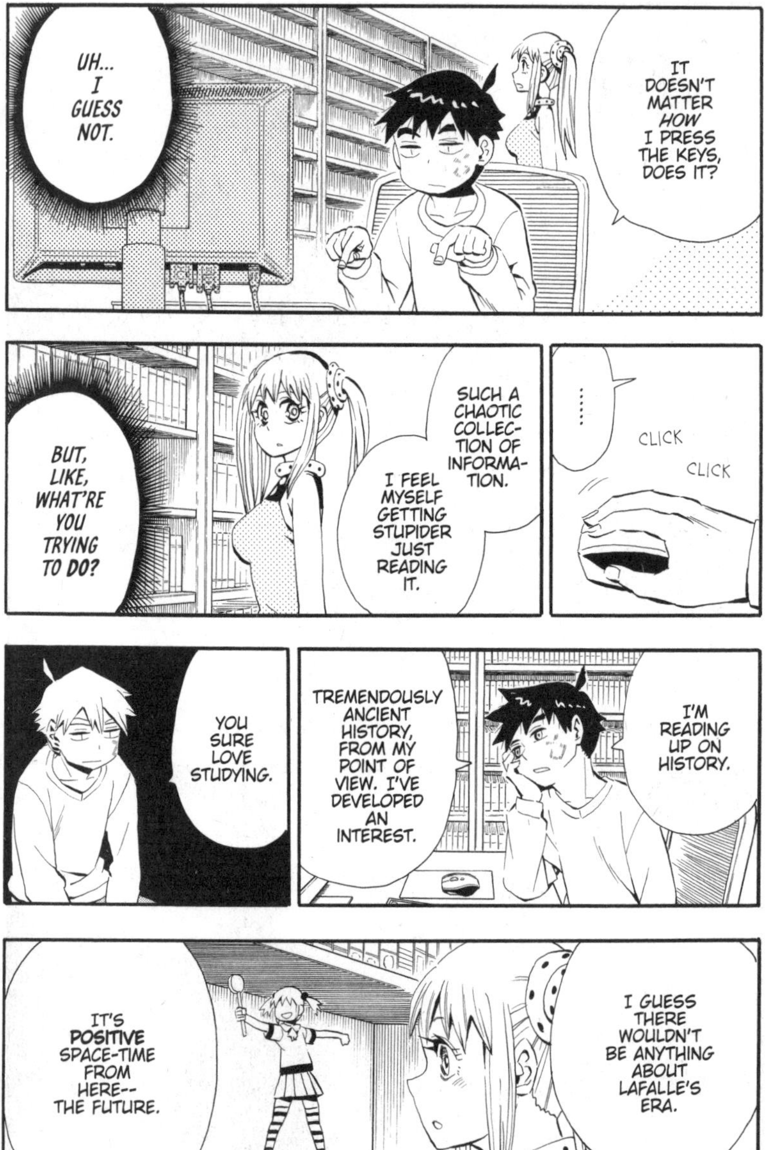
IT DOESN'T MATTER *HOW* I PRESS THE KEYS, DOES IT?
UH... I GUESS NOT.
......
CLICK
CLICK
SUCH A CHAOTIC COLLECTION OF INFORMATION.
I FEEL MYSELF GETTING STUPIDER JUST READING IT.
BUT, LIKE, WHAT'RE YOU TRYING TO DO?
I'M READING UP ON HISTORY.
TREMENDOUSLY ANCIENT HISTORY, FROM MY POINT OF VIEW. I'VE DEVELOPED AN INTEREST.
YOU SURE LOVE STUDYING.
I GUESS THERE WOULDN'T BE ANYTHING ABOUT LAFALLE'S ERA.
IT'S **POSITIVE** SPACE-TIME FROM HERE-- THE FUTURE.

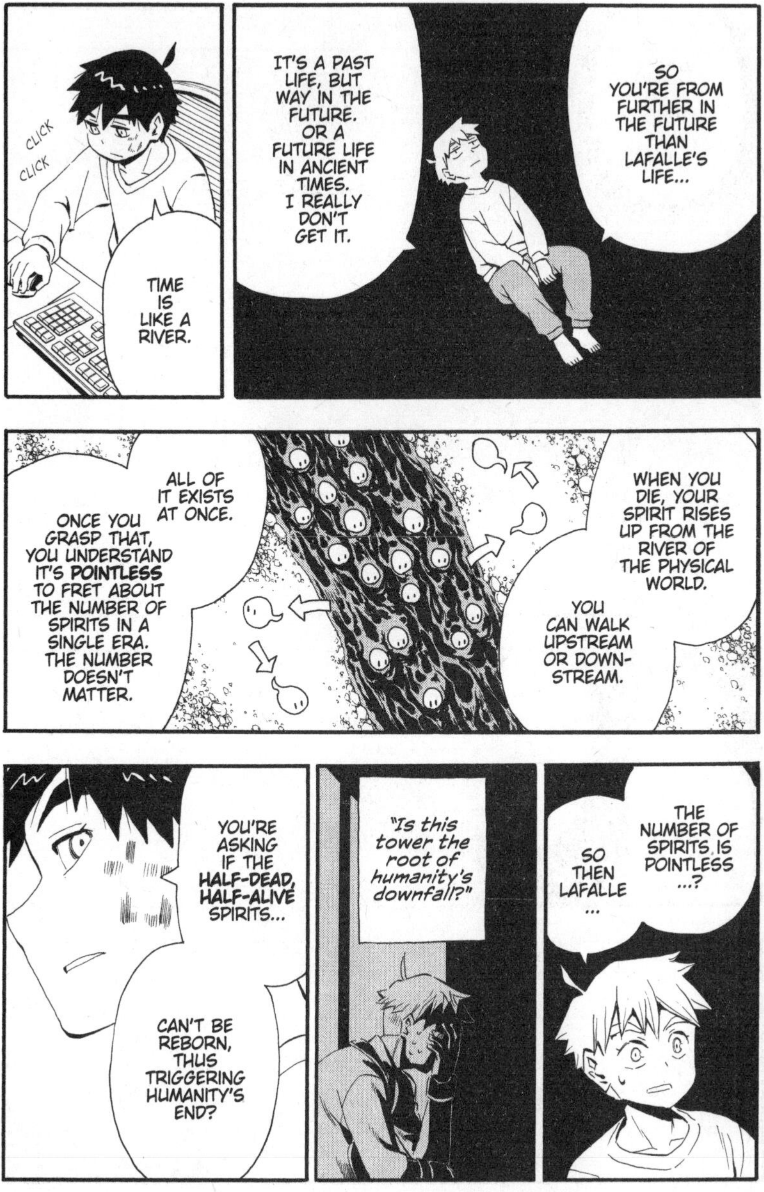
SO YOU'RE FROM FURTHER IN THE FUTURE THAN LAFALLE'S LIFE...
IT'S A PAST LIFE, BUT WAY IN THE FUTURE. OR A FUTURE LIFE IN ANCIENT TIMES. I REALLY DON'T GET IT.
CLICK
CLICK
TIME IS LIKE A RIVER.
WHEN YOU DIE, YOUR SPIRIT RISES UP FROM THE RIVER OF THE PHYSICAL WORLD.
YOU CAN WALK UPSTREAM OR DOWN-STREAM.
ALL OF IT EXISTS AT ONCE.
ONCE YOU GRASP THAT, YOU UNDERSTAND IT'S **POINTLESS** TO FRET ABOUT THE NUMBER OF SPIRITS IN A SINGLE ERA. THE NUMBER DOESN'T MATTER.
THE NUMBER OF SPIRITS IS POINTLESS ...?
SO THEN LAFALLE ...
"Is this tower the root of humanity's downfall?"
YOU'RE ASKING IF THE **HALF-DEAD, HALF-ALIVE** SPIRITS...
CAN'T BE REBORN, THUS TRIGGERING HUMANITY'S END?

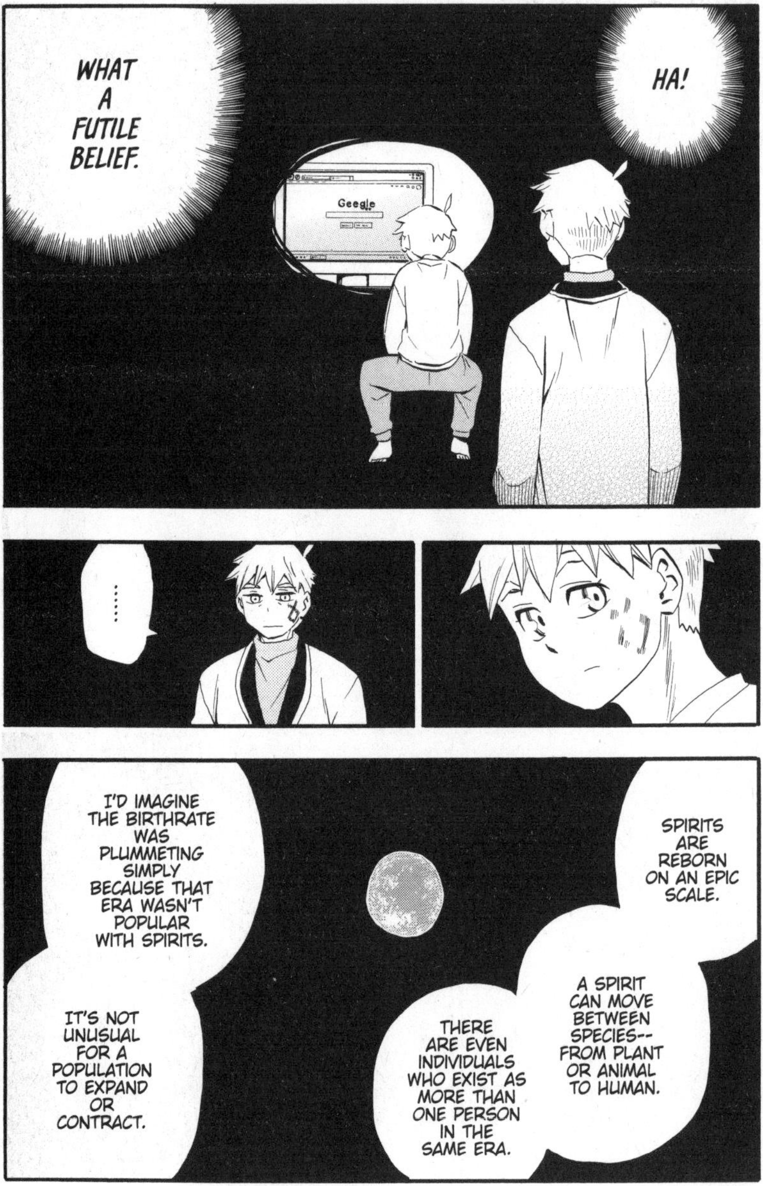
HA!
WHAT A FUTILE BELIEF.
Geegle
......
SPIRITS ARE REBORN ON AN EPIC SCALE.
A SPIRIT CAN MOVE BETWEEN SPECIES-- FROM PLANT OR ANIMAL TO HUMAN.
THERE ARE EVEN INDIVIDUALS WHO EXIST AS MORE THAN ONE PERSON IN THE SAME ERA.
I'D IMAGINE THE BIRTHRATE WAS PLUMMETING SIMPLY BECAUSE THAT ERA WASN'T POPULAR WITH SPIRITS.
IT'S NOT UNUSUAL FOR A POPULATION TO EXPAND OR CONTRACT.

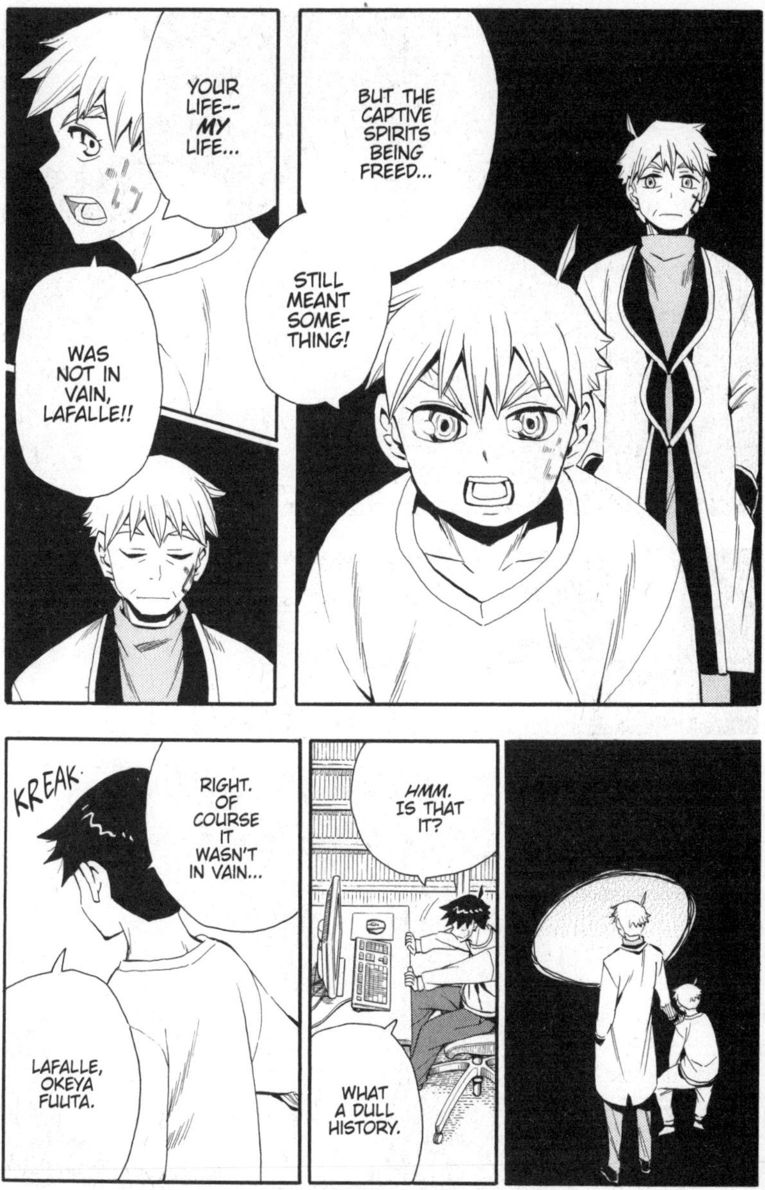
BUT THE CAPTIVE SPIRITS BEING FREED...
STILL MEANT SOMETHING!
YOUR LIFE-- MY LIFE...
WAS NOT IN VAIN, LAFALLE!!
HMM. IS THAT IT?
WHAT A DULL HISTORY.
KREAK
RIGHT. OF COURSE IT WASN'T IN VAIN...
LAFALLE, OKEYA FUUTA.

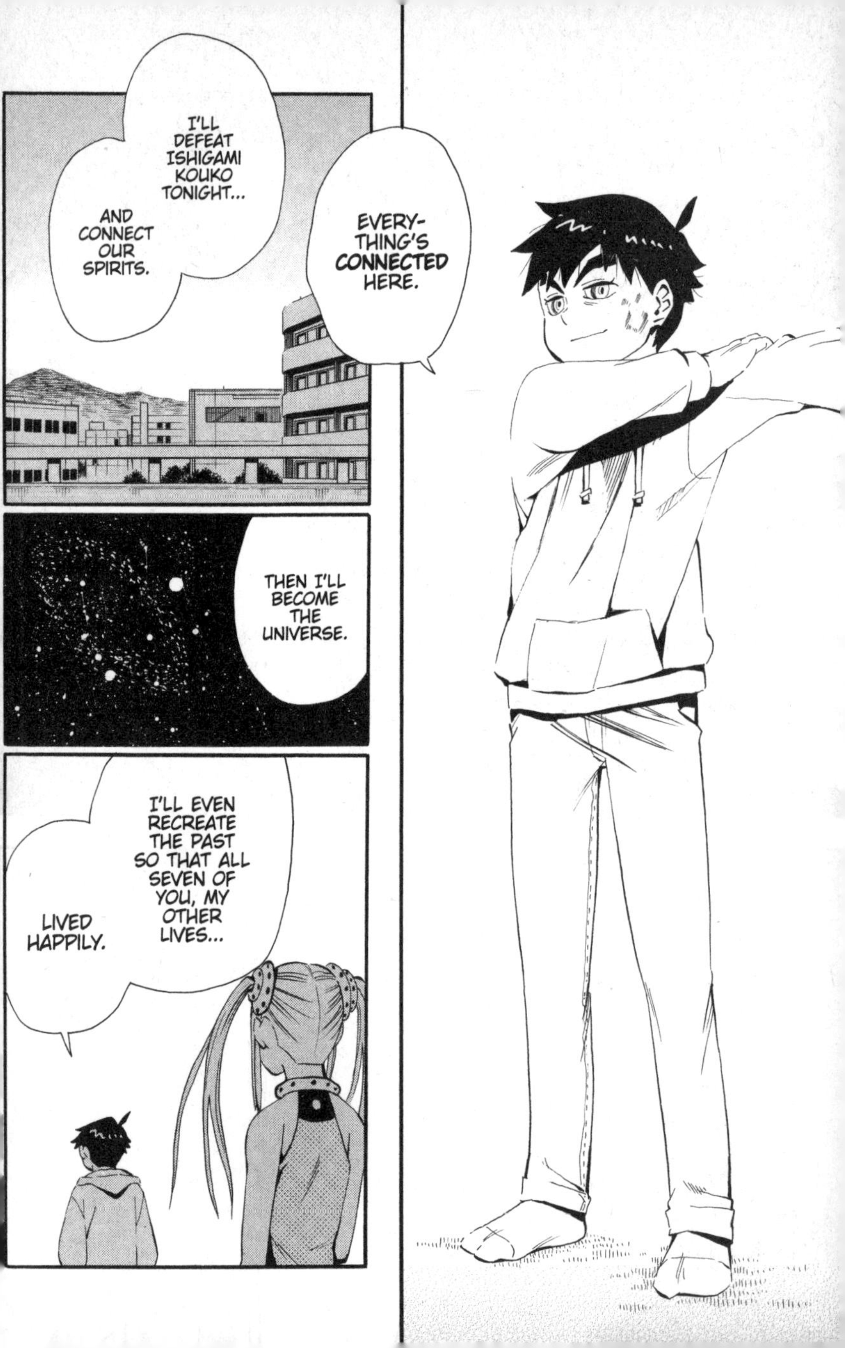
EVERY-THING'S CONNECTED HERE.
I'LL DEFEAT ISHIGAMI KOUKO TONIGHT...
AND CONNECT OUR SPIRITS.
THEN I'LL BECOME THE UNIVERSE.
I'LL EVEN RECREATE THE PAST SO THAT ALL SEVEN OF YOU, MY OTHER LIVES...
LIVED HAPPILY.

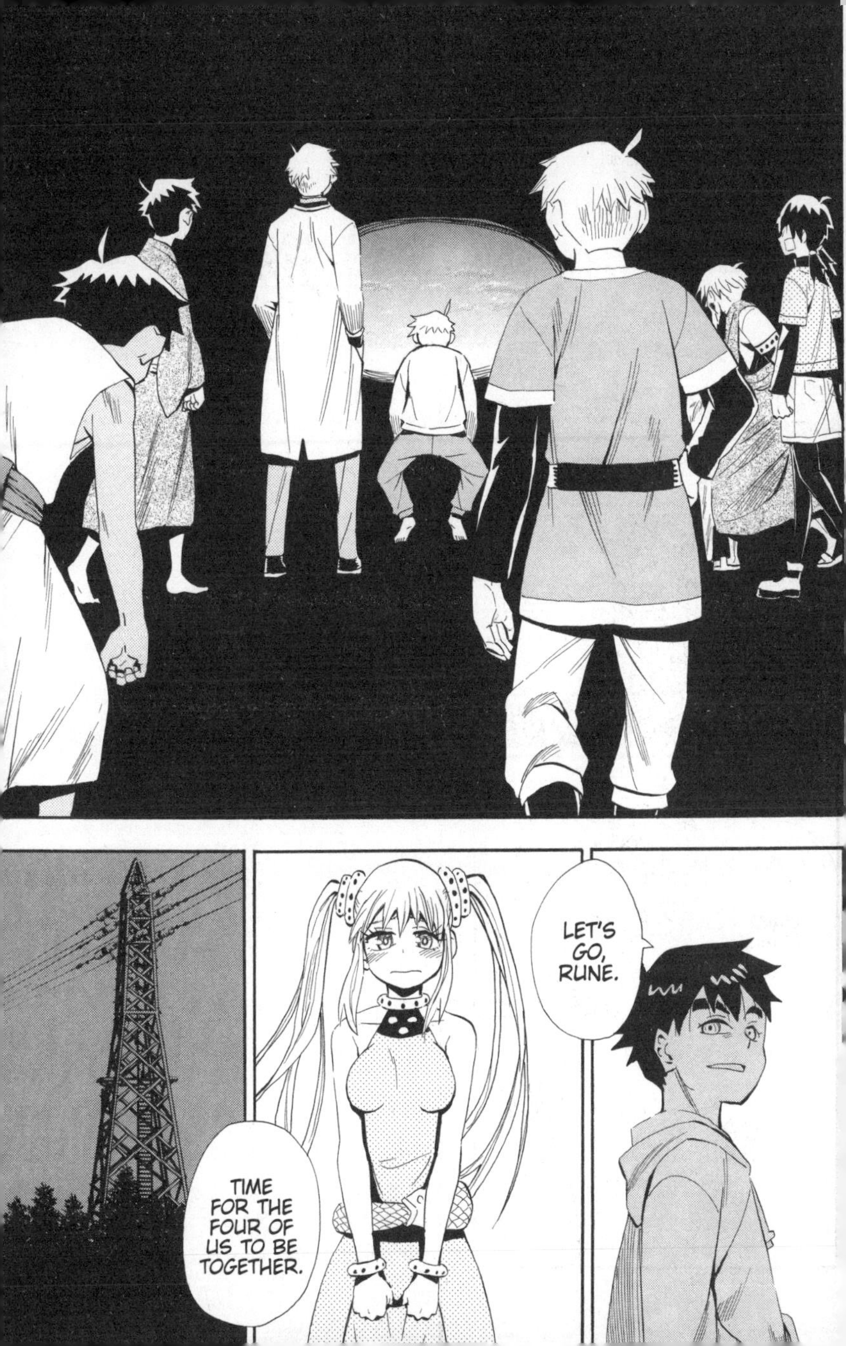
LET'S GO, RUNE.
TIME FOR THE FOUR OF US TO BE TOGETHER.

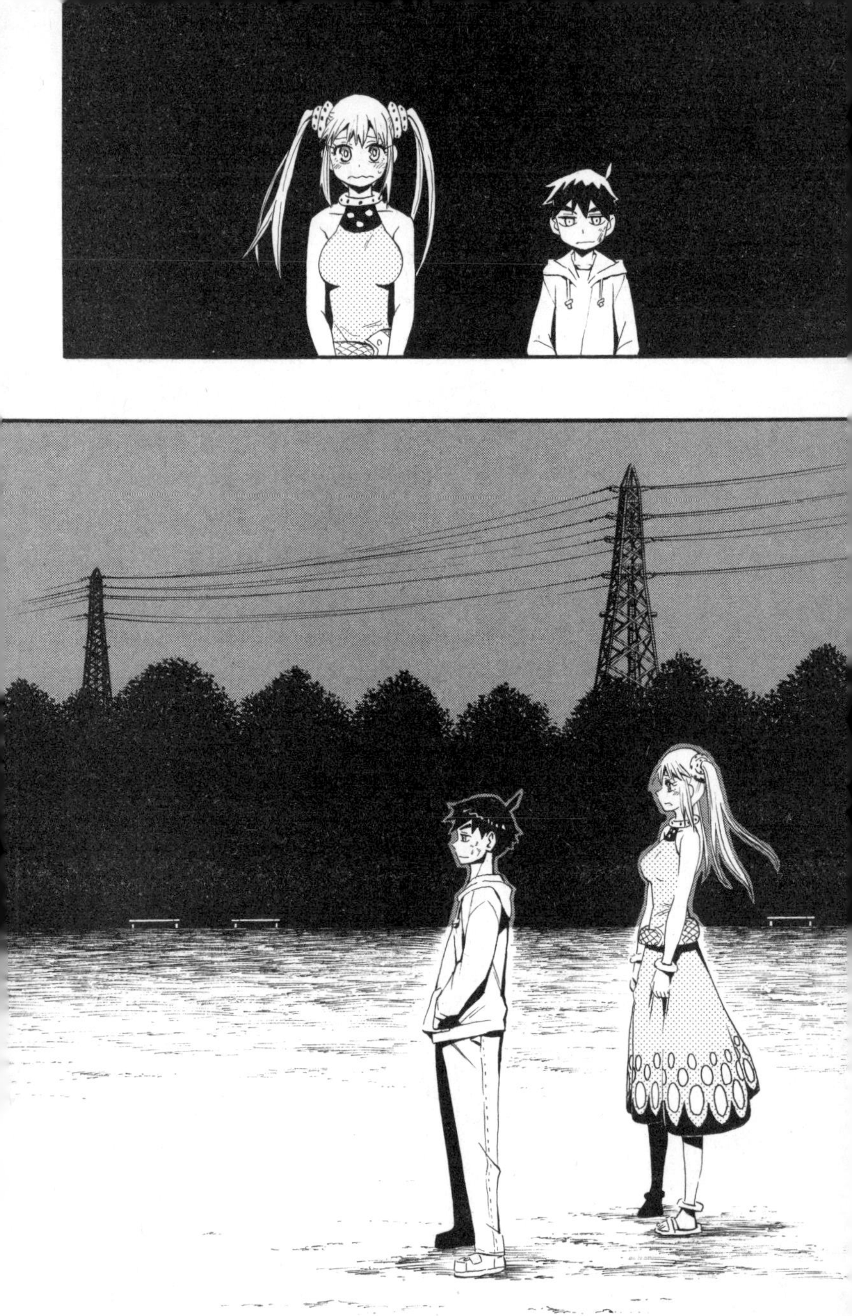

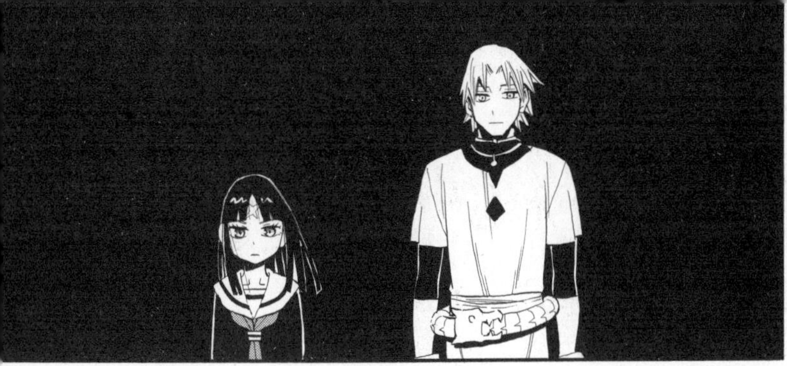
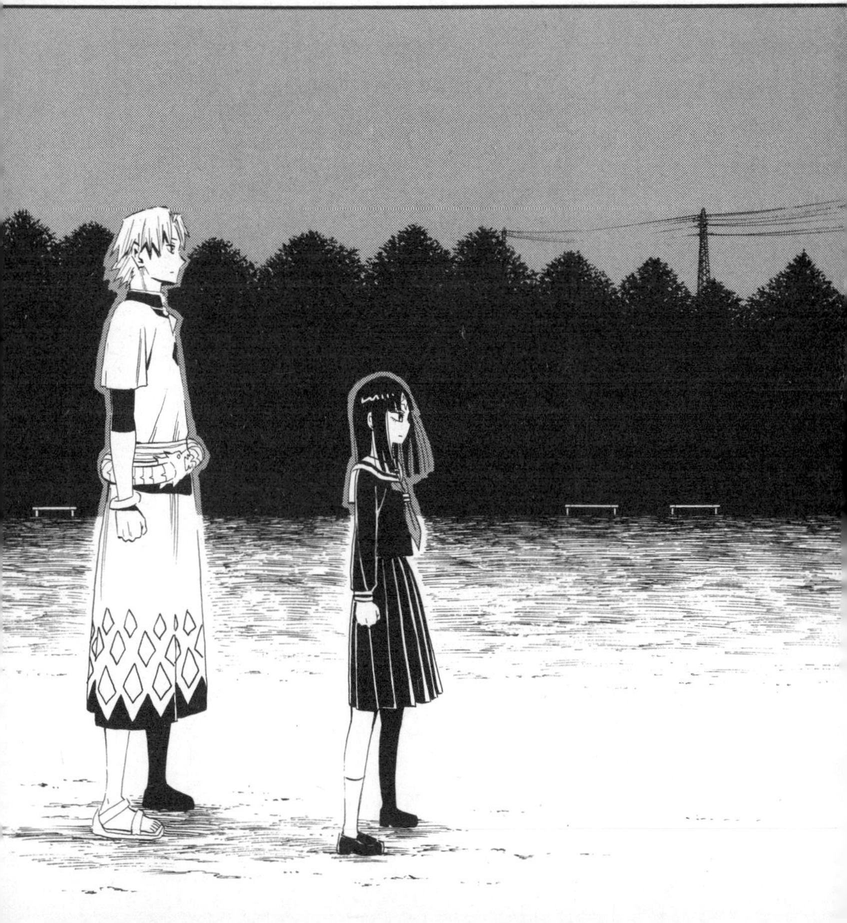

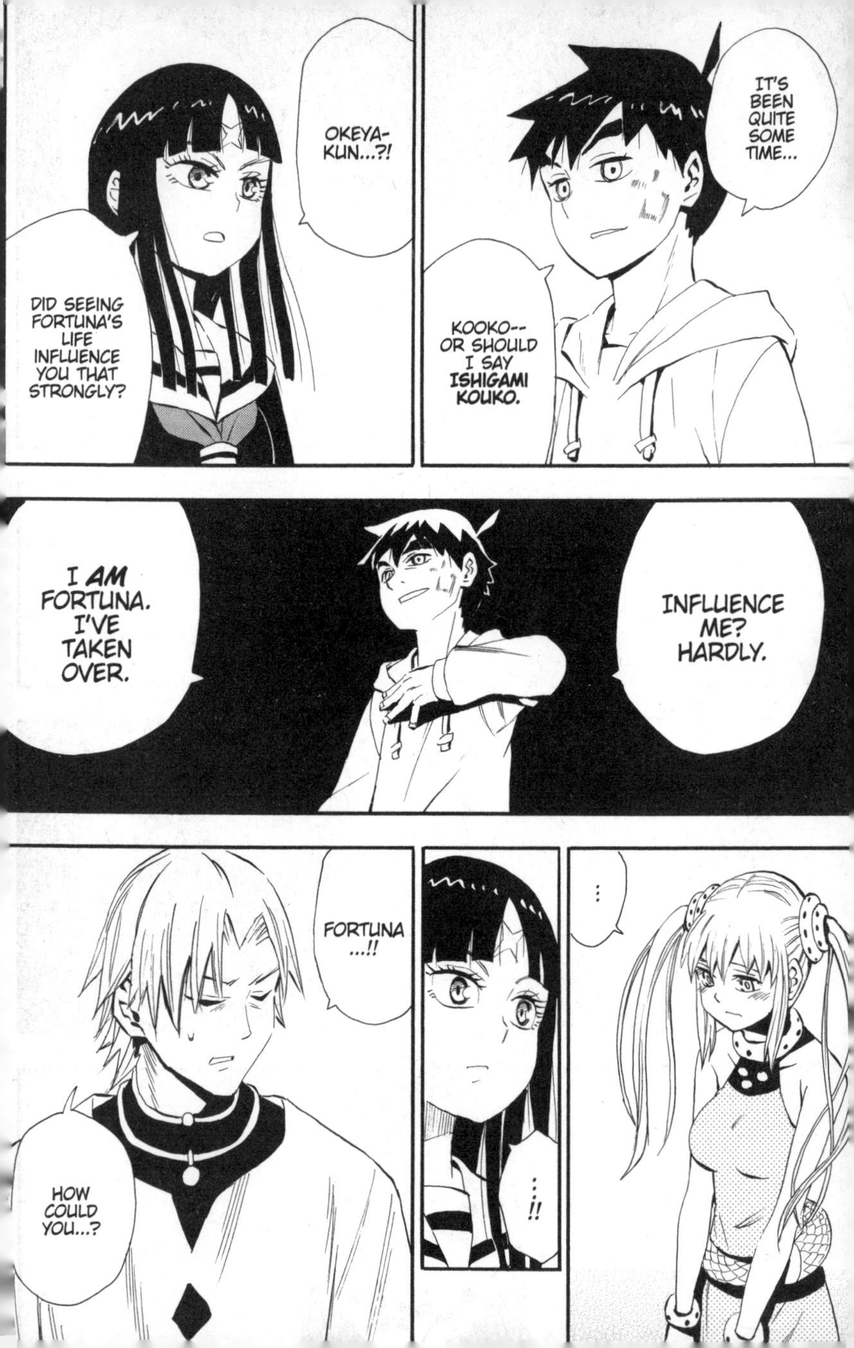
IT'S BEEN QUITE SOME TIME...
KOOKO-- OR SHOULD I SAY **ISHIGAMI KOUKO.**
OKEYA-KUN...?!
DID SEEING FORTUNA'S LIFE INFLUENCE YOU THAT STRONGLY?
INFLUENCE ME? HARDLY.
I ***AM*** FORTUNA. I'VE TAKEN OVER.
...
...!!
FORTUNA ...!!
HOW COULD YOU...?

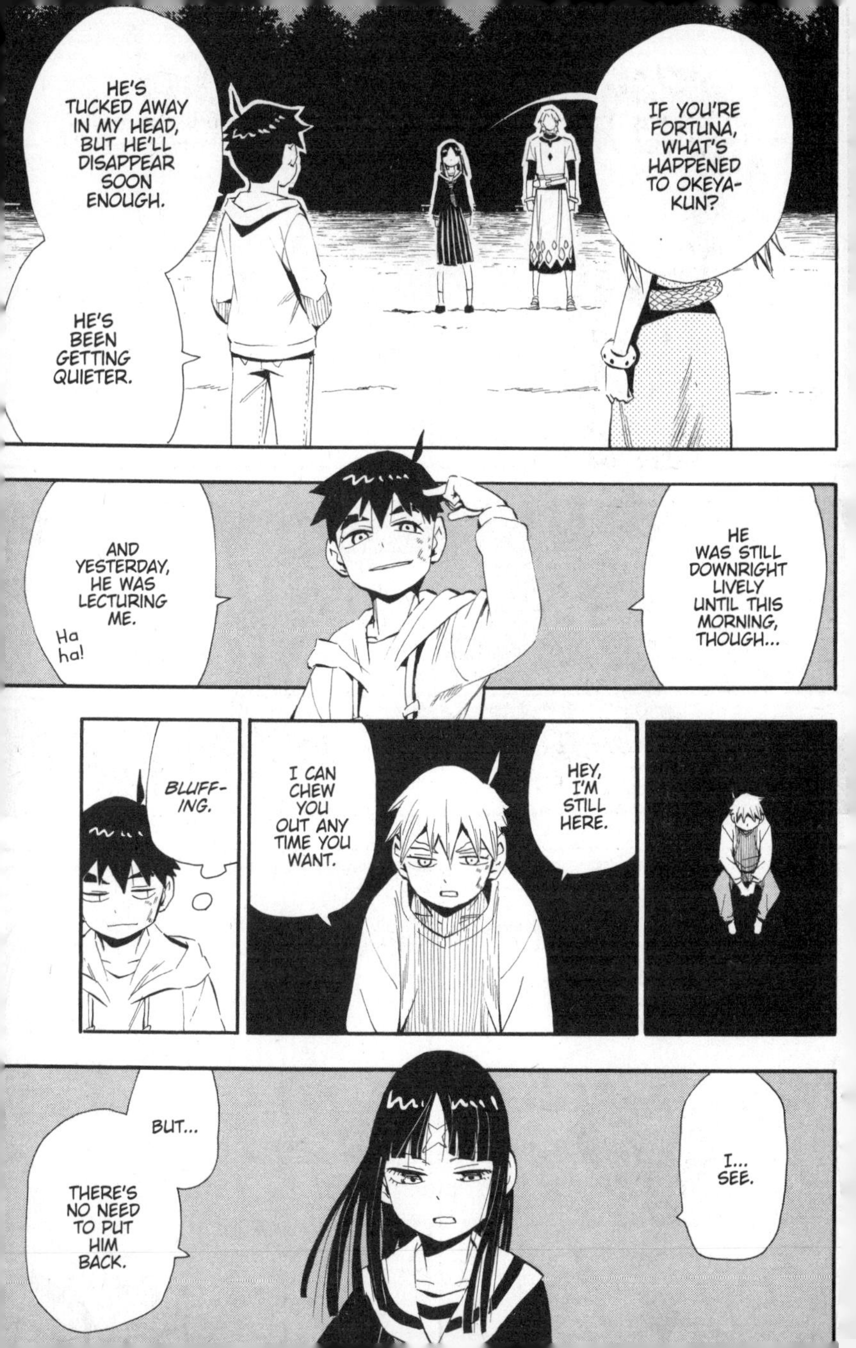
IF YOU'RE FORTUNA, WHAT'S HAPPENED TO OKEYA-KUN?
HE'S TUCKED AWAY IN MY HEAD, BUT HE'LL DISAPPEAR SOON ENOUGH.
HE'S BEEN GETTING QUIETER.
HE WAS STILL DOWNRIGHT LIVELY UNTIL THIS MORNING, THOUGH...
AND YESTERDAY, HE WAS LECTURING ME.
Ha ha!
HEY, I'M STILL HERE.
I CAN CHEW YOU OUT ANY TIME YOU WANT.
BLUFF-ING.
I... SEE.
BUT...
THERE'S NO NEED TO PUT HIM BACK.

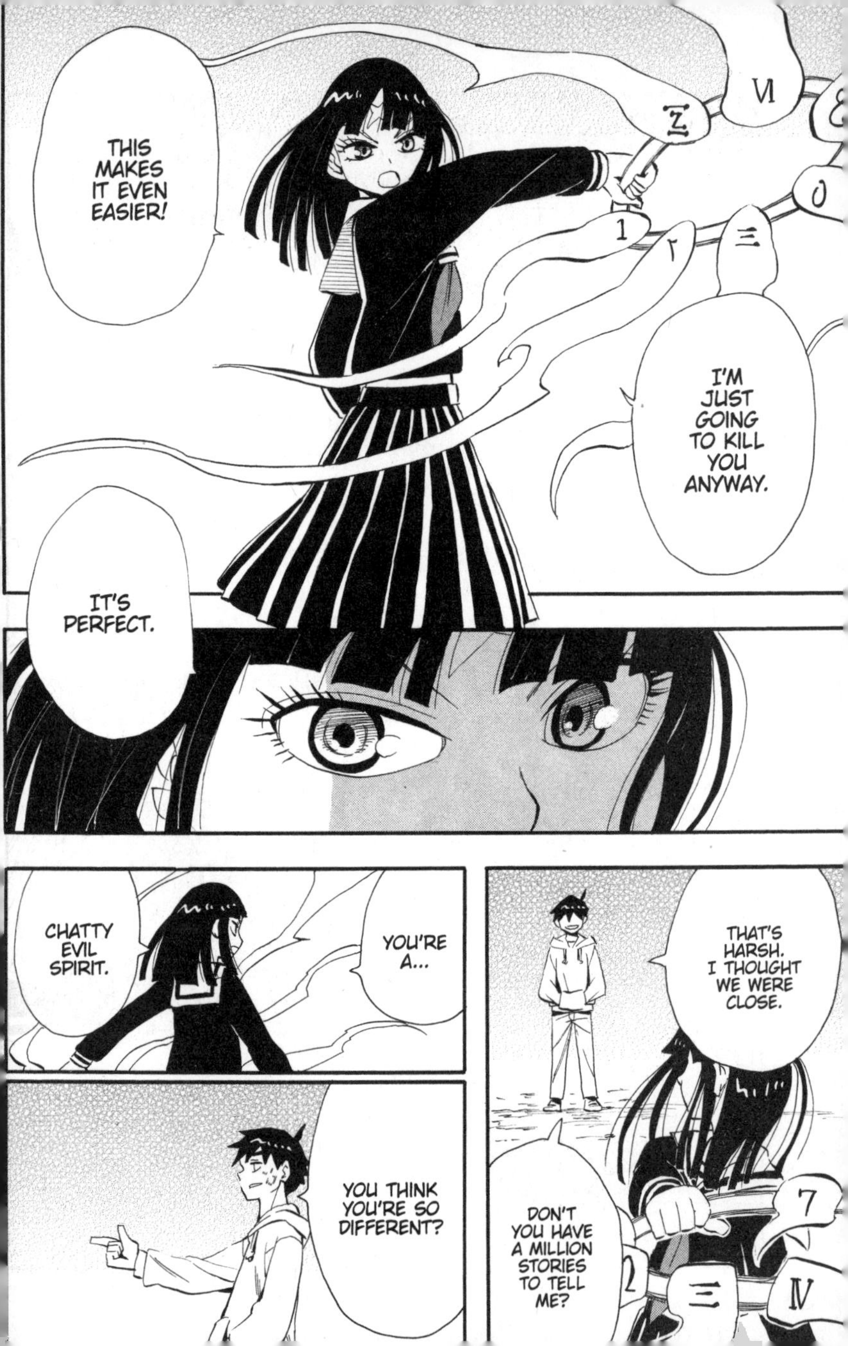
THIS MAKES IT EVEN EASIER!
I'M JUST GOING TO KILL YOU ANYWAY.
IT'S PERFECT.
THAT'S HARSH. I THOUGHT WE WERE CLOSE.
DON'T YOU HAVE A MILLION STORIES TO TELL ME?
YOU'RE A...
CHATTY EVIL SPIRIT.
YOU THINK YOU'RE SO DIFFERENT?

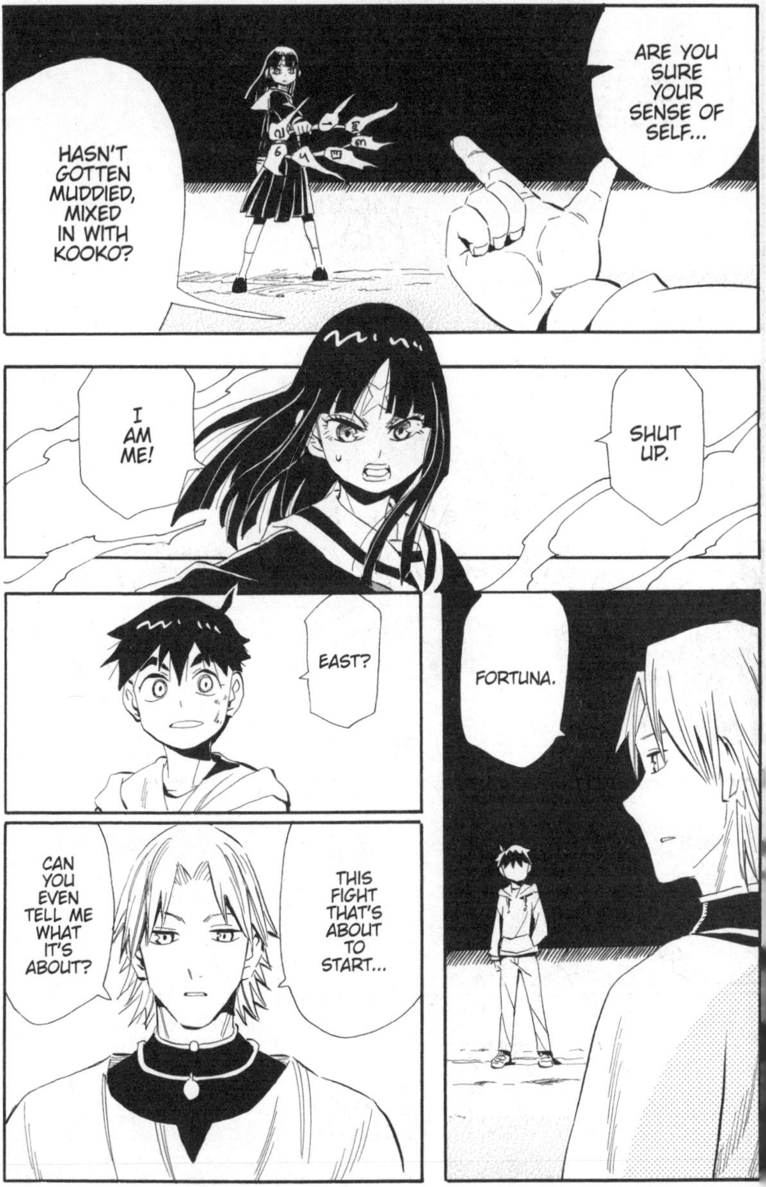
ARE YOU SURE YOUR SENSE OF SELF...
HASN'T GOTTEN MUDDIED, MIXED IN WITH KOOKO?
SHUT UP.
I AM ME!
FORTUNA.
EAST?
THIS FIGHT THAT'S ABOUT TO START...
CAN YOU EVEN TELL ME WHAT IT'S ABOUT?

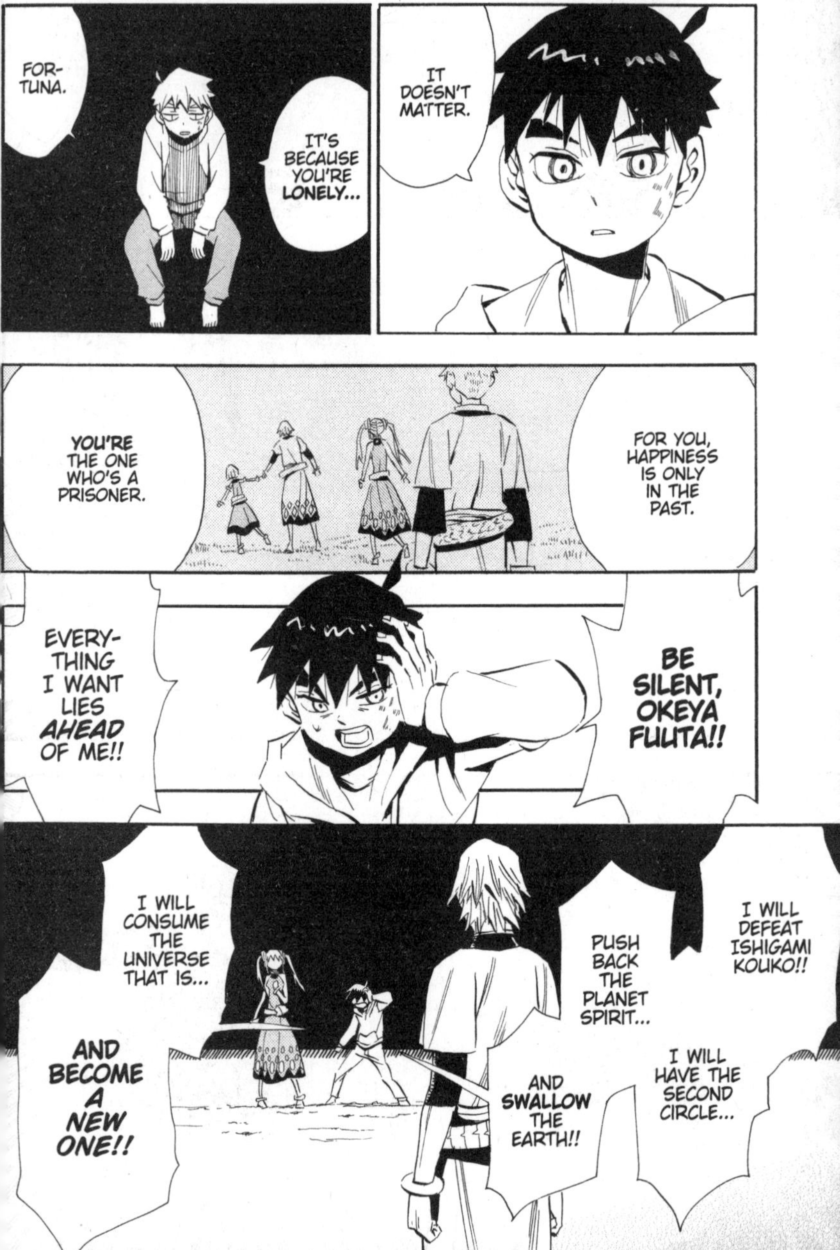
IT DOESN'T MATTER.
FOR-TUNA.
IT'S BECAUSE YOU'RE LONELY...
FOR YOU, HAPPINESS IS ONLY IN THE PAST.
YOU'RE THE ONE WHO'S A PRISONER.
BE SILENT, OKEYA FUUTA!!
EVERY-THING I WANT LIES AHEAD OF ME!!
I WILL DEFEAT ISHIGAMI KOUKO!!
I WILL HAVE THE SECOND CIRCLE...
PUSH BACK THE PLANET SPIRIT...
AND SWALLOW THE EARTH!!
I WILL CONSUME THE UNIVERSE THAT IS...
AND BECOME A NEW ONE!!

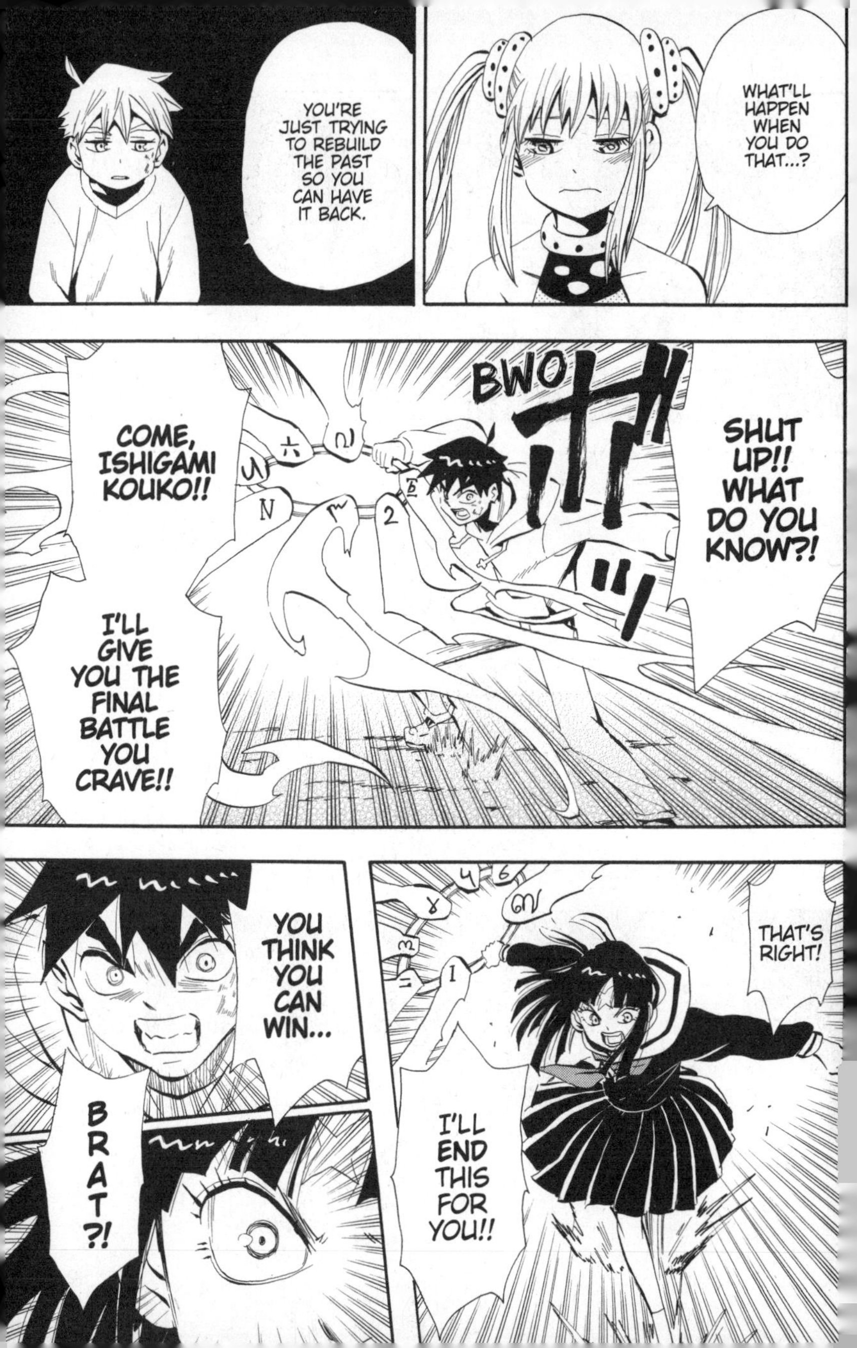
WHAT'LL HAPPEN WHEN YOU DO THAT...?
YOU'RE JUST TRYING TO REBUILD THE PAST SO YOU CAN HAVE IT BACK.
SHUT UP!! WHAT DO YOU KNOW?!
BWO
COME, ISHIGAMI KOUKO!!
I'LL GIVE YOU THE FINAL BATTLE YOU CRAVE!!
THAT'S RIGHT!
I'LL END THIS FOR YOU!!
YOU THINK YOU CAN WIN...
BRAT?!

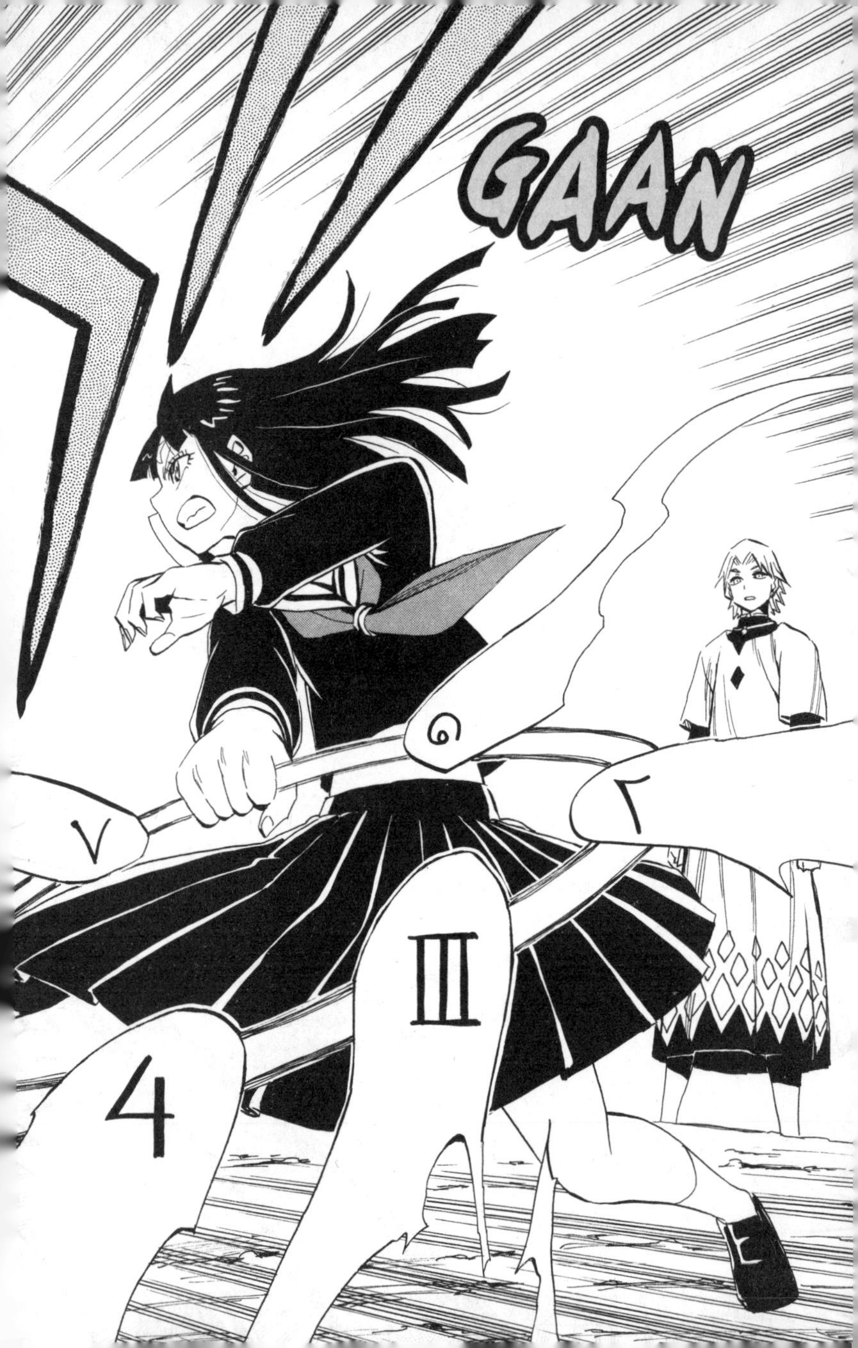
GAAN

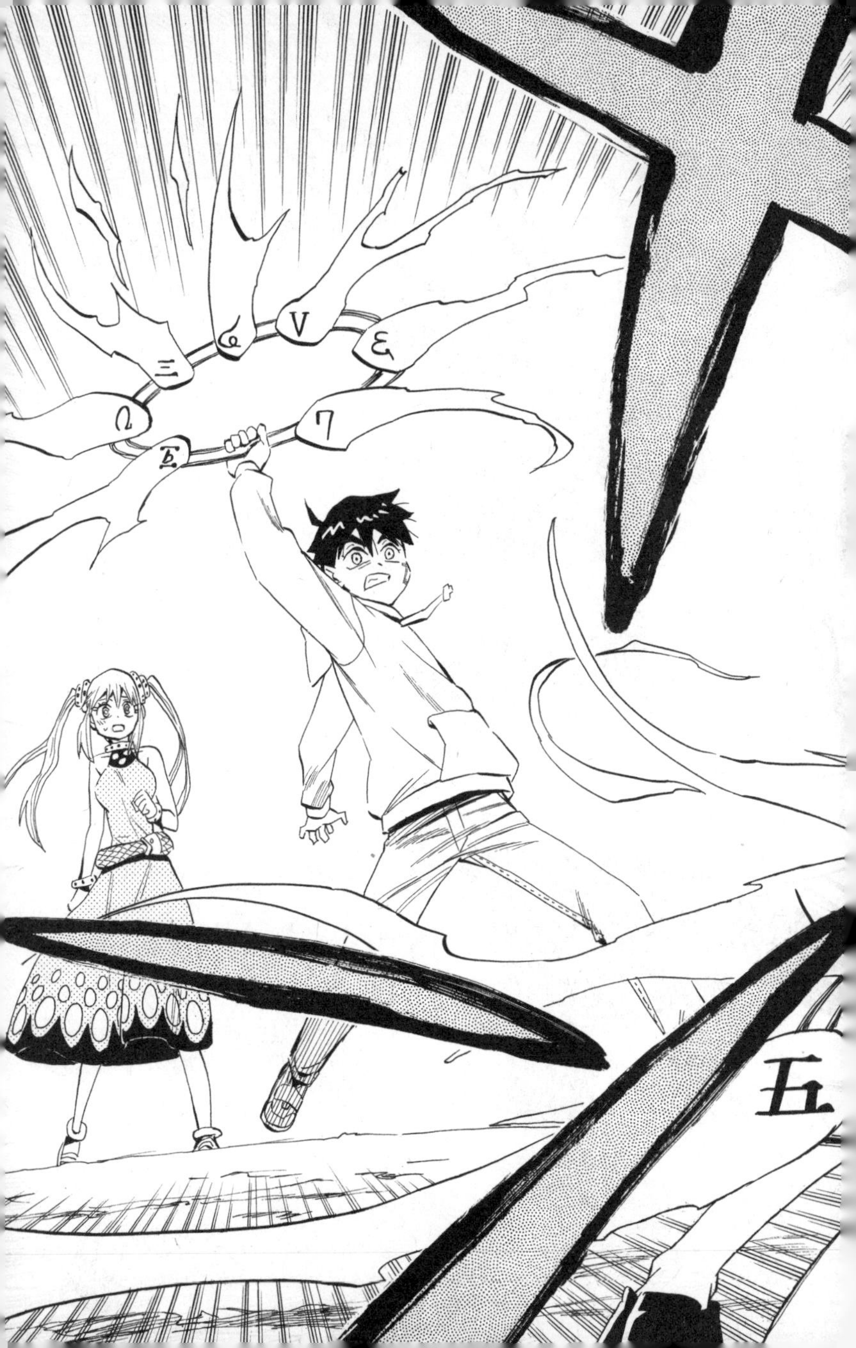

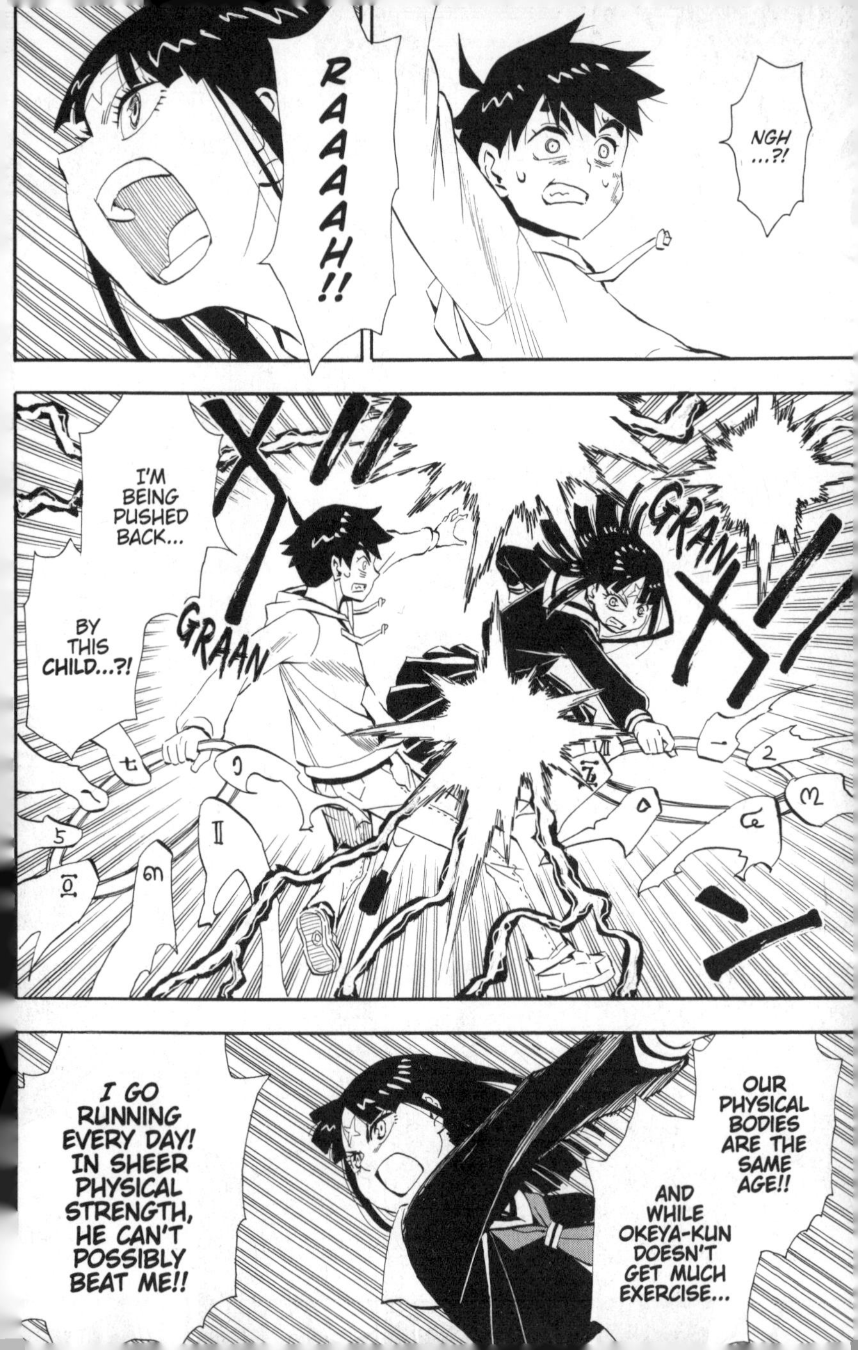
NGH ...?!
RAAAAAH!!
GRAN
I'M BEING PUSHED BACK...
GRAAN
BY THIS CHILD...?!
OUR PHYSICAL BODIES ARE THE SAME AGE!!
AND WHILE OKEYA-KUN DOESN'T GET MUCH EXERCISE...
I GO RUNNING EVERY DAY! IN SHEER PHYSICAL STRENGTH, HE CAN'T POSSIBLY BEAT ME!!

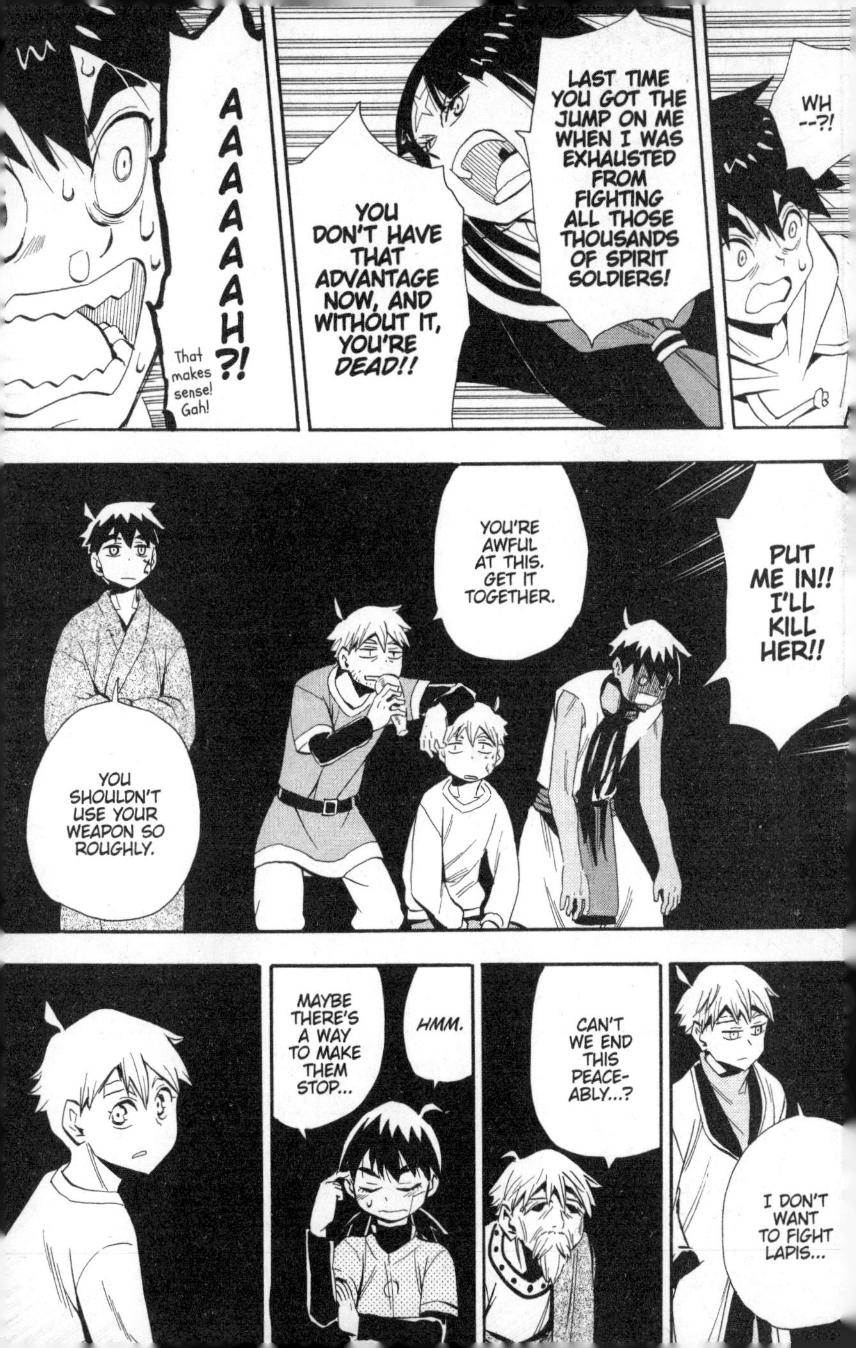
WH--?!
LAST TIME YOU GOT THE JUMP ON ME WHEN I WAS EXHAUSTED FROM FIGHTING ALL THOSE THOUSANDS OF SPIRIT SOLDIERS!
YOU DON'T HAVE THAT ADVANTAGE NOW, AND WITHOUT IT, YOU'RE *DEAD!!*
AAAAAAAH?!
That makes sense! Gah!
PUT ME IN!! I'LL KILL HER!!
YOU'RE AWFUL AT THIS. GET IT TOGETHER.
YOU SHOULDN'T USE YOUR WEAPON SO ROUGHLY.
I DON'T WANT TO FIGHT LAPIS...
CAN'T WE END THIS PEACEABLY...?
HMM.
MAYBE THERE'S A WAY TO MAKE THEM STOP...

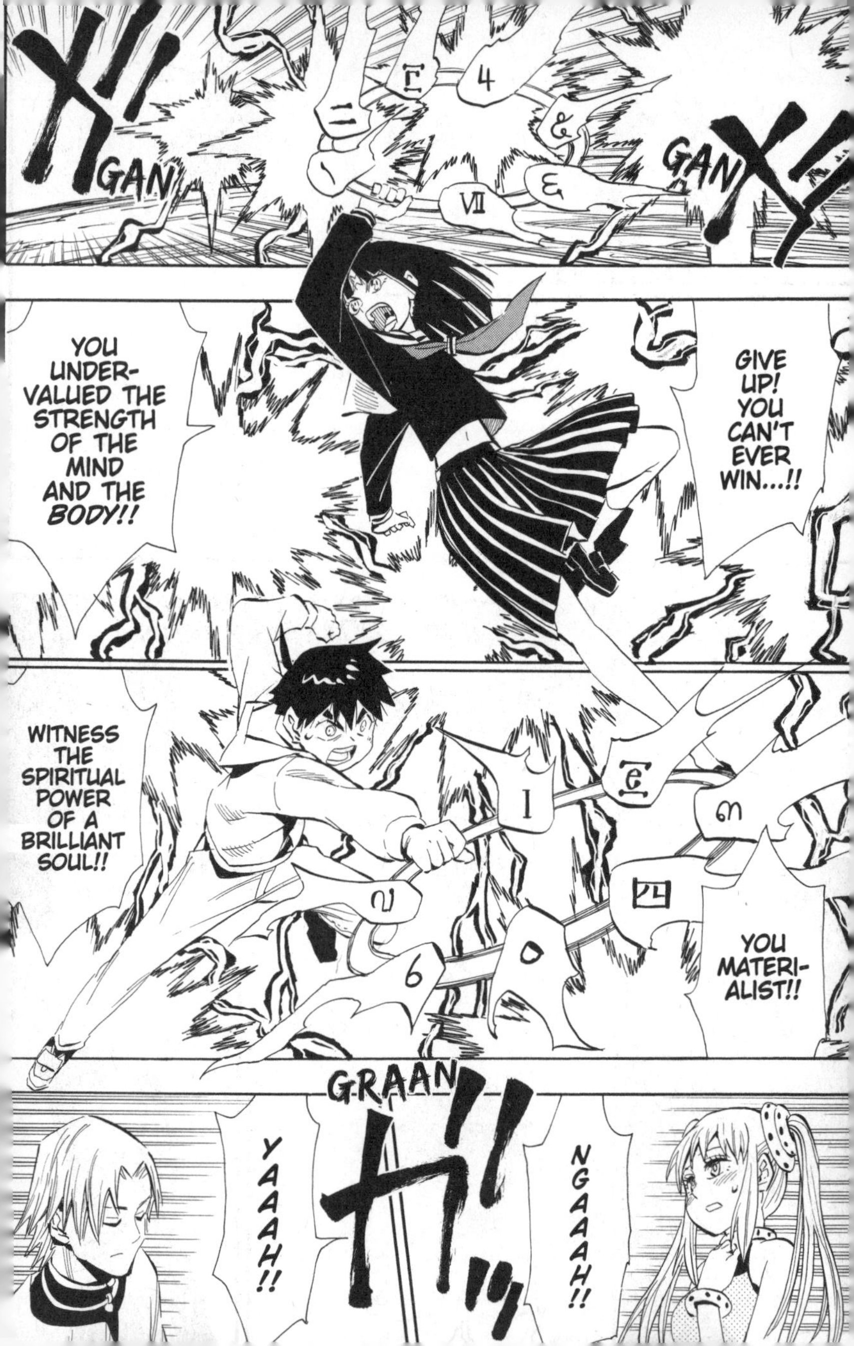
GAN
GAN
GIVE UP! YOU CAN'T EVER WIN...!!
YOU UNDER-VALUED THE STRENGTH OF THE MIND AND THE *BODY*!!
YOU MATERI-ALIST!!
WITNESS THE SPIRITUAL POWER OF A BRILLIANT SOUL!!
GRAAN
NGAAAAH!!
YAAAAH!!

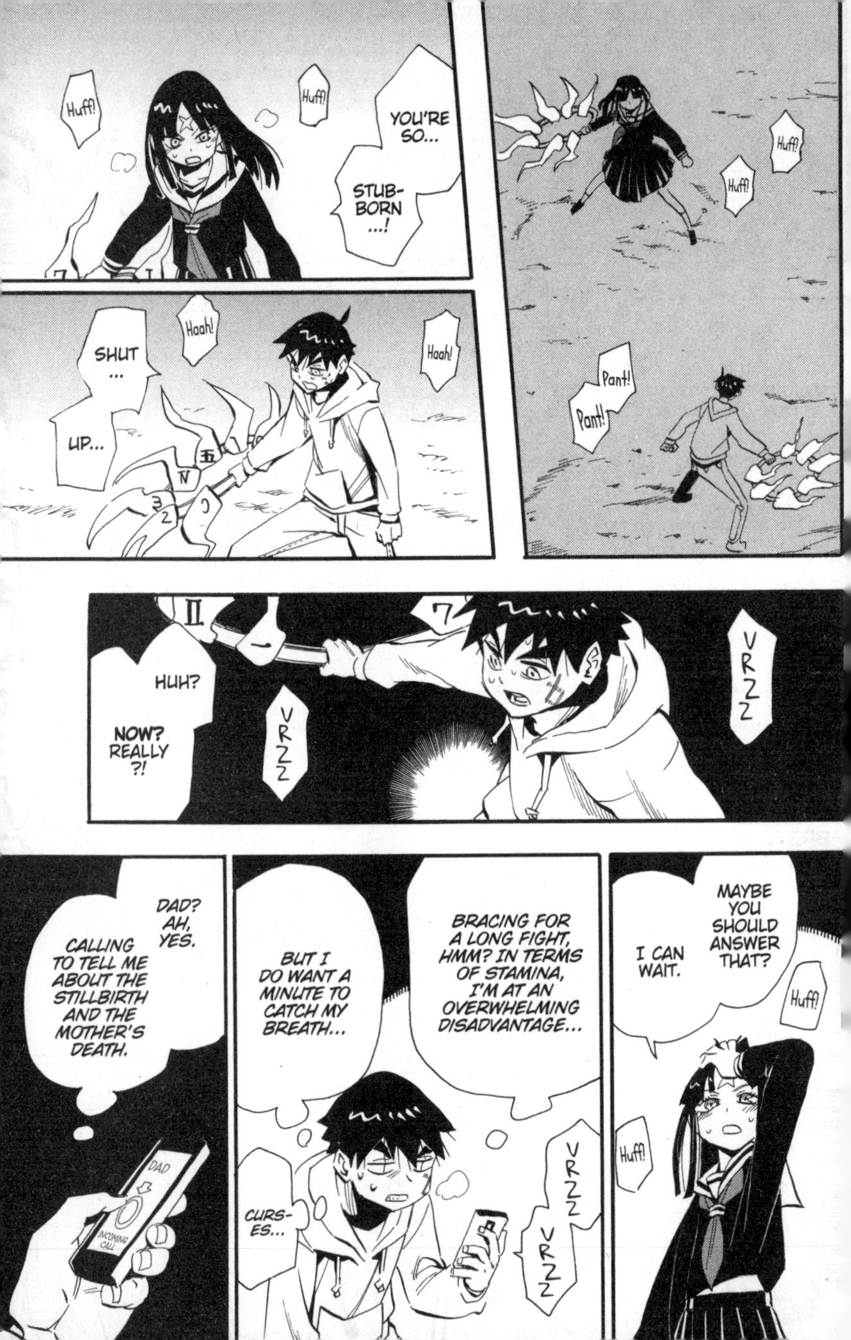
Huff!
Huff!
Pant!
Pant!
Huff!
Huff!
YOU'RE SO...
STUB-BORN ...!
Haah!
Haah!
SHUT ...
UP...
VRZZ
HUH?
NOW? REALLY ?!
VRZZ
MAYBE YOU SHOULD ANSWER THAT?
I CAN WAIT.
Huff!
Huff!
BRACING FOR A LONG FIGHT, HMM? IN TERMS OF STAMINA, I'M AT AN OVERWHELMING DISADVANTAGE...
BUT I DO WANT A MINUTE TO CATCH MY BREATH...
VRZZ
VRZZ
CURS-ES...
DAD? AH, YES.
CALLING TO TELL ME ABOUT THE STILLBIRTH AND THE MOTHER'S DEATH.
DAD
INCOMING CALL

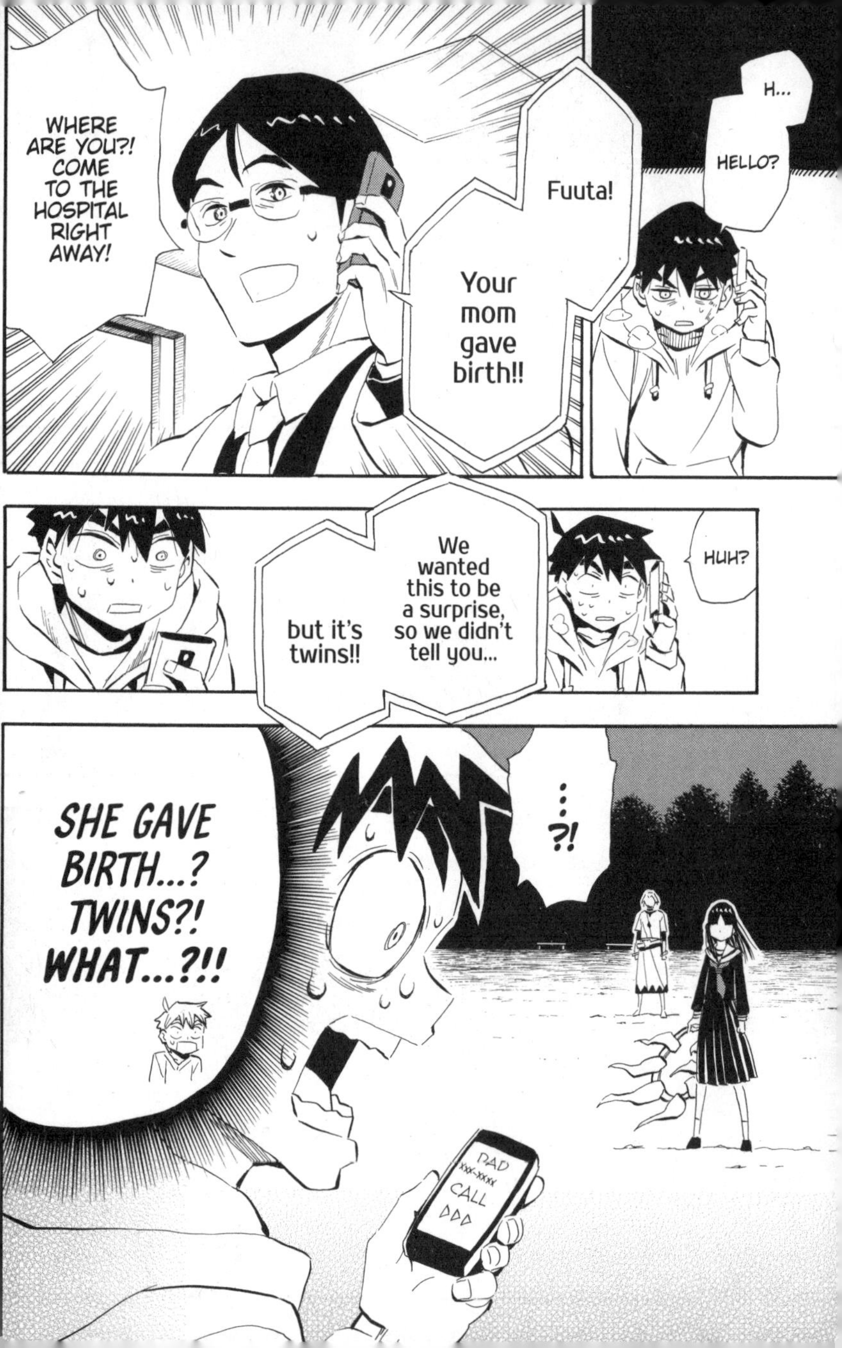
H...
HELLO?
Fuuta!
Your mom gave birth!!
WHERE ARE YOU?! COME TO THE HOSPITAL RIGHT AWAY!
HUH?
We wanted this to be a surprise, so we didn't tell you...
but it's twins!!
...?!
SHE GAVE BIRTH...? TWINS?! WHAT...?!!
DAD
xxx-xxxx
CALL

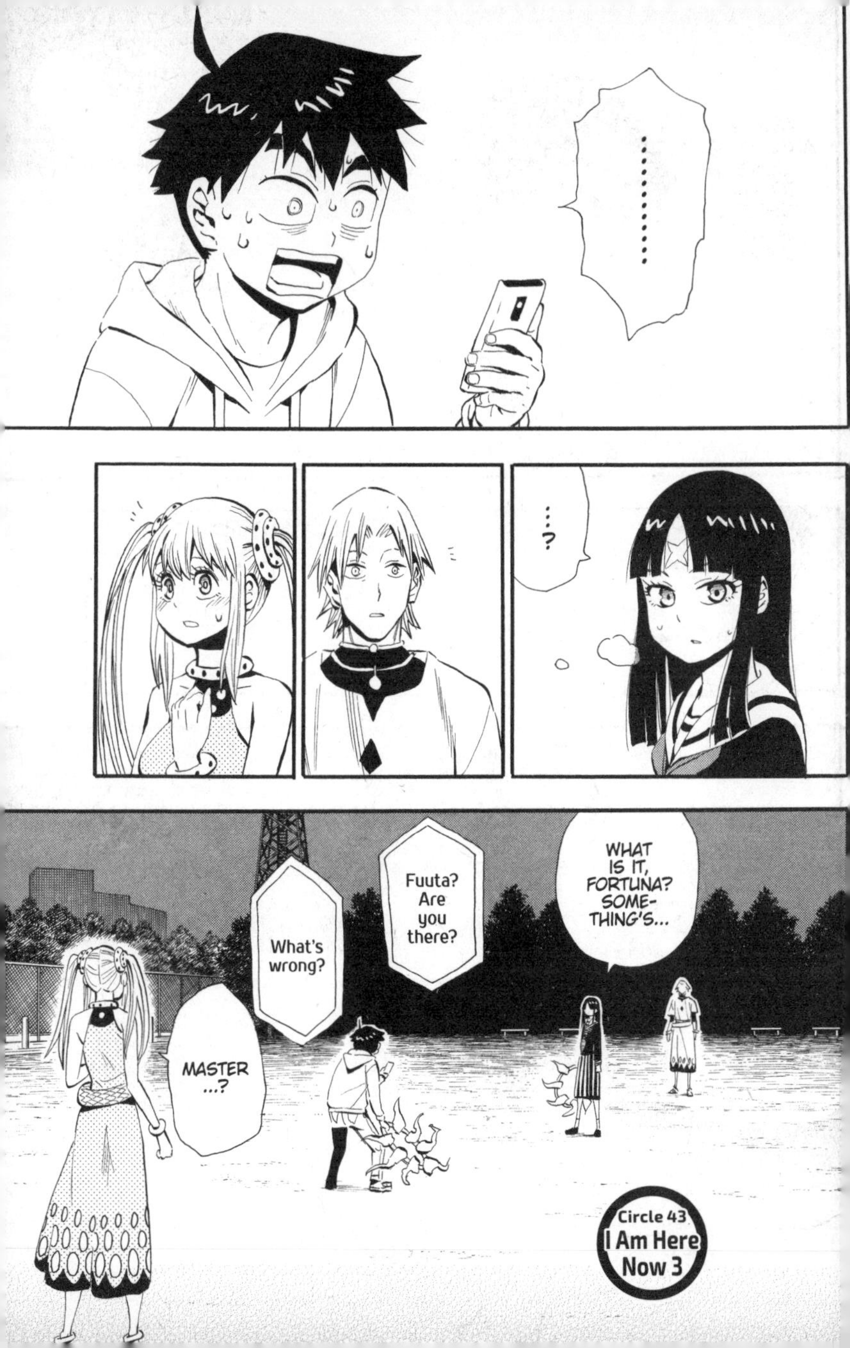
……
…?
WHAT IS IT, FORTUNA? SOME-THING'S…
Fuuta? Are you there?
What's wrong?
MASTER …?
Circle 43
I Am Here Now 3

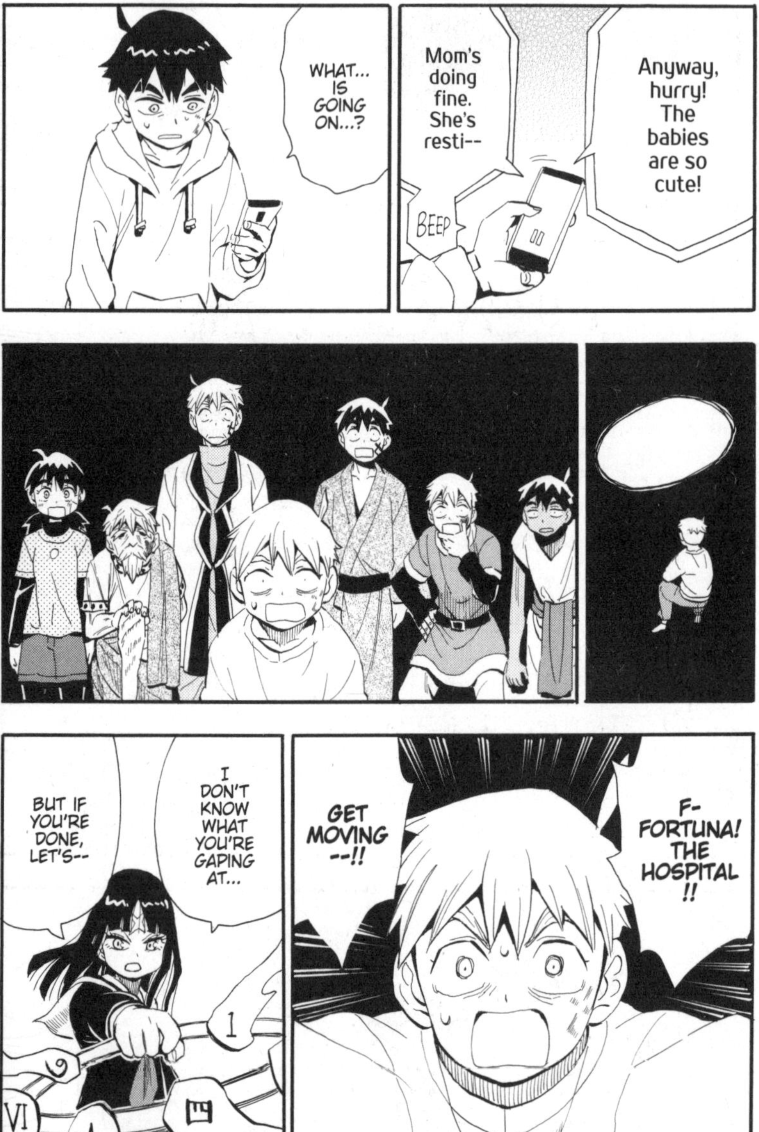
Anyway, hurry! The babies are so cute!
Mom's doing fine. She's resti--
BEEP
WHAT... IS GOING ON...?
F- FORTUNA! THE HOSPITAL !!
GET MOVING --!!
I DON'T KNOW WHAT YOU'RE GAPING AT...
BUT IF YOU'RE DONE, LET'S--

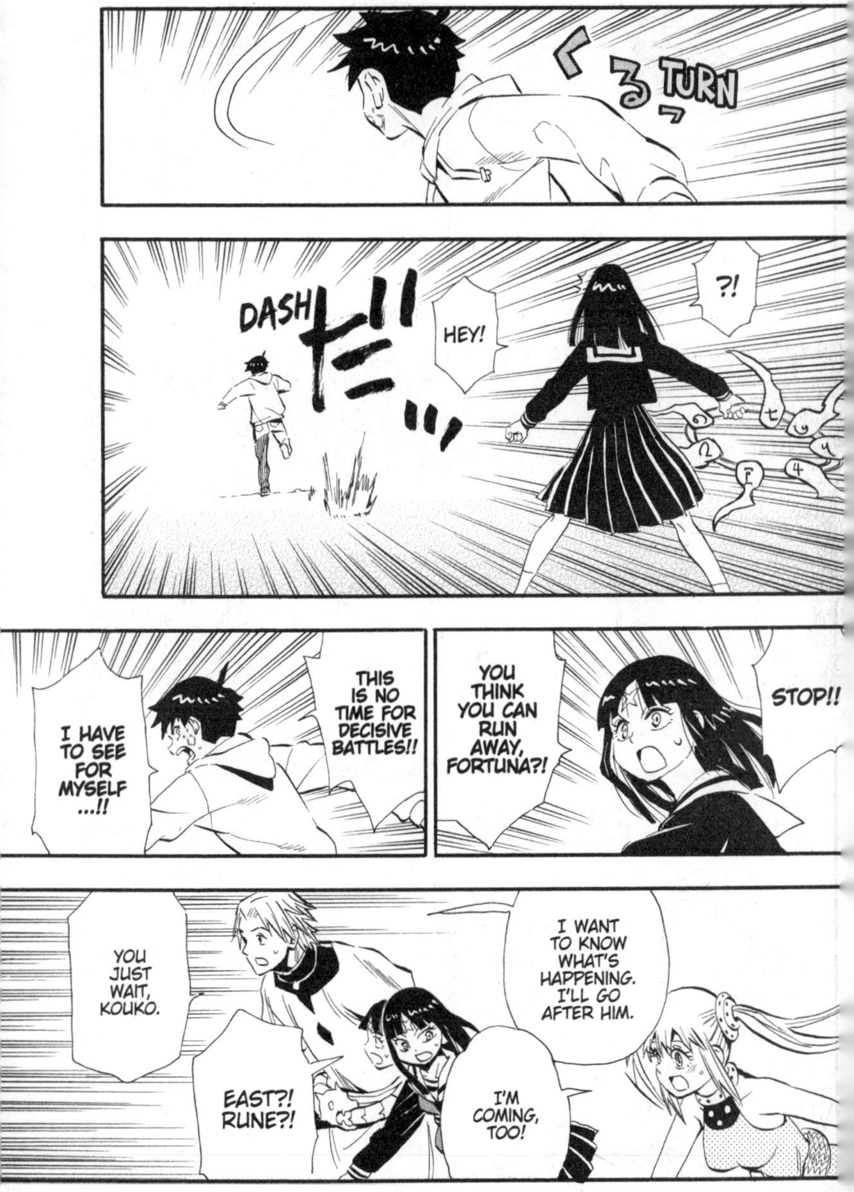
TURN
?!
HEY!
DASH
STOP!!
YOU THINK YOU CAN RUN AWAY, FORTUNA?!
THIS IS NO TIME FOR DECISIVE BATTLES!!
I HAVE TO SEE FOR MYSELF ...!!
I WANT TO KNOW WHAT'S HAPPENING. I'LL GO AFTER HIM.
I'M COMING, TOO!
YOU JUST WAIT, KOUKO.
EAST?! RUNE?!

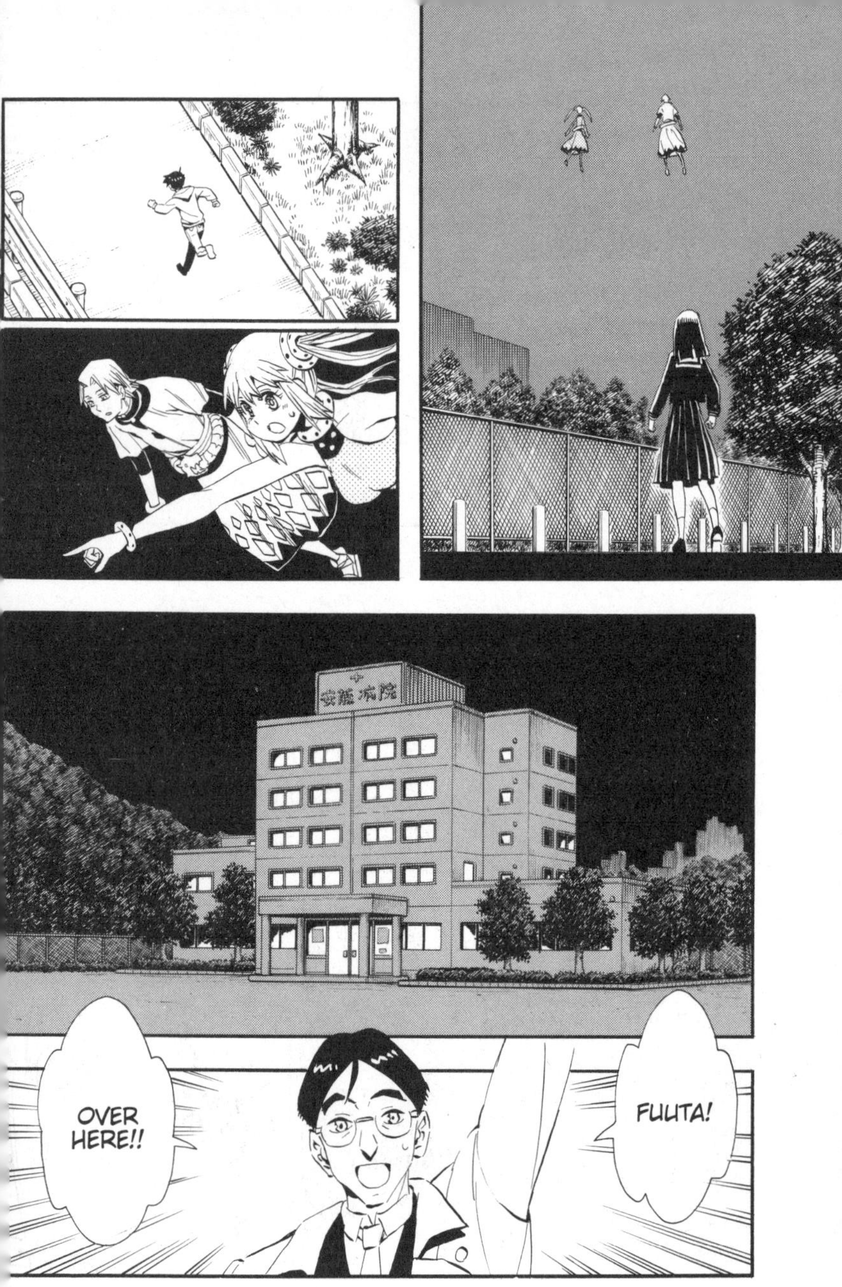
FUUTA!
OVER HERE!!

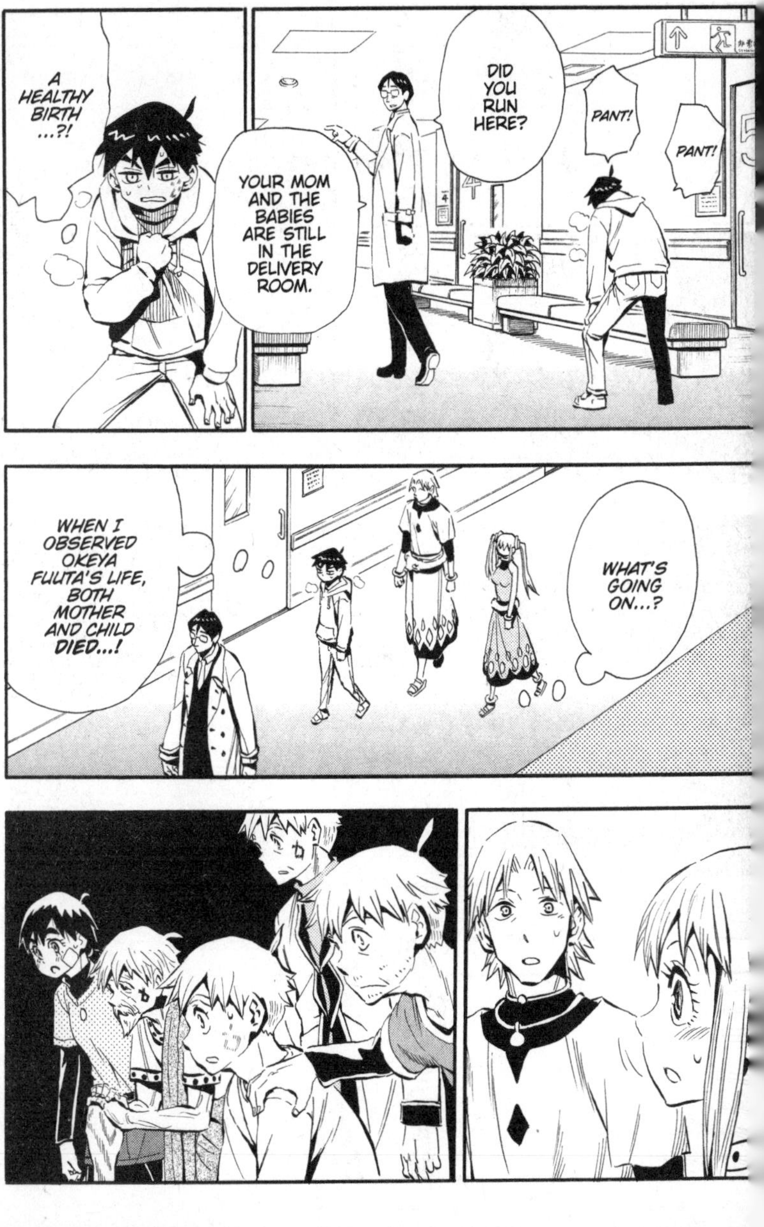
PANT!
PANT!
DID YOU RUN HERE?
YOUR MOM AND THE BABIES ARE STILL IN THE DELIVERY ROOM.
A HEALTHY BIRTH ...?!
WHAT'S GOING ON...?
WHEN I OBSERVED OKEYA FUUTA'S LIFE, BOTH MOTHER AND CHILD DIED...!

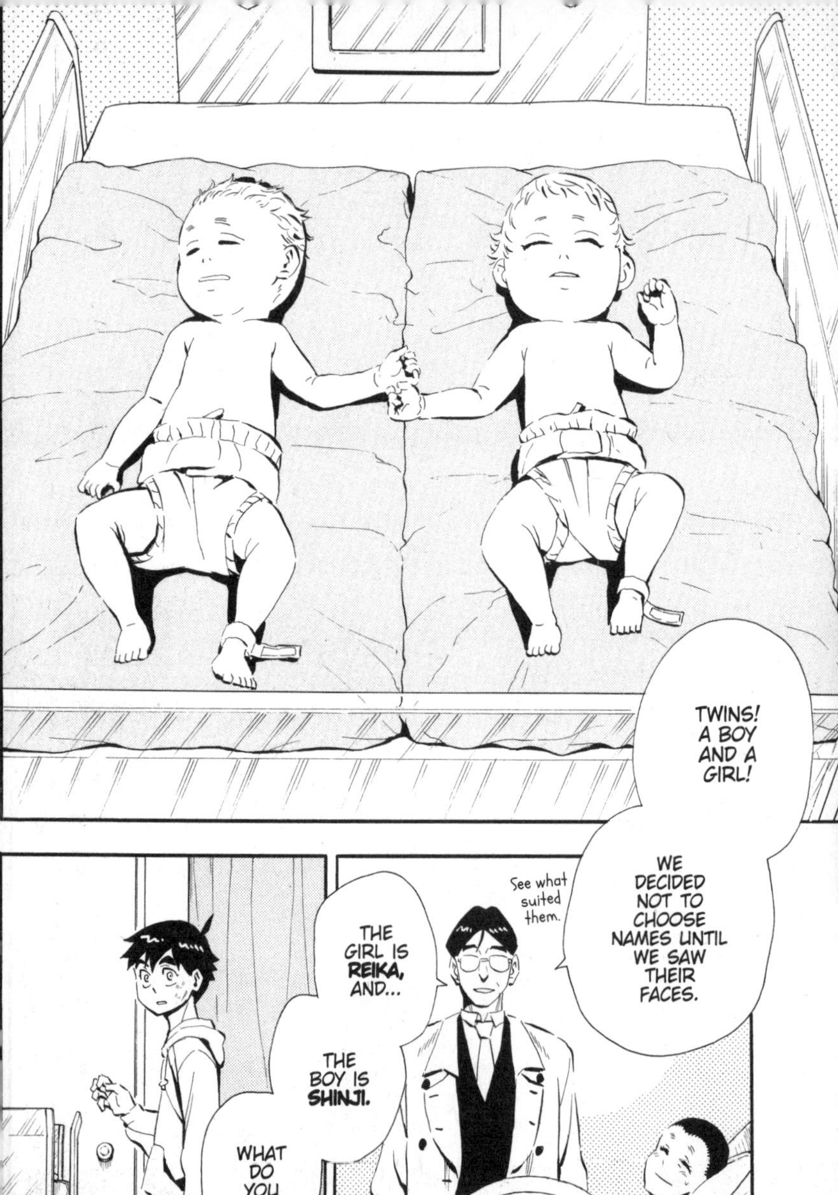
TWINS! A BOY AND A GIRL!
WE DECIDED NOT TO CHOOSE NAMES UNTIL WE SAW THEIR FACES.
See what suited them.
THE GIRL IS **REIKA,** AND...
THE BOY IS **SHINJI.**
WHAT DO YOU THINK?

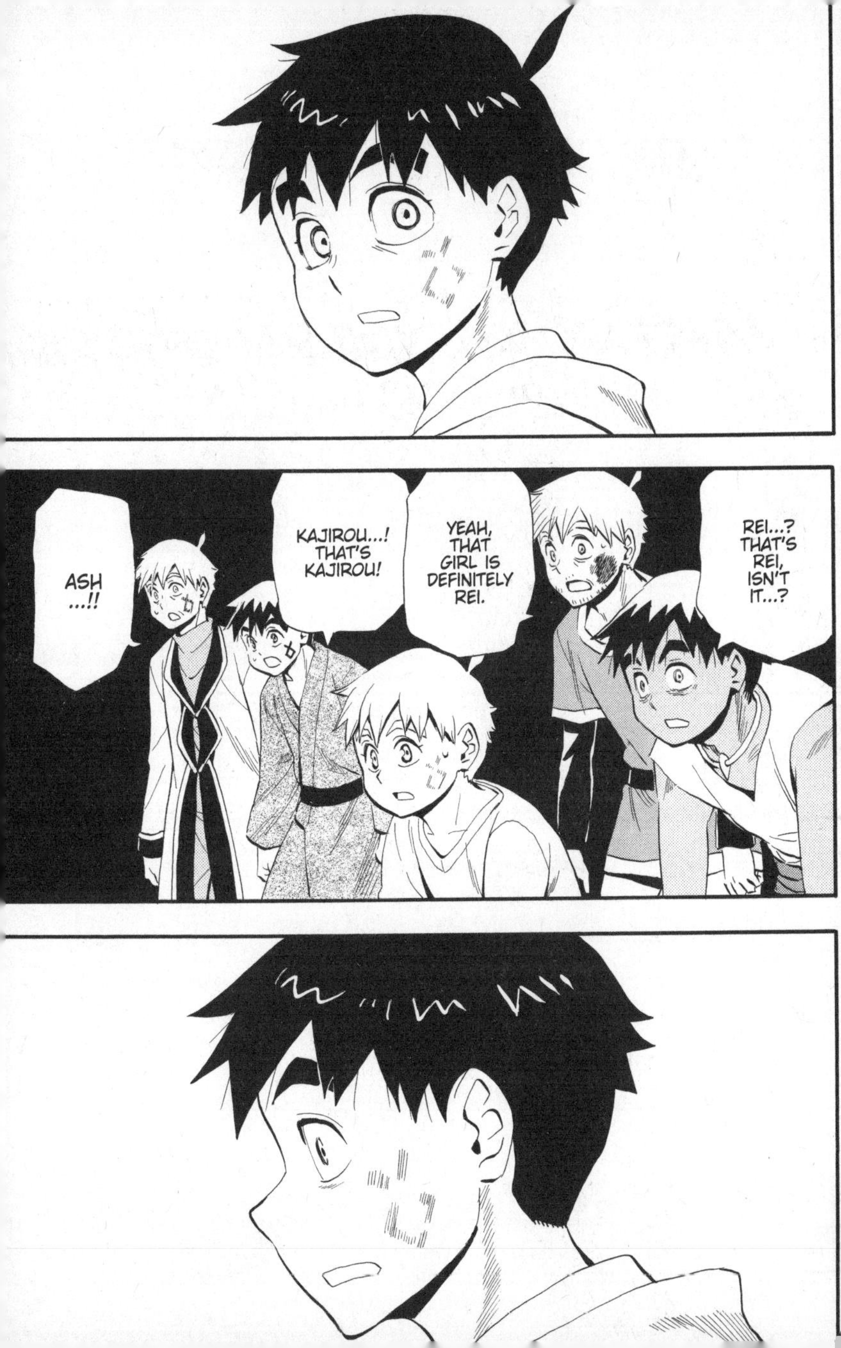
REI...? THAT'S REI, ISN'T IT...?
YEAH, THAT GIRL IS DEFINITELY REI.
KAJIROU...! THAT'S KAJIROU!
ASH ...!!

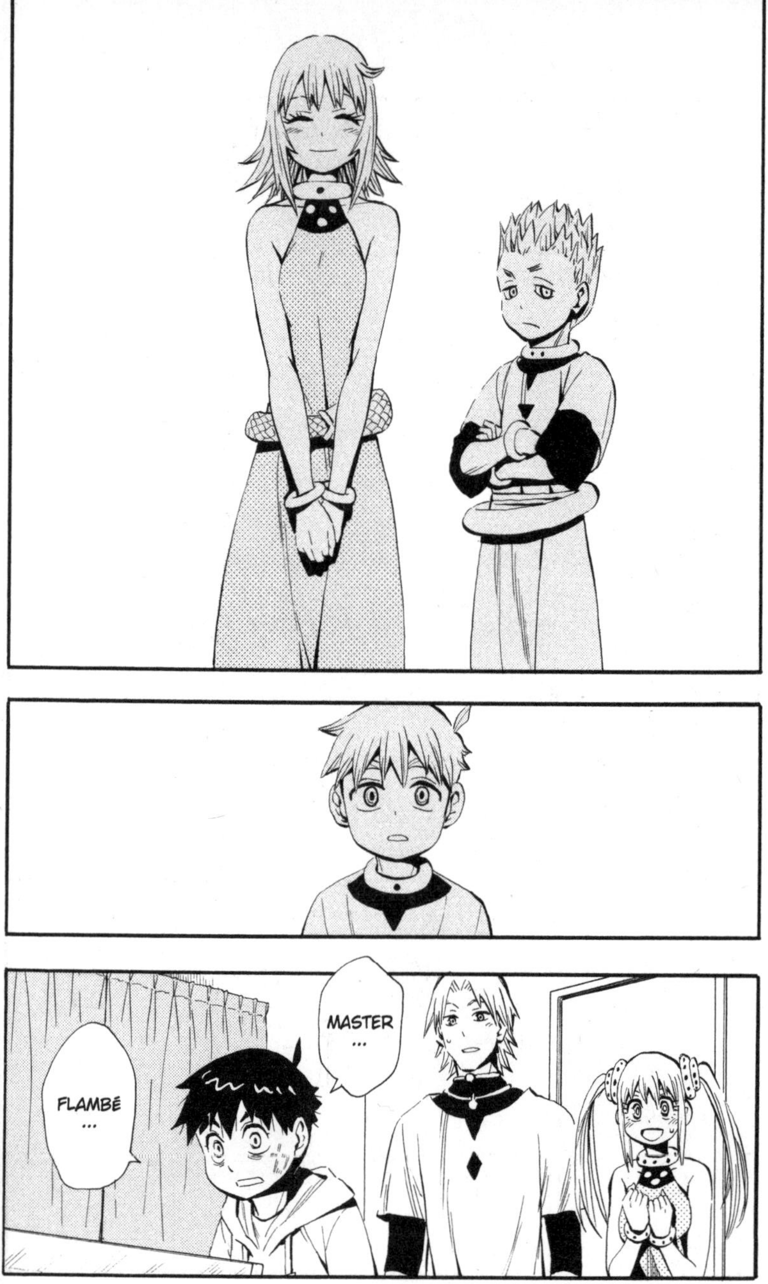
MASTER ...
FLAMBÉ ...

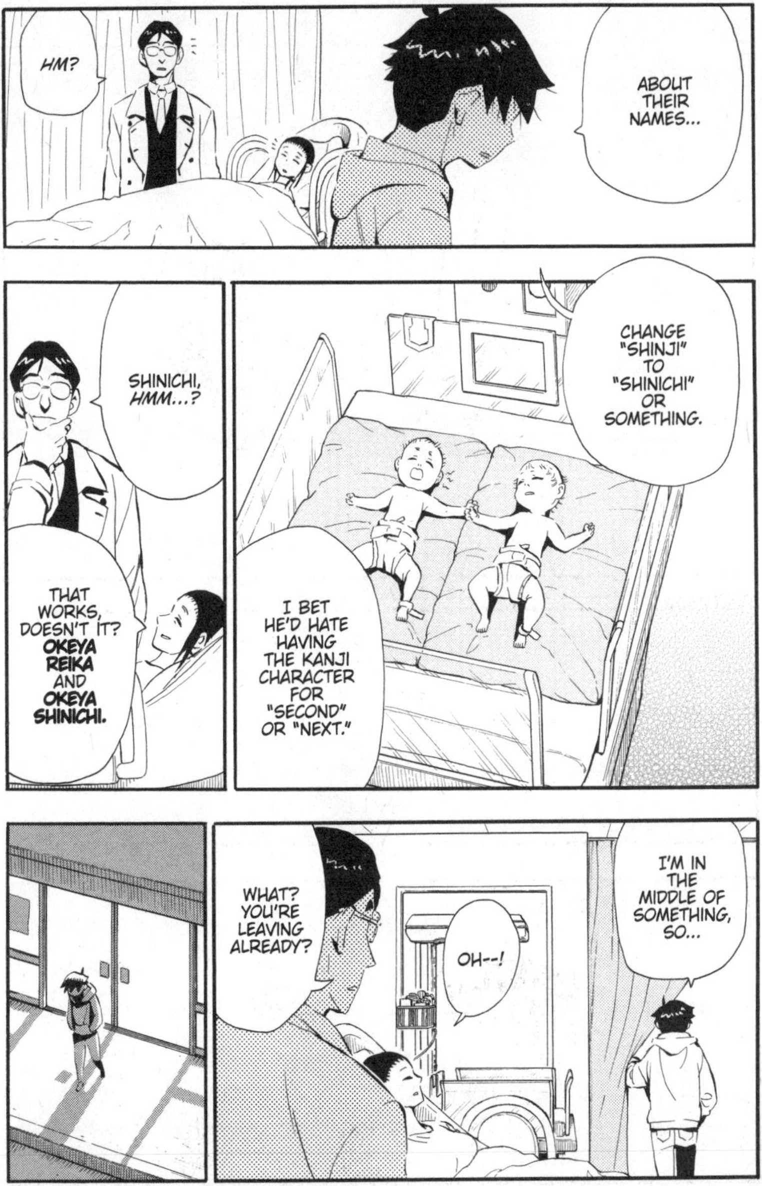
ABOUT THEIR NAMES...
HM?
CHANGE "SHINJI" TO "SHINICHI" OR SOMETHING.
I BET HE'D HATE HAVING THE KANJI CHARACTER FOR "SECOND" OR "NEXT."
SHINICHI, HMM...?
THAT WORKS, DOESN'T IT? OKEYA REIKA AND OKEYA SHINICHI.
I'M IN THE MIDDLE OF SOMETHING, SO...
OH--!
WHAT? YOU'RE LEAVING ALREADY?

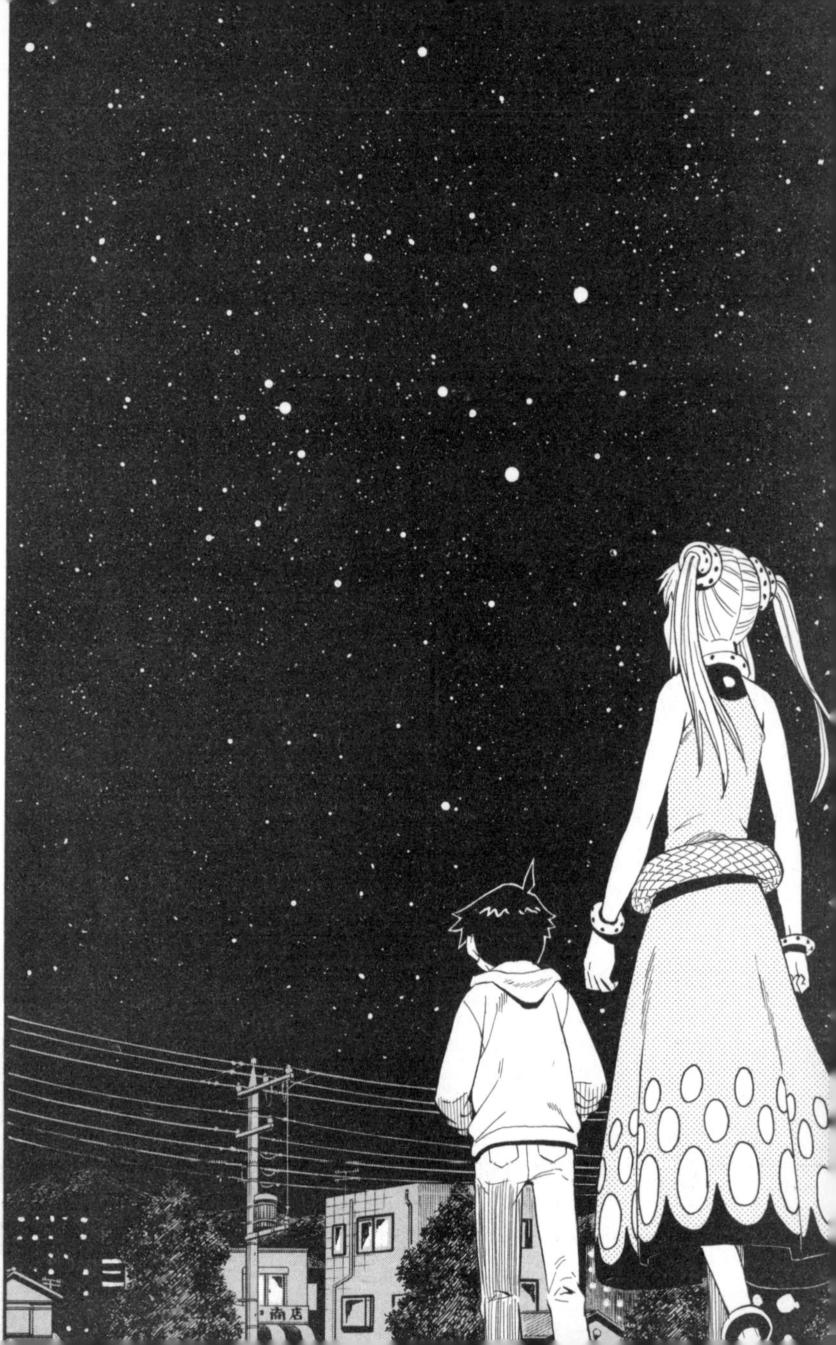
商店

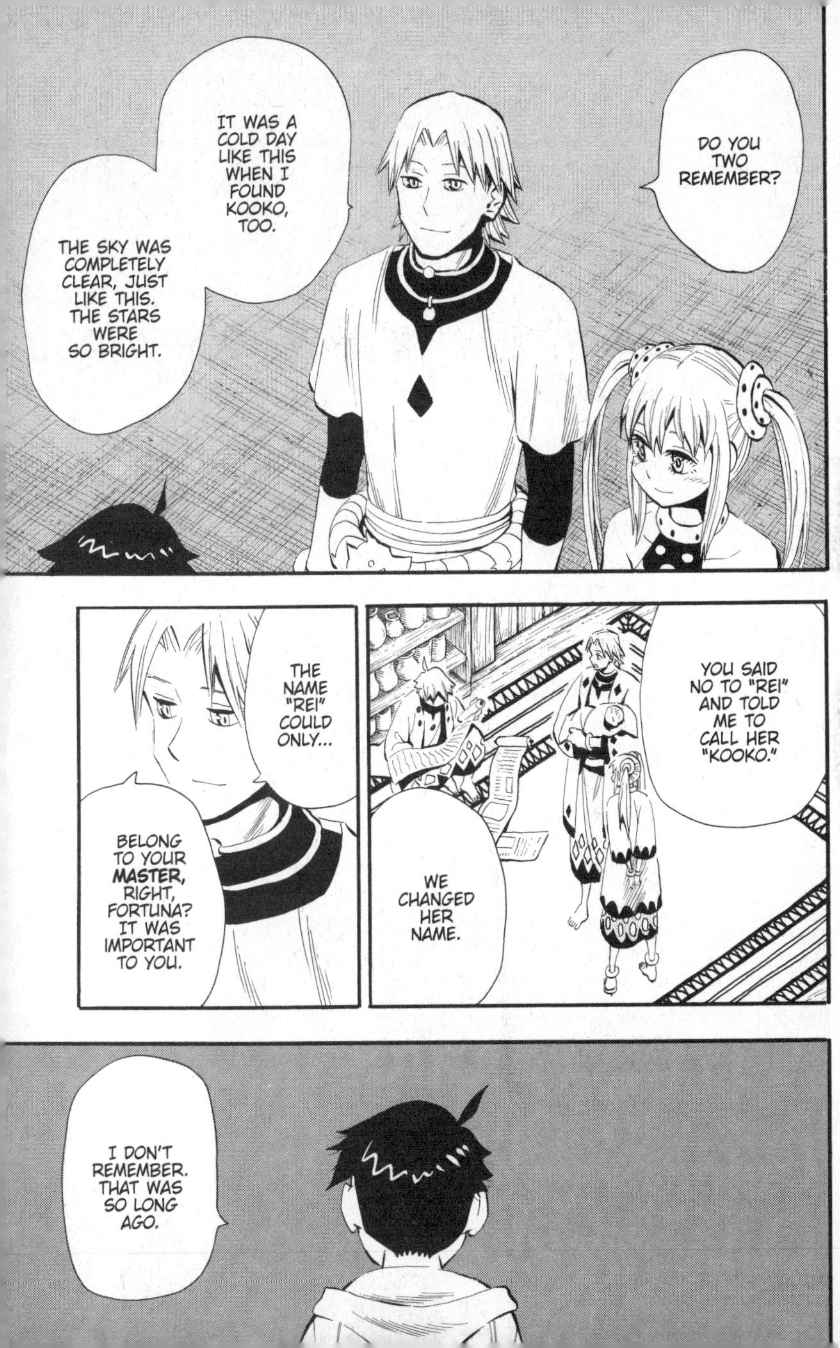
DO YOU TWO REMEMBER?
IT WAS A COLD DAY LIKE THIS WHEN I FOUND KOOKO, TOO.
THE SKY WAS COMPLETELY CLEAR, JUST LIKE THIS. THE STARS WERE SO BRIGHT.
YOU SAID NO TO "REI" AND TOLD ME TO CALL HER "KOOKO."
WE CHANGED HER NAME.
THE NAME "REI" COULD ONLY...
BELONG TO YOUR **MASTER,** RIGHT, FORTUNA? IT WAS IMPORTANT TO YOU.
I DON'T REMEMBER. THAT WAS SO LONG AGO.

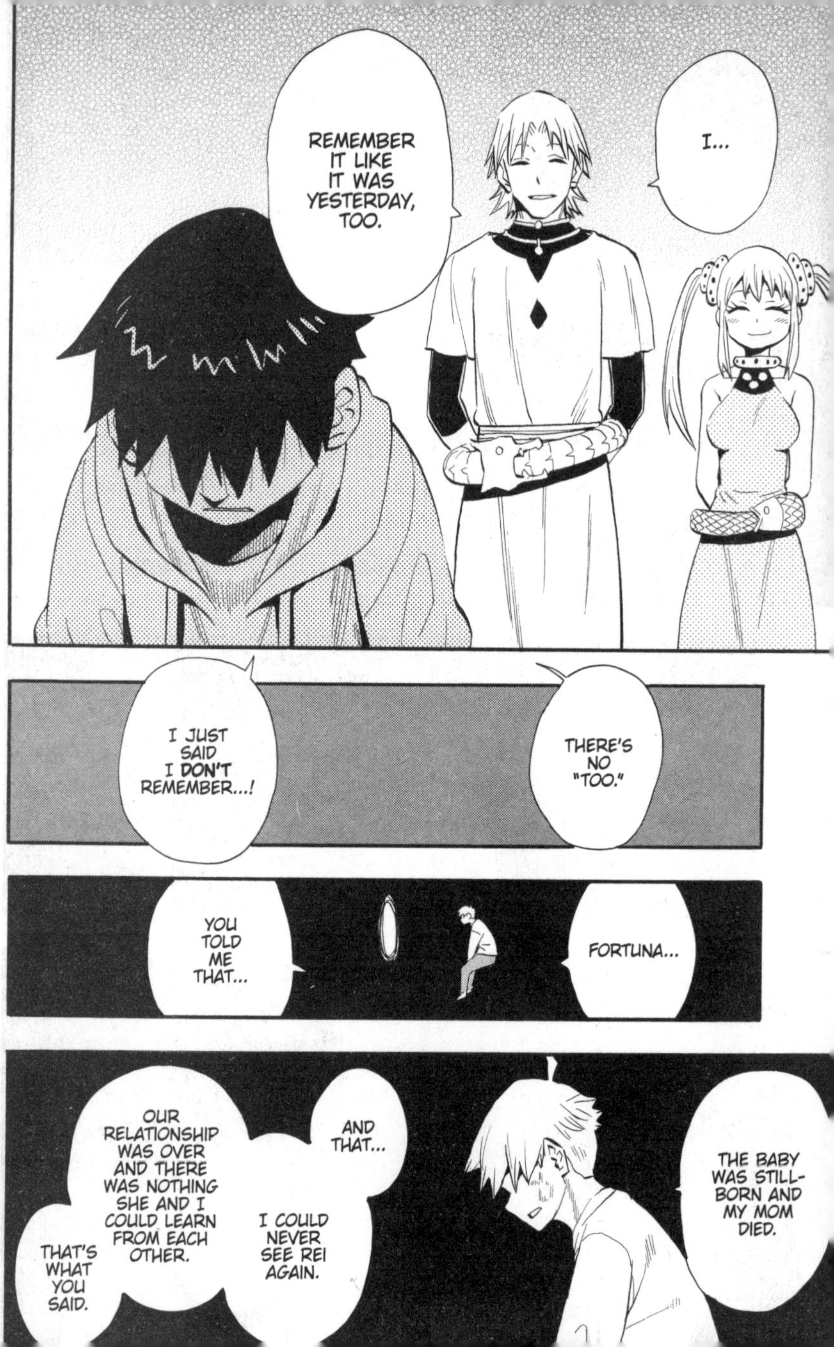
I...
REMEMBER IT LIKE IT WAS YESTERDAY, TOO.
THERE'S NO "TOO."
I JUST SAID I **DON'T** REMEMBER...!
FORTUNA...
YOU TOLD ME THAT...
THE BABY WAS STILL-BORN AND MY MOM DIED.
AND THAT...
I COULD NEVER SEE REI AGAIN.
OUR RELATIONSHIP WAS OVER AND THERE WAS NOTHING SHE AND I COULD LEARN FROM EACH OTHER.
THAT'S WHAT YOU SAID.

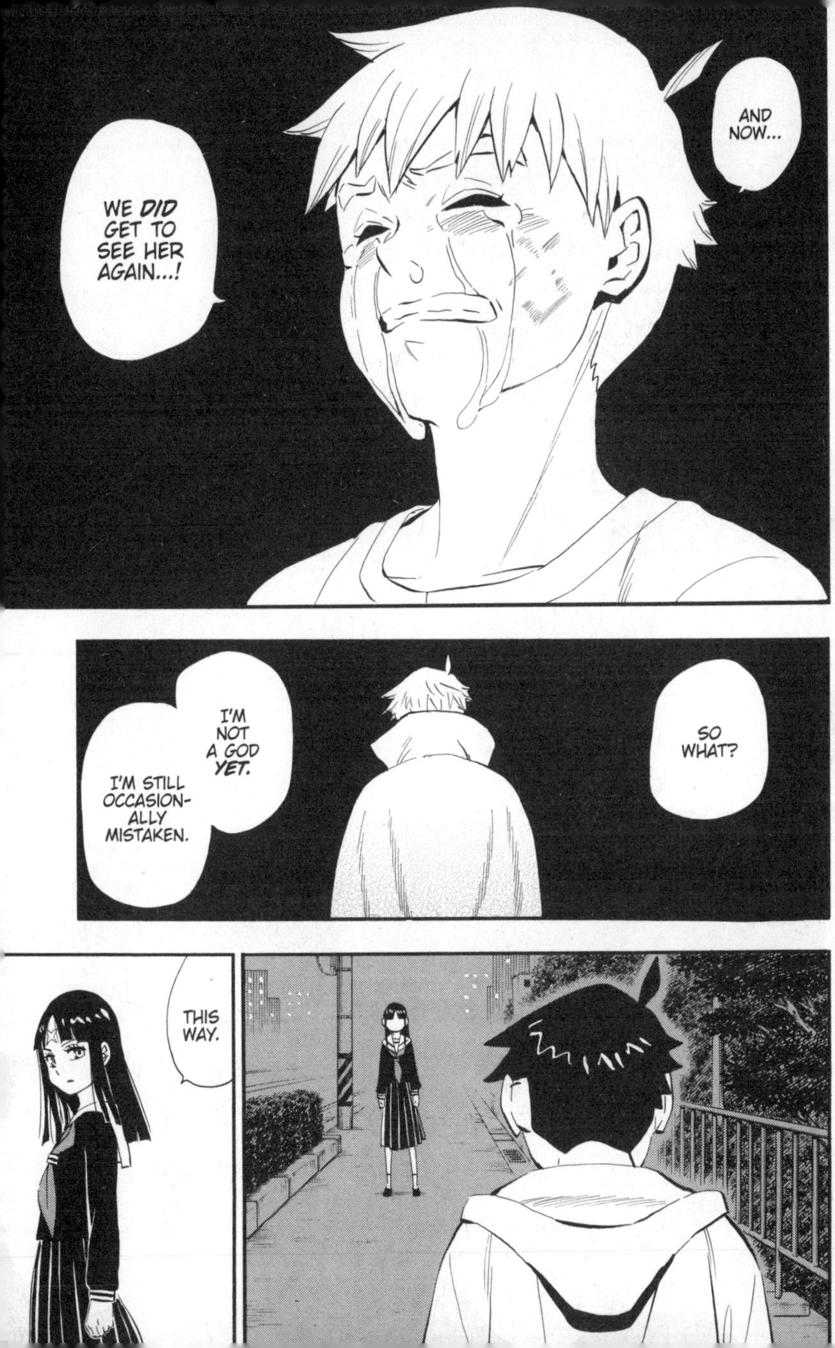
AND NOW...
WE *DID* GET TO SEE HER AGAIN...!
SO WHAT?
I'M NOT A GOD *YET*.
I'M STILL OCCASION-ALLY MISTAKEN.
THIS WAY.

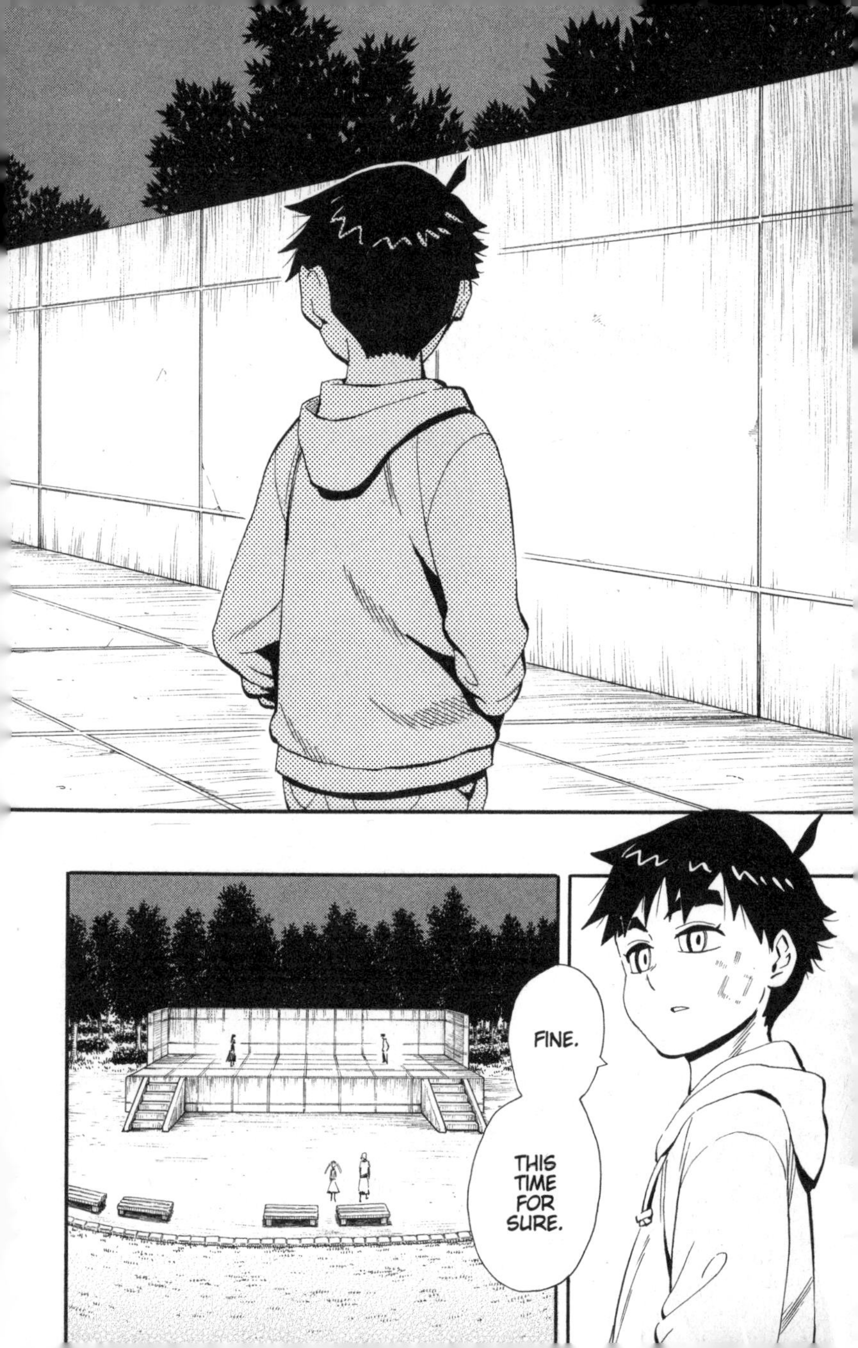
FINE.
THIS TIME FOR SURE.

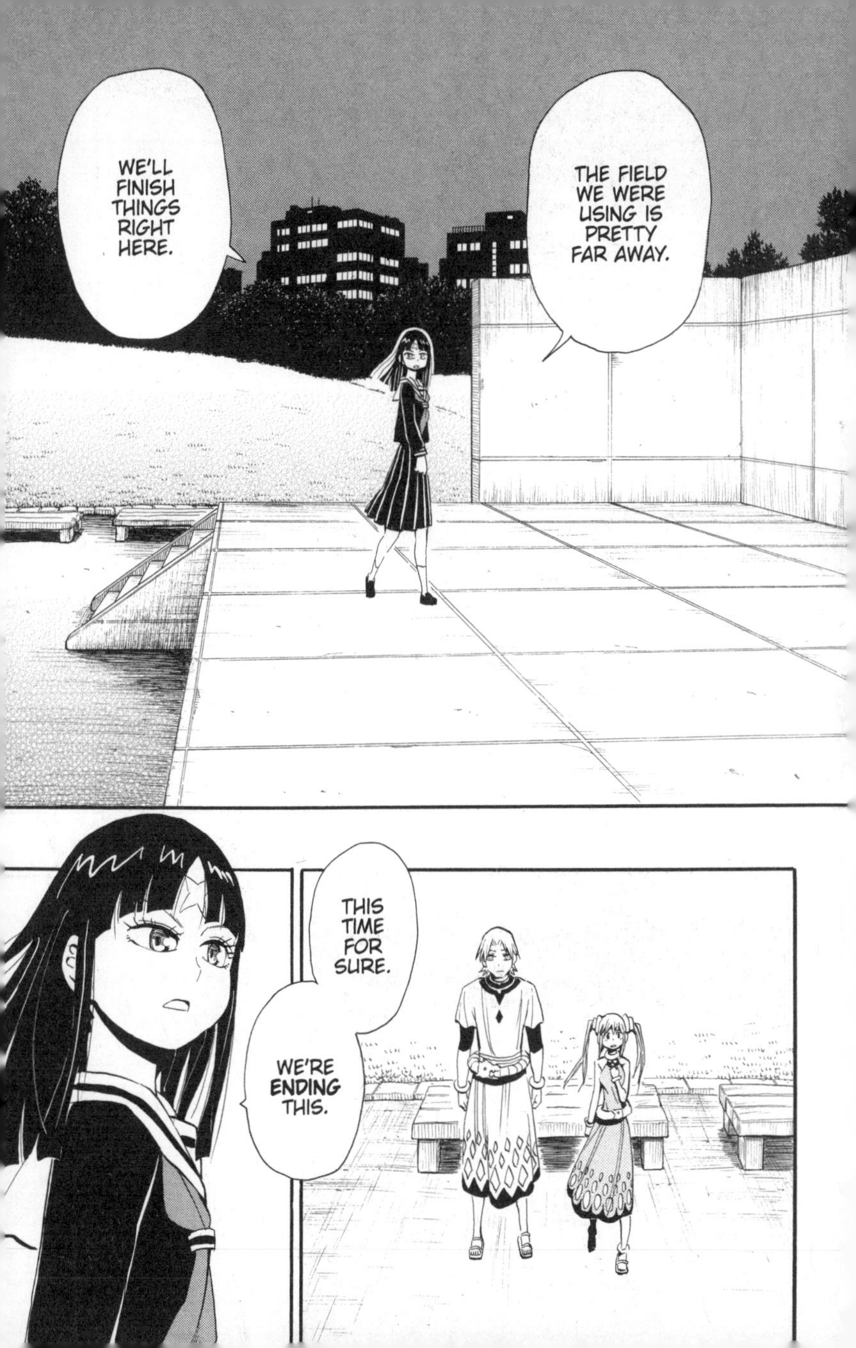
THE FIELD WE WERE USING IS PRETTY FAR AWAY.
WE'LL FINISH THINGS RIGHT HERE.
THIS TIME FOR SURE.
WE'RE ENDING THIS.

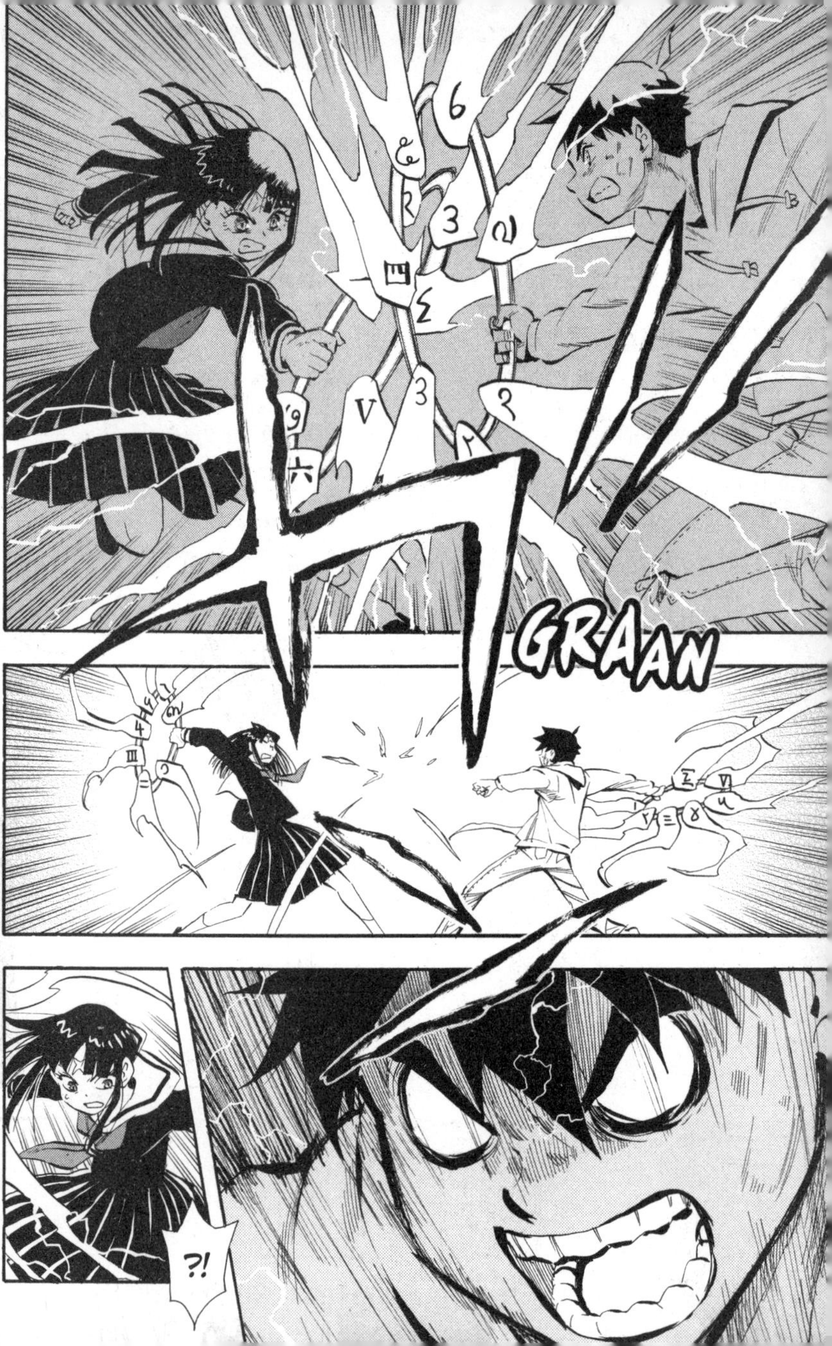
GRAAN
?!

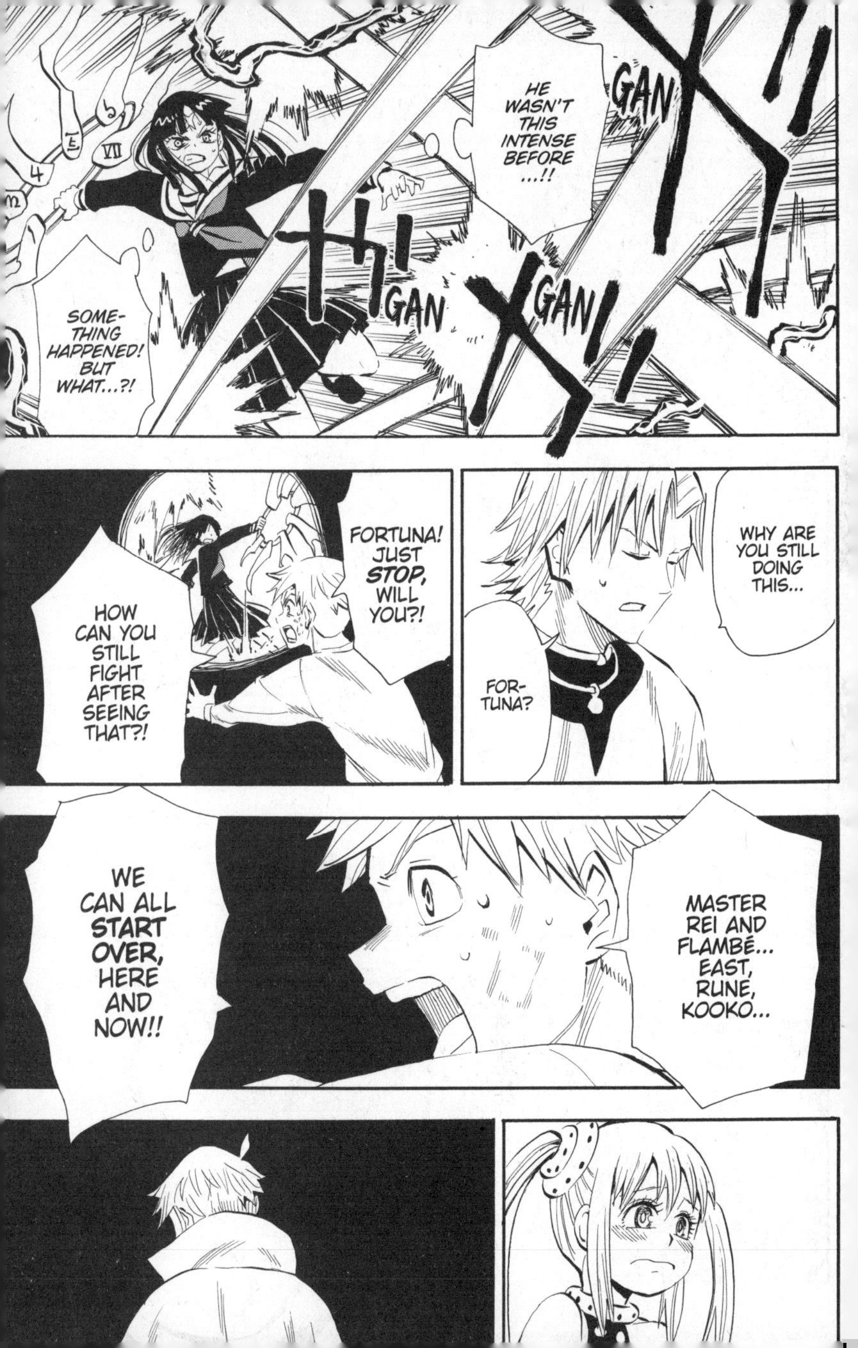
GAN
HE WASN'T THIS INTENSE BEFORE ...!!
GAN
GAN
SOME-THING HAPPENED! BUT WHAT...?!
WHY ARE YOU STILL DOING THIS...
FOR-TUNA?
FORTUNA! JUST STOP, WILL YOU?!
HOW CAN YOU STILL FIGHT AFTER SEEING THAT?!
MASTER REI AND FLAMBÉ... EAST, RUNE, KOOKO...
WE CAN ALL START OVER, HERE AND NOW!!

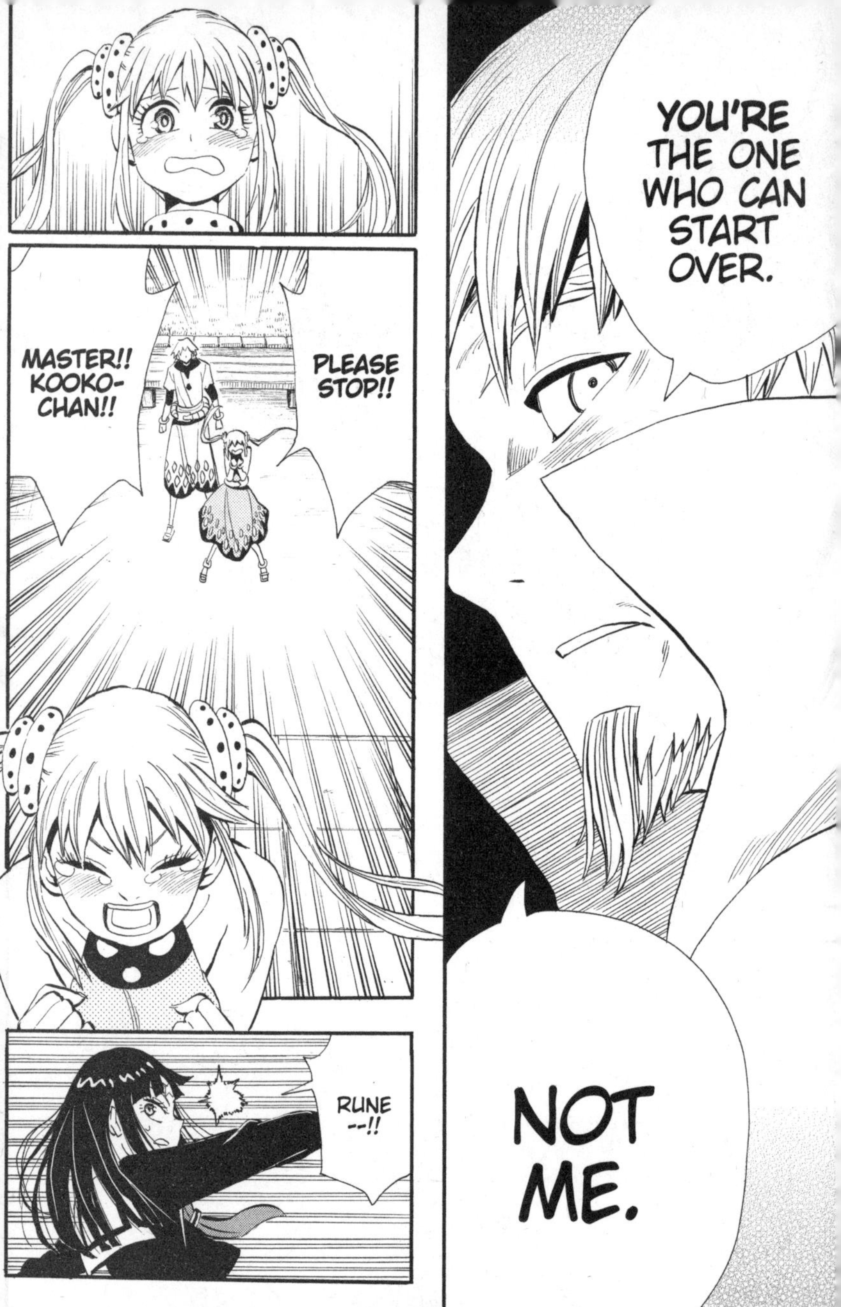
YOU'RE THE ONE WHO CAN START OVER.
NOT ME.
PLEASE STOP!!
MASTER!! KOOKO-CHAN!!
RUNE --!!

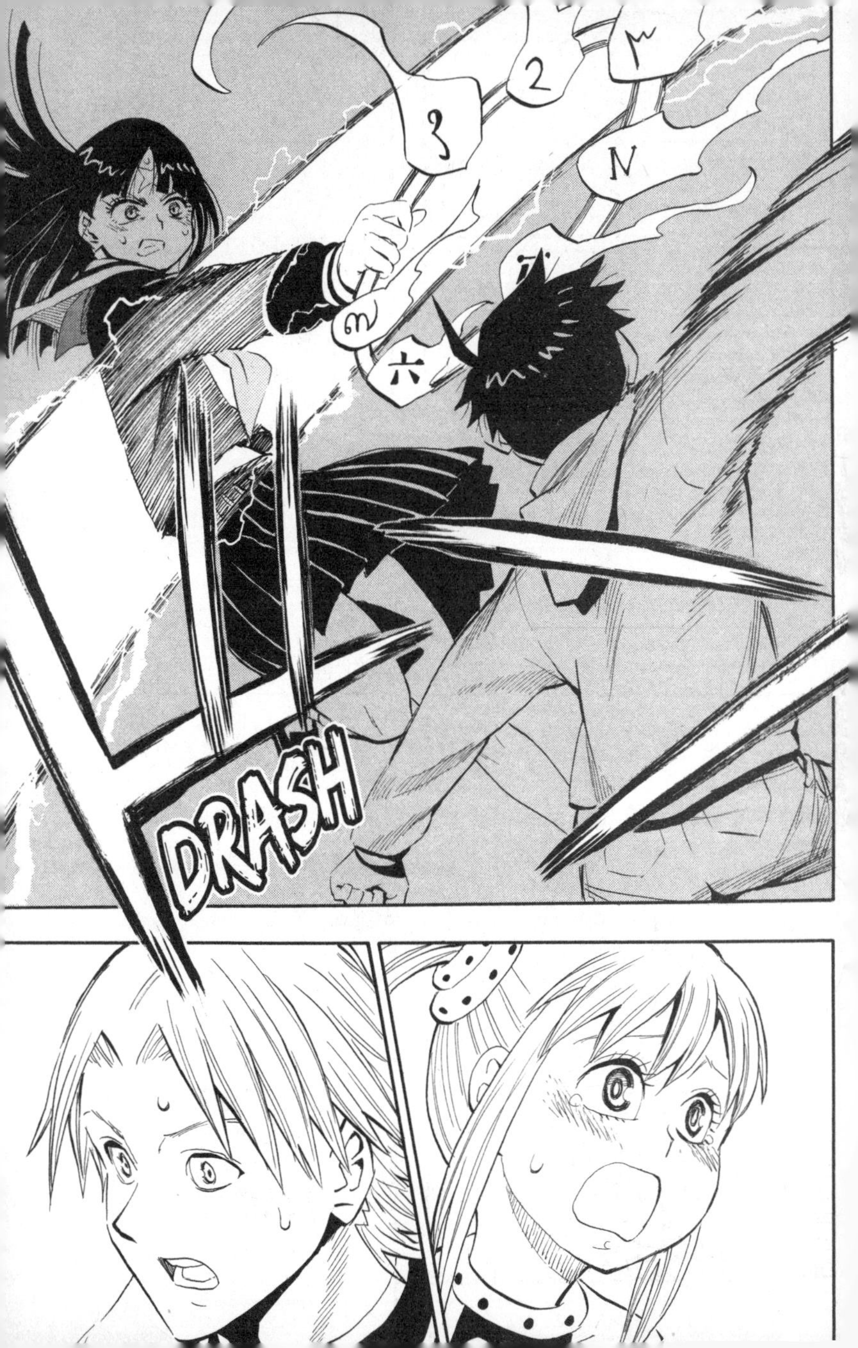
DRASH

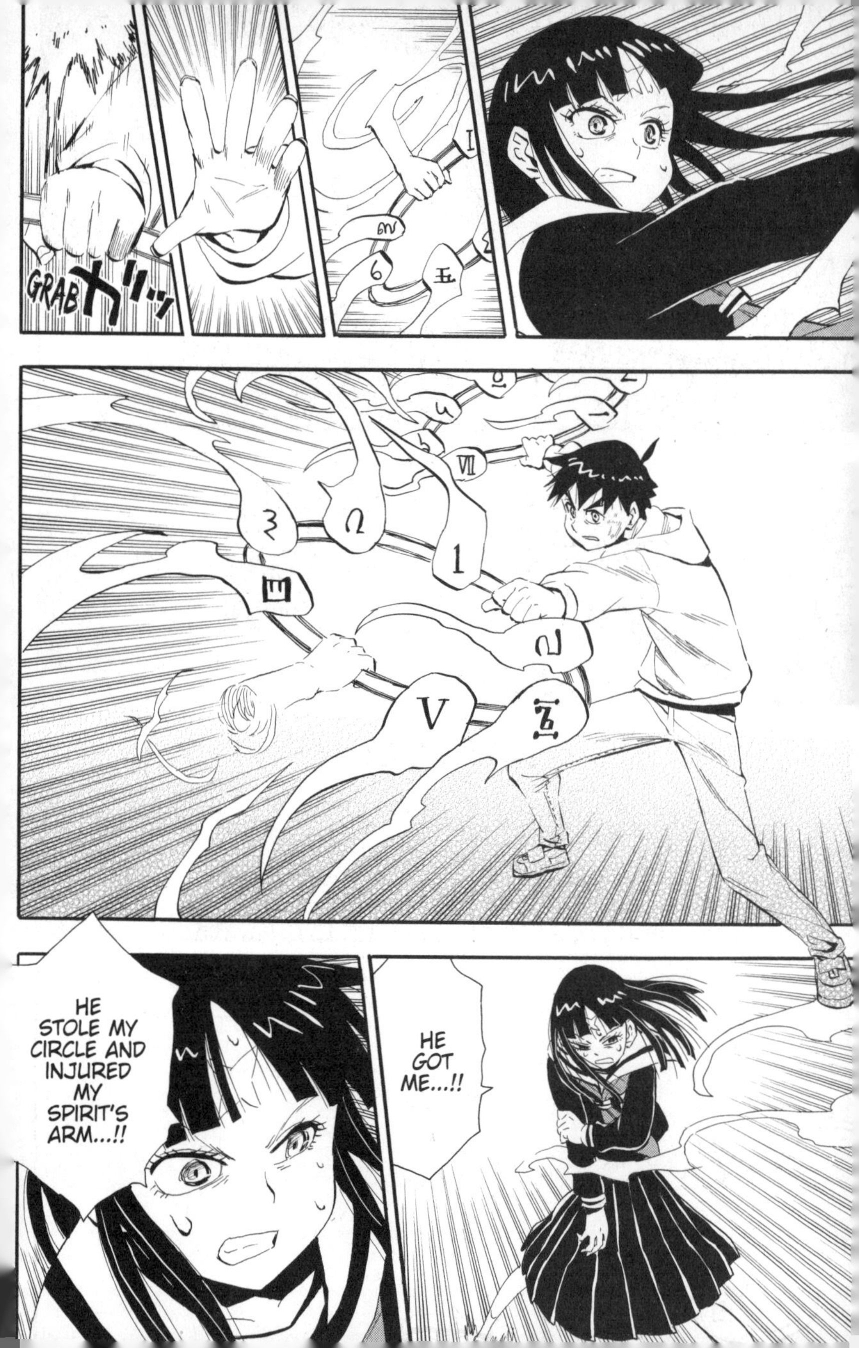
GRAB ガッ
HE GOT ME...!!
HE STOLE MY CIRCLE AND INJURED MY SPIRIT'S ARM...!!

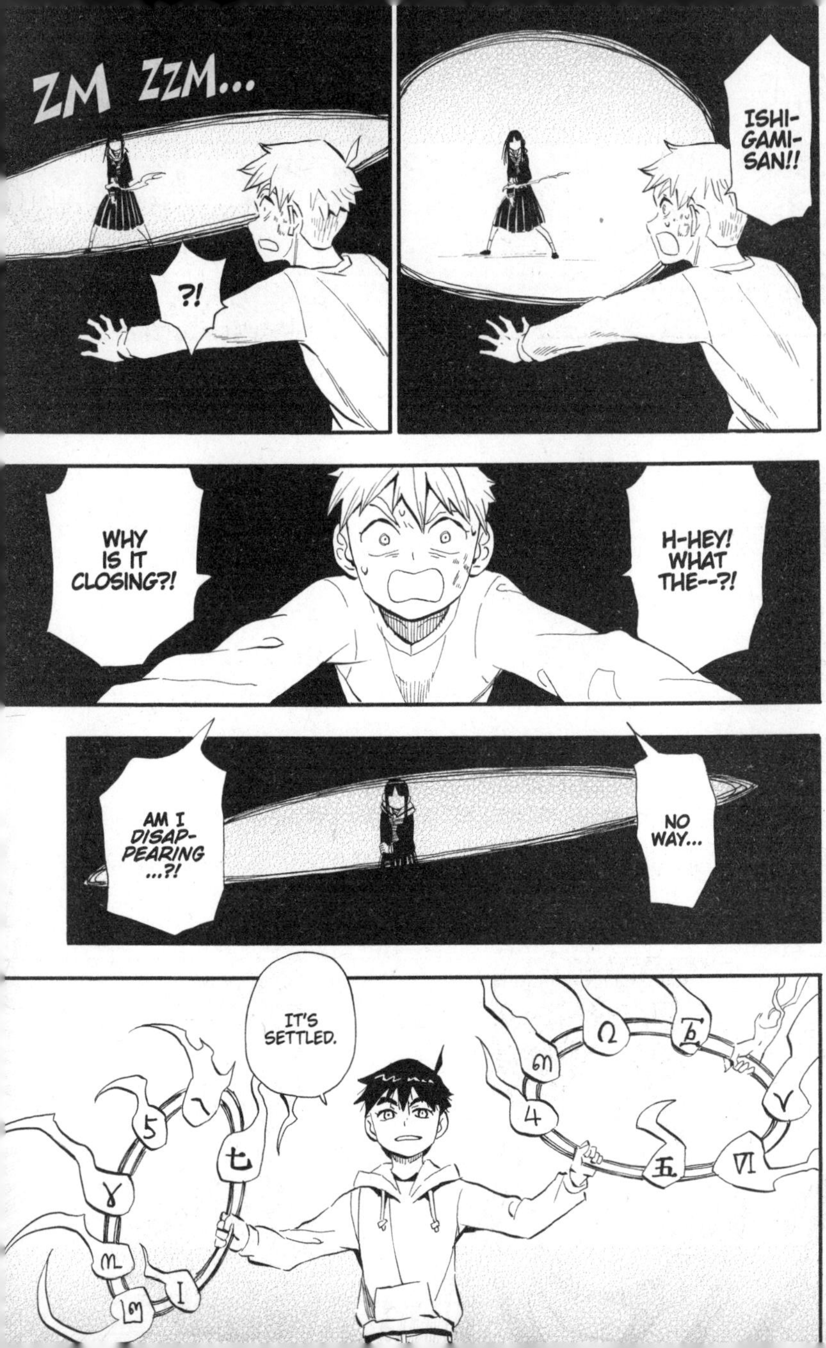
ISHI-GAMI-SAN!!
ZM ZZM...
?!
H-HEY! WHAT THE--?!
WHY IS IT CLOSING?!
NO WAY...
AM I DISAP-PEARING ...?!
IT'S SETTLED.

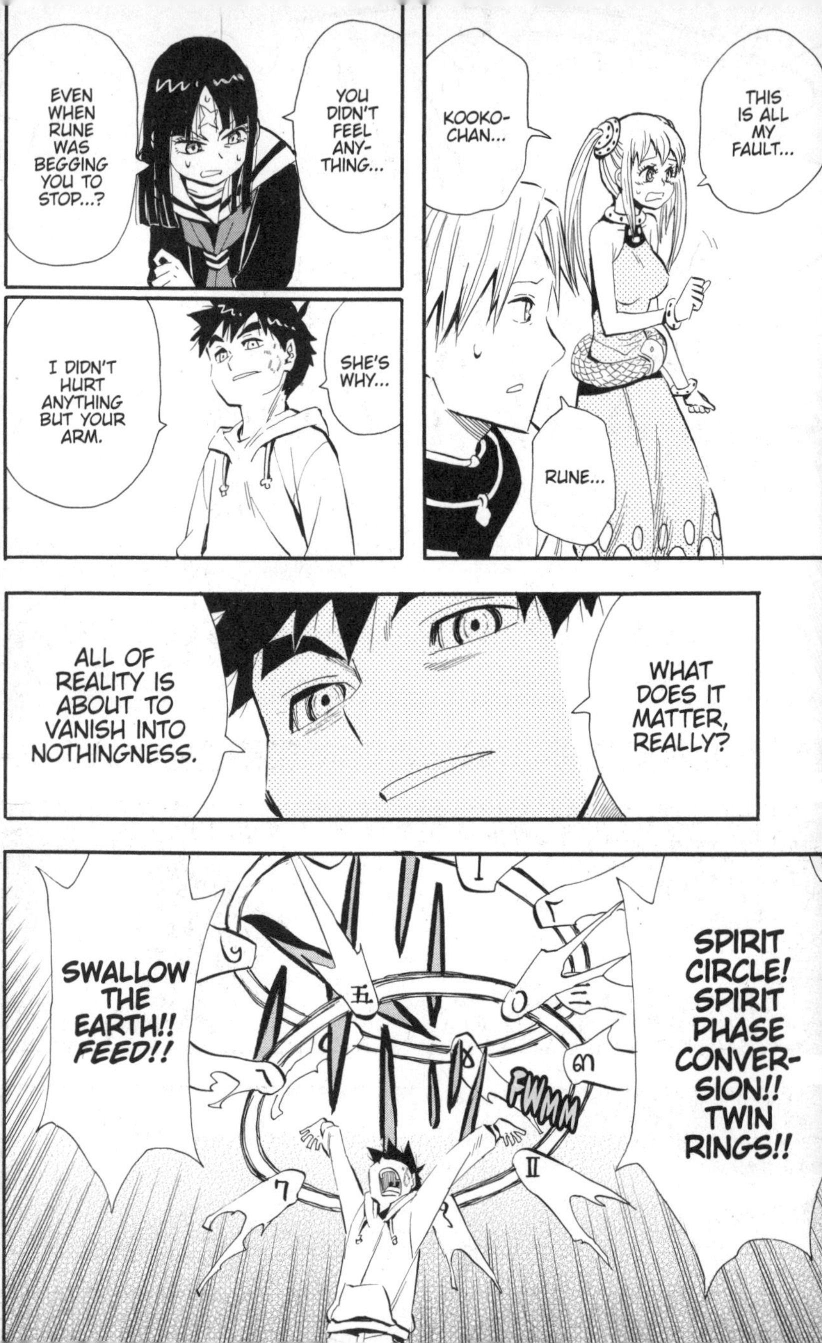
THIS IS ALL MY FAULT...
KOOKO-CHAN...
RUNE...
YOU DIDN'T FEEL ANYTHING...
EVEN WHEN RUNE WAS BEGGING YOU TO STOP...?
SHE'S WHY...
I DIDN'T HURT ANYTHING BUT YOUR ARM.
WHAT DOES IT MATTER, REALLY?
ALL OF REALITY IS ABOUT TO VANISH INTO NOTHINGNESS.
SPIRIT CIRCLE! SPIRIT PHASE CONVERSION!! TWIN RINGS!!
FWMM
SWALLOW THE EARTH!! FEED!!

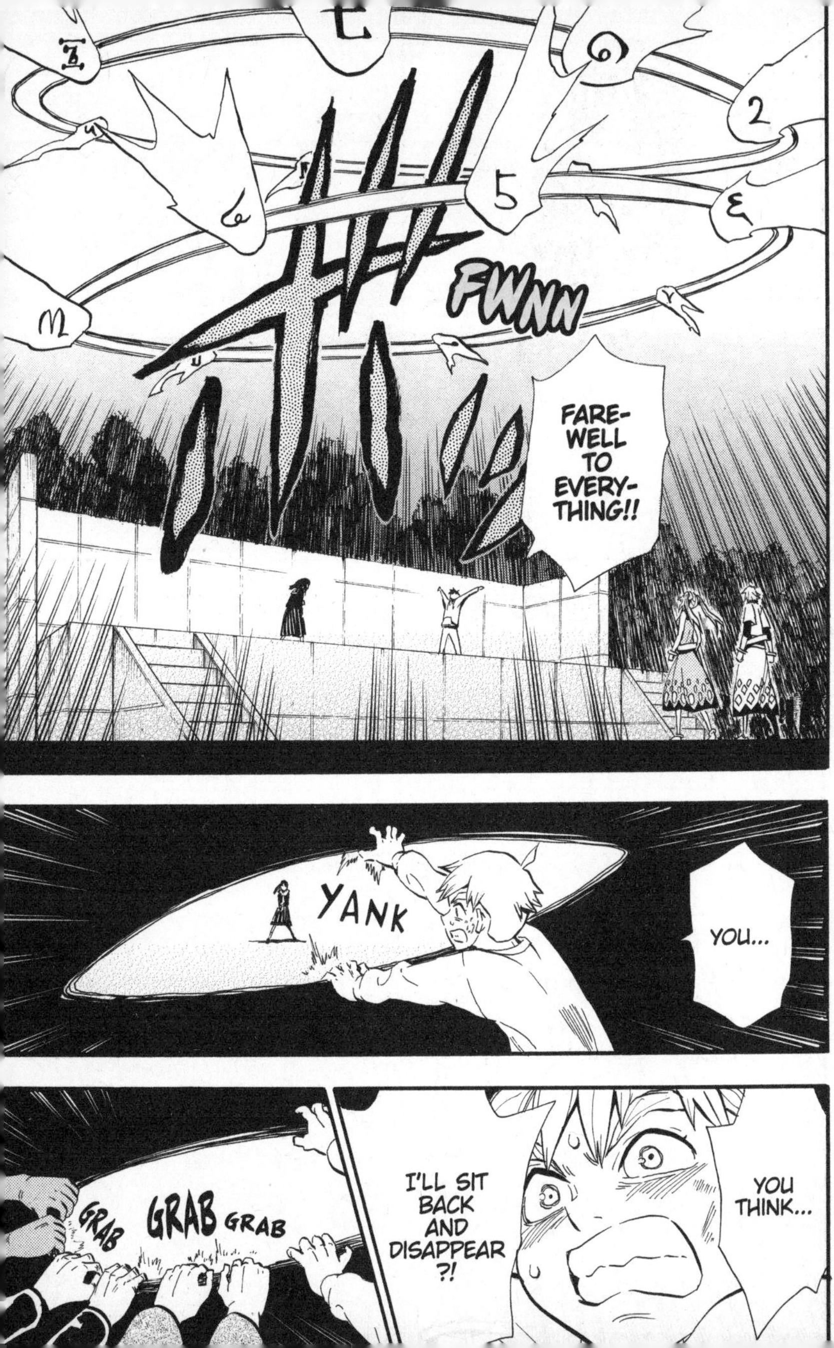
FWNN
FARE-WELL TO EVERY-THING!!
YOU...
YANK
YOU THINK...
I'LL SIT BACK AND DISAPPEAR ?!
GRAB
GRAB
GRAB

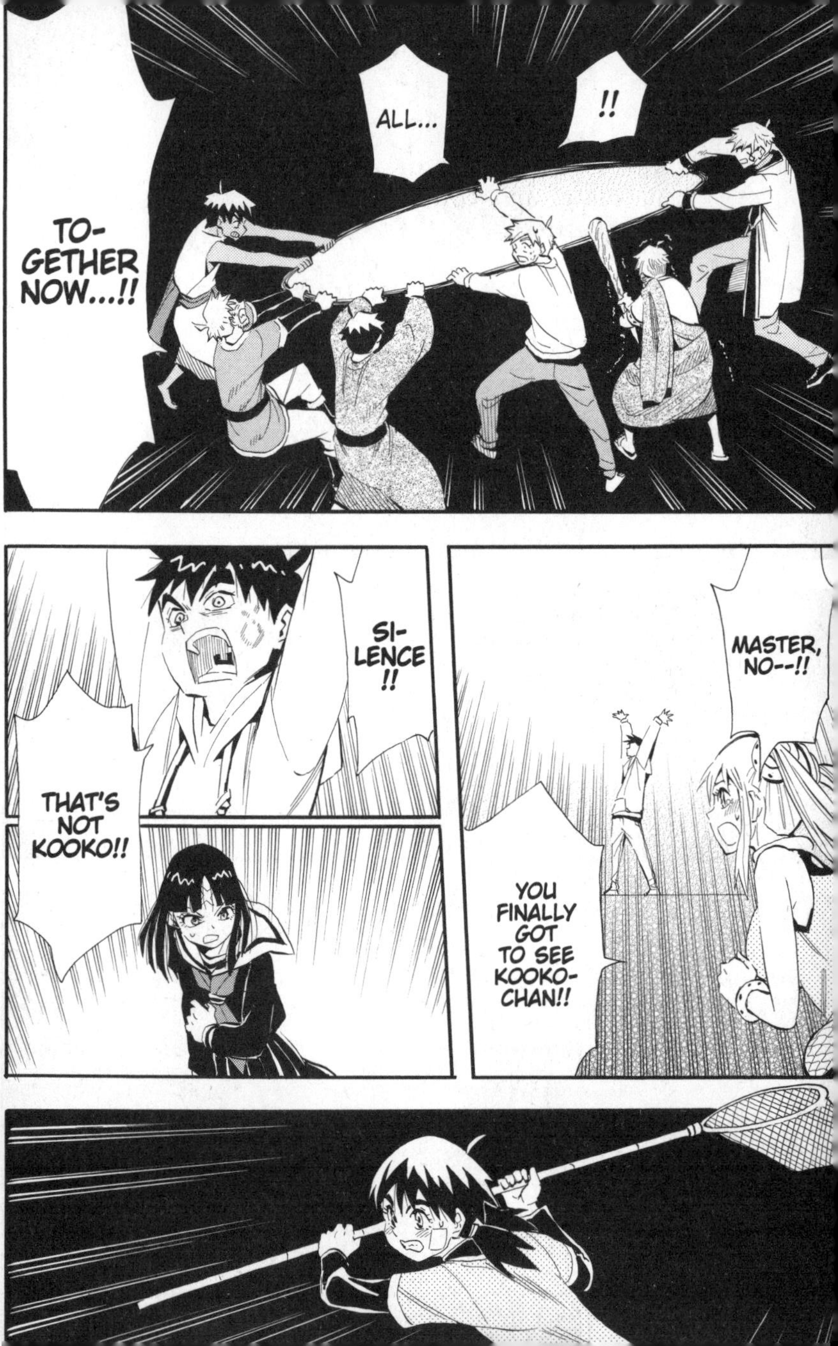
!!
ALL...
TO-GETHER NOW...!!
MASTER, NO--!!
YOU FINALLY GOT TO SEE KOOKO-CHAN!!
SI-LENCE !!
THAT'S NOT KOOKO!!

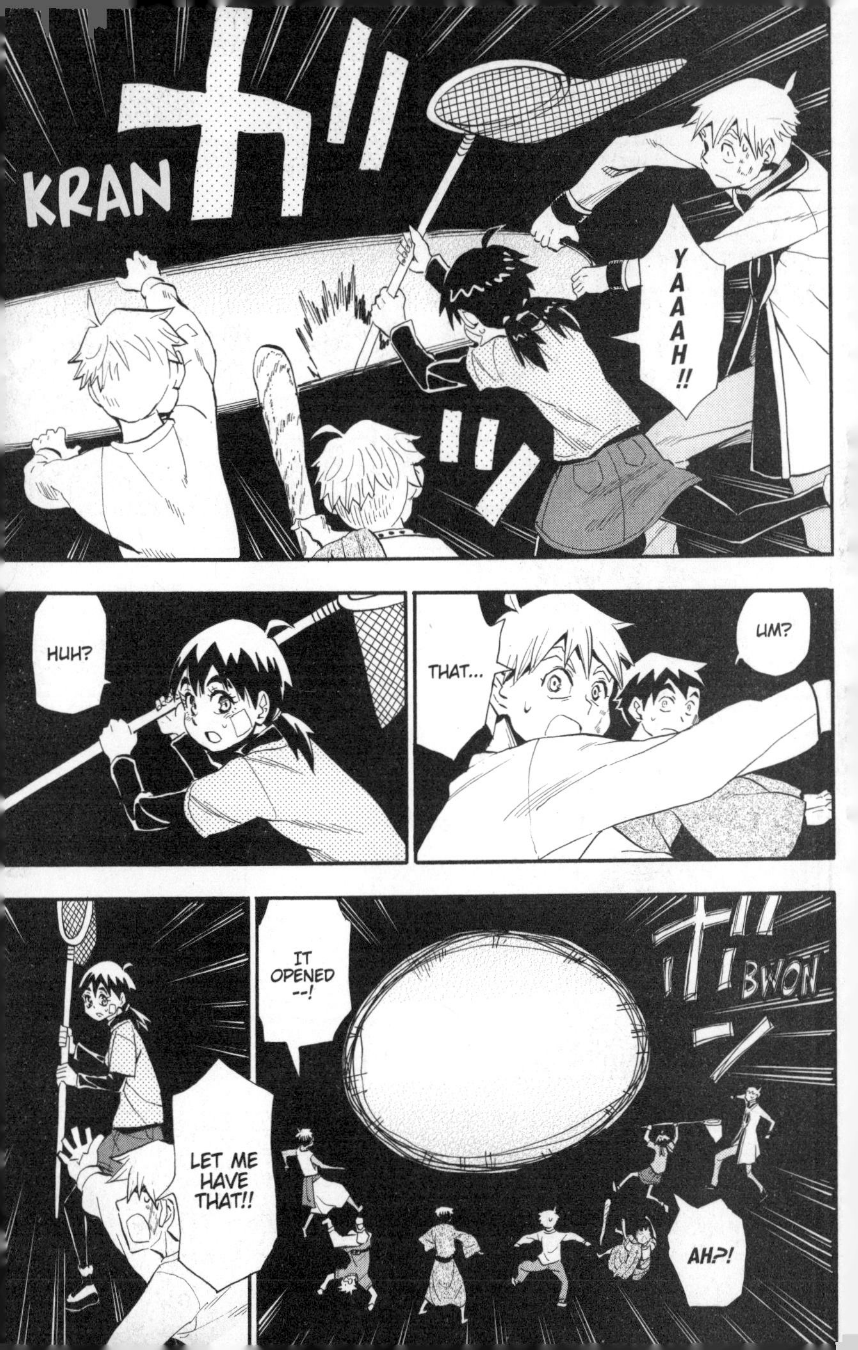
KRAN
YAAAAH!!
UM?
THAT...
HUH?
BWON
IT OPENED --!
LET ME HAVE THAT!!
AH?!

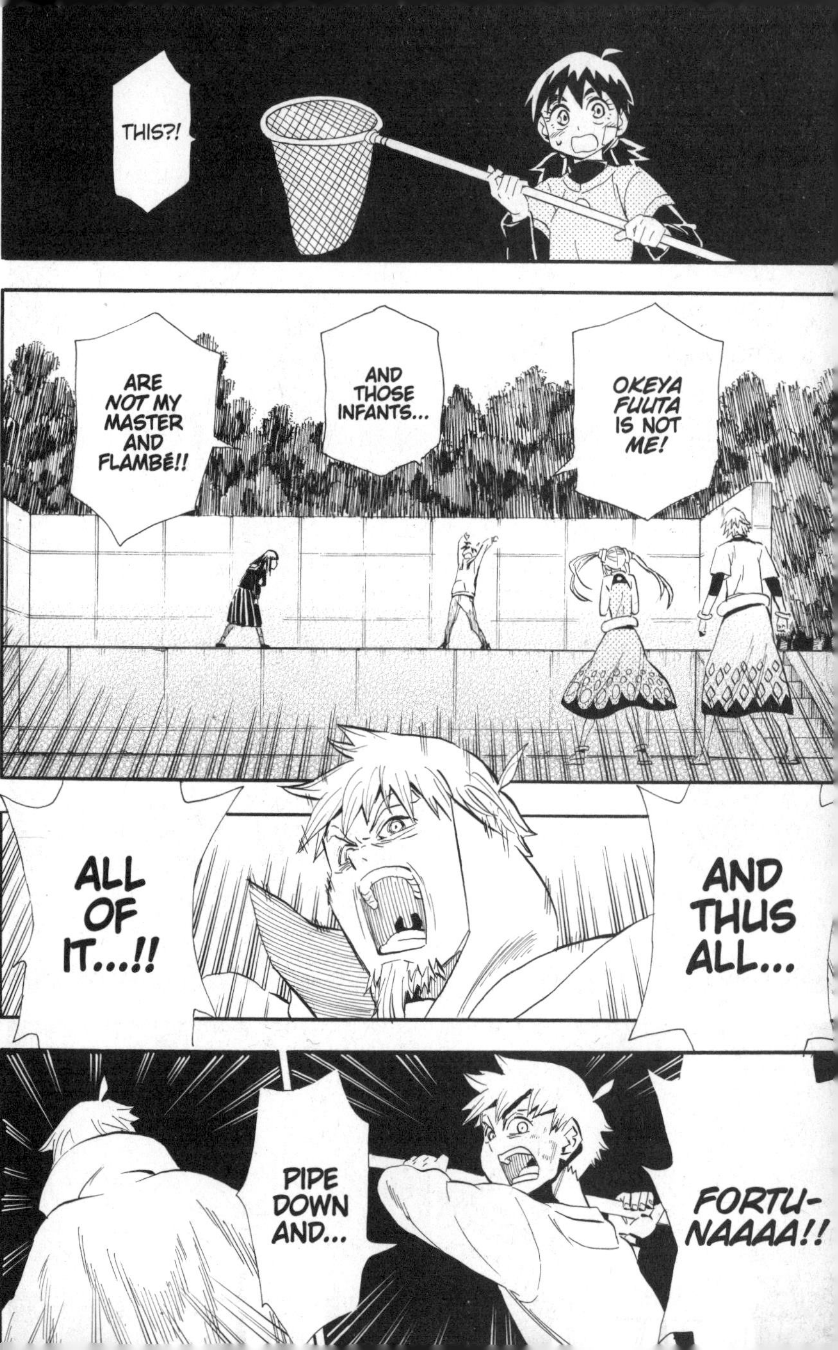
THIS?!
OKEYA FUUTA IS NOT ME!
AND THOSE INFANTS...
ARE NOT MY MASTER AND FLAMBÉ!!
AND THUS ALL...
ALL OF IT...!!
FORTU-NAAAA!!
PIPE DOWN AND...

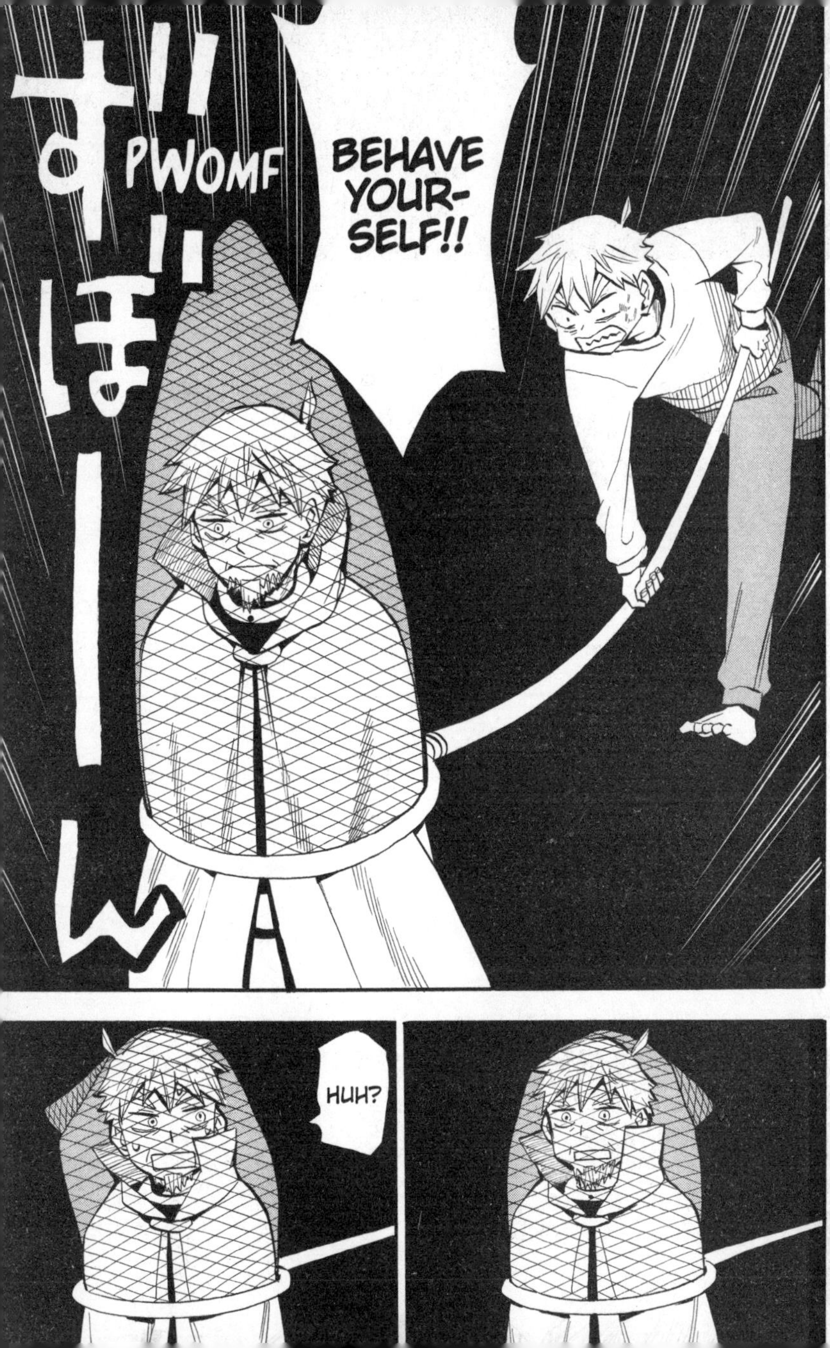
BEHAVE YOUR-SELF!!
すぽーん
PWOMF
HUH?

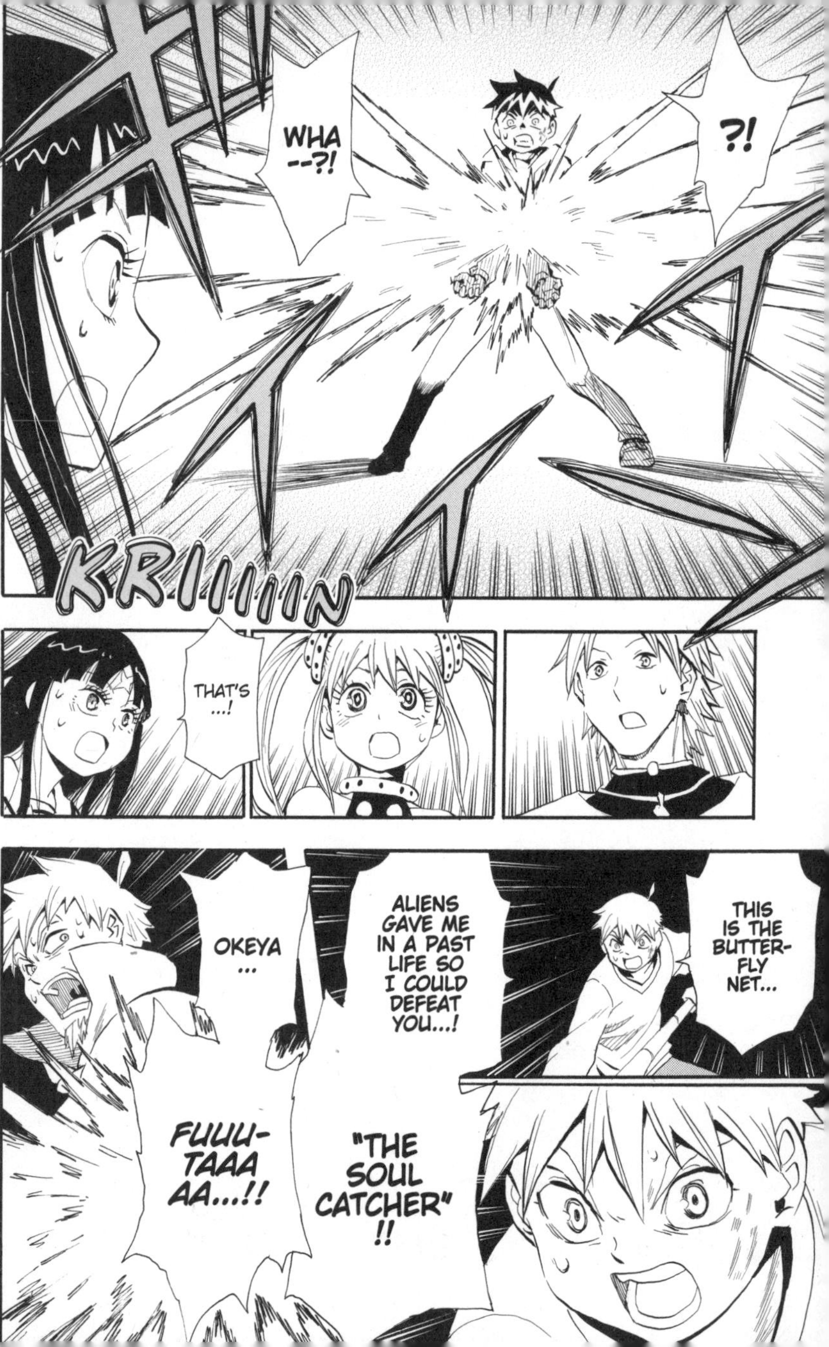
?!
WHA --?!
KRIIIIIN
THAT'S ...!
THIS IS THE BUTTER-FLY NET...
ALIENS GAVE ME IN A PAST LIFE SO I COULD DEFEAT YOU...!
"THE SOUL CATCHER" !!
OKEYA ...
FUUU-TAAAA AA...!!

Circle 43/END

Spirit Circle

Spirit Circle

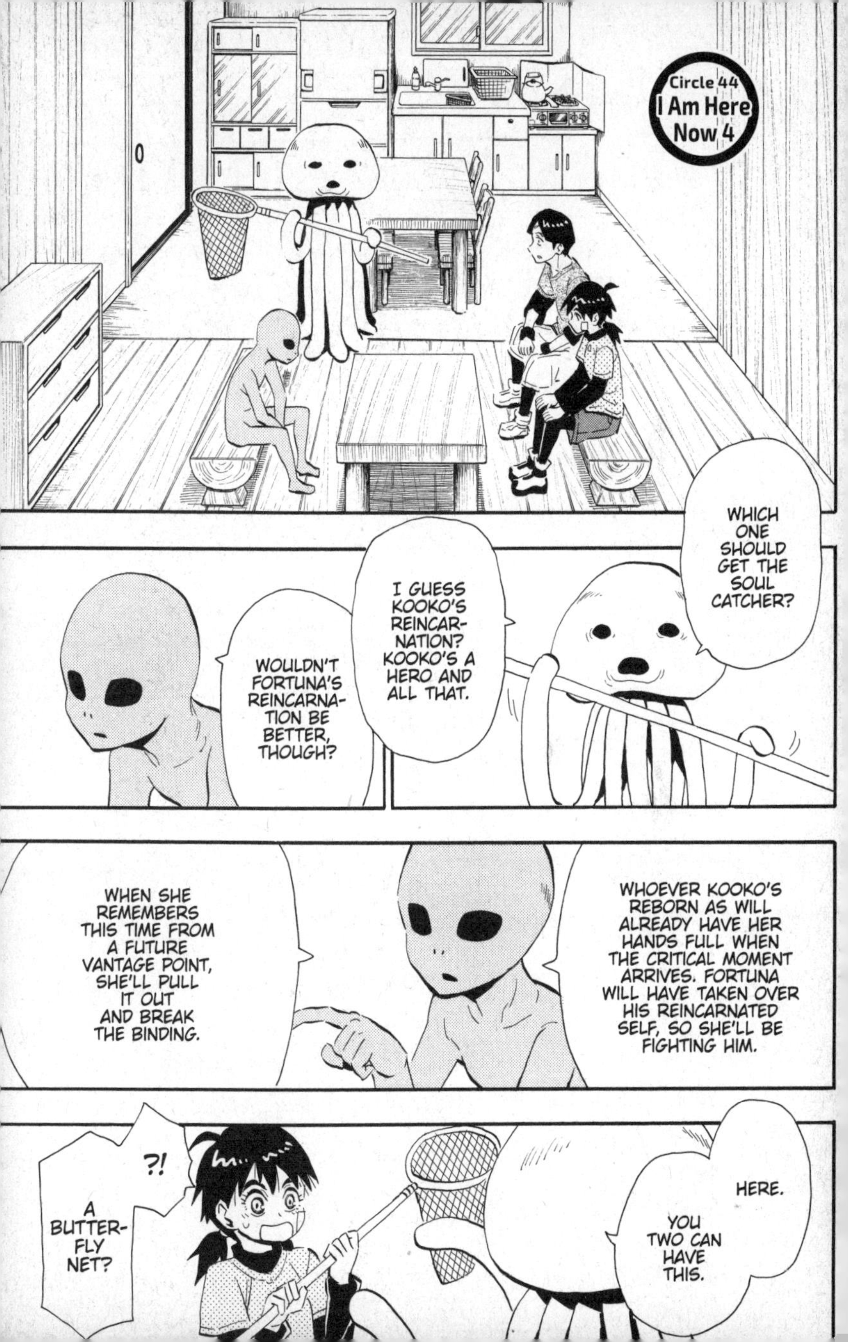
Circle 44
I Am Here Now 4
WHICH ONE SHOULD GET THE SOUL CATCHER?
I GUESS KOOKO'S REINCARNATION? KOOKO'S A HERO AND ALL THAT.
WOULDN'T FORTUNA'S REINCARNATION BE BETTER, THOUGH?
WHOEVER KOOKO'S REBORN AS WILL ALREADY HAVE HER HANDS FULL WHEN THE CRITICAL MOMENT ARRIVES. FORTUNA WILL HAVE TAKEN OVER HIS REINCARNATED SELF, SO SHE'LL BE FIGHTING HIM.
WHEN SHE REMEMBERS THIS TIME FROM A FUTURE VANTAGE POINT, SHE'LL PULL IT OUT AND BREAK THE BINDING.
HERE.
YOU TWO CAN HAVE THIS.
?!
A BUTTER-FLY NET?

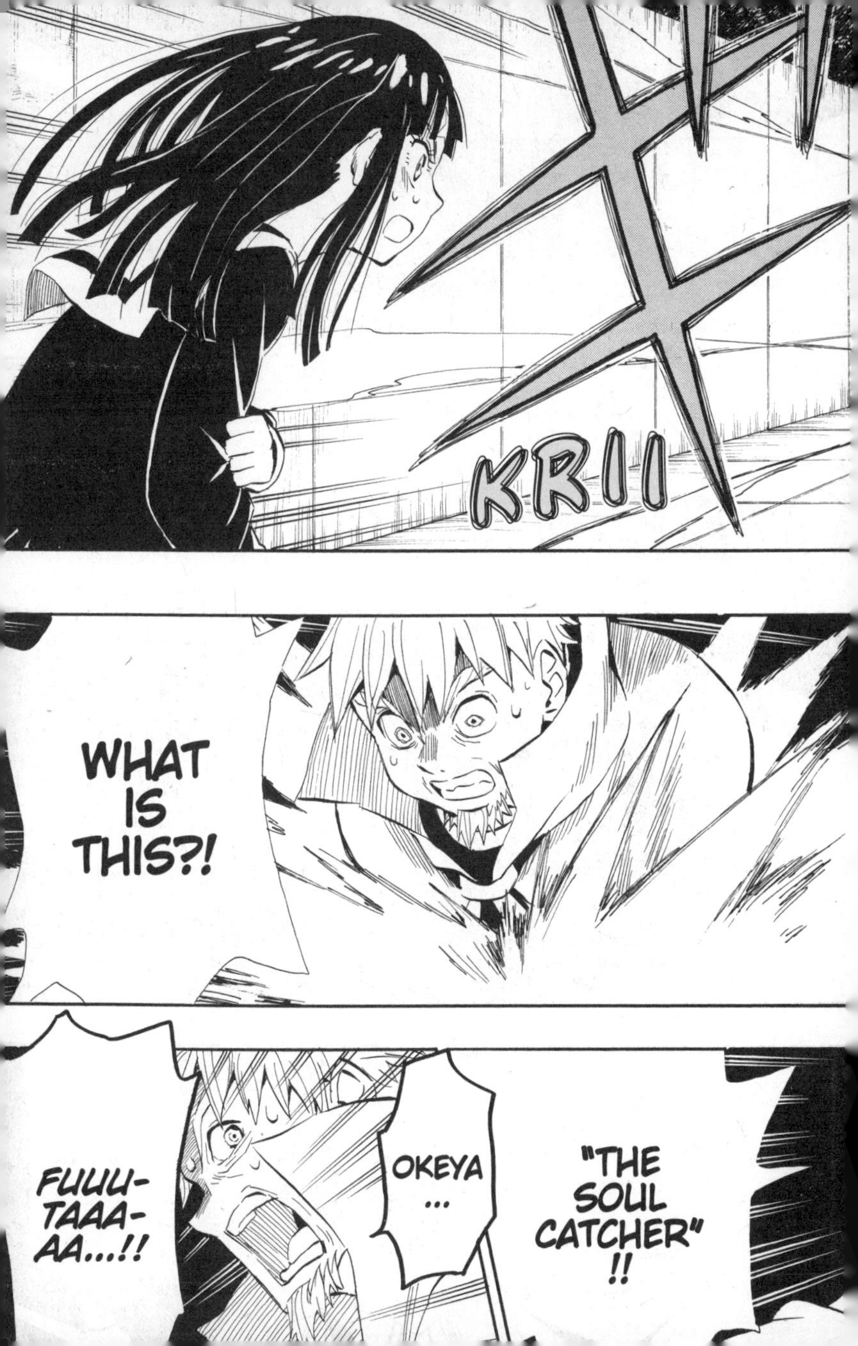
KRII
WHAT IS THIS?!
"THE SOUL CATCHER"!!
OKEYA...
FUUU-TAAAA-AA...!!

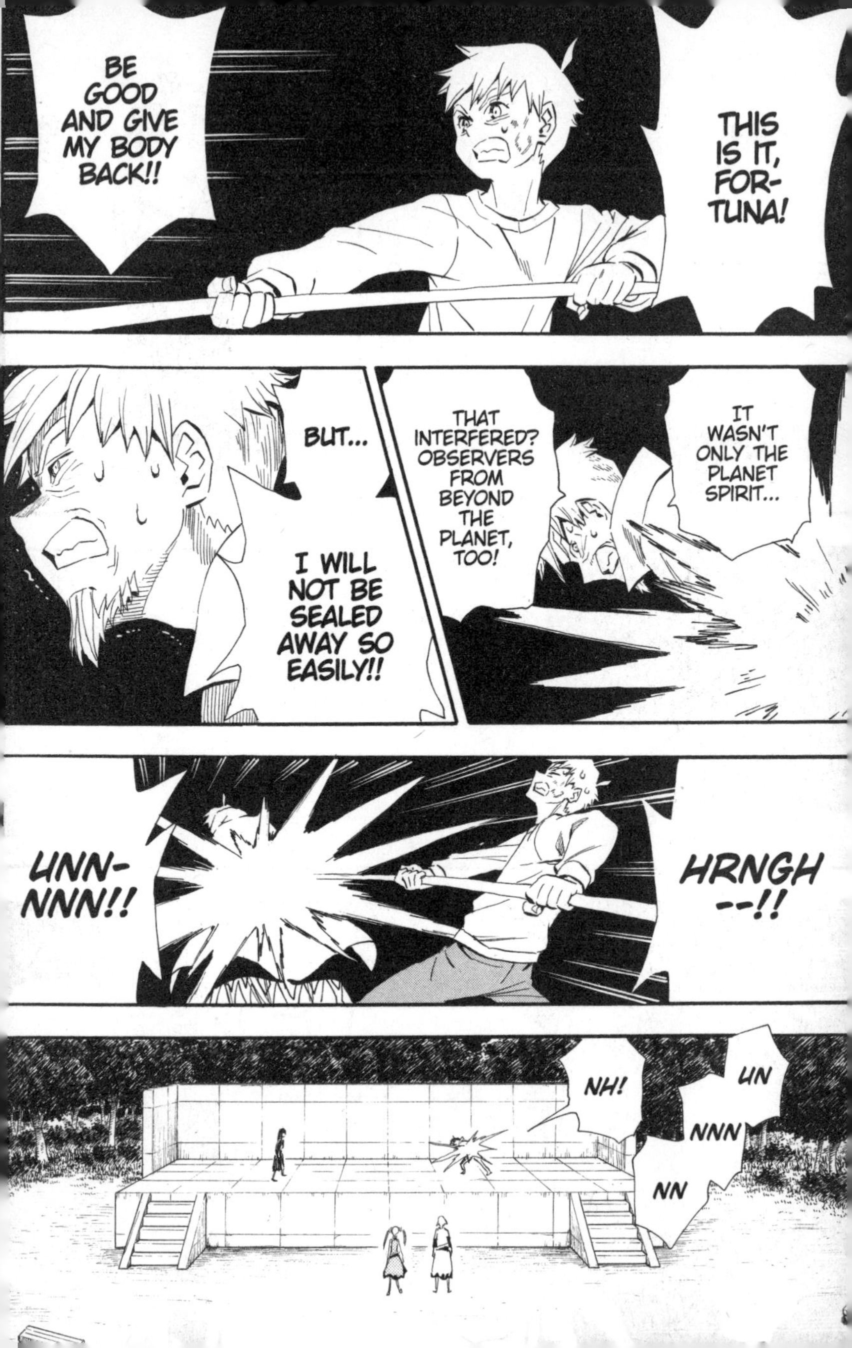
THIS IS IT, FOR-TUNA!
BE GOOD AND GIVE MY BODY BACK!!
IT WASN'T ONLY THE PLANET SPIRIT...
THAT INTERFERED? OBSERVERS FROM BEYOND THE PLANET, TOO!
BUT...
I WILL NOT BE SEALED AWAY SO EASILY!!
HRNGH --!!
UNN-NNN!!
UN
NNN
NN
NH!

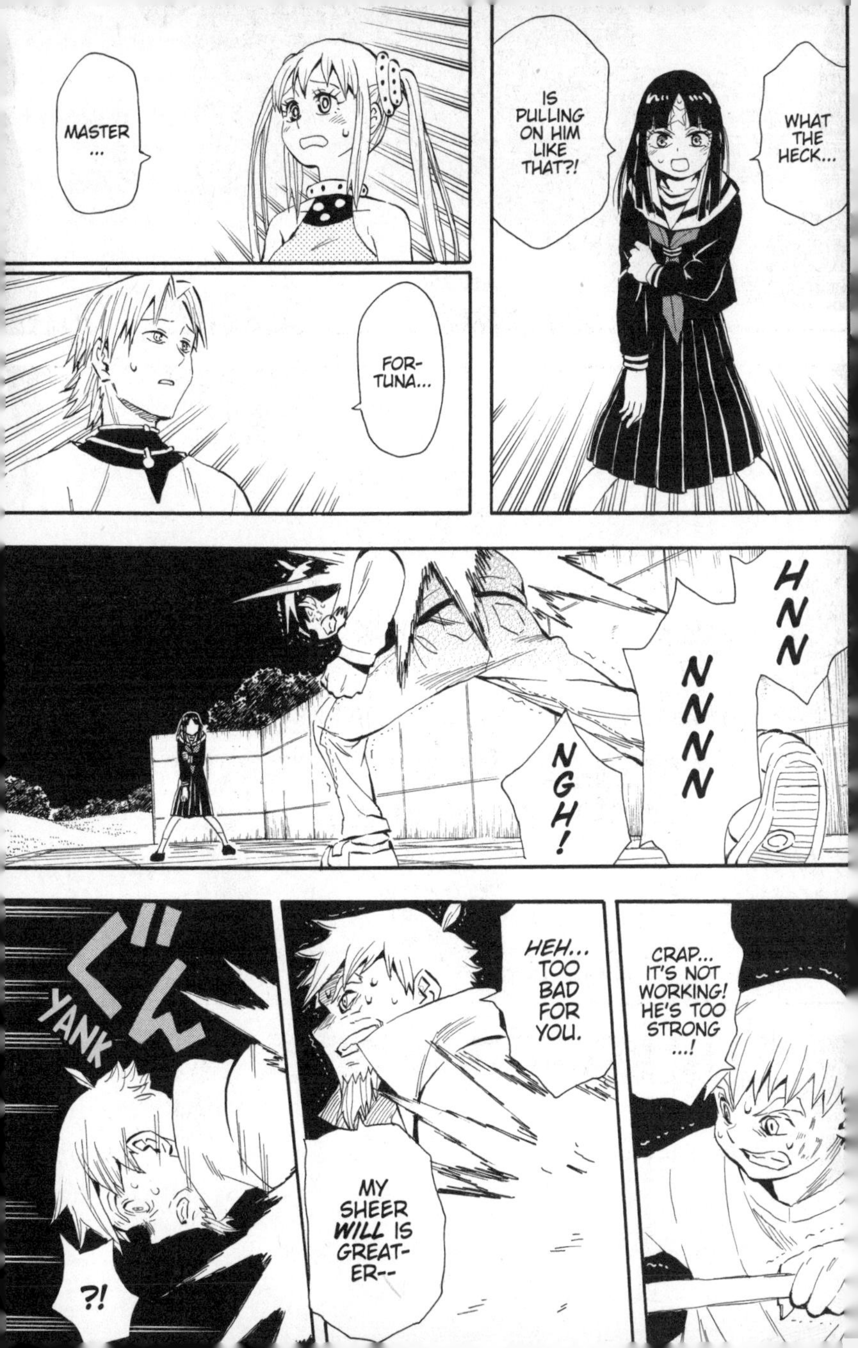
WHAT THE HECK...
IS PULLING ON HIM LIKE THAT?!
MASTER ...
FOR-TUNA...
HNN
NNNN
NGH!
CRAP... IT'S NOT WORKING! HE'S TOO STRONG ...!
HEH... TOO BAD FOR YOU.
MY SHEER WILL IS GREATER--
ぐん
YANK
?!

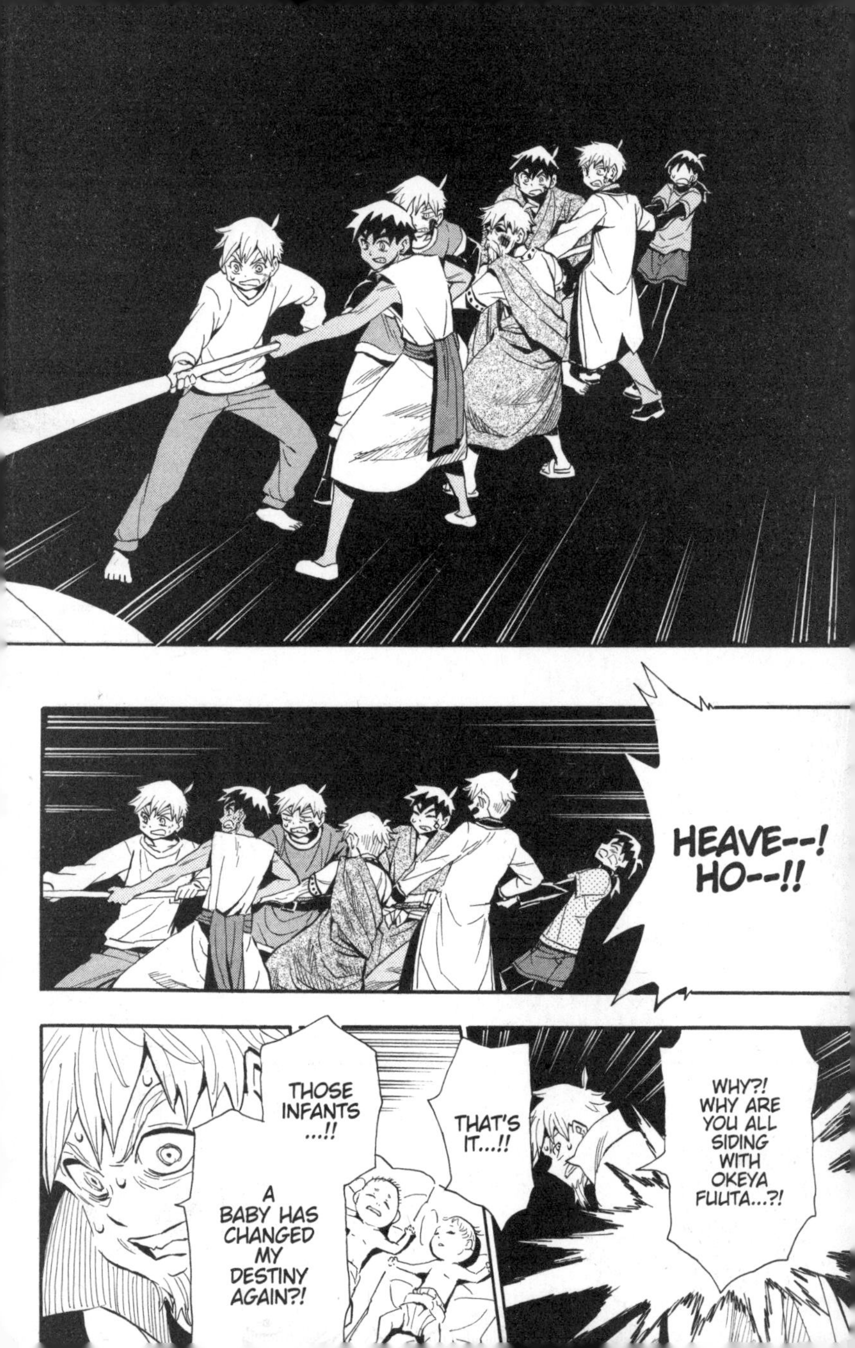
HEAVE--! HO--!!
WHY?! WHY ARE YOU ALL SIDING WITH OKEYA FUUTA...?!
THAT'S IT...!!
THOSE INFANTS ...!!
A BABY HAS CHANGED MY DESTINY AGAIN?!

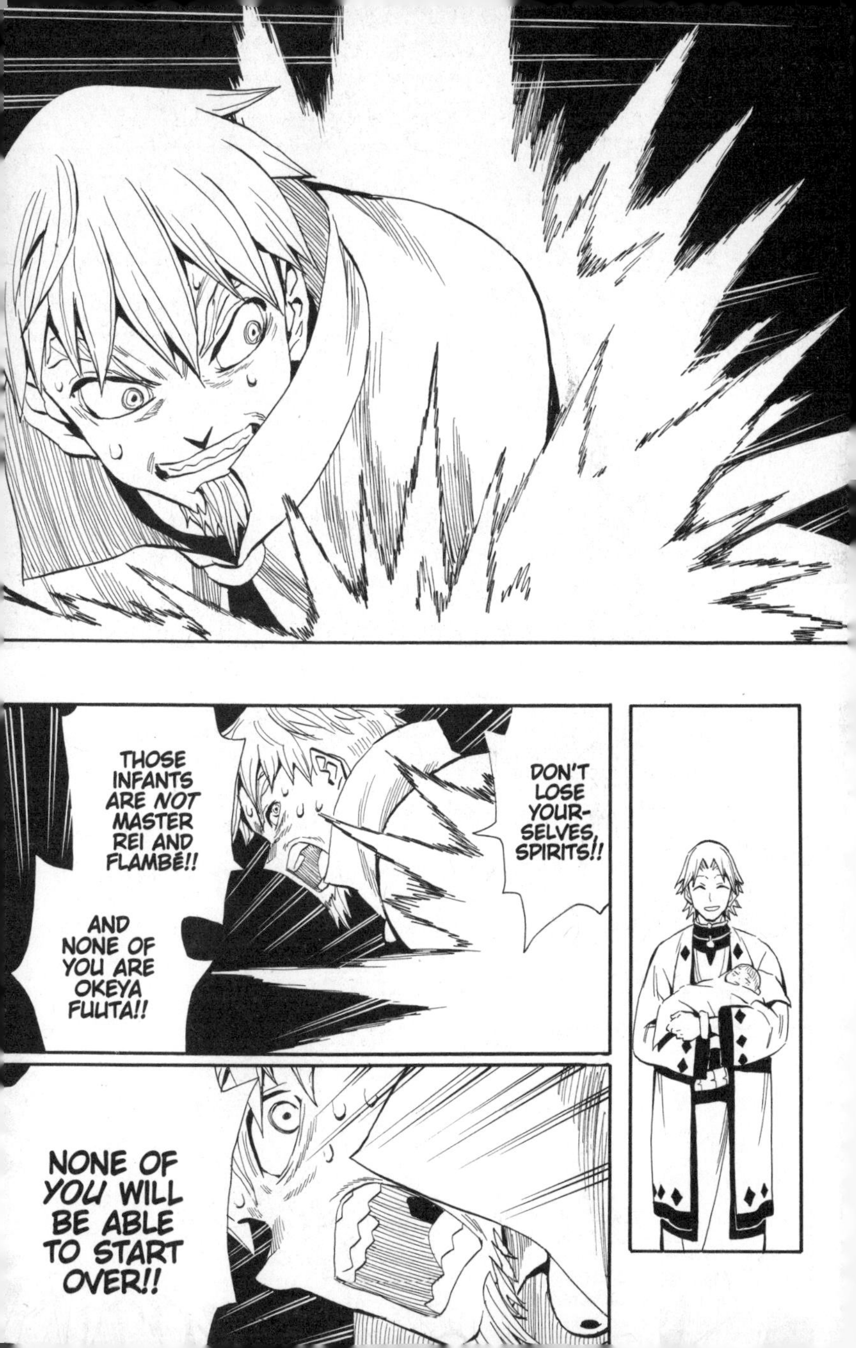
DON'T LOSE YOUR-SELVES, SPIRITS!!
THOSE INFANTS ARE NOT MASTER REI AND FLAMBÉ!!
AND NONE OF YOU ARE OKEYA FUUTA!!
NONE OF YOU WILL BE ABLE TO START OVER!!

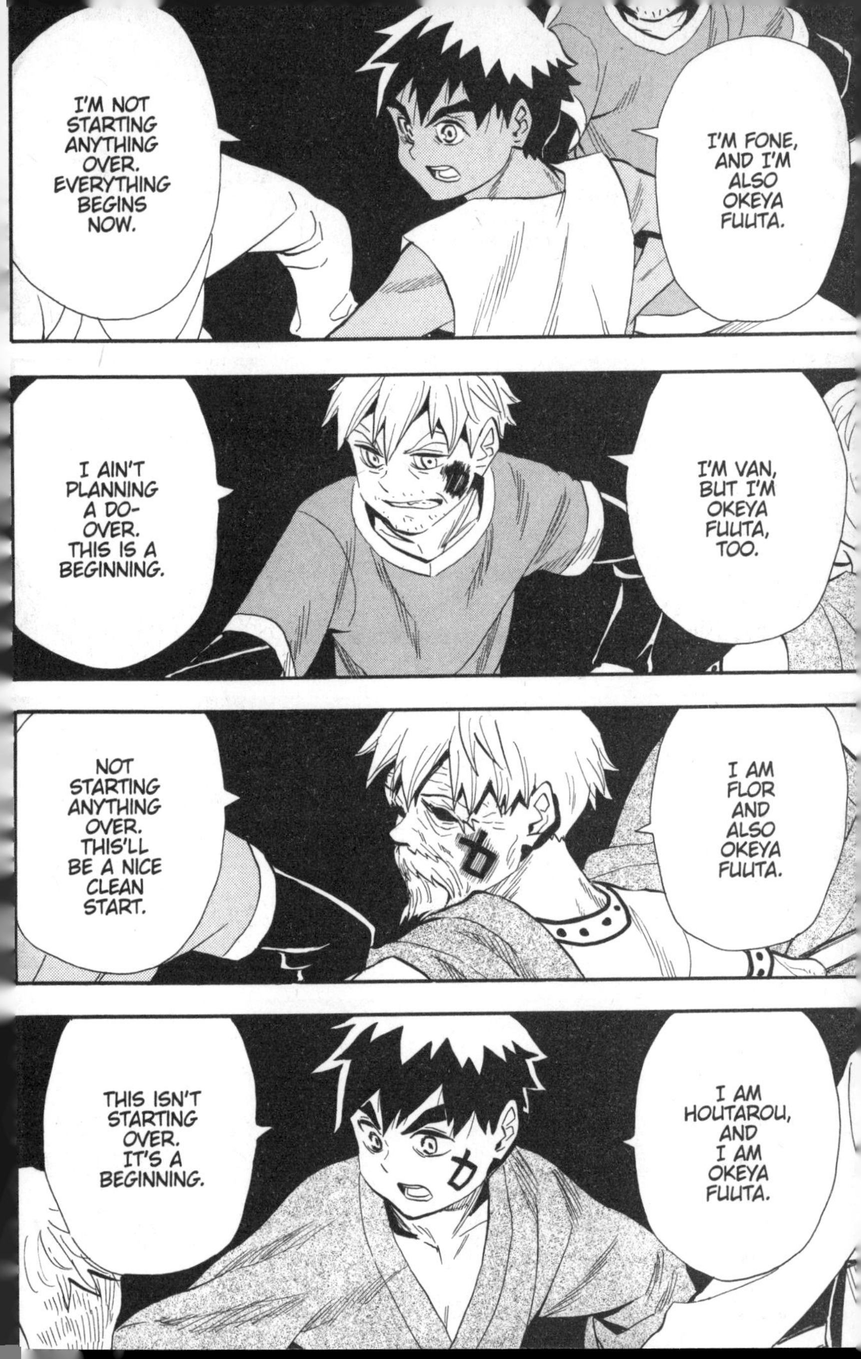

I'M FONE, AND I'M ALSO OKEYA FUUTA.
I'M NOT STARTING ANYTHING OVER. EVERYTHING BEGINS NOW.
I'M VAN, BUT I'M OKEYA FUUTA, TOO.
I AIN'T PLANNING A DO-OVER. THIS IS A BEGINNING.
I AM FLOR AND ALSO OKEYA FUUTA.
NOT STARTING ANYTHING OVER. THIS'LL BE A NICE CLEAN START.
I AM HOUTAROU, AND I AM OKEYA FUUTA.
THIS ISN'T STARTING OVER. IT'S A BEGINNING.

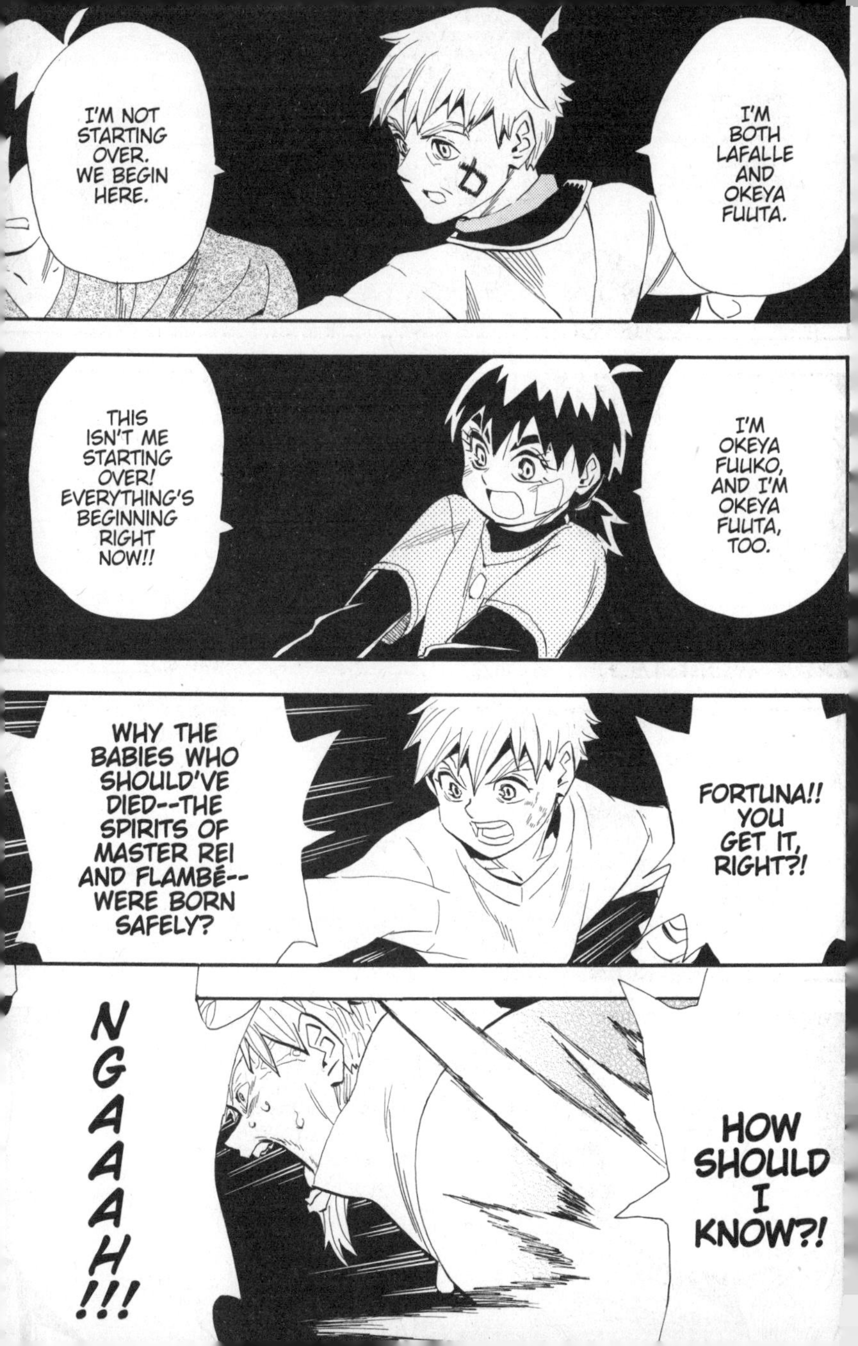
I'M BOTH LAFALLE AND OKEYA FUUTA.
I'M NOT STARTING OVER. WE BEGIN HERE.
I'M OKEYA FUUKO, AND I'M OKEYA FUUTA, TOO.
THIS ISN'T ME STARTING OVER! EVERYTHING'S BEGINNING RIGHT NOW!!
FORTUNA!! YOU GET IT, RIGHT?!
WHY THE BABIES WHO SHOULD'VE DIED--THE SPIRITS OF MASTER REI AND FLAMBÉ--WERE BORN SAFELY?
HOW SHOULD I KNOW?!
NGAAAAH!!!

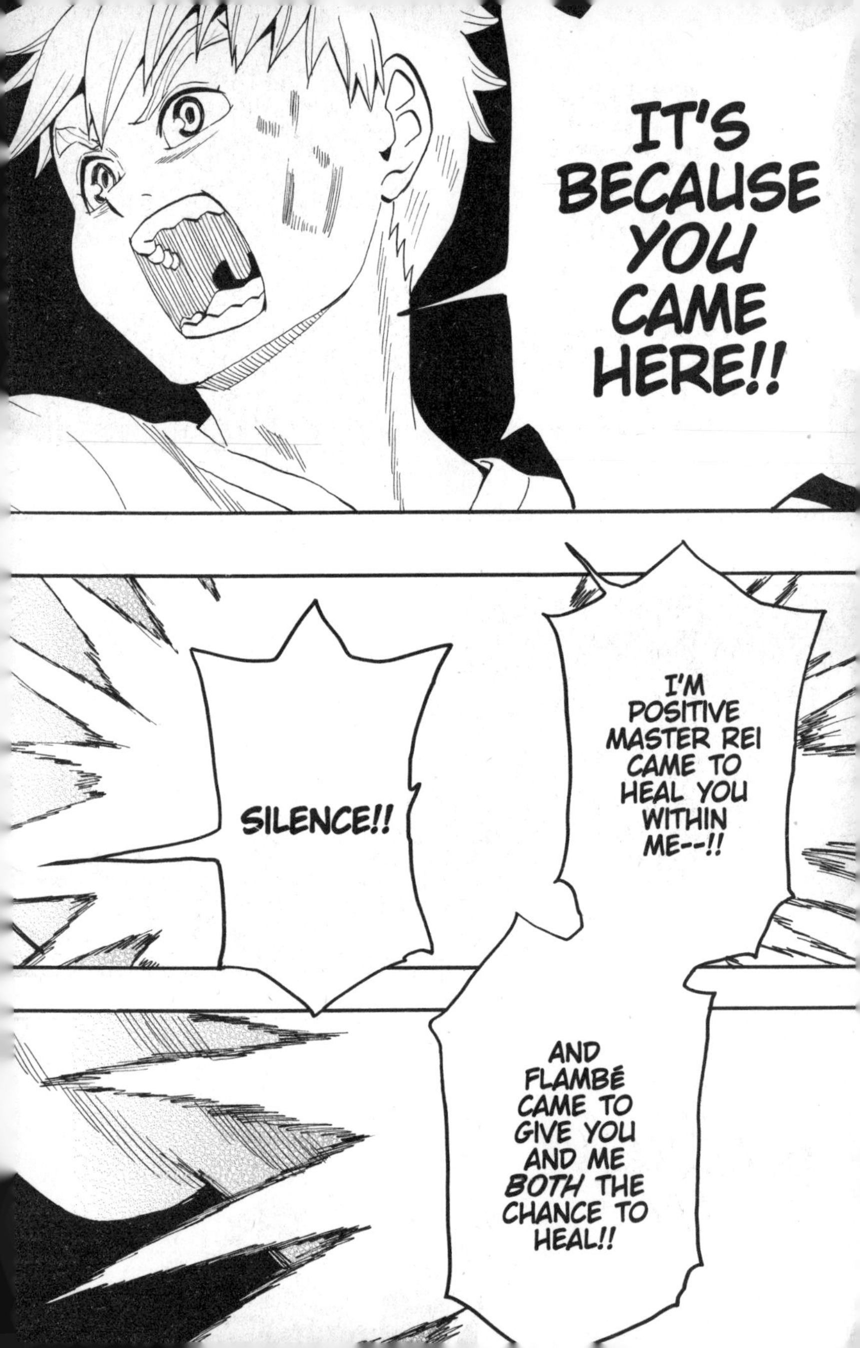
IT'S BECAUSE YOU CAME HERE!!
I'M POSITIVE MASTER REI CAME TO HEAL YOU WITHIN ME--!!
SILENCE!!
AND FLAMBÉ CAME TO GIVE YOU AND ME *BOTH* THE CHANCE TO HEAL!!

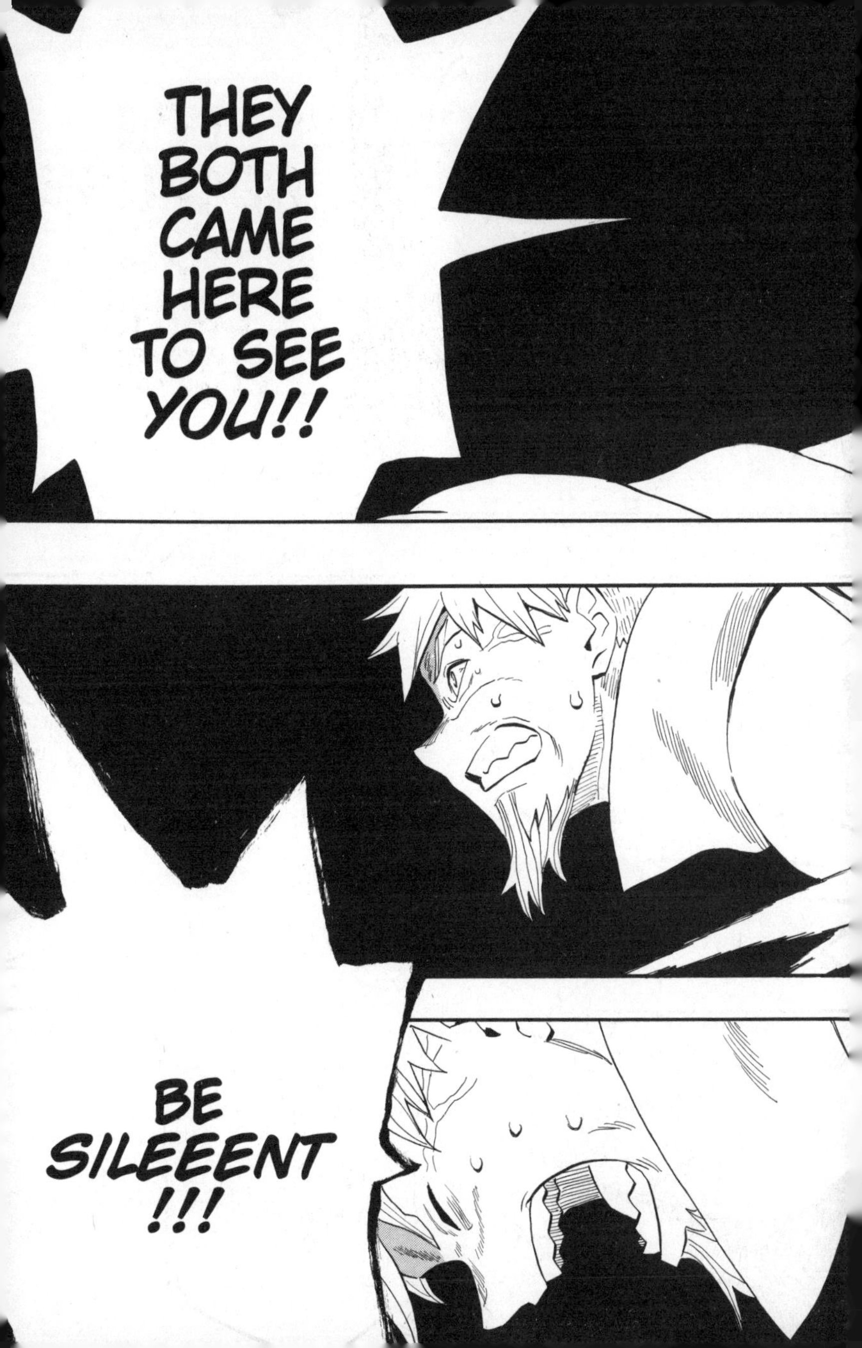
THEY BOTH CAME HERE TO SEE YOU!!
BE SILEEENT !!!

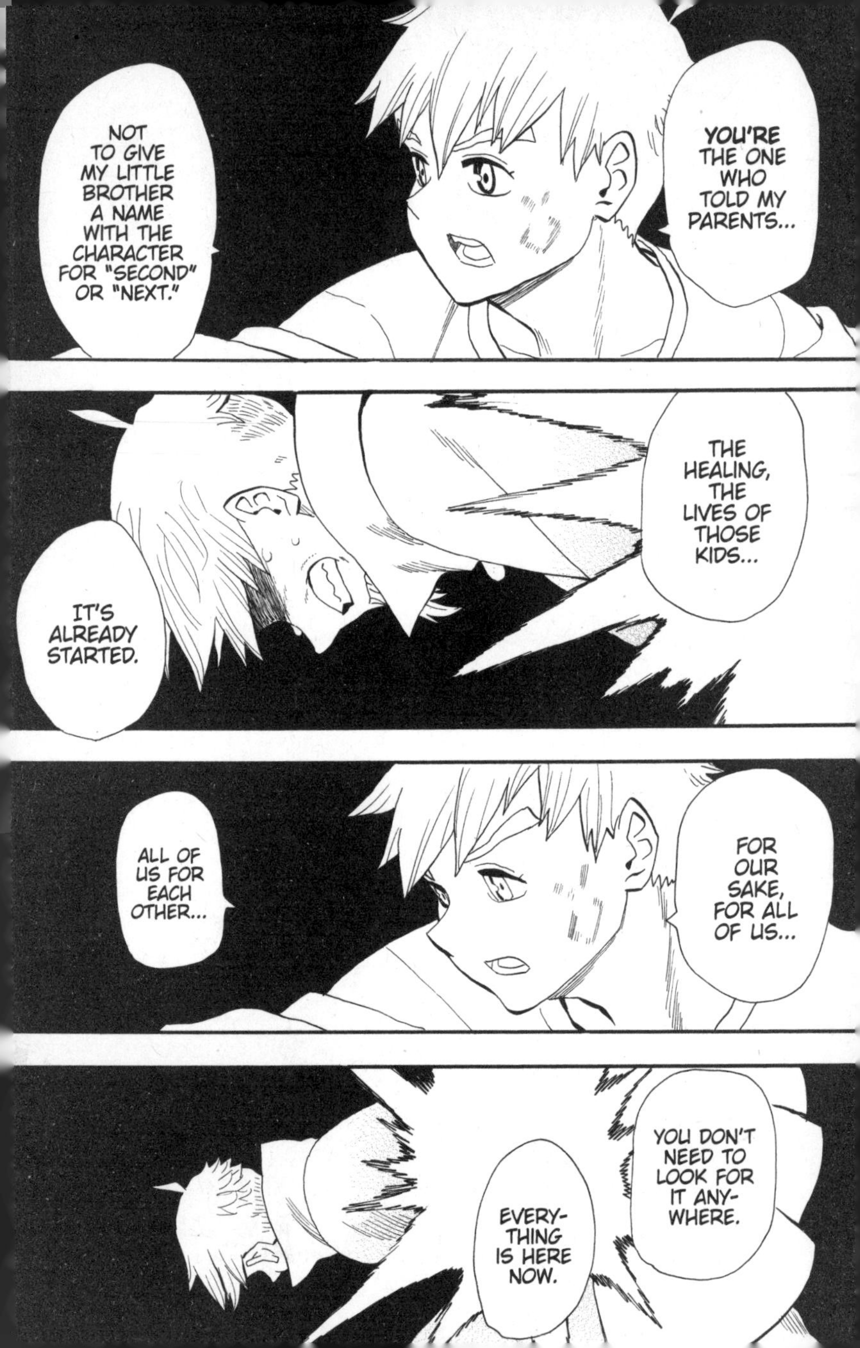
YOU'RE THE ONE WHO TOLD MY PARENTS...
NOT TO GIVE MY LITTLE BROTHER A NAME WITH THE CHARACTER FOR "SECOND" OR "NEXT."
THE HEALING, THE LIVES OF THOSE KIDS...
IT'S ALREADY STARTED.
FOR OUR SAKE, FOR ALL OF US...
ALL OF US FOR EACH OTHER...
YOU DON'T NEED TO LOOK FOR IT ANY-WHERE.
EVERY-THING IS HERE NOW.

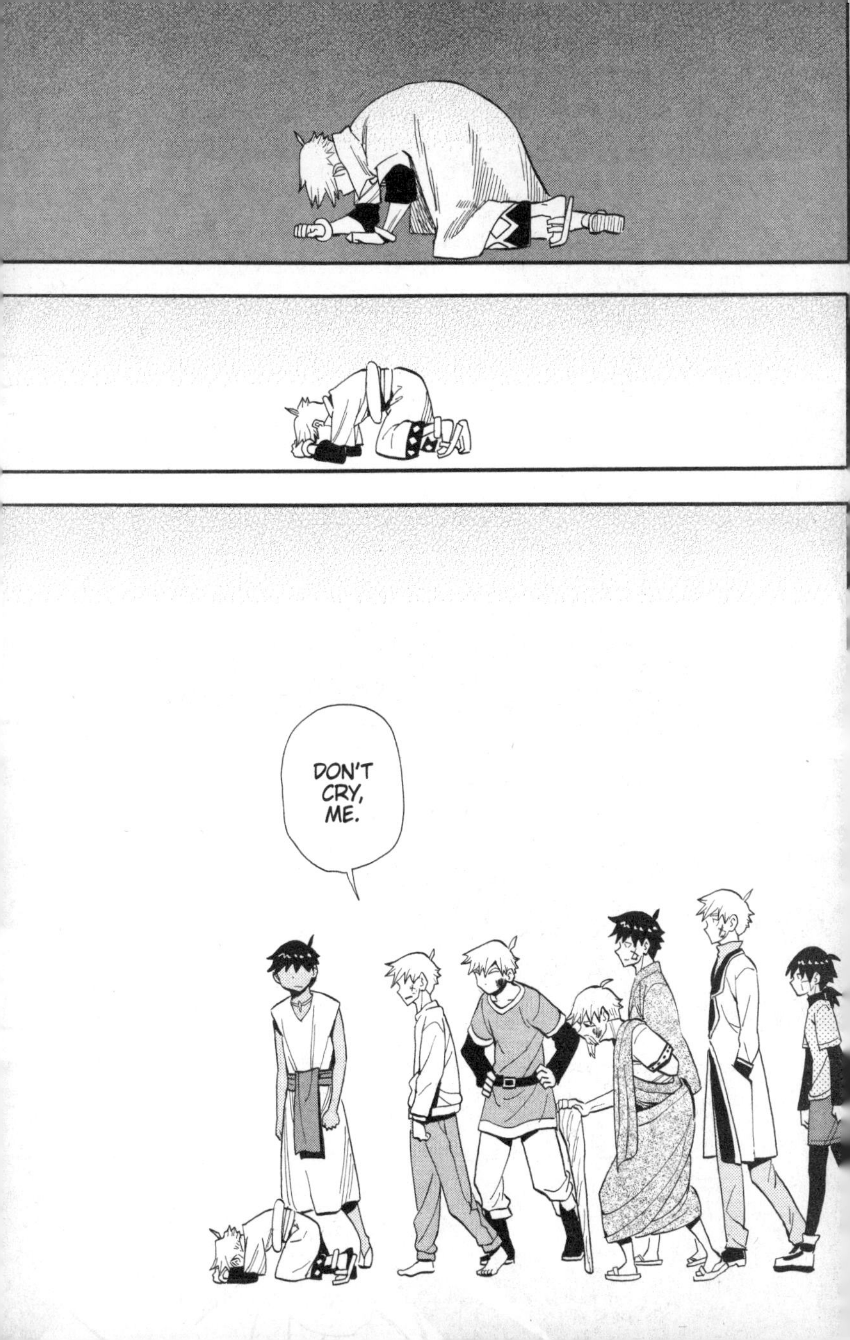
DON'T CRY, ME.

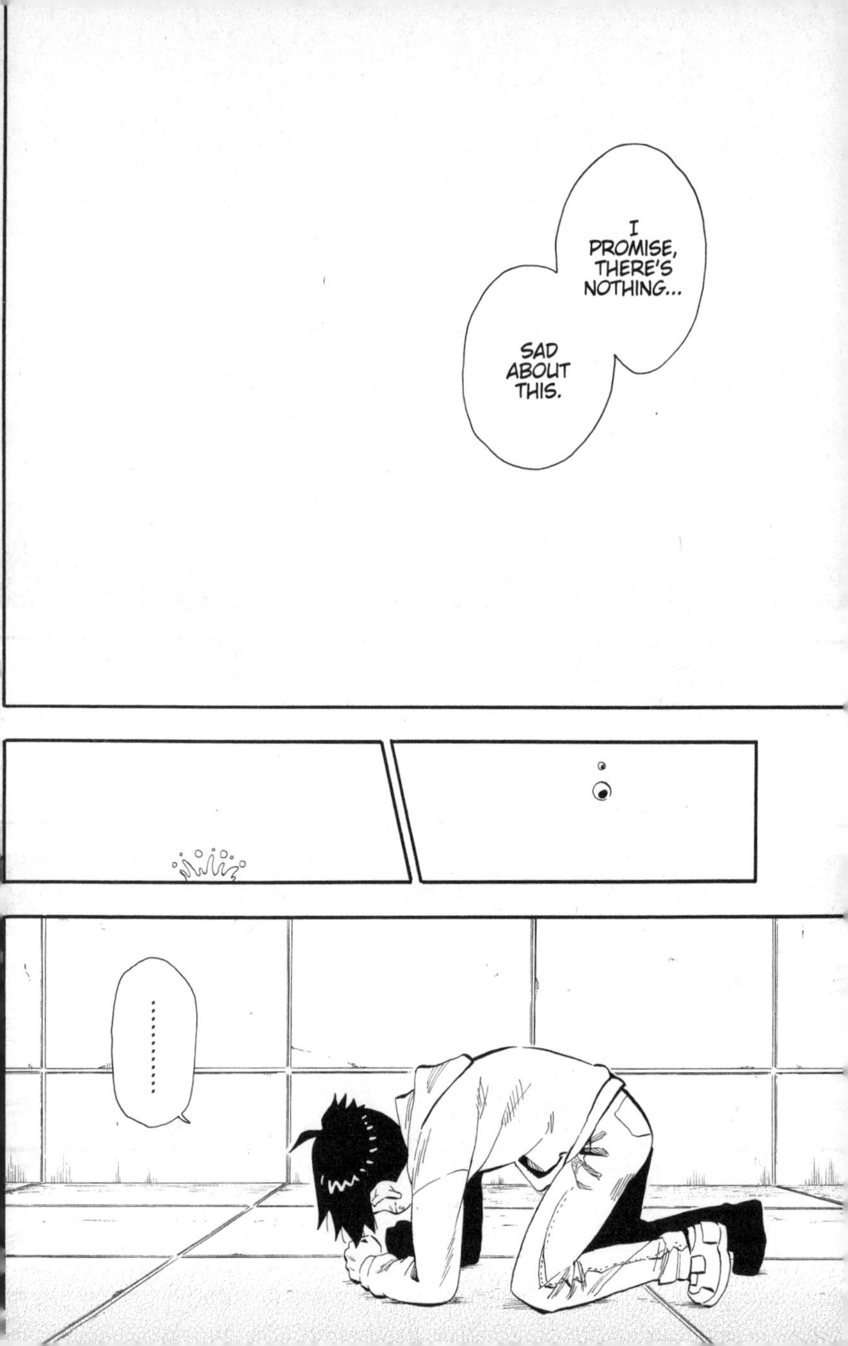
I PROMISE, THERE'S NOTHING...
SAD ABOUT THIS.
......

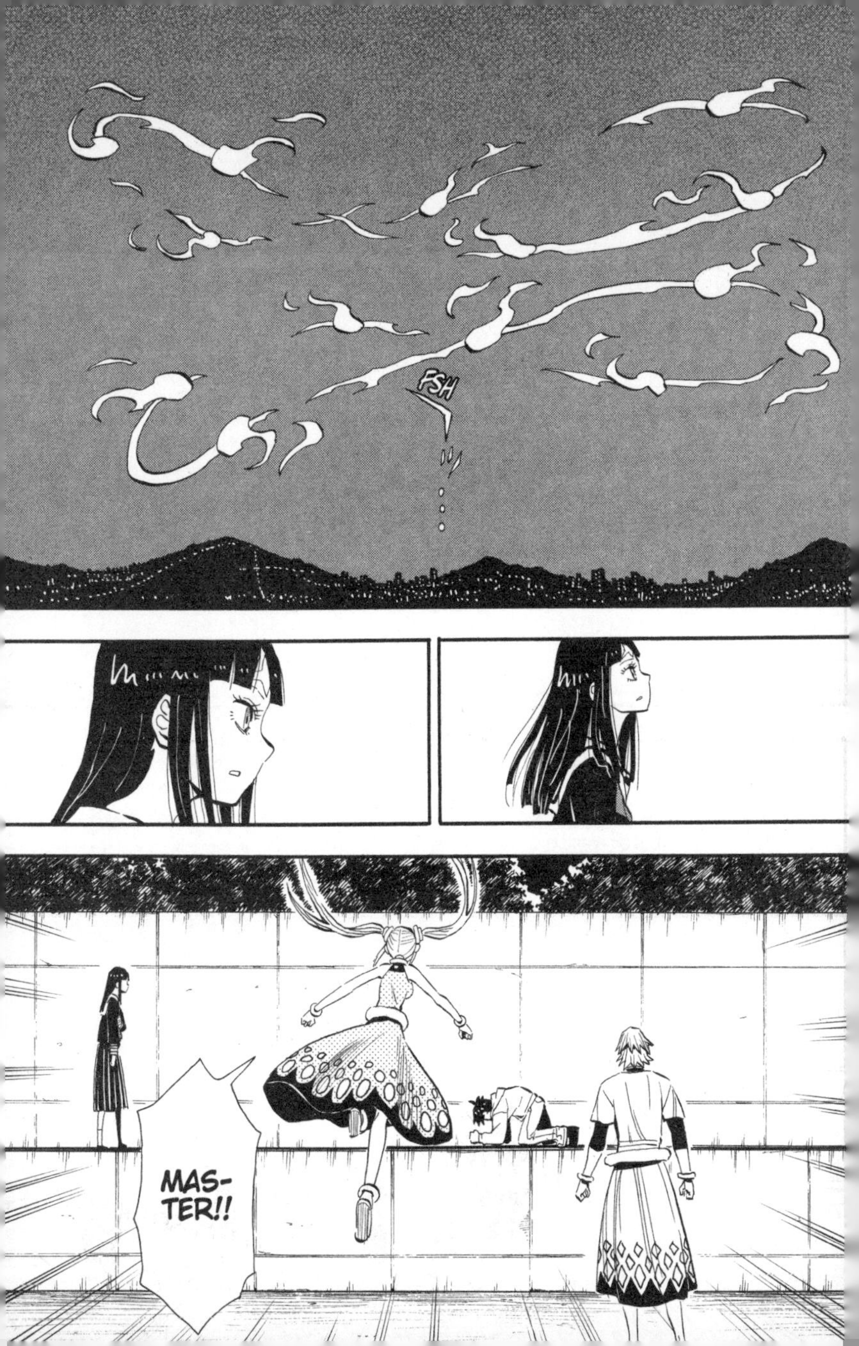
FSH
MAS-
TER!!

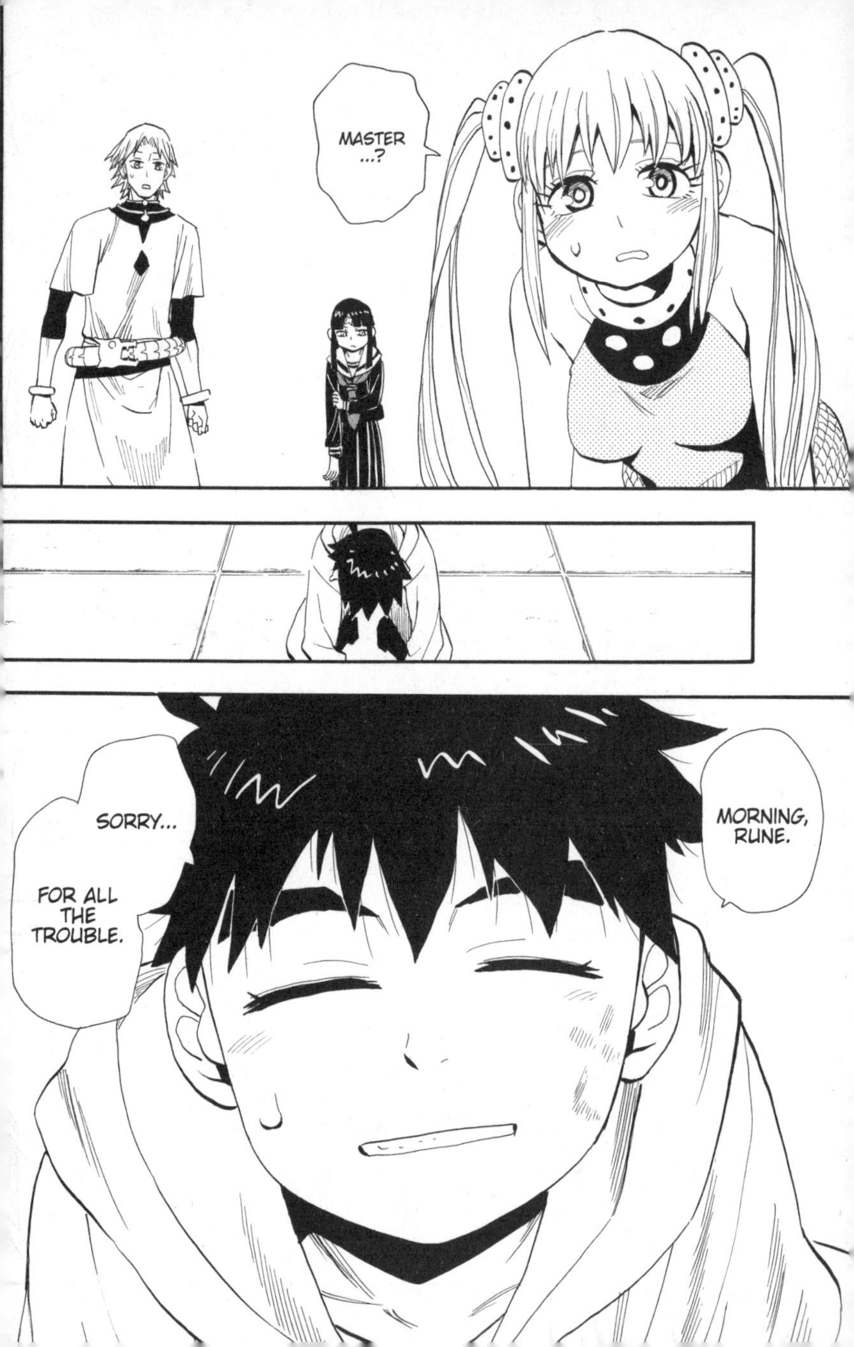
MASTER ...?
MORNING, RUNE.
SORRY...
FOR ALL THE TROUBLE.

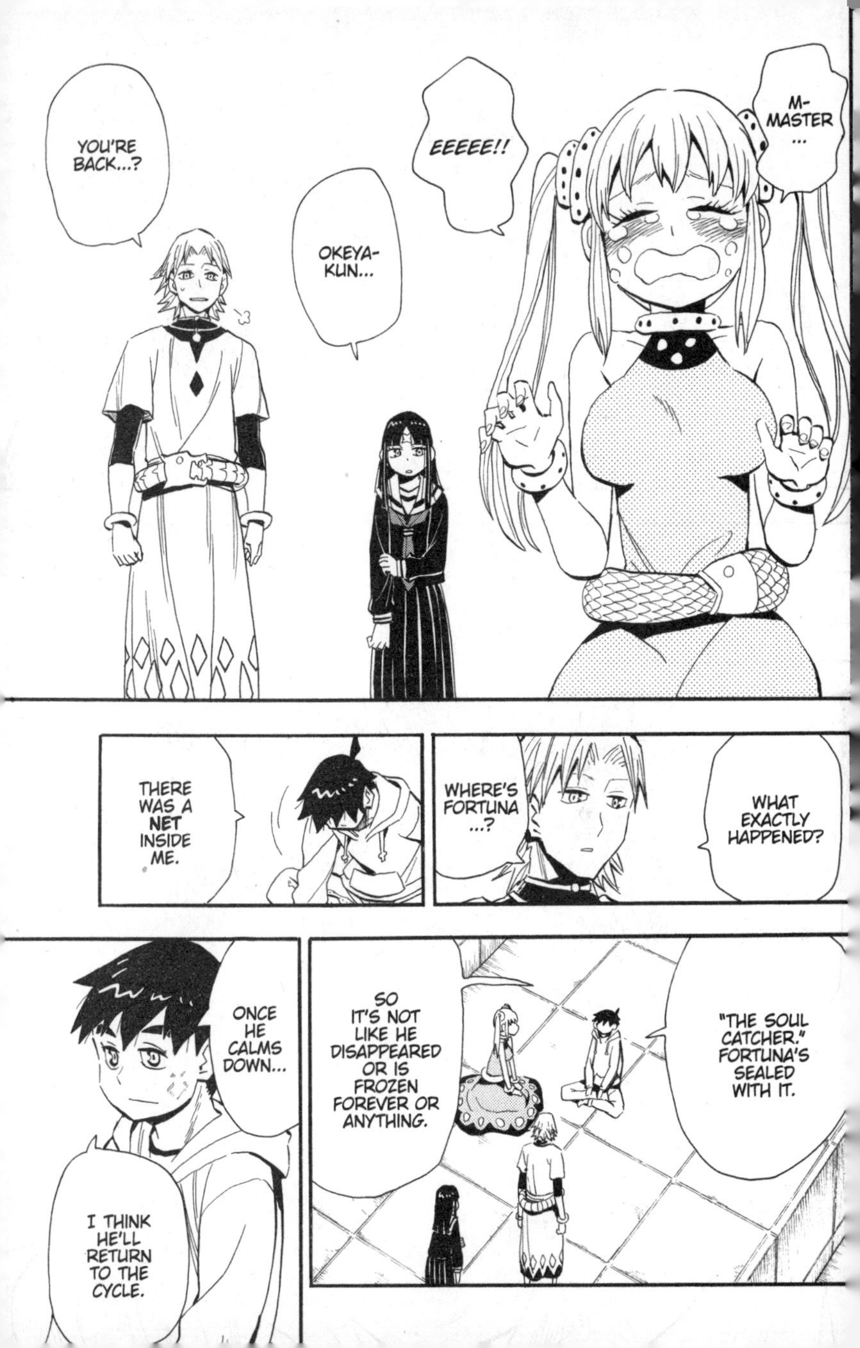
M-MASTER...
EEEEE!!
OKEYA-KUN...
YOU'RE BACK...?
WHAT EXACTLY HAPPENED?
WHERE'S FORTUNA...?
THERE WAS A NET INSIDE ME.
"THE SOUL CATCHER." FORTUNA'S SEALED WITH IT.
SO IT'S NOT LIKE HE DISAPPEARED OR IS FROZEN FOREVER OR ANYTHING.
ONCE HE CALMS DOWN...
I THINK HE'LL RETURN TO THE CYCLE.

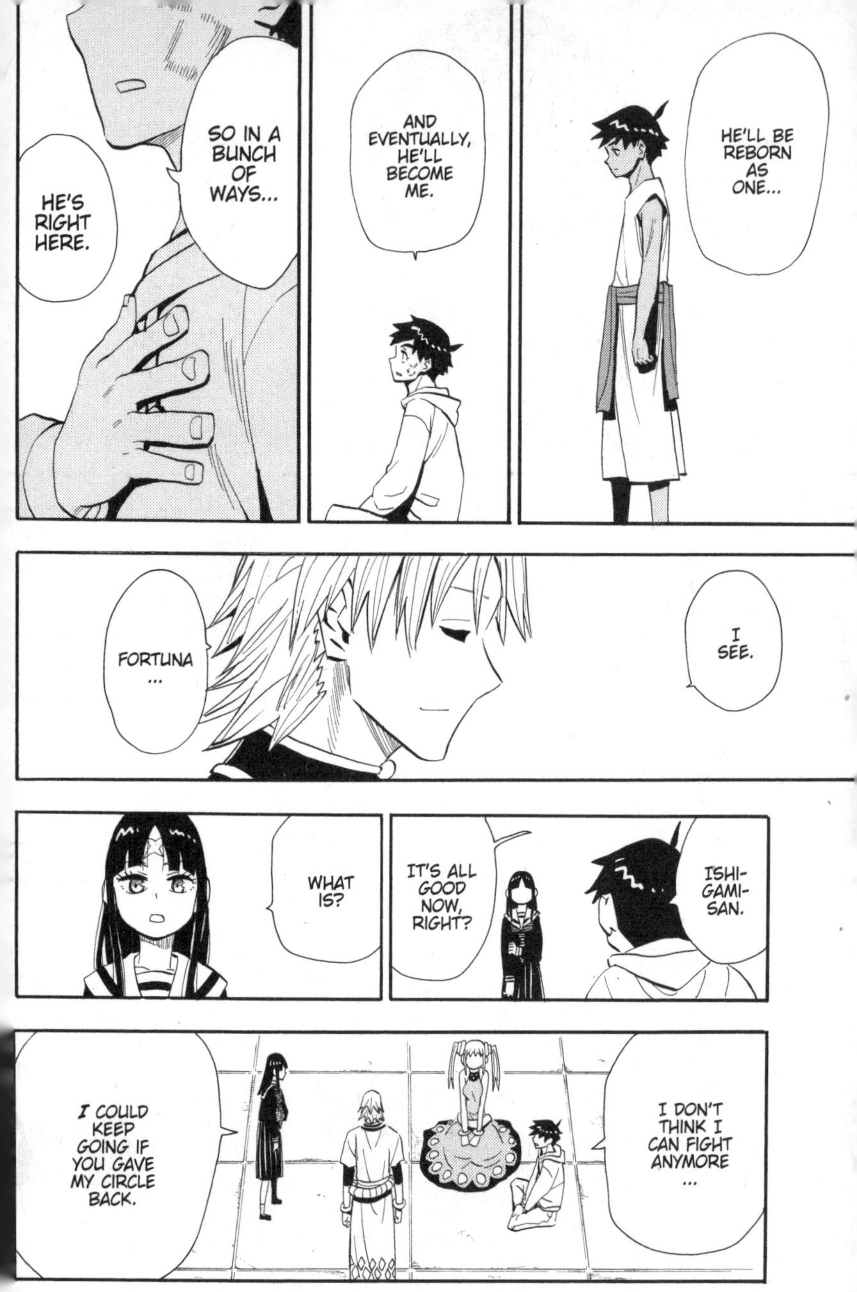
HE'LL BE REBORN AS ONE...
AND EVENTUALLY, HE'LL BECOME ME.
SO IN A BUNCH OF WAYS...
HE'S RIGHT HERE.
I SEE.
FORTUNA...
ISHI-GAMI-SAN.
IT'S ALL GOOD NOW, RIGHT?
WHAT IS?
I DON'T THINK I CAN FIGHT ANYMORE...
I COULD KEEP GOING IF YOU GAVE MY CIRCLE BACK.

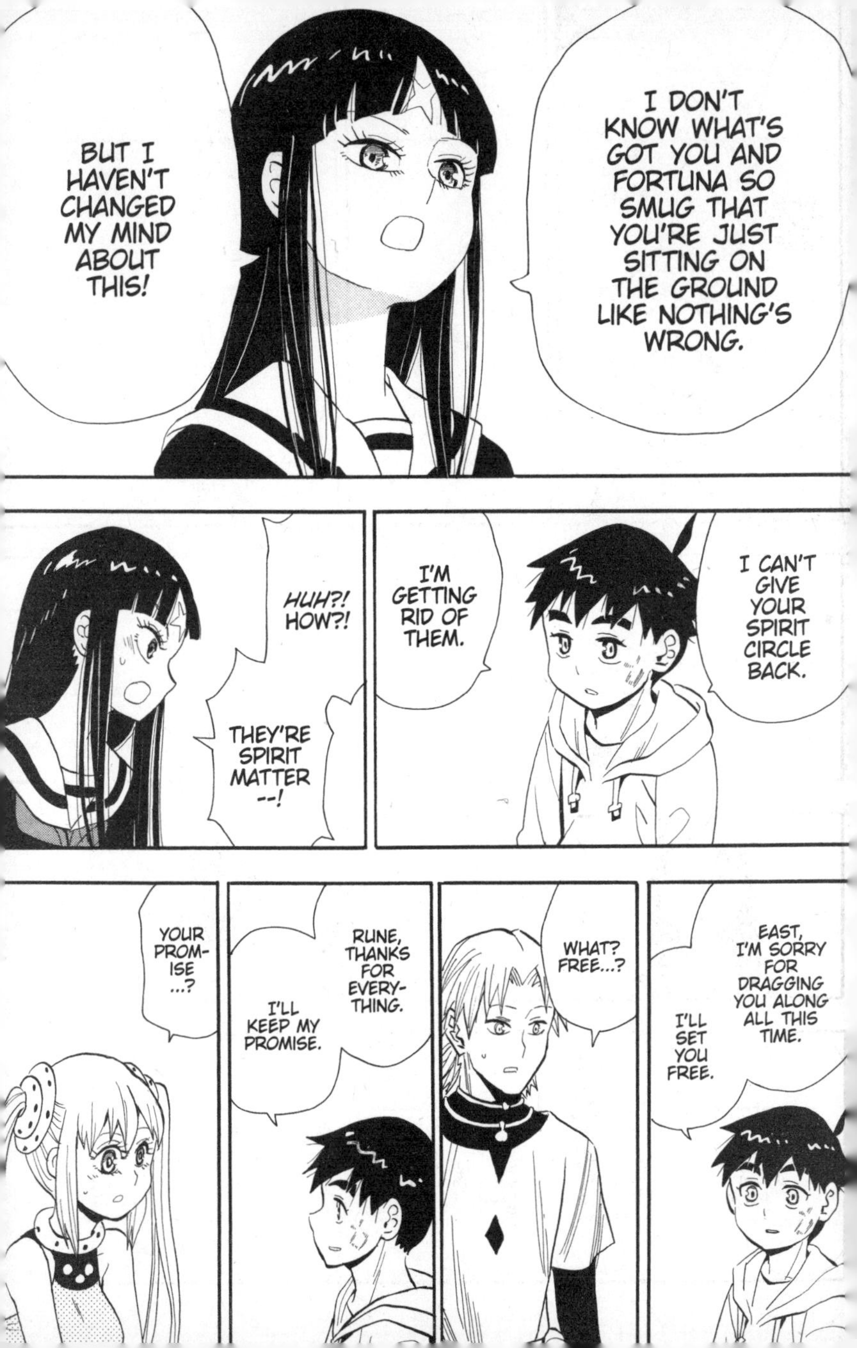
I DON'T KNOW WHAT'S GOT YOU AND FORTUNA SO SMUG THAT YOU'RE JUST SITTING ON THE GROUND LIKE NOTHING'S WRONG.
BUT I HAVEN'T CHANGED MY MIND ABOUT THIS!
I CAN'T GIVE YOUR SPIRIT CIRCLE BACK.
I'M GETTING RID OF THEM.
HUH?! HOW?!
THEY'RE SPIRIT MATTER --!
EAST, I'M SORRY FOR DRAGGING YOU ALONG ALL THIS TIME.
I'LL SET YOU FREE.
WHAT? FREE...?
RUNE, THANKS FOR EVERYTHING.
I'LL KEEP MY PROMISE.
YOUR PROMISE...?

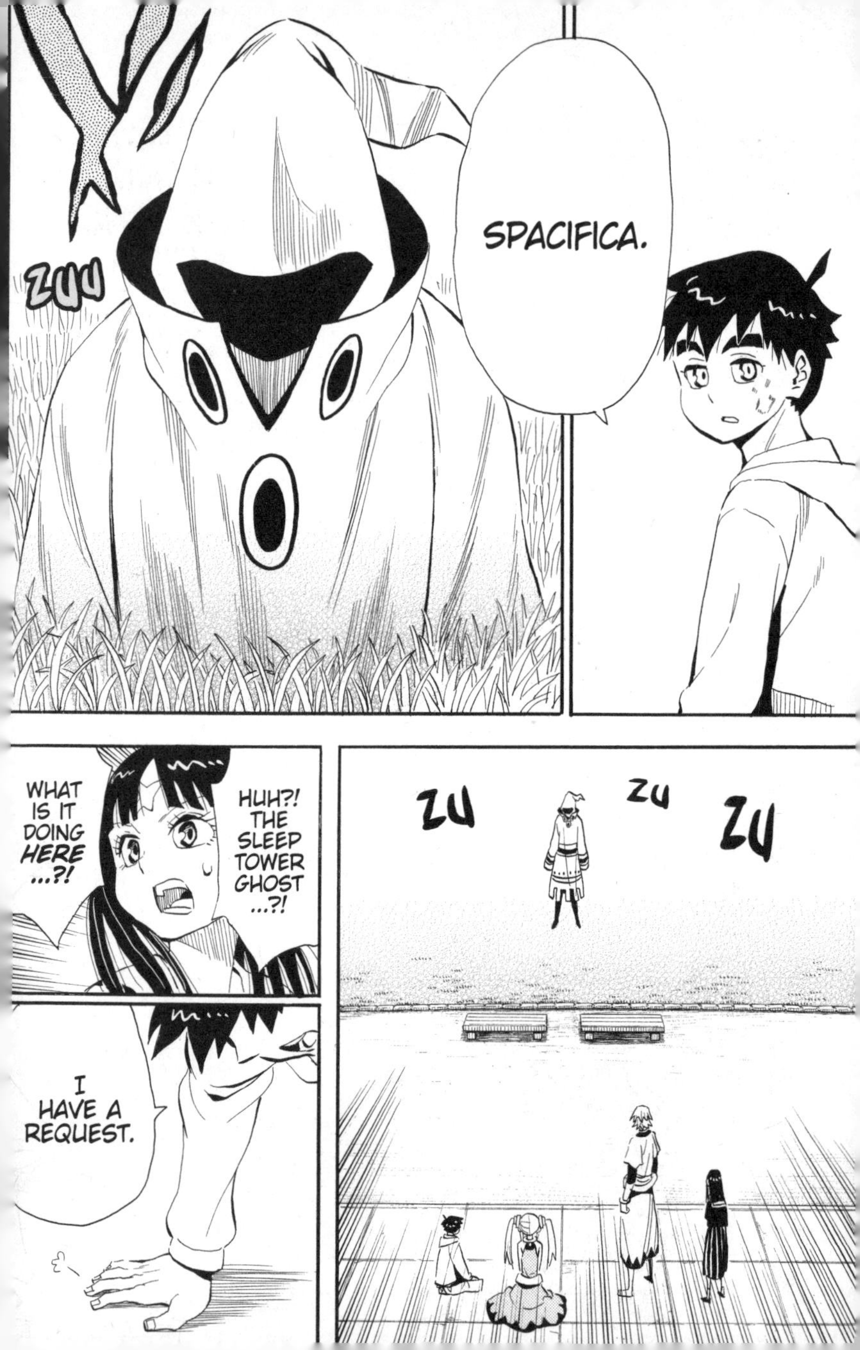
SPACIFICA.
ZUU
ZU
ZU
ZU
HUH?! THE SLEEP TOWER GHOST ...?!
WHAT IS IT DOING *HERE* ...?!
I HAVE A REQUEST.

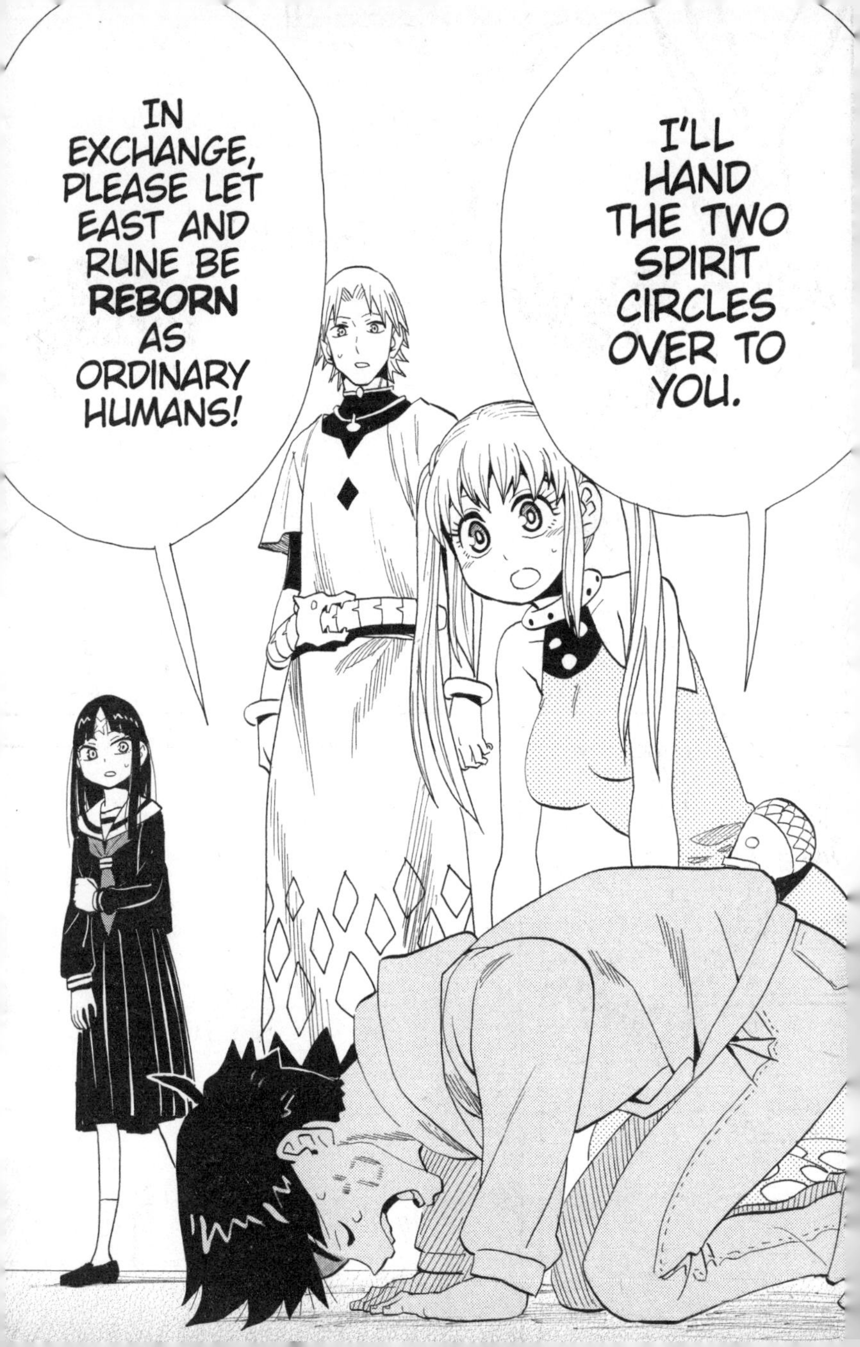
I'LL HAND THE TWO SPIRIT CIRCLES OVER TO YOU.
IN EXCHANGE, PLEASE LET EAST AND RUNE BE REBORN AS ORDINARY HUMANS!

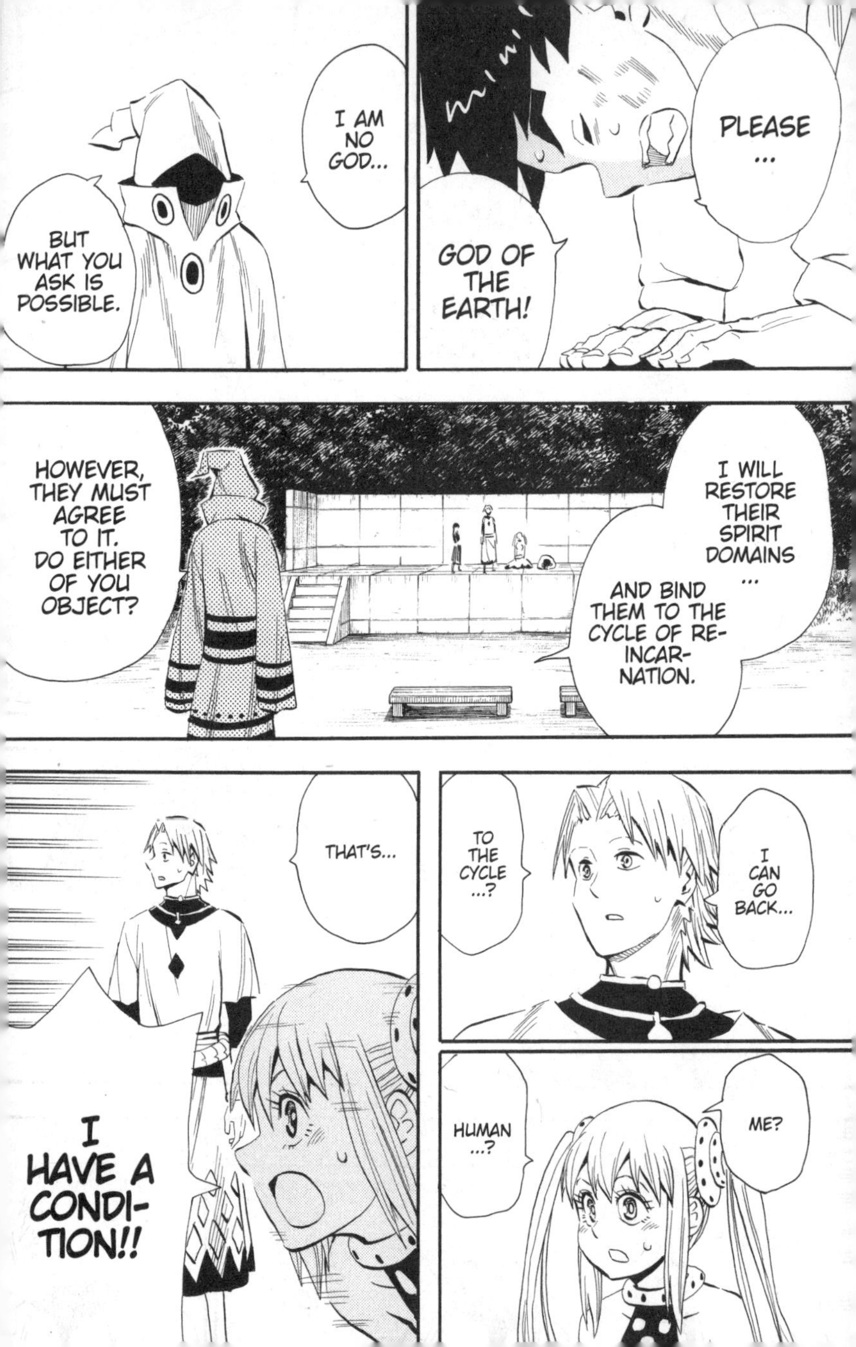
PLEASE ...
GOD OF THE EARTH!
I AM NO GOD...
BUT WHAT YOU ASK IS POSSIBLE.
I WILL RESTORE THEIR SPIRIT DOMAINS ...
AND BIND THEM TO THE CYCLE OF RE-INCARNATION.
HOWEVER, THEY MUST AGREE TO IT. DO EITHER OF YOU OBJECT?
I CAN GO BACK...
TO THE CYCLE ...?
ME?
HUMAN ...?
THAT'S...
I HAVE A CONDITION!!

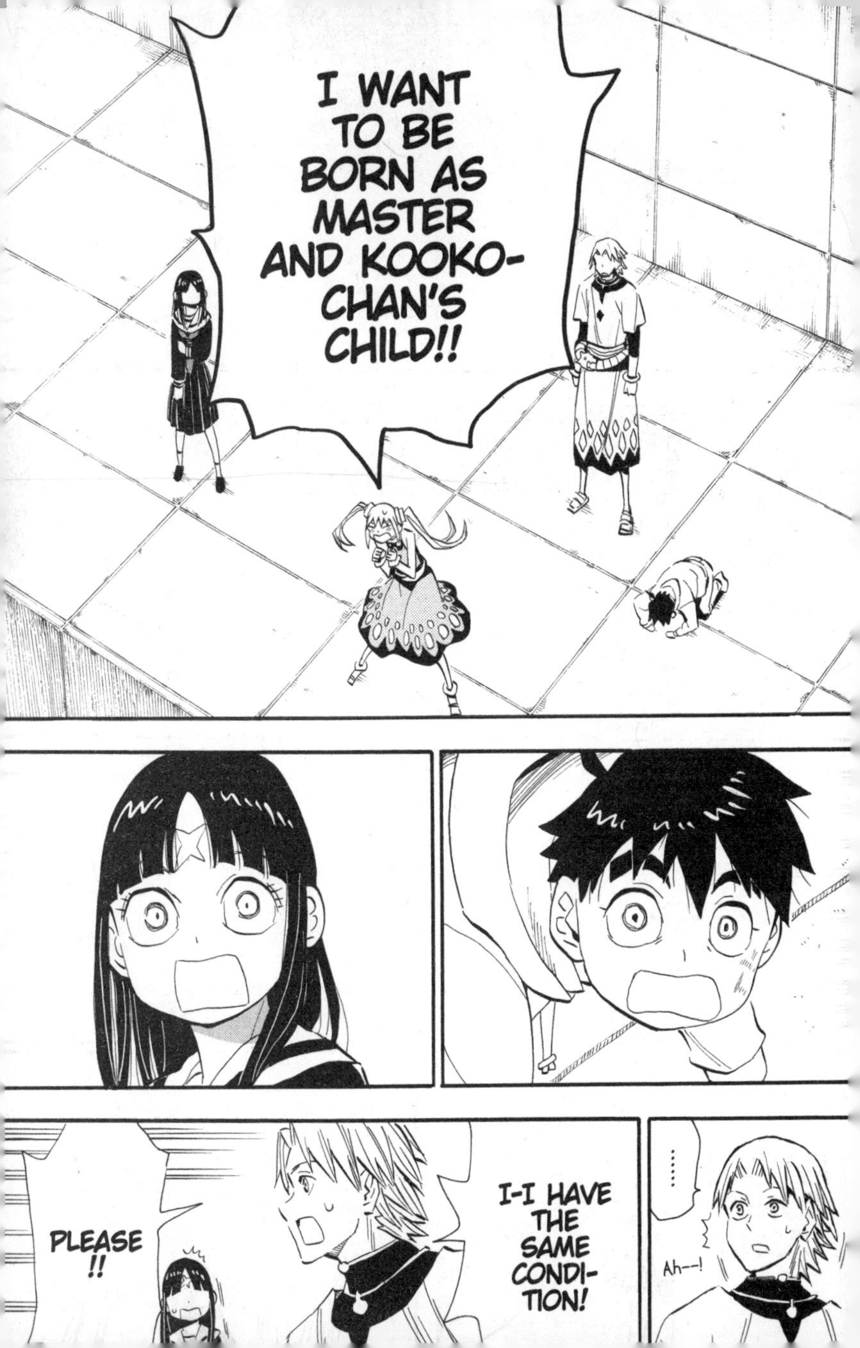
I WANT TO BE BORN AS MASTER AND KOOKO-CHAN'S CHILD!!
......
Ah--!
I-I HAVE THE SAME CONDITION!
PLEASE!!

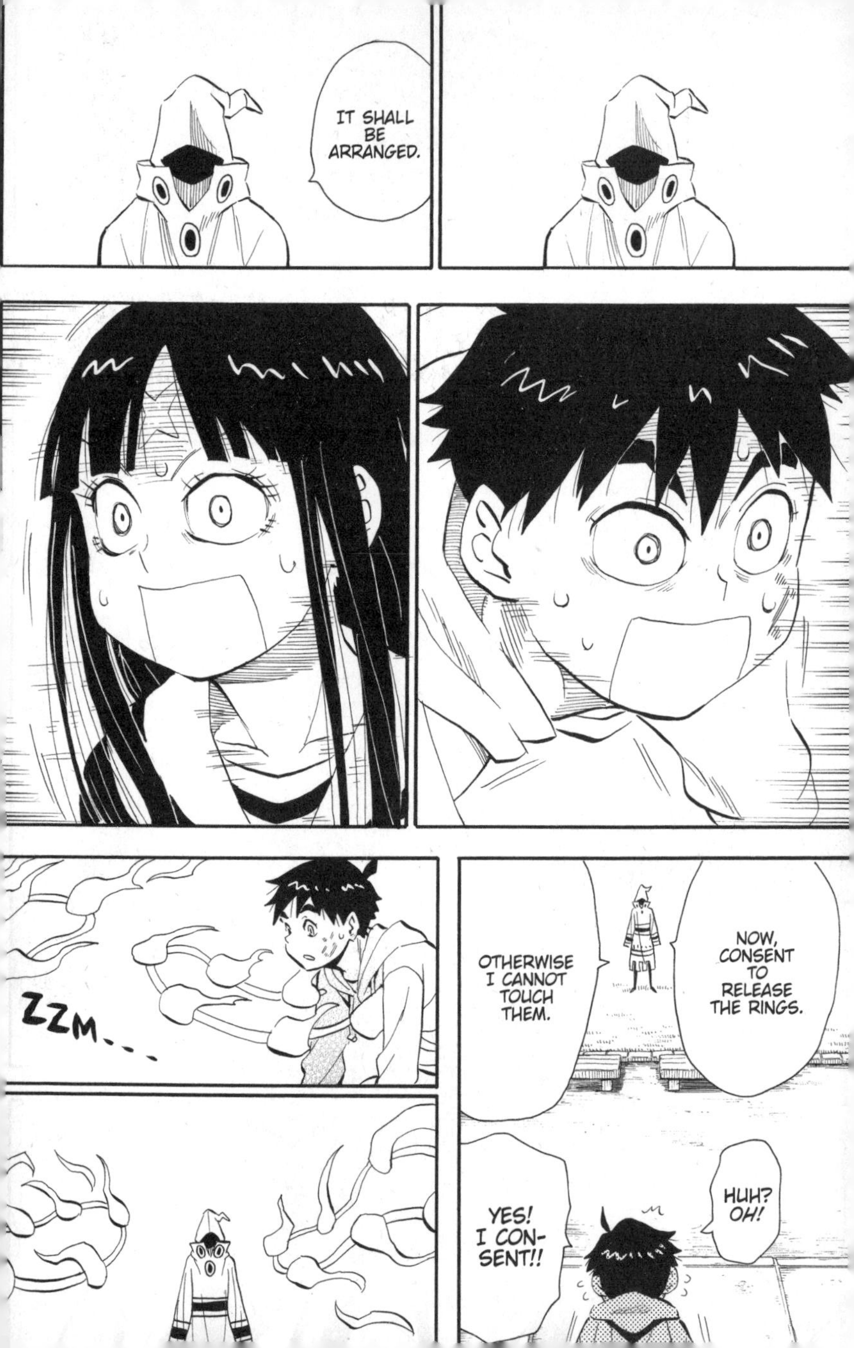
IT SHALL BE ARRANGED.
NOW, CONSENT TO RELEASE THE RINGS.
OTHERWISE I CANNOT TOUCH THEM.
HUH? OH!
YES! I CON-SENT!!
ZZM....

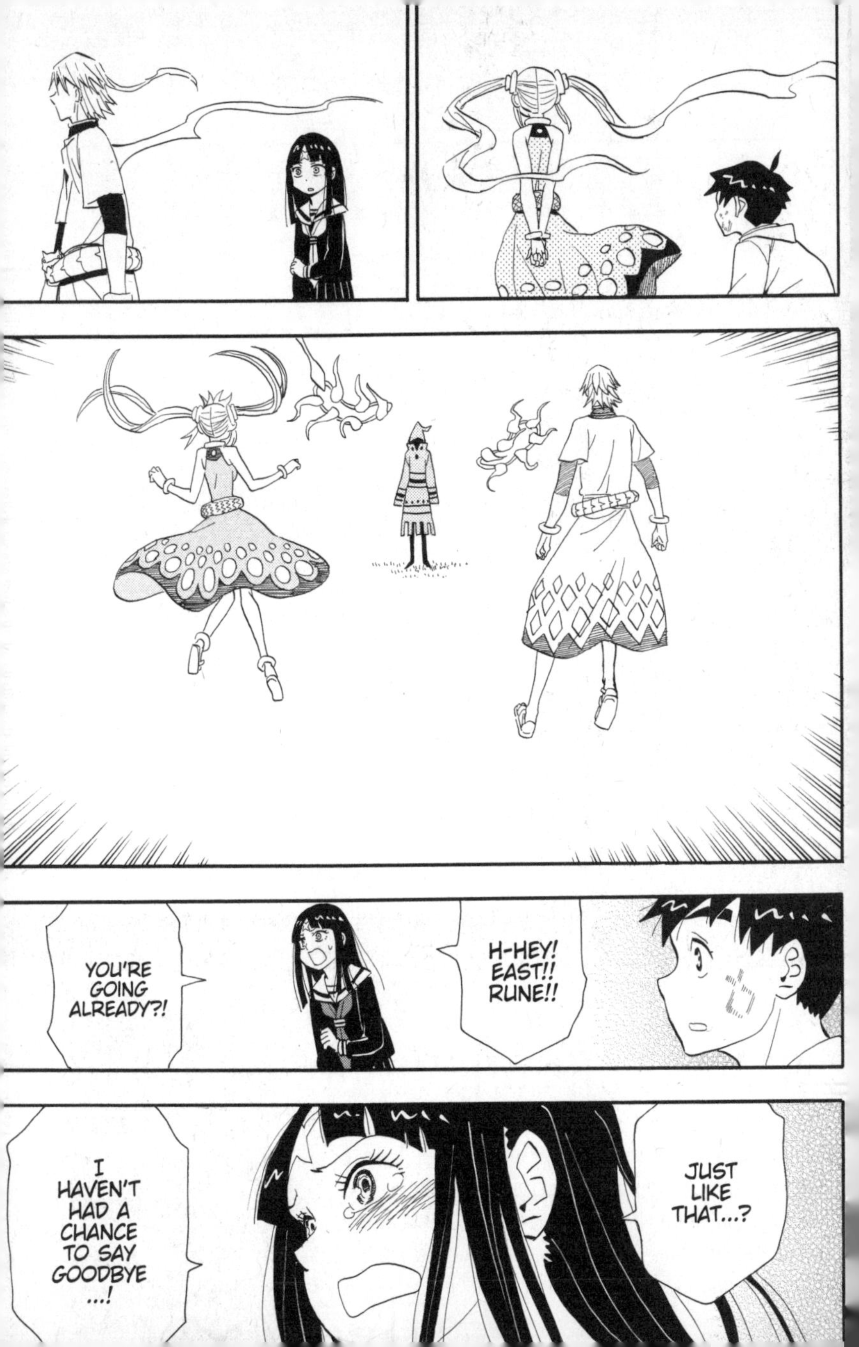
H-HEY! EAST!! RUNE!!
YOU'RE GOING ALREADY?!
JUST LIKE THAT...?
I HAVEN'T HAD A CHANCE TO SAY GOODBYE...!

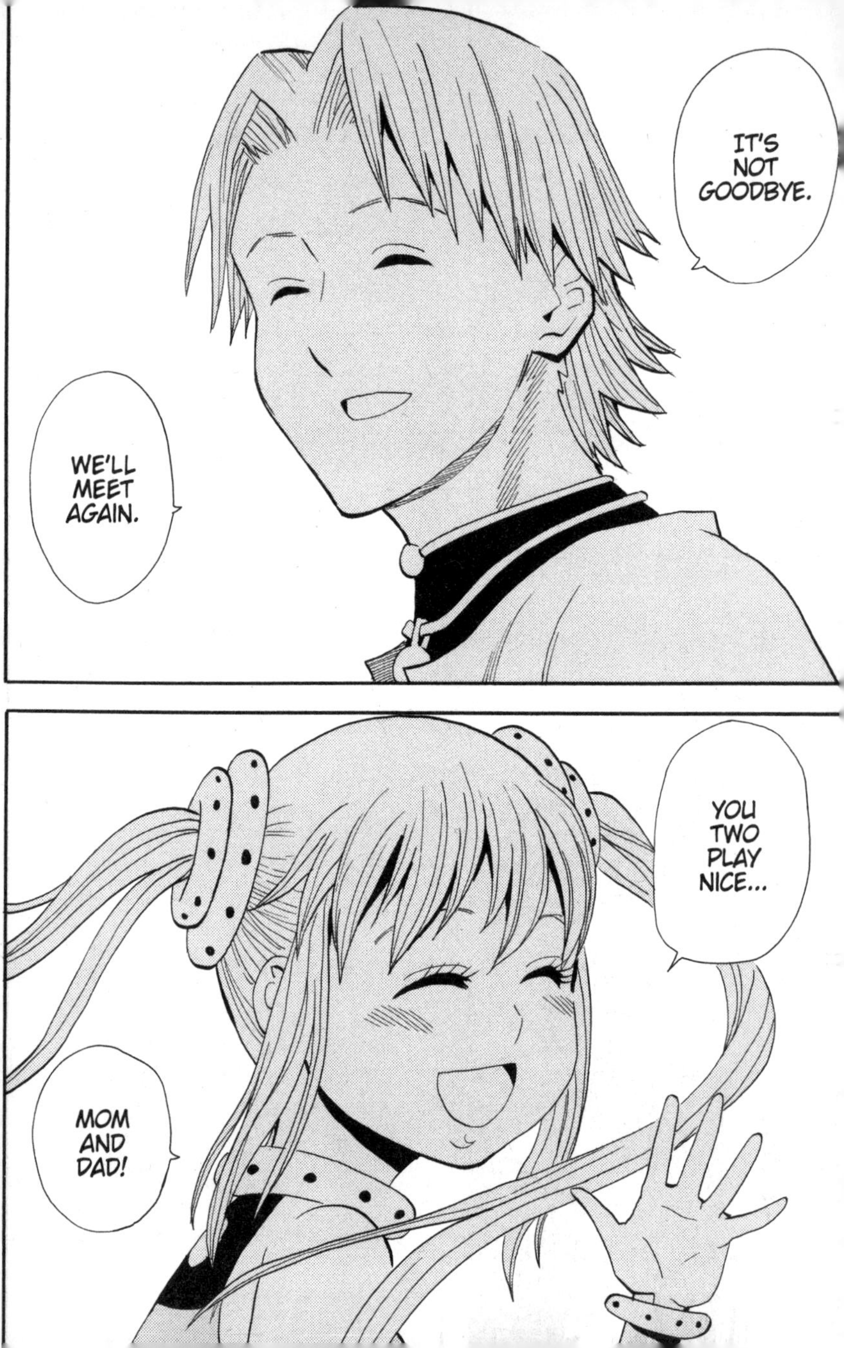
IT'S NOT GOODBYE.
WE'LL MEET AGAIN.
YOU TWO PLAY NICE...
MOM AND DAD!

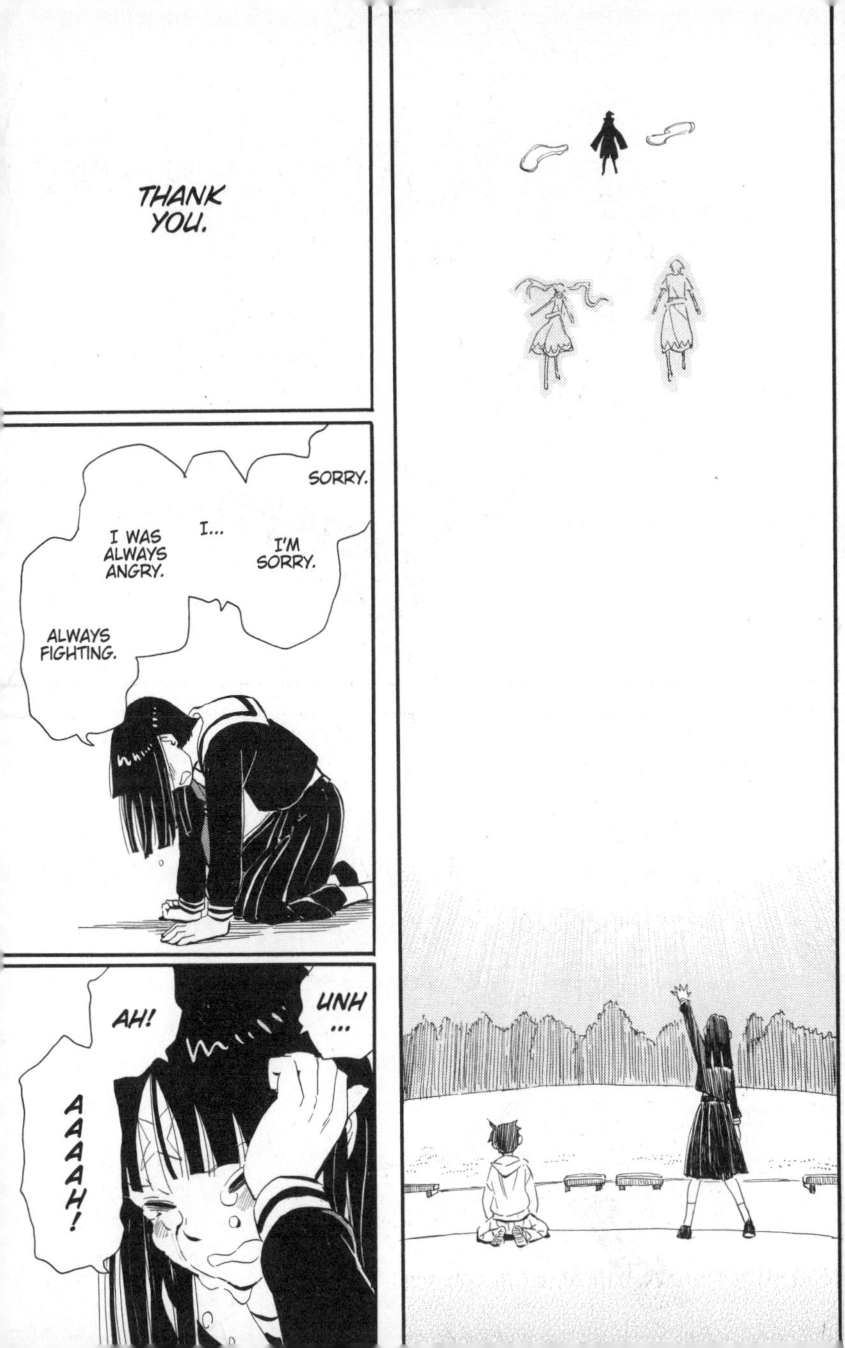
THANK YOU.
SORRY.
I'M SORRY.
I...
I WAS ALWAYS ANGRY.
ALWAYS FIGHTING.
UNH ...
AH!
AAAAAH!

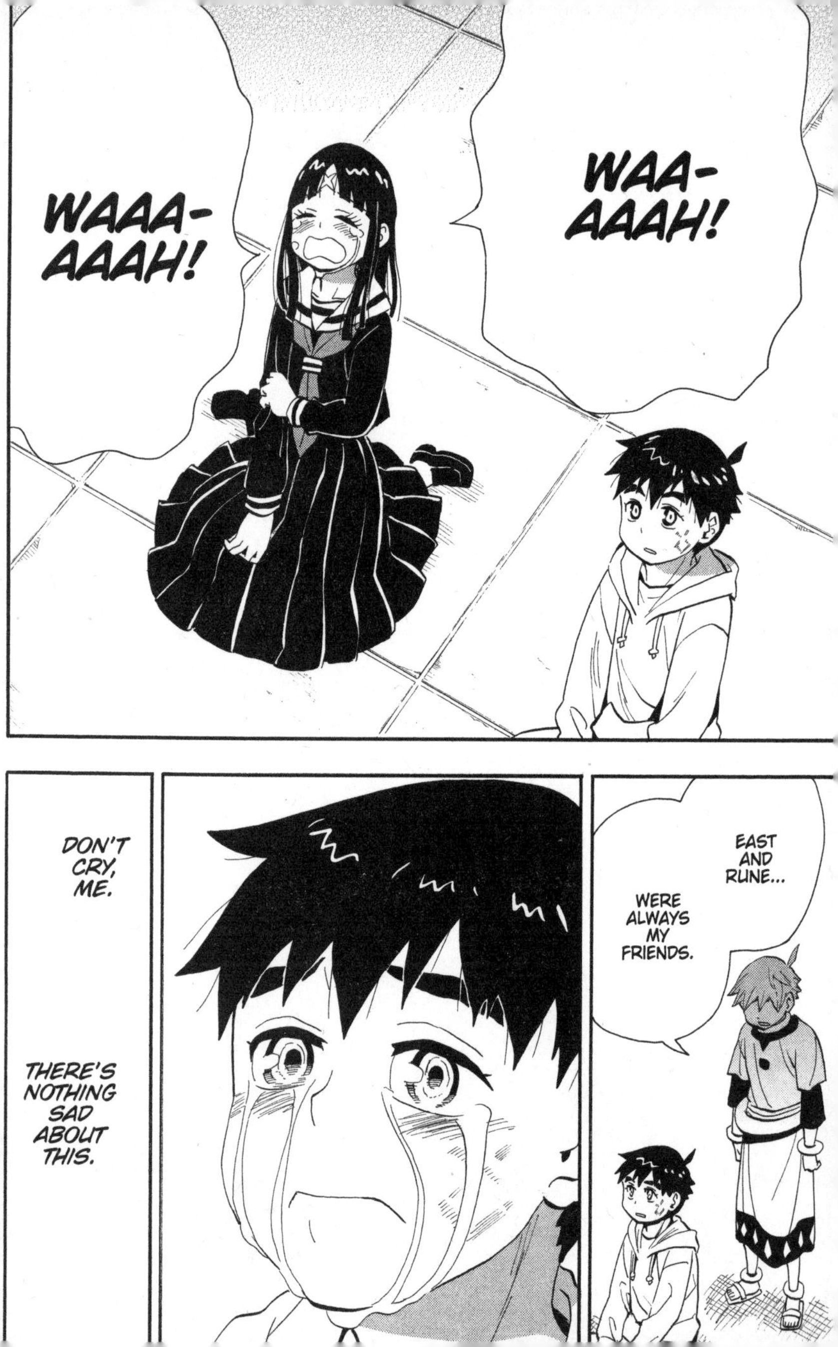
WAA-AAAH!
WAAAA-AAAH!
EAST AND RUNE...
WERE ALWAYS MY FRIENDS.
DON'T CRY, ME.
THERE'S NOTHING SAD ABOUT THIS.

Spirit Circle

Spirit Circle

Circle 45

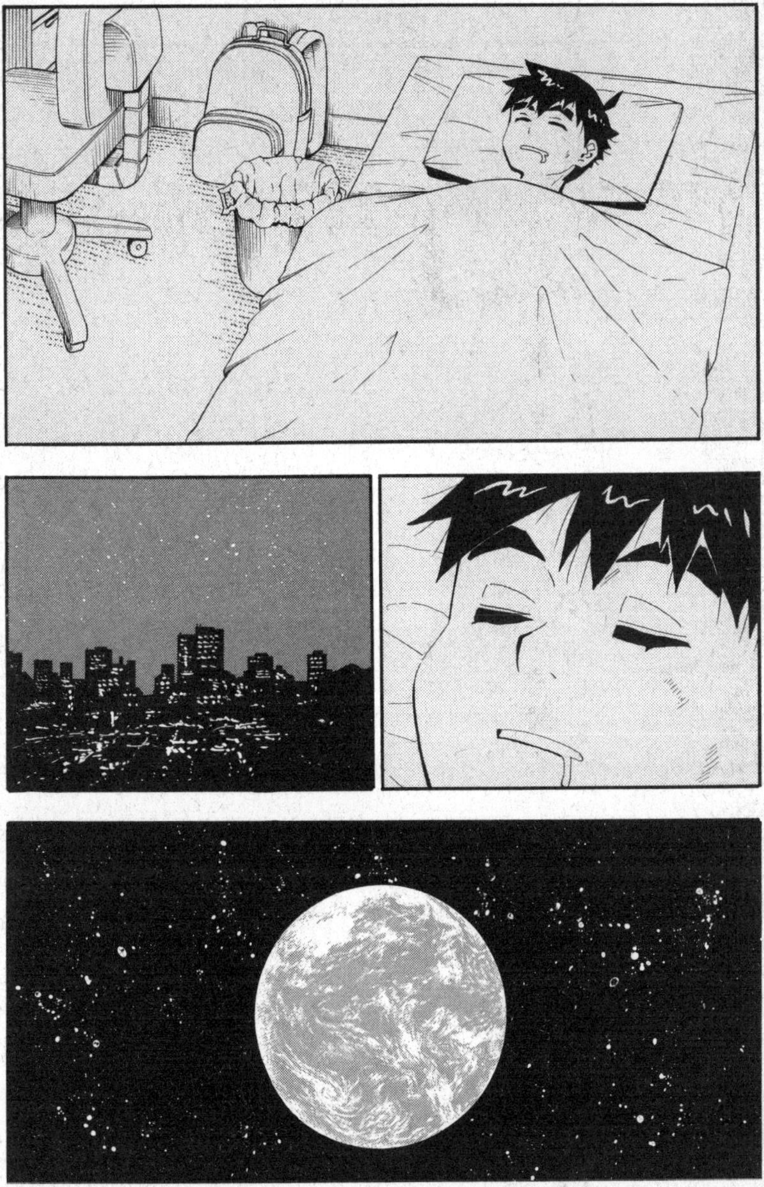

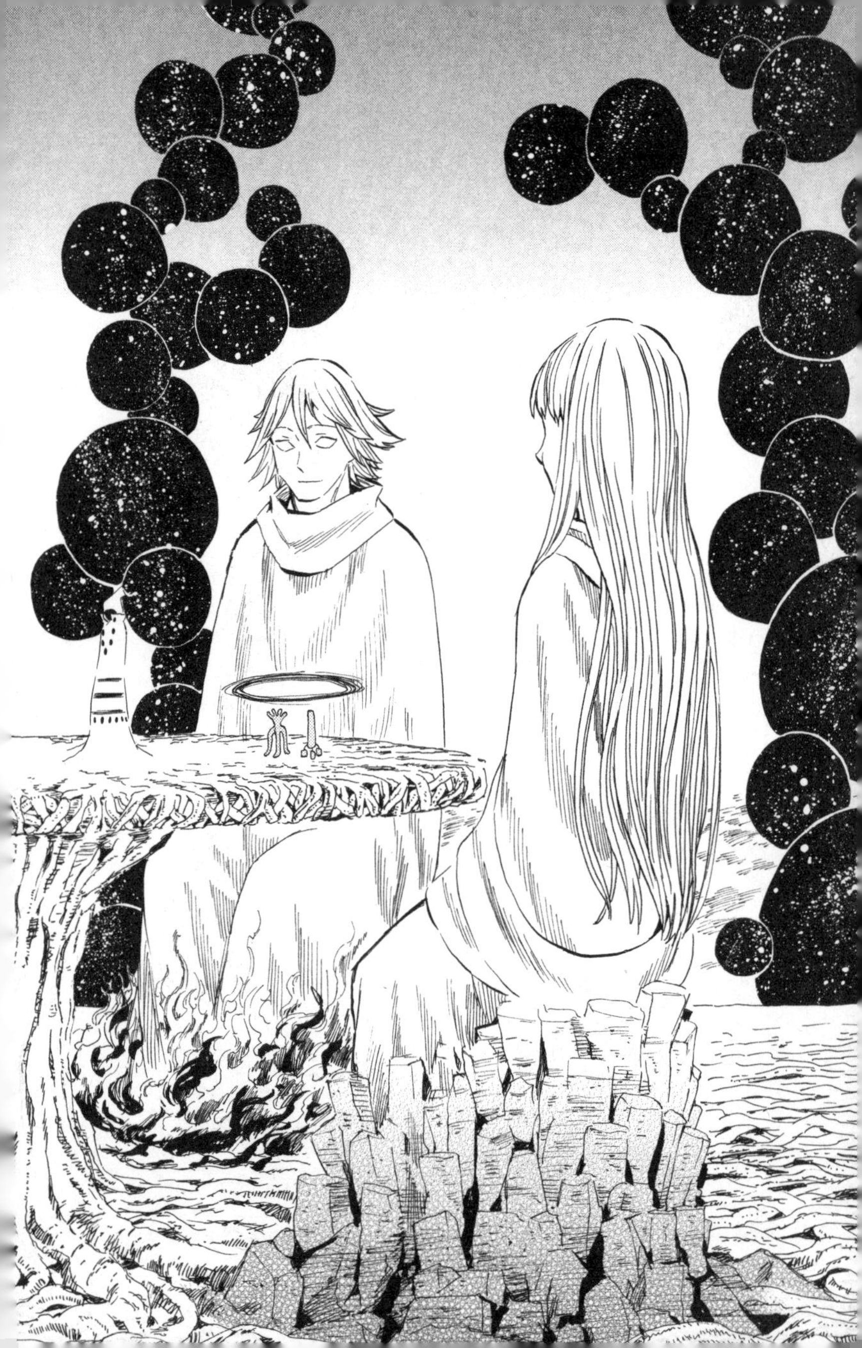

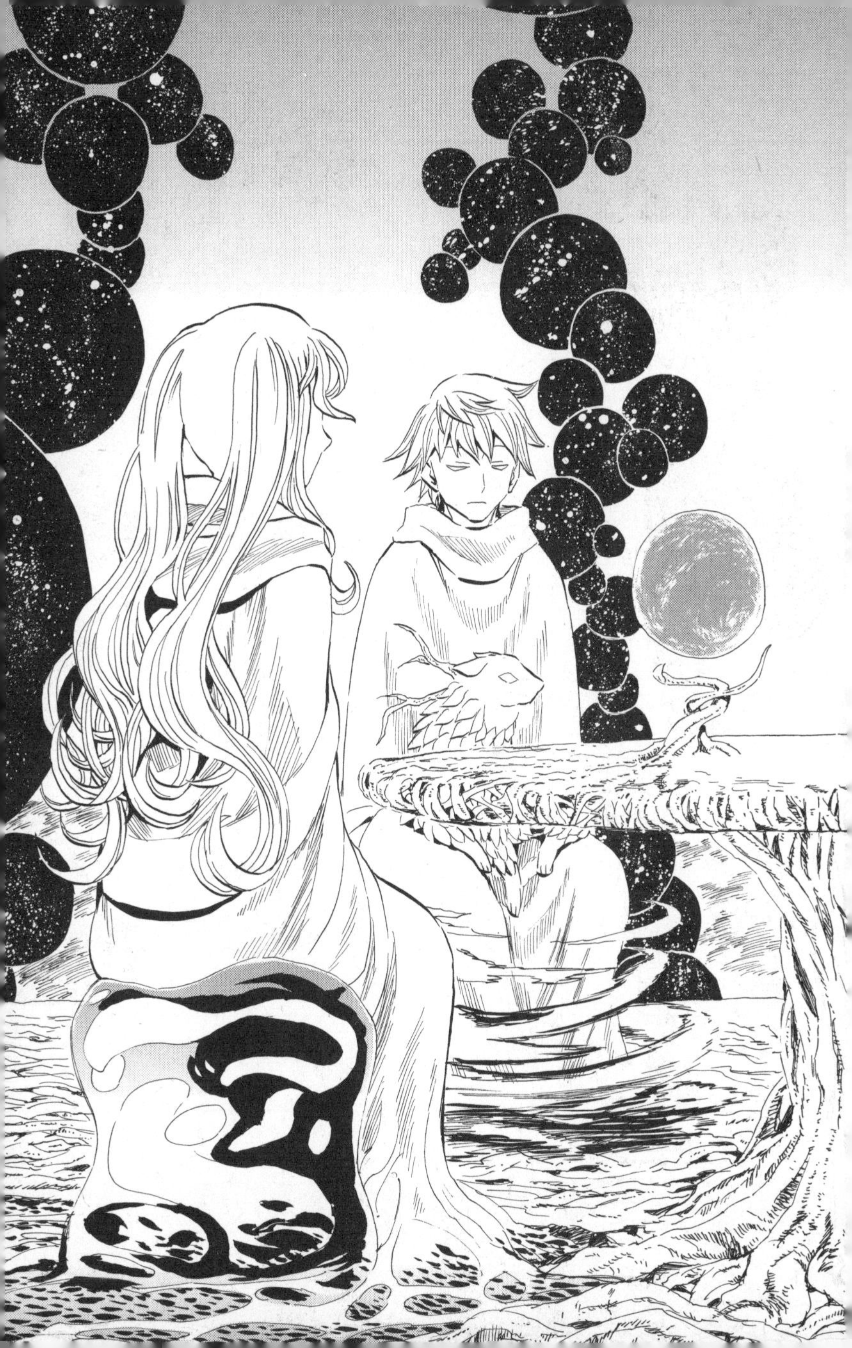

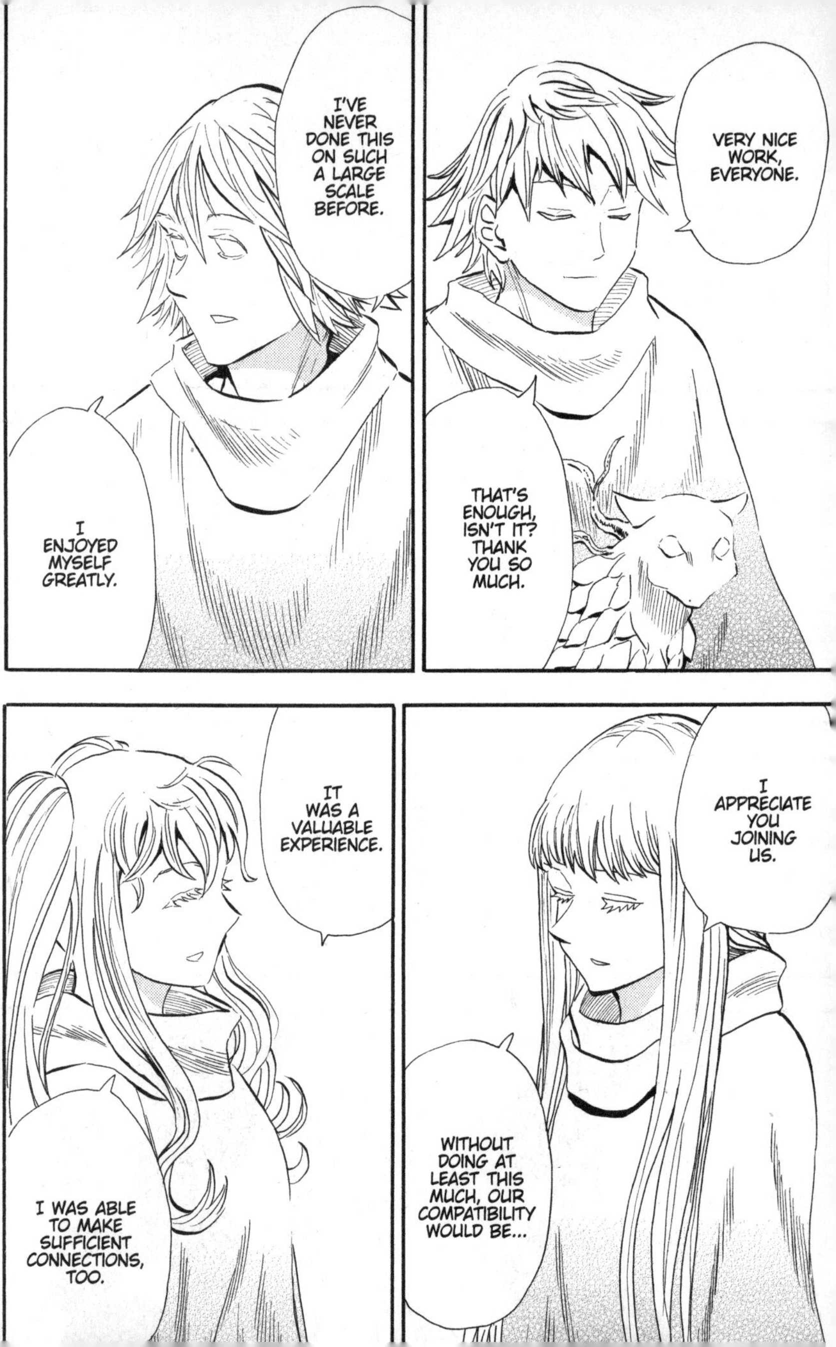
VERY NICE WORK, EVERYONE.
THAT'S ENOUGH, ISN'T IT? THANK YOU SO MUCH.
I'VE NEVER DONE THIS ON SUCH A LARGE SCALE BEFORE.
I ENJOYED MYSELF GREATLY.
I APPRECIATE YOU JOINING US.
WITHOUT DOING AT LEAST THIS MUCH, OUR COMPATIBILITY WOULD BE...
IT WAS A VALUABLE EXPERIENCE.
I WAS ABLE TO MAKE SUFFICIENT CONNECTIONS, TOO.

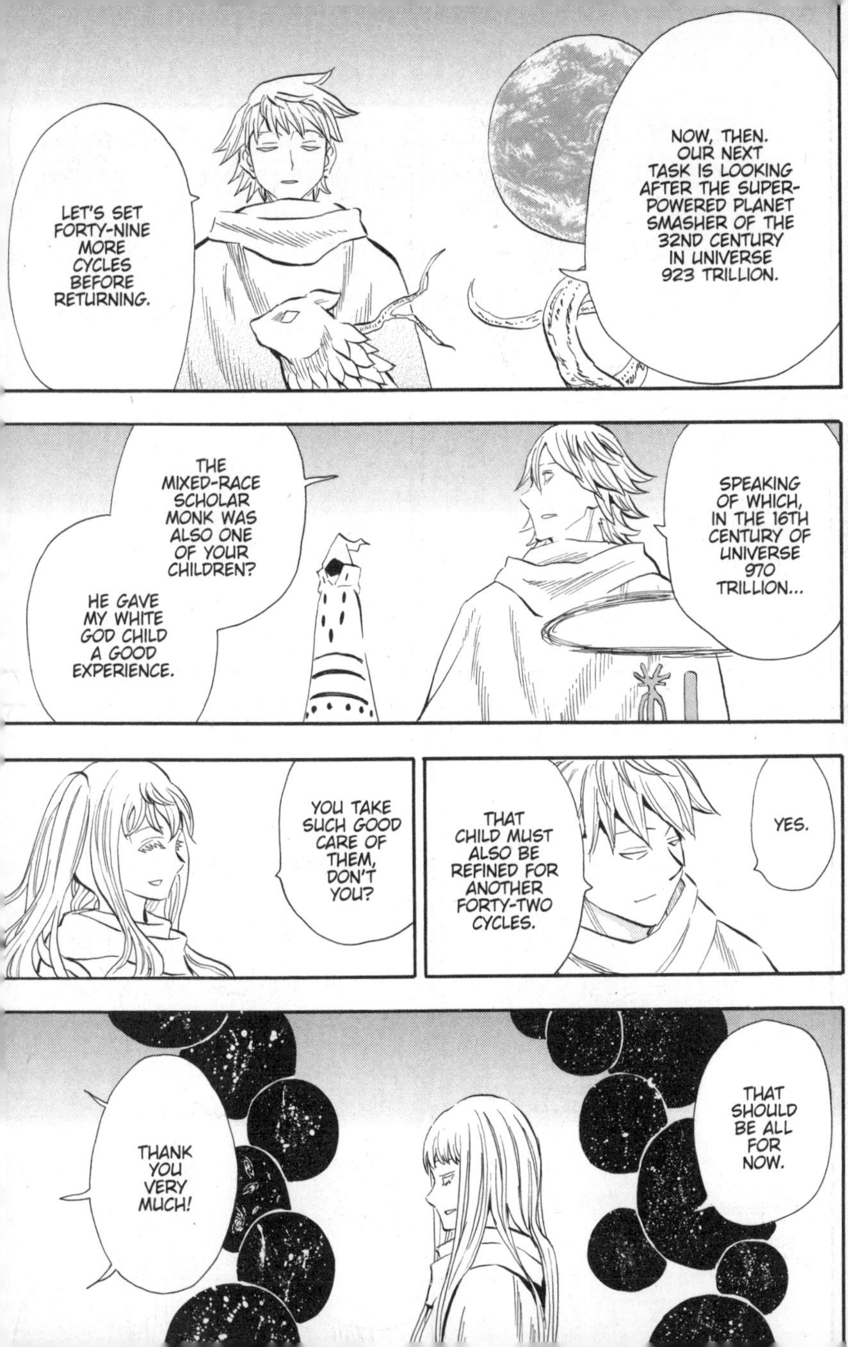
NOW, THEN. OUR NEXT TASK IS LOOKING AFTER THE SUPER-POWERED PLANET SMASHER OF THE 32ND CENTURY IN UNIVERSE 923 TRILLION.
LET'S SET FORTY-NINE MORE CYCLES BEFORE RETURNING.
SPEAKING OF WHICH, IN THE 16TH CENTURY OF UNIVERSE 970 TRILLION...
THE MIXED-RACE SCHOLAR MONK WAS ALSO ONE OF YOUR CHILDREN?
HE GAVE MY WHITE GOD CHILD A GOOD EXPERIENCE.
YES.
THAT CHILD MUST ALSO BE REFINED FOR ANOTHER FORTY-TWO CYCLES.
YOU TAKE SUCH GOOD CARE OF THEM, DON'T YOU?
THAT SHOULD BE ALL FOR NOW.
THANK YOU VERY MUCH!

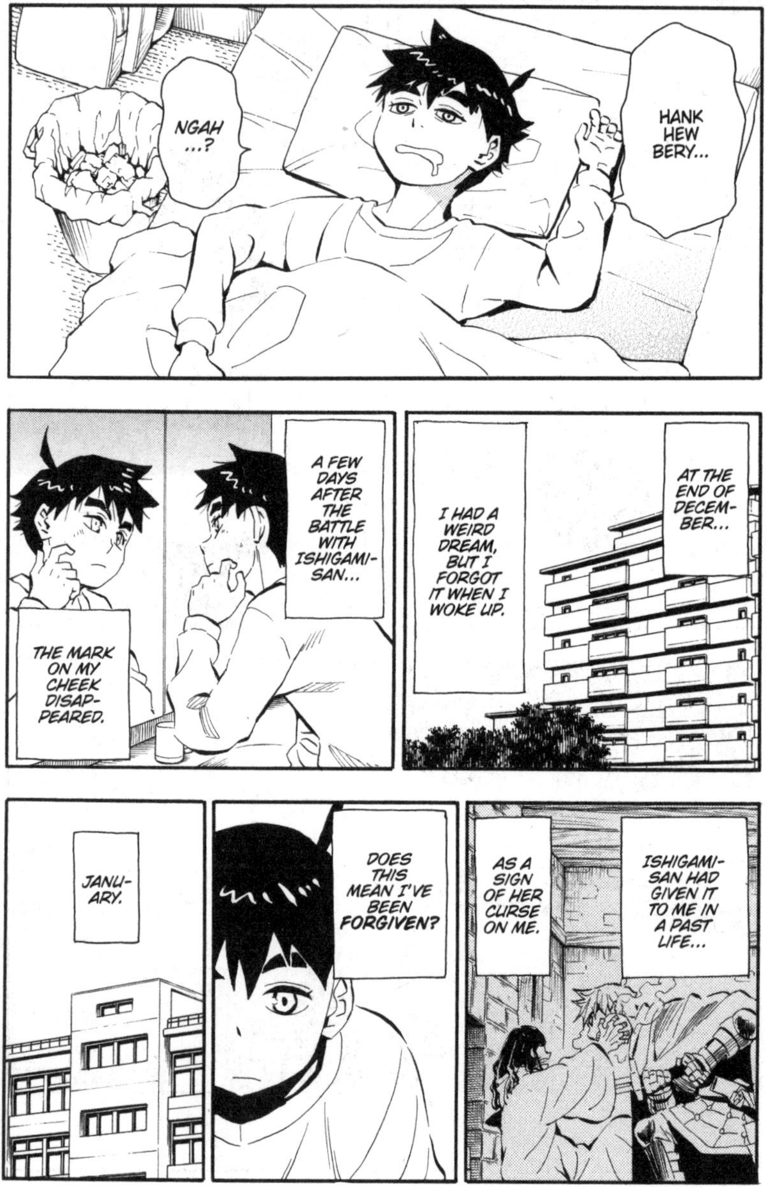
HANK HEW BERY...
NGAH ...?
AT THE END OF DECEMBER...
I HAD A WEIRD DREAM, BUT I FORGOT IT WHEN I WOKE UP.
A FEW DAYS AFTER THE BATTLE WITH ISHIGAMI-SAN...
THE MARK ON MY CHEEK DISAPPEARED.
ISHIGAMI-SAN HAD GIVEN IT TO ME IN A PAST LIFE...
AS A SIGN OF HER CURSE ON ME.
DOES THIS MEAN I'VE BEEN FORGIVEN?
JANUARY.

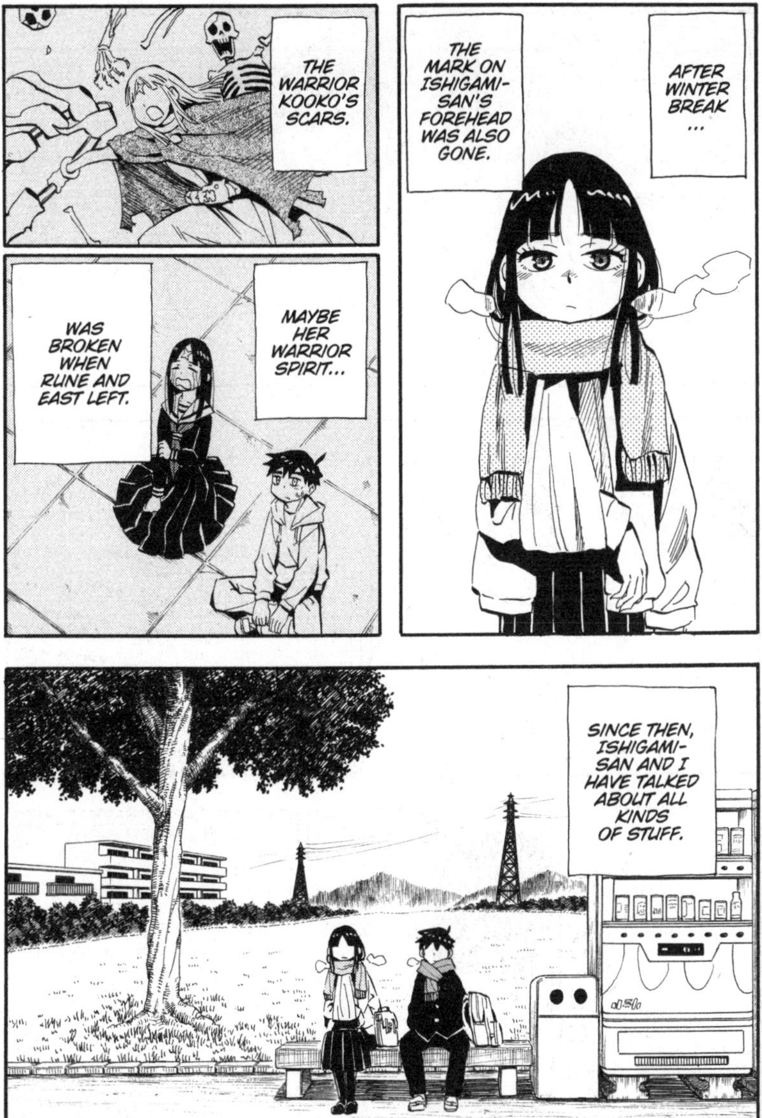
AFTER WINTER BREAK ...
THE MARK ON ISHIGAMI-SAN'S FOREHEAD WAS ALSO GONE.
THE WARRIOR KOOKO'S SCARS.
MAYBE HER WARRIOR SPIRIT...
WAS BROKEN WHEN RUNE AND EAST LEFT.
SINCE THEN, ISHIGAMI-SAN AND I HAVE TALKED ABOUT ALL KINDS OF STUFF.

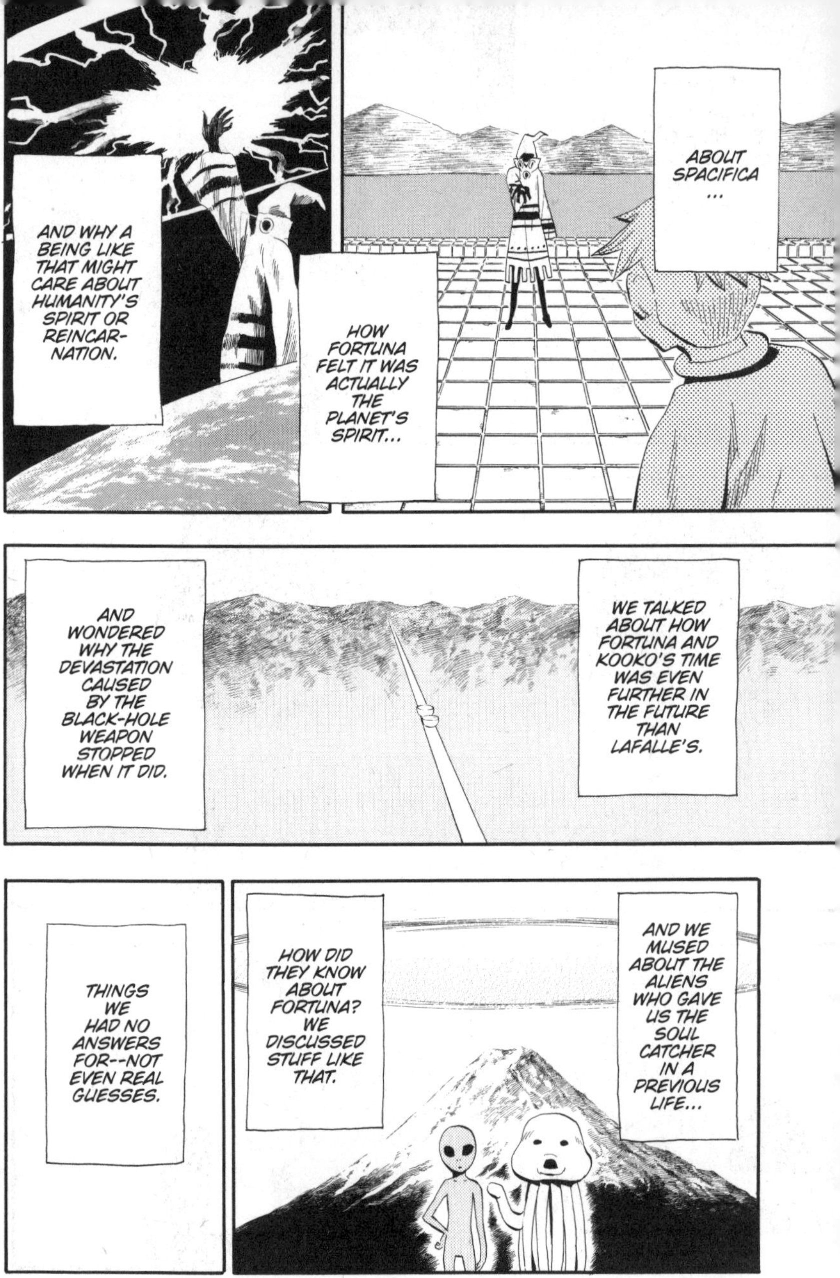
ABOUT SPACIFICA ...
HOW FORTUNA FELT IT WAS ACTUALLY THE PLANET'S SPIRIT...
AND WHY A BEING LIKE THAT MIGHT CARE ABOUT HUMANITY'S SPIRIT OR REINCAR-NATION.
WE TALKED ABOUT HOW FORTUNA AND KOOKO'S TIME WAS EVEN FURTHER IN THE FUTURE THAN LAFALLE'S.
AND WONDERED WHY THE DEVASTATION CAUSED BY THE BLACK-HOLE WEAPON STOPPED WHEN IT DID.
AND WE MUSED ABOUT THE ALIENS WHO GAVE US THE SOUL CATCHER IN A PREVIOUS LIFE...
HOW DID THEY KNOW ABOUT FORTUNA? WE DISCUSSED STUFF LIKE THAT.
THINGS WE HAD NO ANSWERS FOR--NOT EVEN REAL GUESSES.

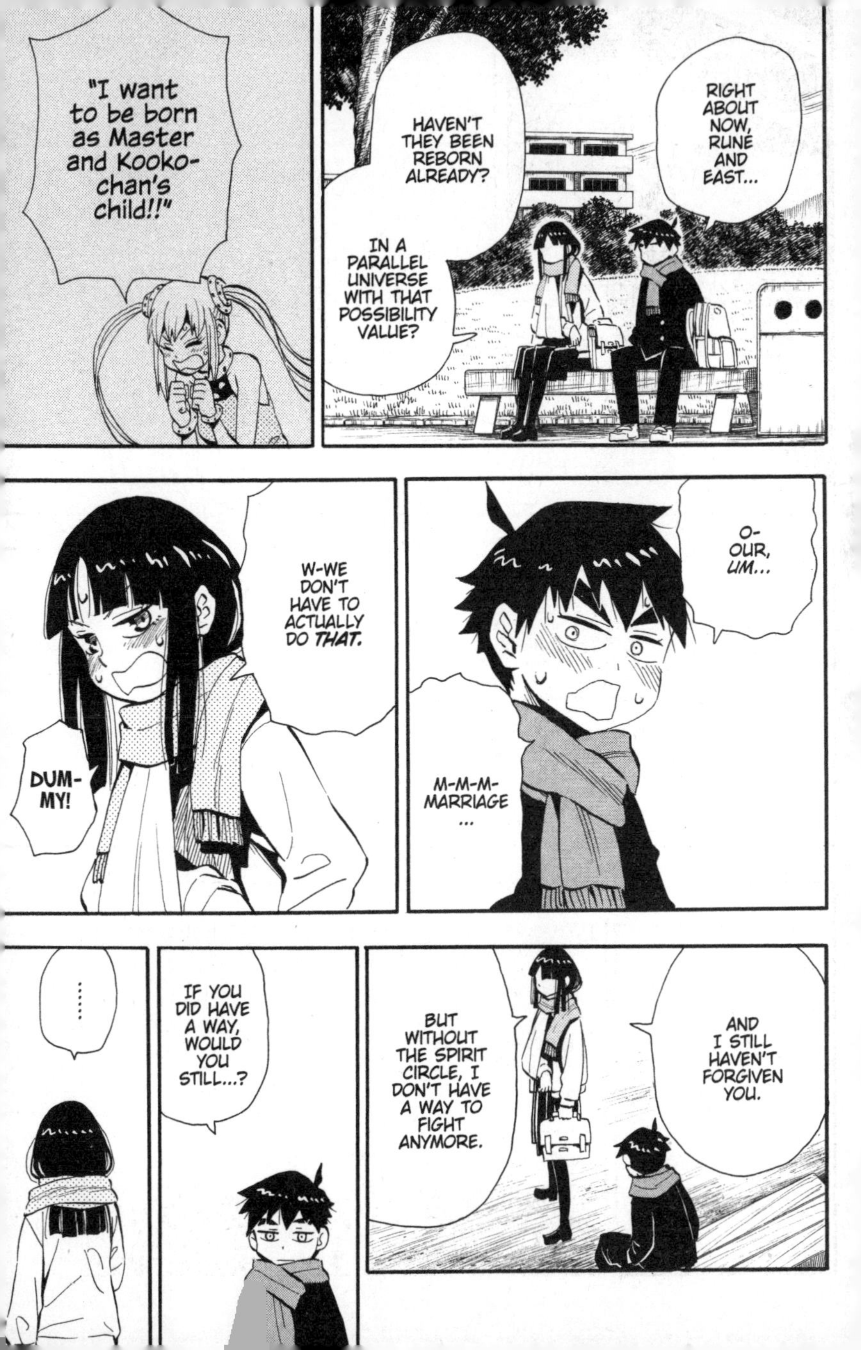
RIGHT ABOUT NOW, RUNE AND EAST...
HAVEN'T THEY BEEN REBORN ALREADY?
IN A PARALLEL UNIVERSE WITH THAT POSSIBILITY VALUE?
"I want to be born as Master and Kooko-chan's child!!"
O-OUR, UM...
M-M-M-MARRIAGE...
W-WE DON'T HAVE TO ACTUALLY DO *THAT.*
DUM-MY!
AND I STILL HAVEN'T FORGIVEN YOU.
BUT WITHOUT THE SPIRIT CIRCLE, I DON'T HAVE A WAY TO FIGHT ANYMORE.
IF YOU DID HAVE A WAY, WOULD YOU STILL...?
......

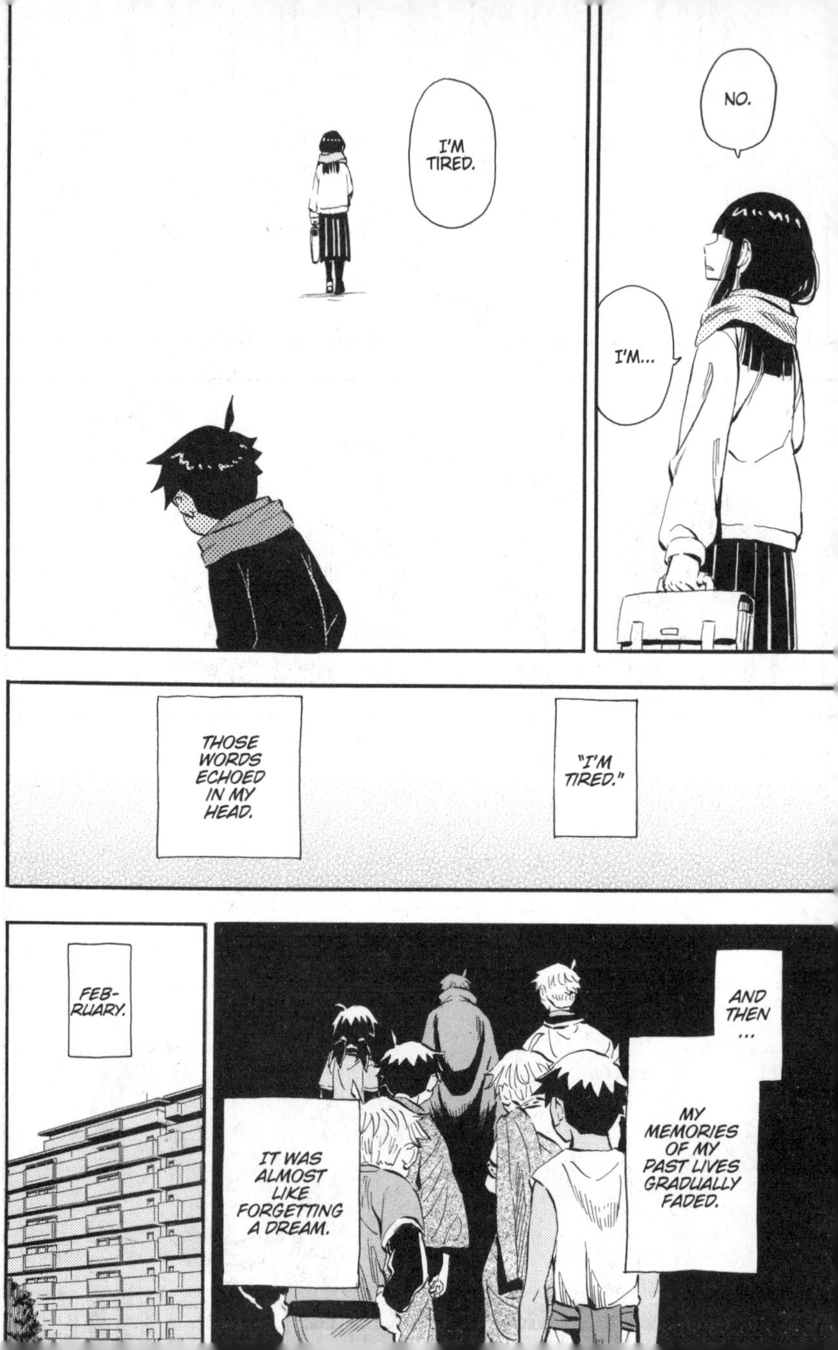
NO.
I'M...
I'M TIRED.
"I'M TIRED."
THOSE WORDS ECHOED IN MY HEAD.
AND THEN...
MY MEMORIES OF MY PAST LIVES GRADUALLY FADED.
IT WAS ALMOST LIKE FORGETTING A DREAM.
FEB-RUARY.

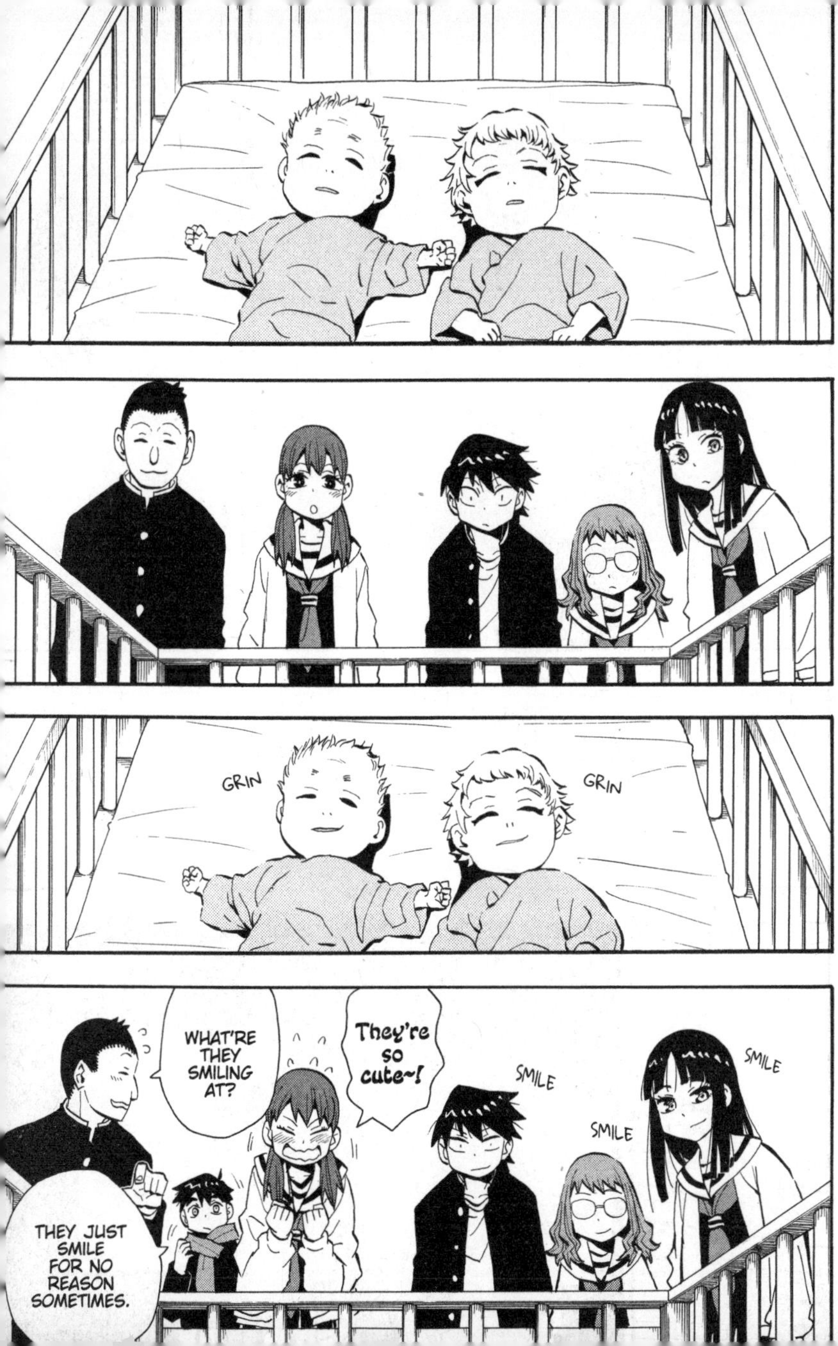
GRIN
GRIN
SMILE
SMILE
SMILE
They're so cute~!
WHAT'RE THEY SMILING AT?
THEY JUST SMILE FOR NO REASON SOMETIMES.

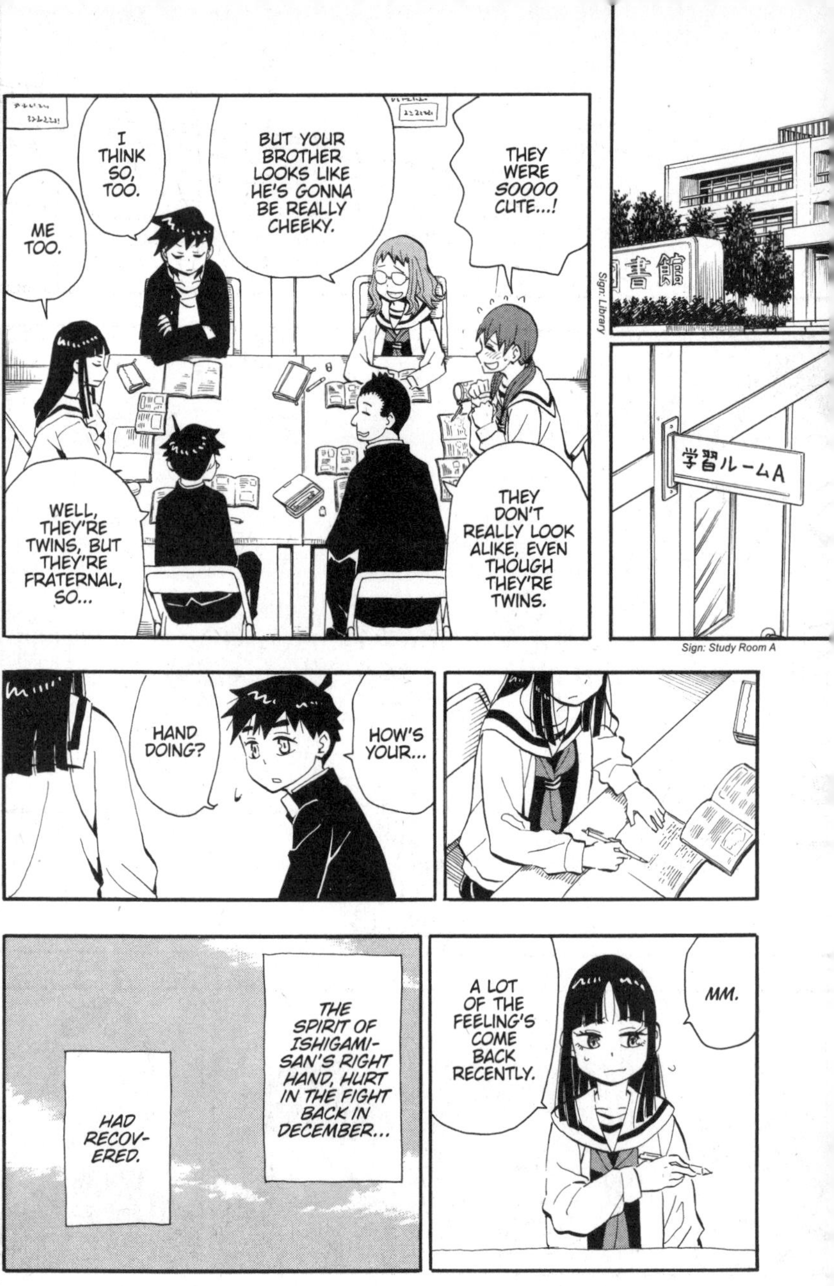

図書館
Sign: Library
学習ルームA
Sign: Study Room A
THEY WERE SOOOO CUTE...!
THEY DON'T REALLY LOOK ALIKE, EVEN THOUGH THEY'RE TWINS.
WELL, THEY'RE TWINS, BUT THEY'RE FRATERNAL, SO...
BUT YOUR BROTHER LOOKS LIKE HE'S GONNA BE REALLY CHEEKY.
I THINK SO, TOO.
ME TOO.
HOW'S YOUR...
HAND DOING?
MM.
A LOT OF THE FEELING'S COME BACK RECENTLY.
THE SPIRIT OF ISHIGAMI-SAN'S RIGHT HAND, HURT IN THE FIGHT BACK IN DECEMBER...
HAD RECOVERED.

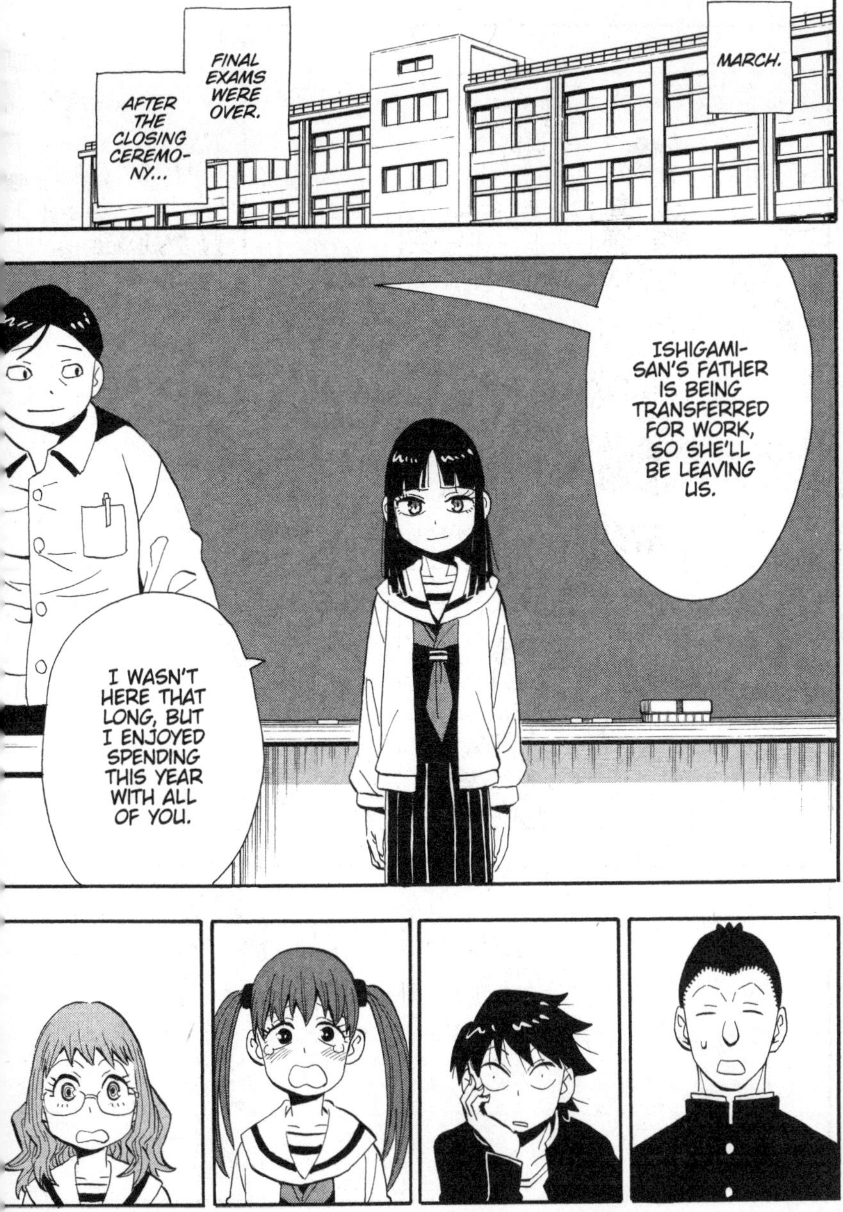
MARCH.
FINAL EXAMS WERE OVER.
AFTER THE CLOSING CEREMO-NY...
ISHIGAMI-SAN'S FATHER IS BEING TRANSFERRED FOR WORK, SO SHE'LL BE LEAVING US.
I WASN'T HERE THAT LONG, BUT I ENJOYED SPENDING THIS YEAR WITH ALL OF YOU.

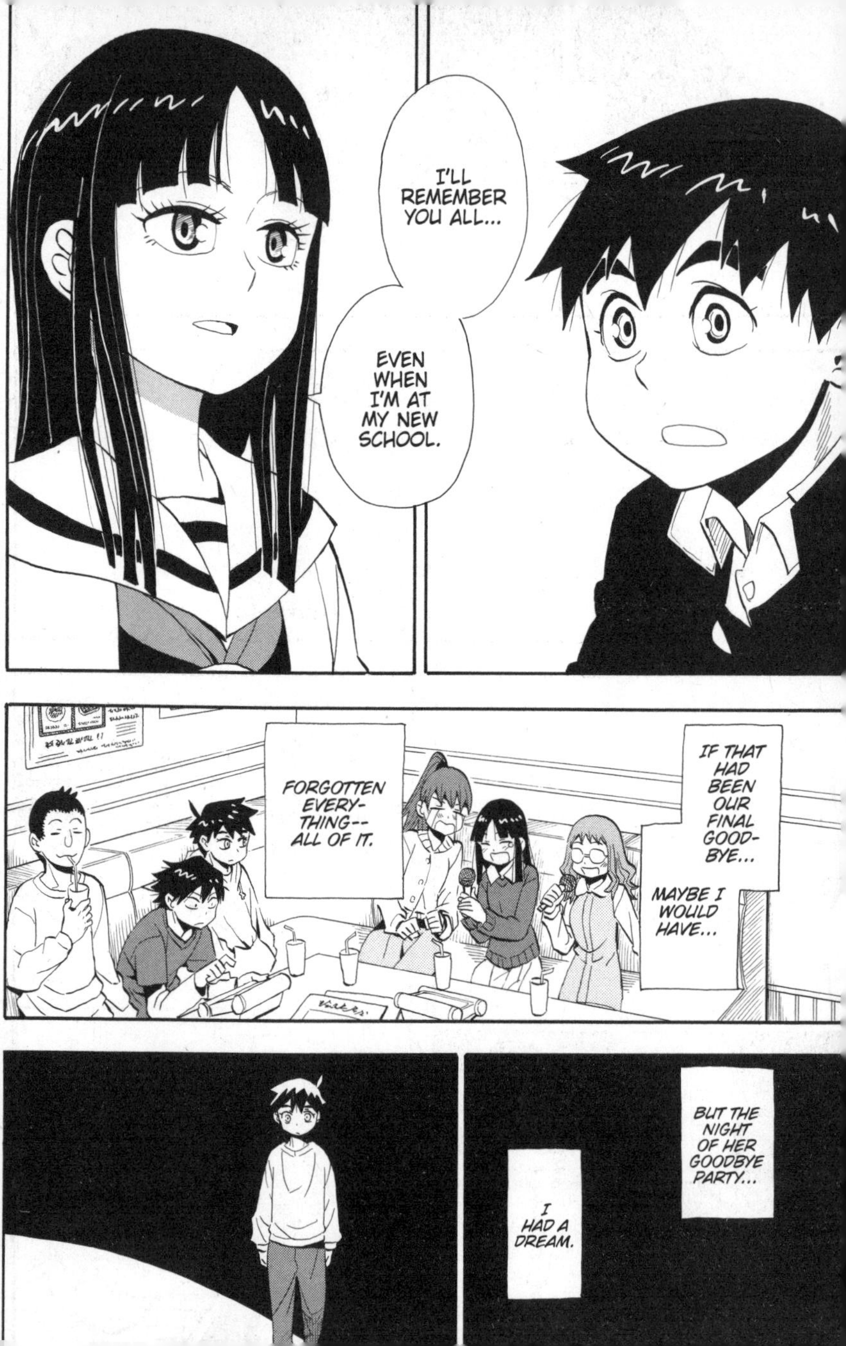
I'LL REMEMBER YOU ALL...
EVEN WHEN I'M AT MY NEW SCHOOL.
IF THAT HAD BEEN OUR FINAL GOOD-BYE...
MAYBE I WOULD HAVE...
FORGOTTEN EVERY-THING--ALL OF IT.
BUT THE NIGHT OF HER GOODBYE PARTY...
I HAD A DREAM.

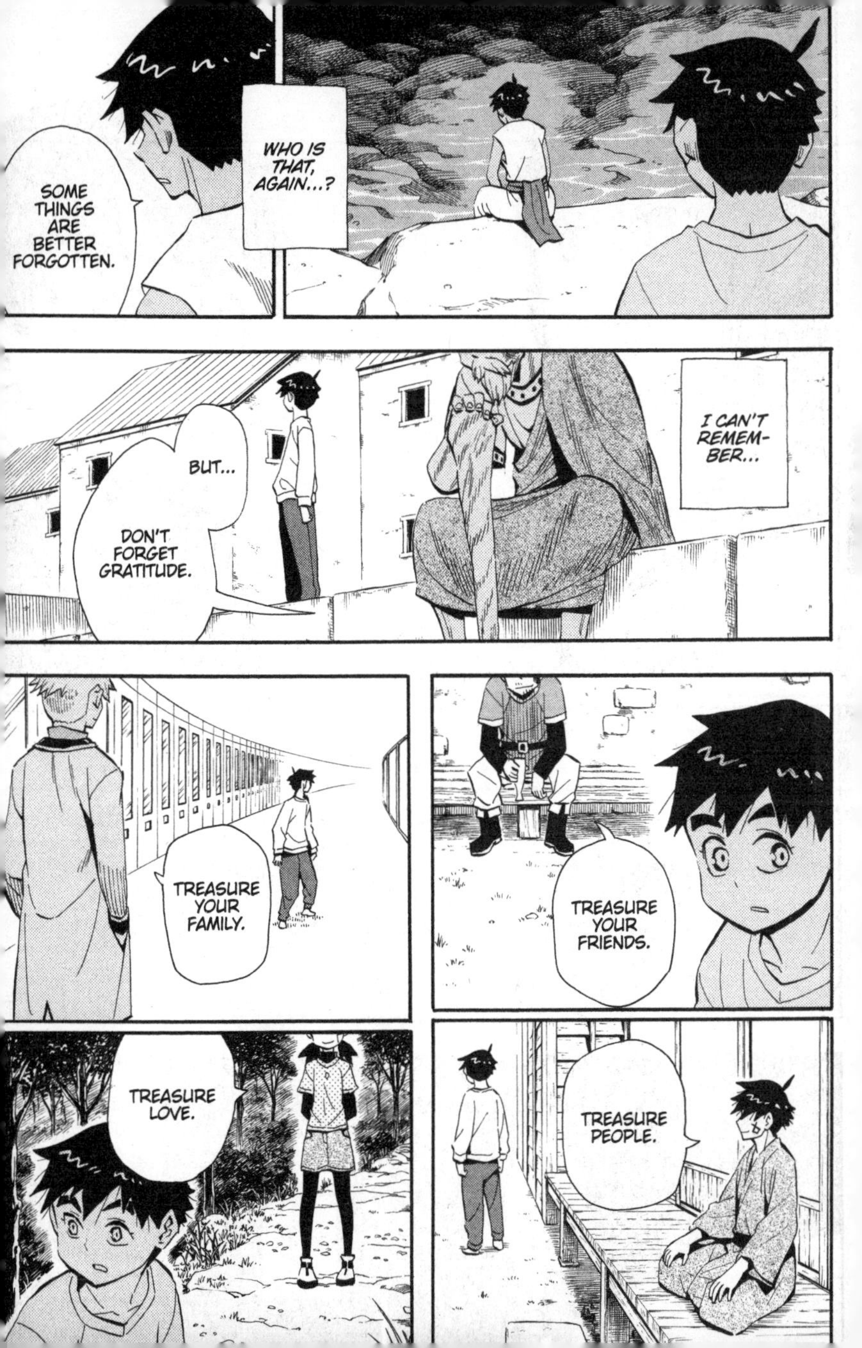
WHO IS THAT, AGAIN...?
SOME THINGS ARE BETTER FORGOTTEN.
I CAN'T REMEMBER...
BUT...
DON'T FORGET GRATITUDE.
TREASURE YOUR FRIENDS.
TREASURE YOUR FAMILY.
TREASURE PEOPLE.
TREASURE LOVE.

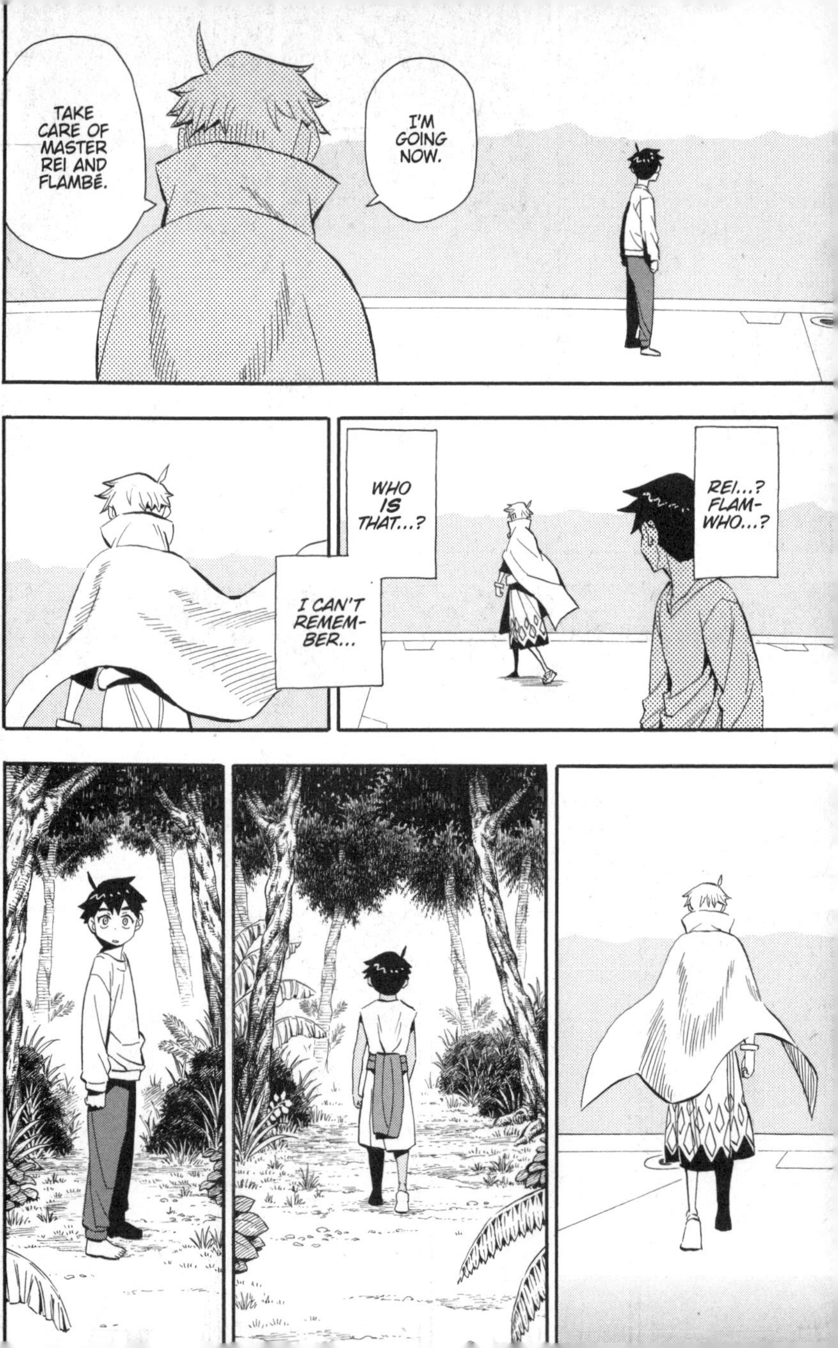
I'M GOING NOW.
TAKE CARE OF MASTER REI AND FLAMBÉ.
REI...? FLAM-WHO...?
WHO IS THAT...?
I CAN'T REMEMBER...

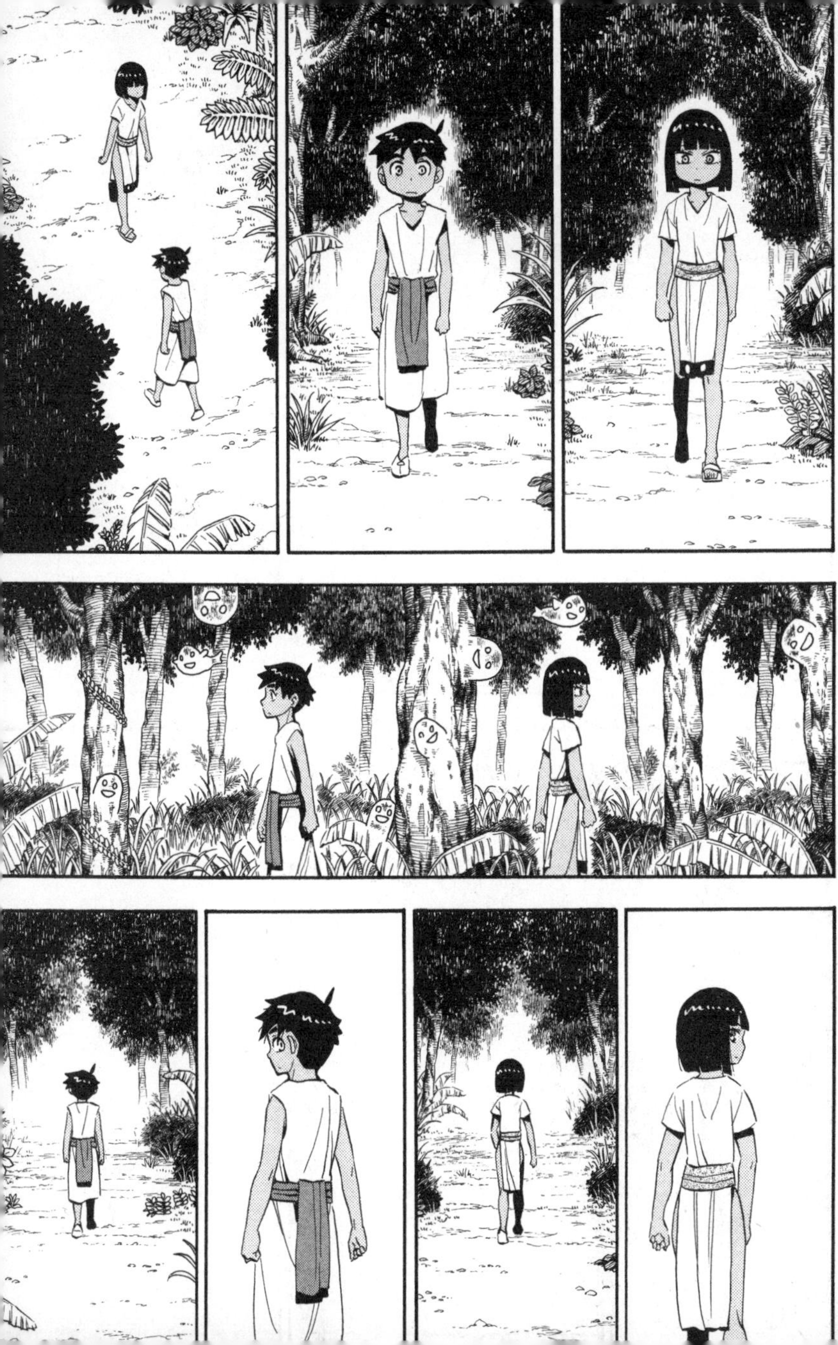

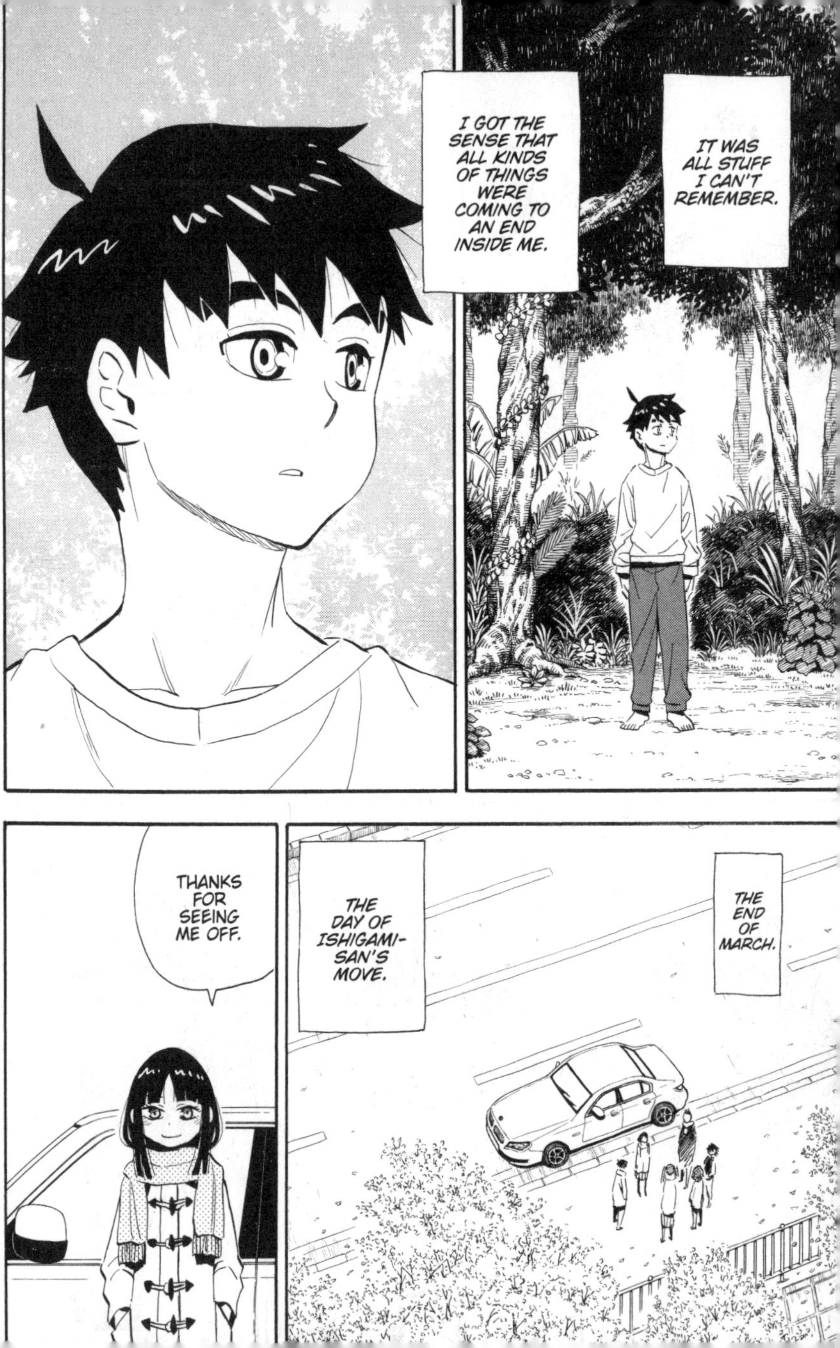
IT WAS ALL STUFF I CAN'T REMEMBER.
I GOT THE SENSE THAT ALL KINDS OF THINGS WERE COMING TO AN END INSIDE ME.
THE END OF MARCH.
THE DAY OF ISHIGAMI-SAN'S MOVE.
THANKS FOR SEEING ME OFF.

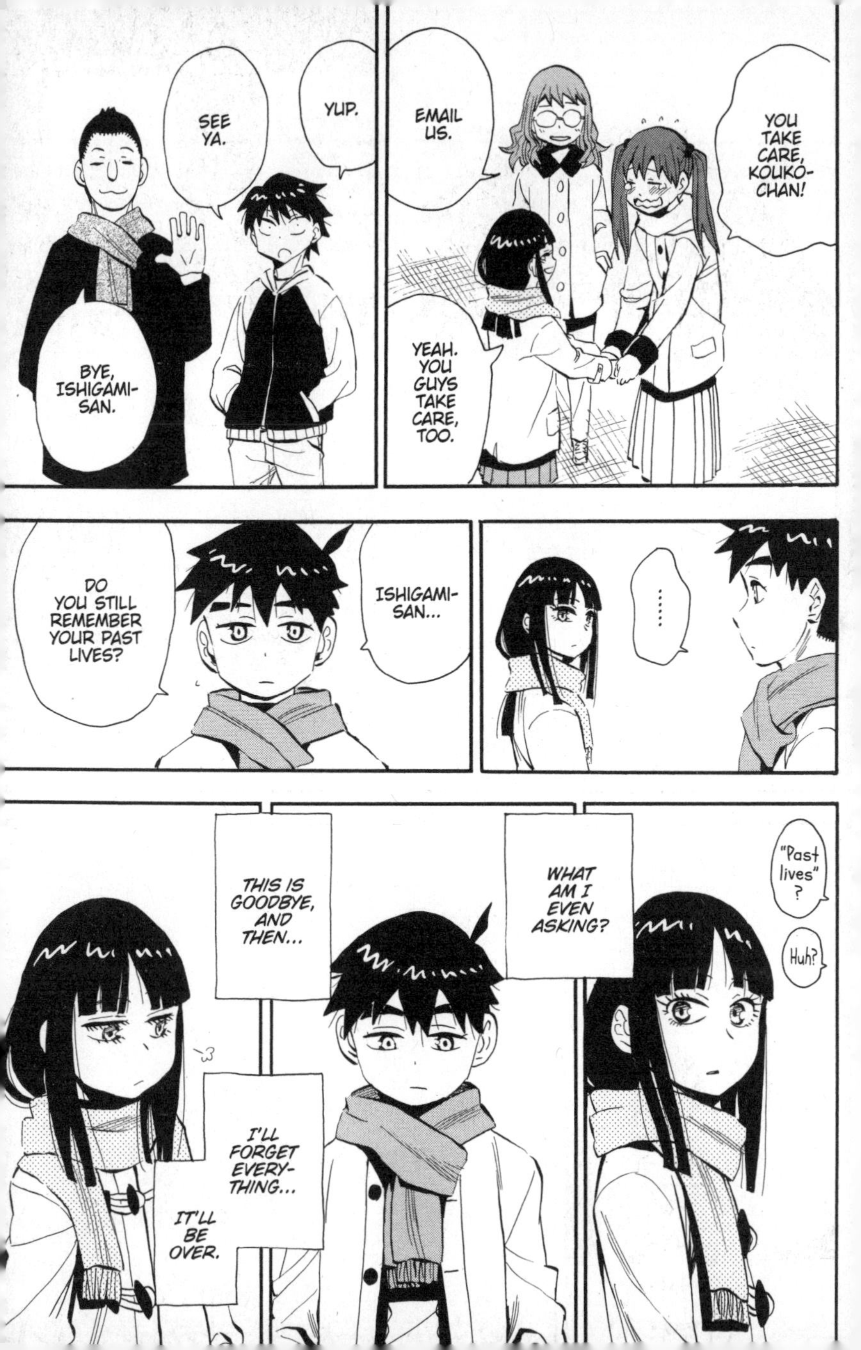
YOU TAKE CARE, KOUKO-CHAN!
EMAIL US.
YEAH. YOU GUYS TAKE CARE, TOO.
YUP.
SEE YA.
BYE, ISHIGAMI-SAN.
......
ISHIGAMI-SAN...
DO YOU STILL REMEMBER YOUR PAST LIVES?
"Past lives"?
Huh?
WHAT AM I EVEN ASKING?
THIS IS GOODBYE, AND THEN...
I'LL FORGET EVERYTHING...
IT'LL BE OVER.

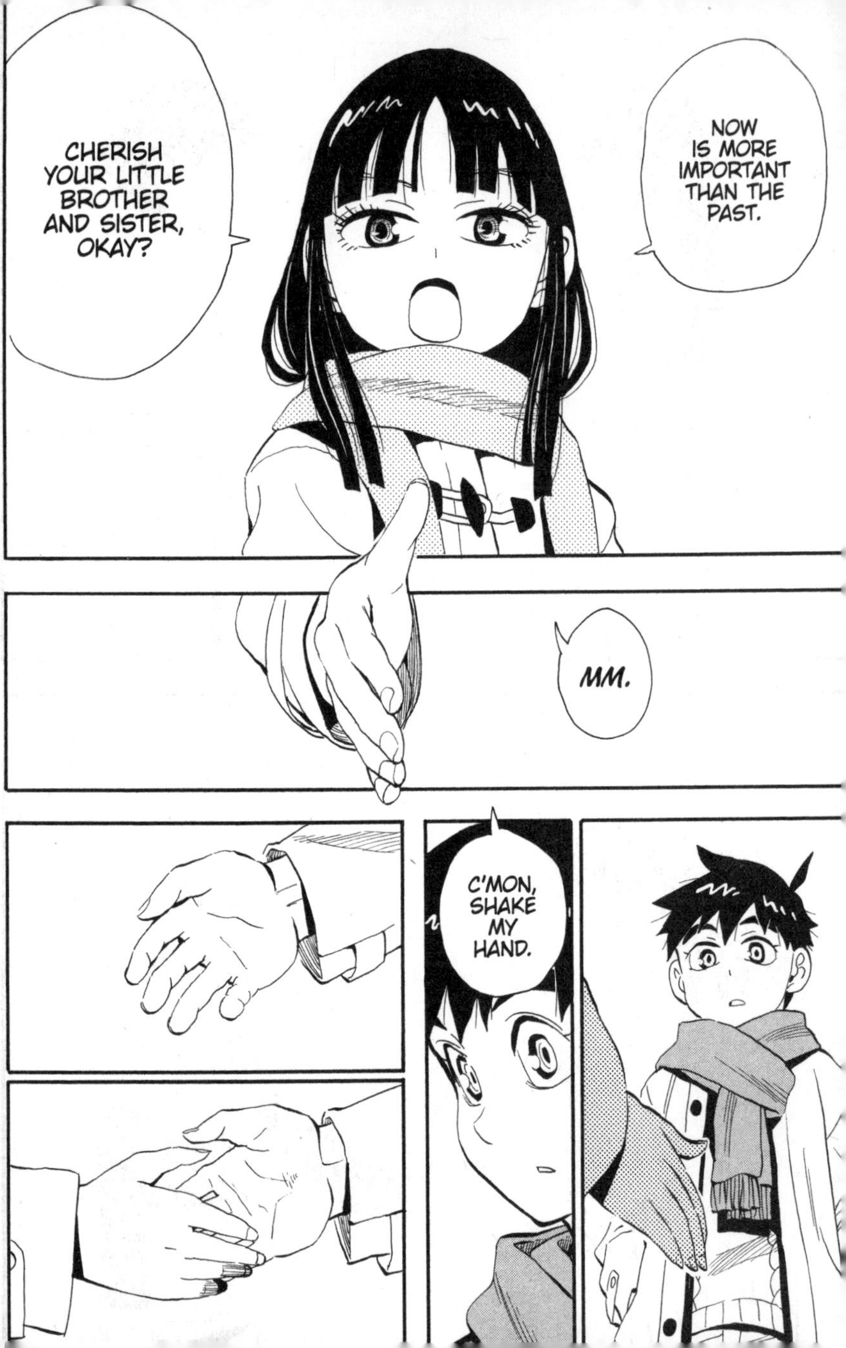
NOW IS MORE IMPORTANT THAN THE PAST.
CHERISH YOUR LITTLE BROTHER AND SISTER, OKAY?
MM.
C'MON, SHAKE MY HAND.

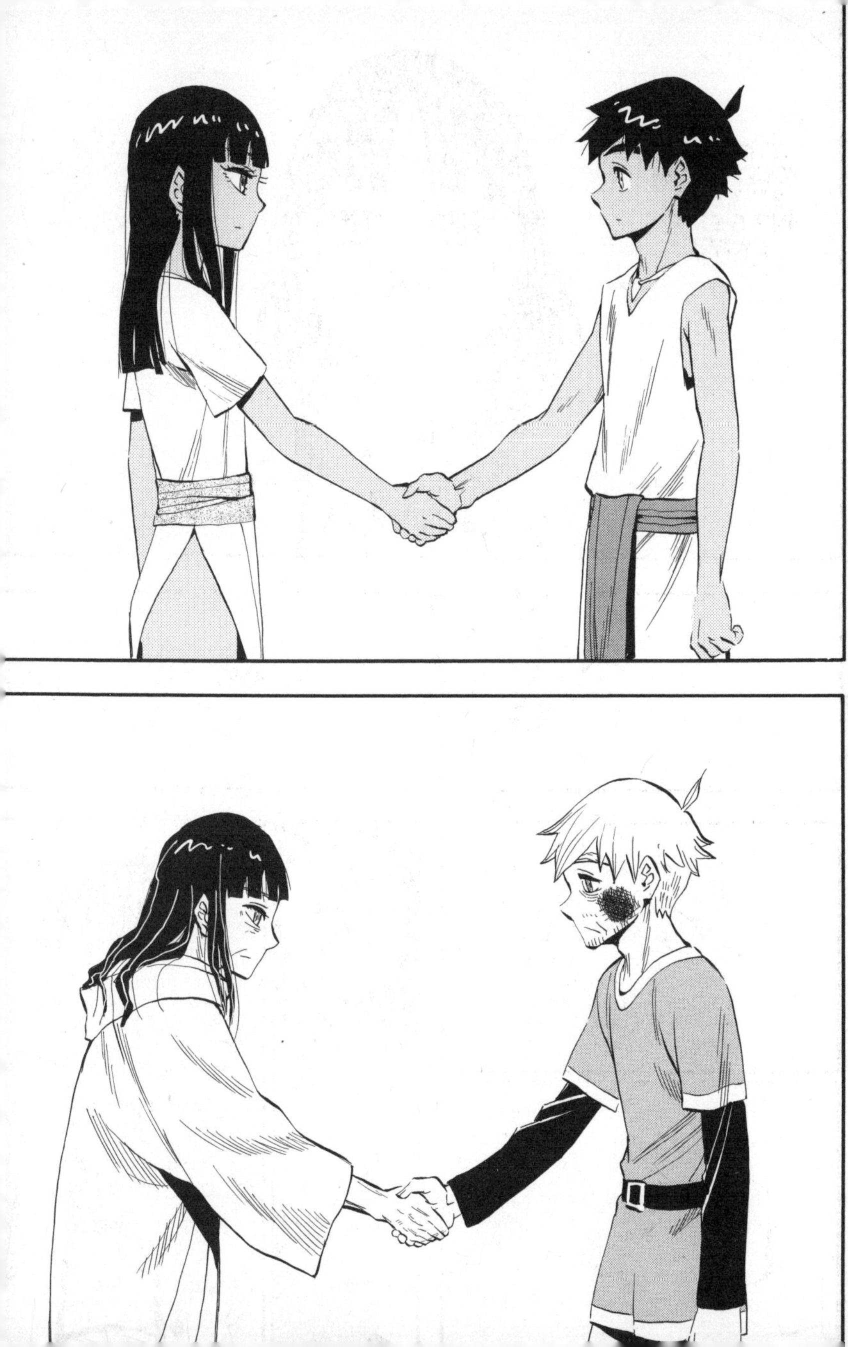

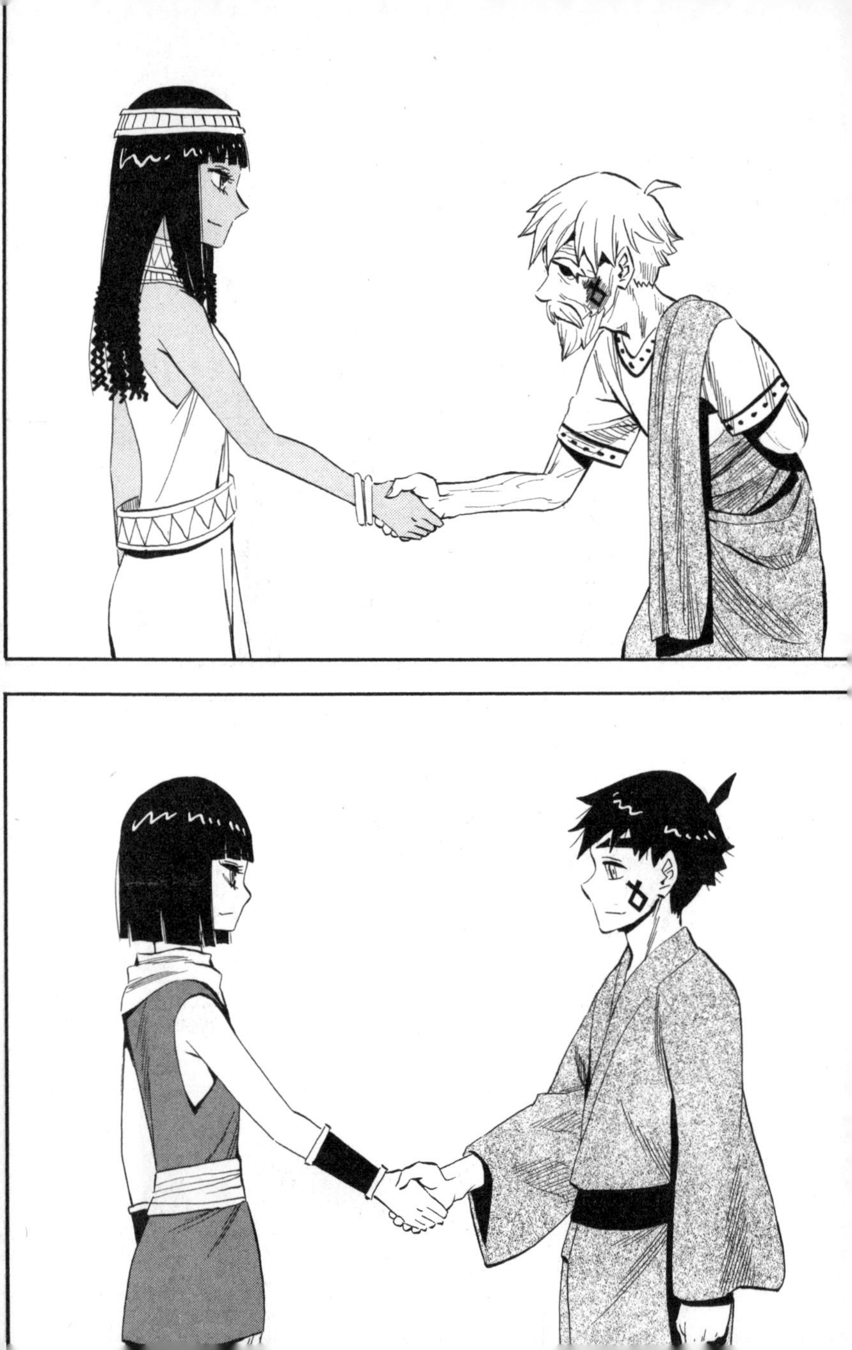

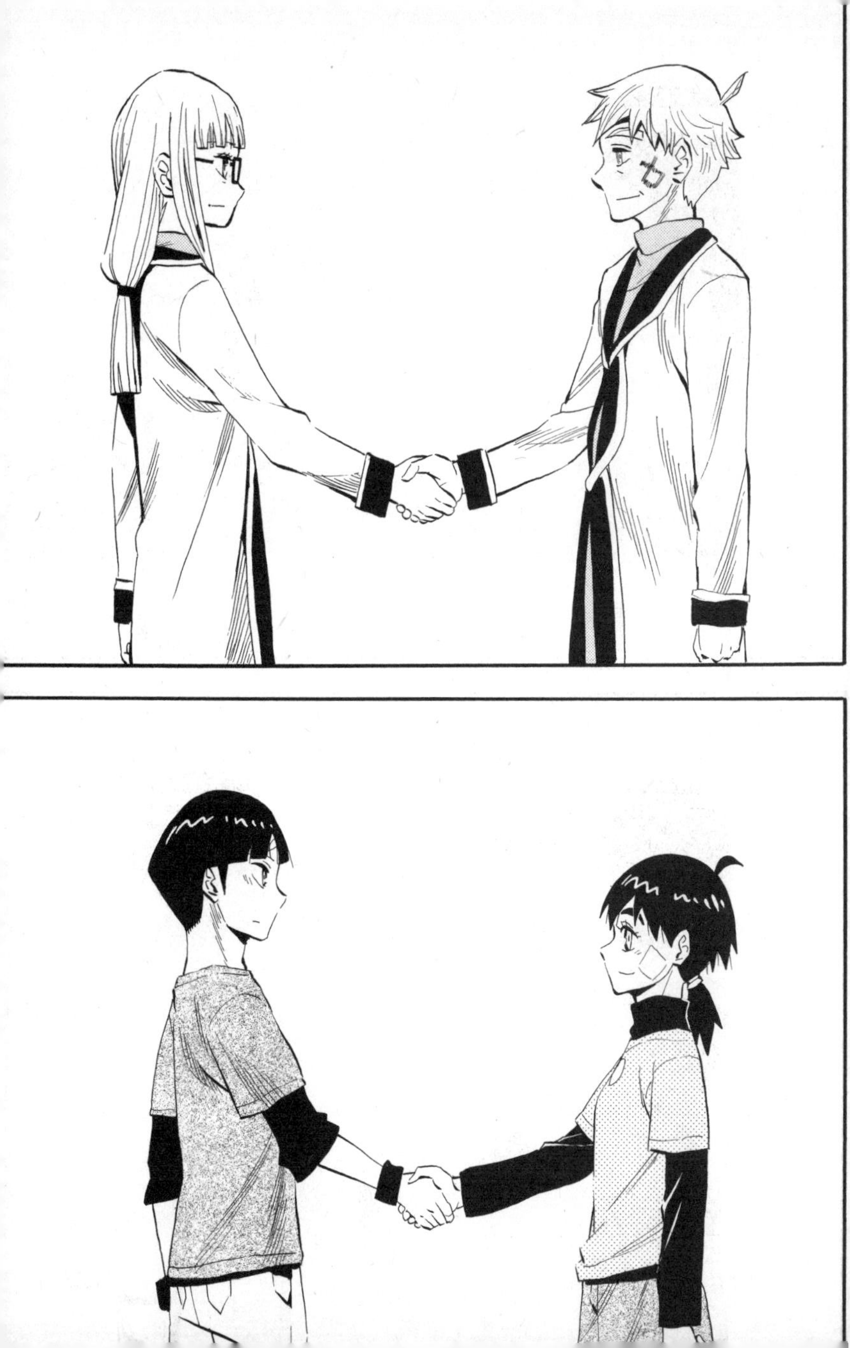

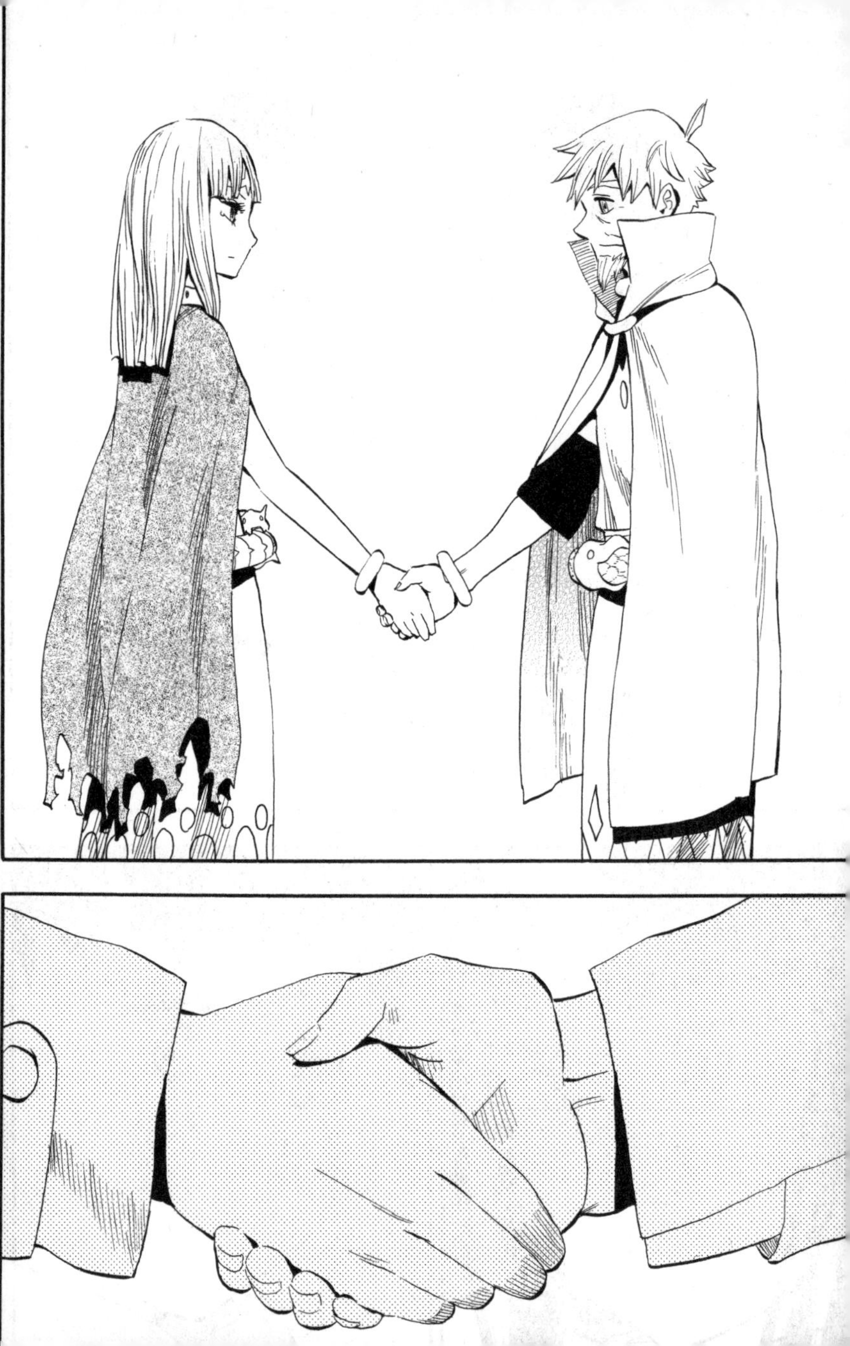

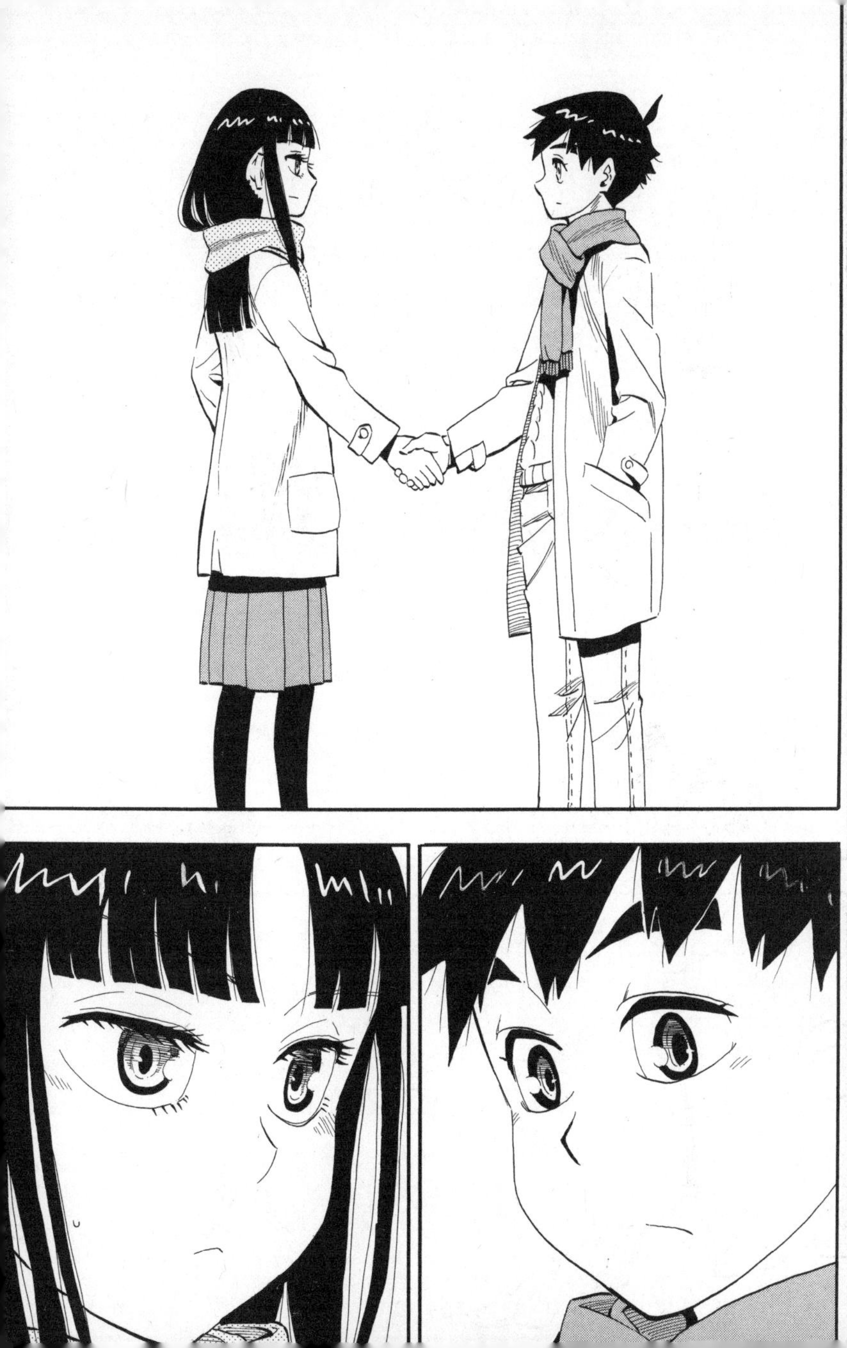

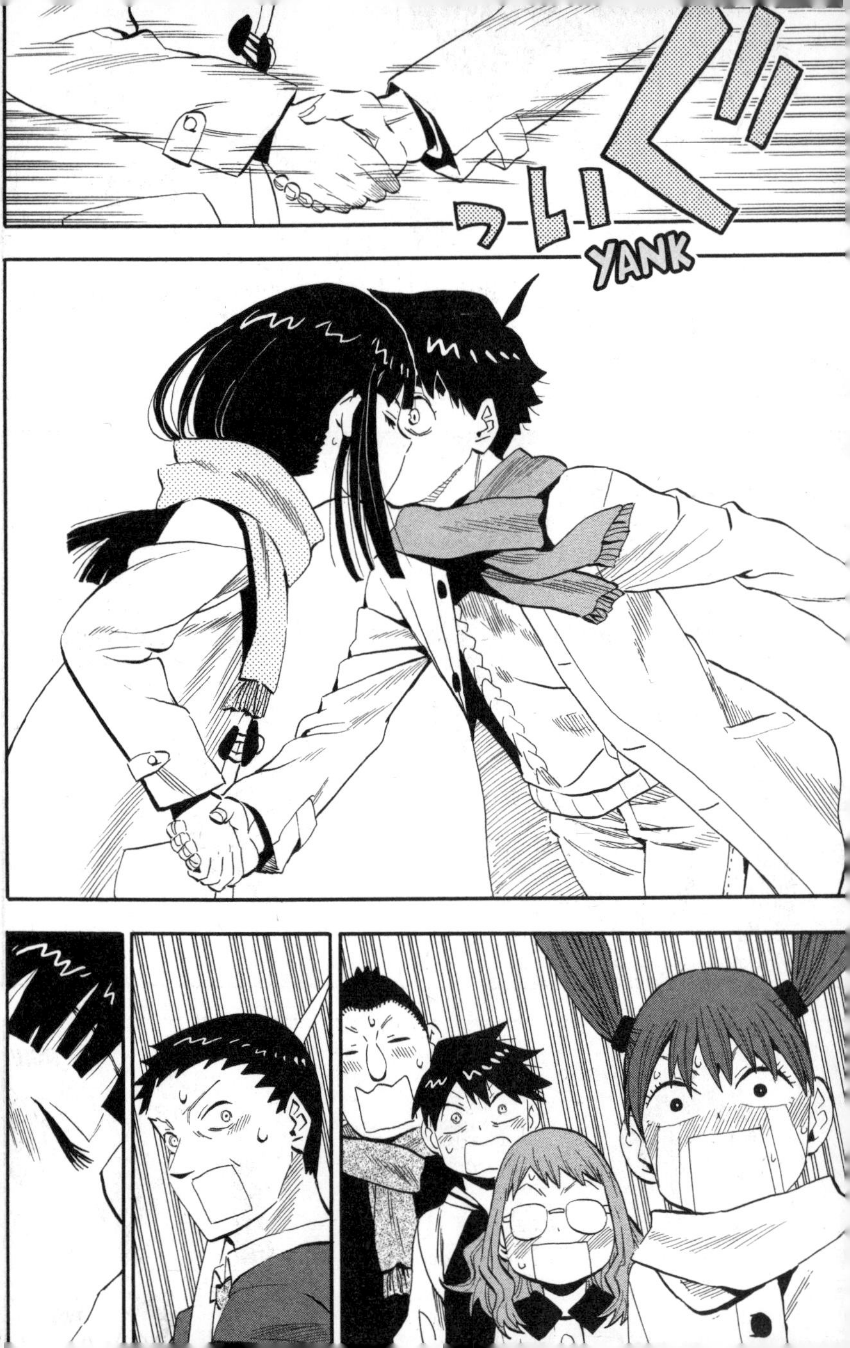
ぐいっ
YANK

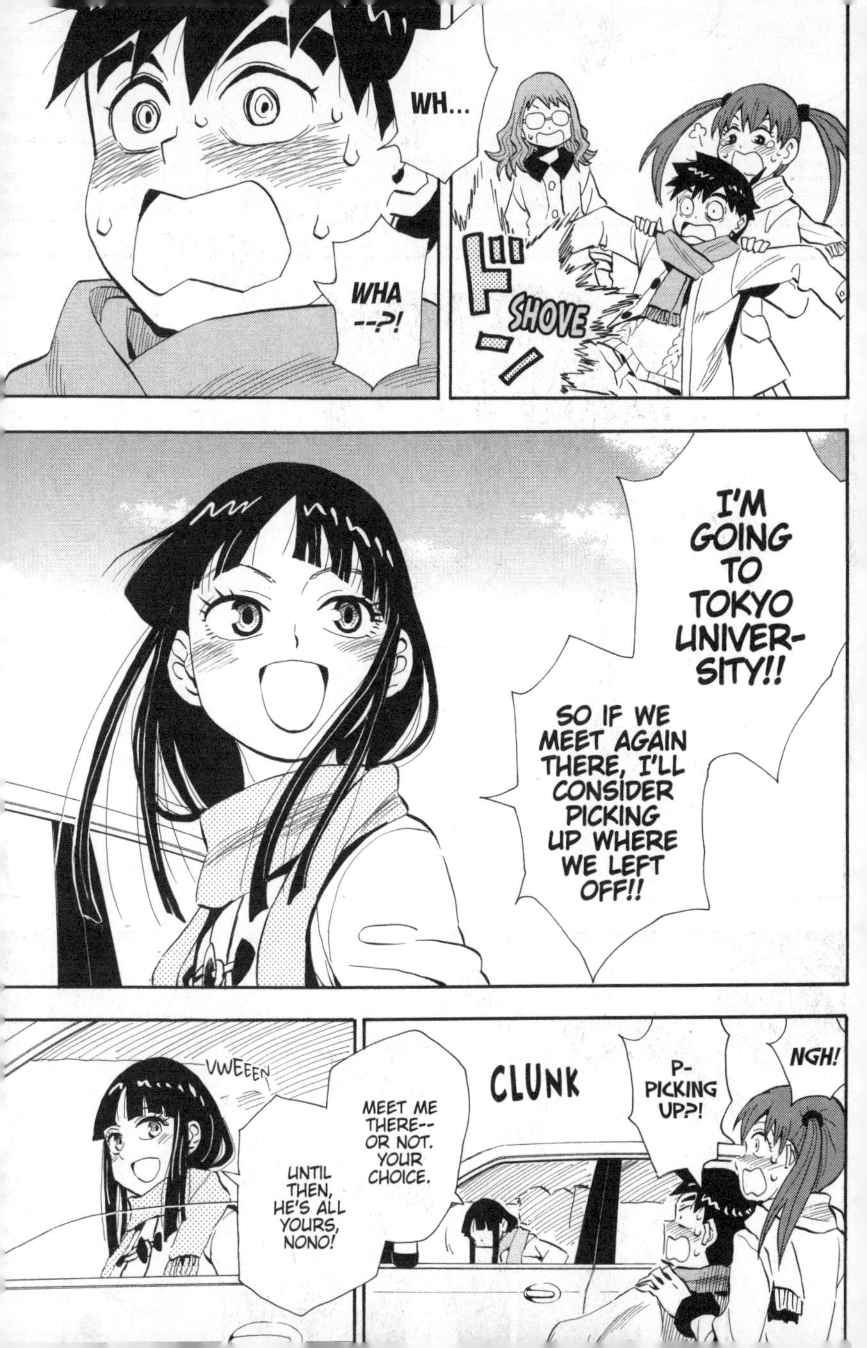
SHOVE
WH...
WHA --?!
I'M GOING TO TOKYO UNIVERSITY!!
SO IF WE MEET AGAIN THERE, I'LL CONSIDER PICKING UP WHERE WE LEFT OFF!!
NGH!
P-PICKING UP?!
CLUNK
MEET ME THERE-- OR NOT. YOUR CHOICE.
UNTIL THEN, HE'S ALL YOURS, NONO!
VWEEEN

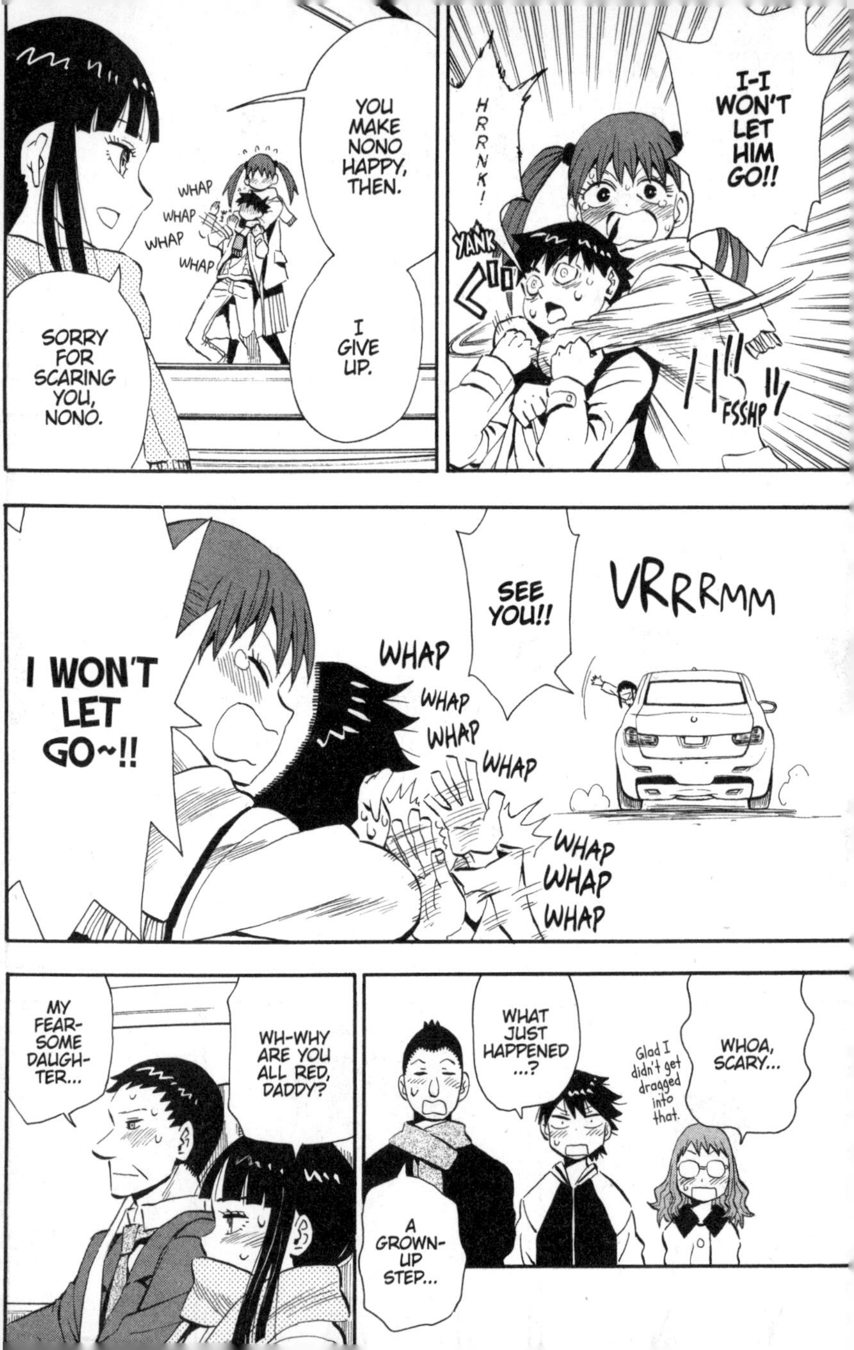
I-I WON'T LET HIM GO!!
HRRRNK!
YANK
FSSHP
YOU MAKE NONO HAPPY, THEN.
WHAP
WHAP
WHAP
WHAP
I GIVE UP.
SORRY FOR SCARING YOU, NONO.
VRRRMM
SEE YOU!!
WHAP
WHAP
WHAP
WHAP
I WON'T LET GO~!!
WHAP
WHAP
WHAP
WHOA, SCARY...
Glad I didn't get dragged into that.
WHAT JUST HAPPENED ...?
WH-WHY ARE YOU ALL RED, DADDY?
MY FEAR-SOME DAUGH-TER...
A GROWN-UP STEP...

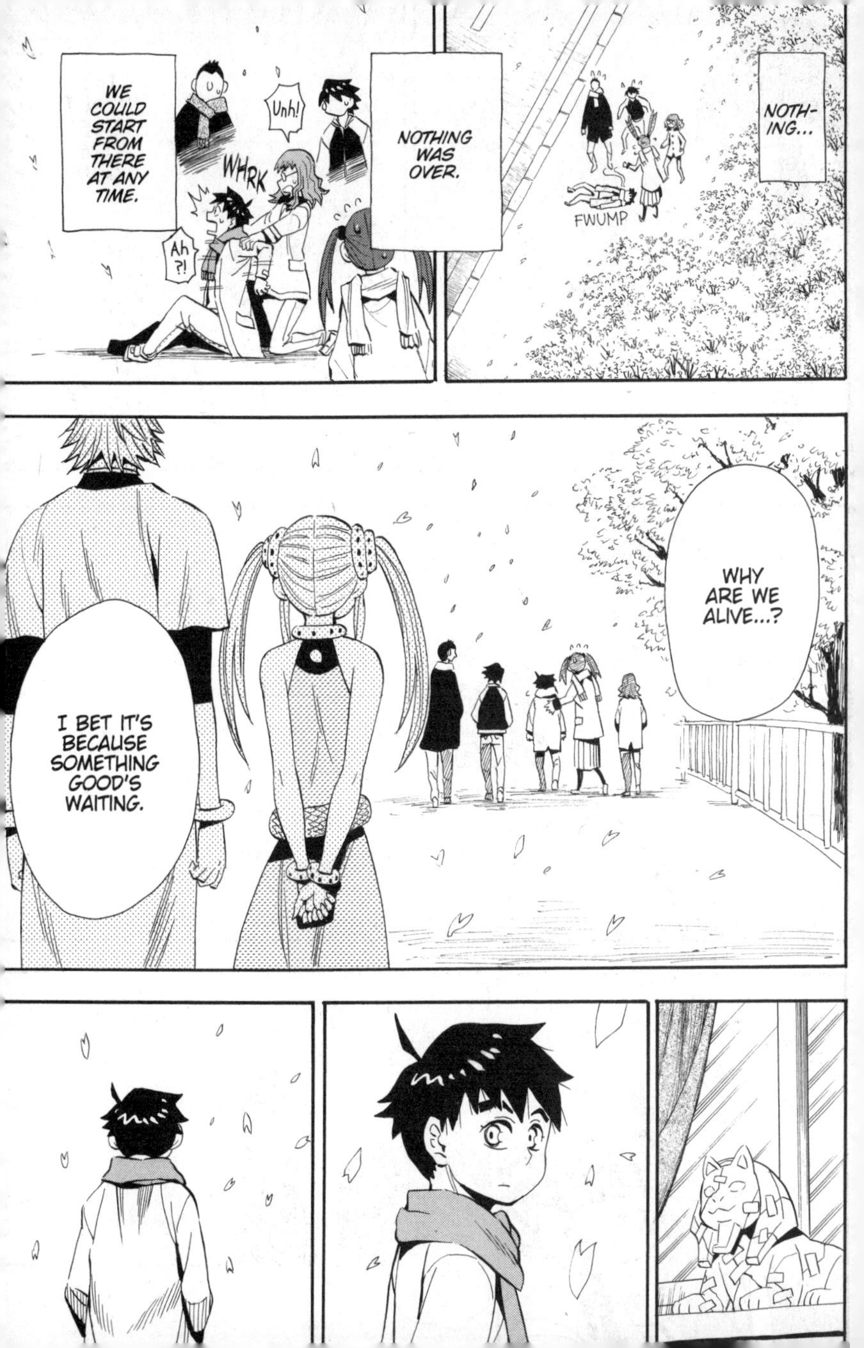
NOTHING...
FWUMP
NOTHING WAS OVER.
Unh!
WHRK
WE COULD START FROM THERE AT ANY TIME.
Ah?!
WHY ARE WE ALIVE...?
I BET IT'S BECAUSE SOMETHING GOOD'S WAITING.

Circle 45
Fuuta 1

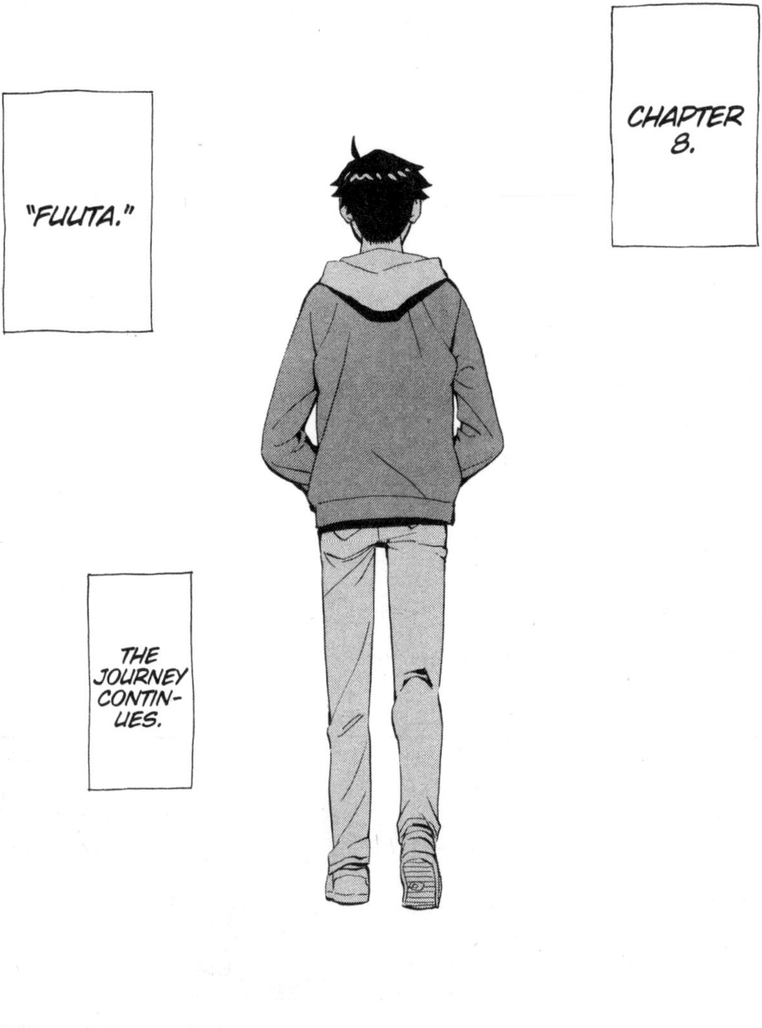
CHAPTER 8.
"FUUTA."
THE JOURNEY CONTIN-UES.

Circle 45/END

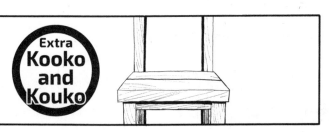

Extra Kooko and Kouko
IN THE COURSE OF A SPIRIT'S JOURNEY, A PERSON'S SEVEN LIVES...
ARE THE MOST FLEETING OF THINGS.

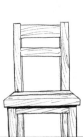

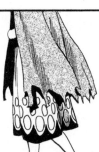

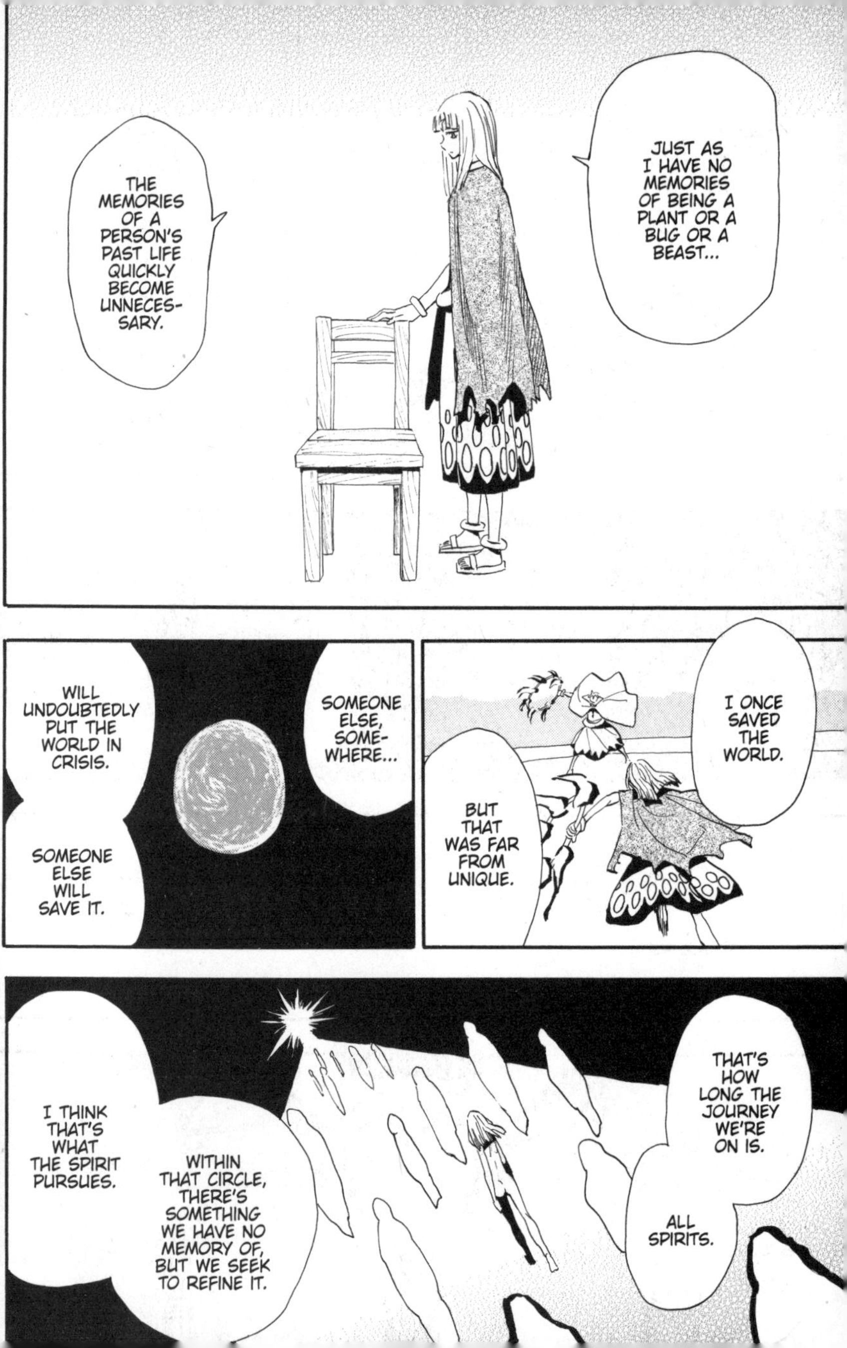
JUST AS I HAVE NO MEMORIES OF BEING A PLANT OR A BUG OR A BEAST...
THE MEMORIES OF A PERSON'S PAST LIFE QUICKLY BECOME UNNECES-SARY.
I ONCE SAVED THE WORLD.
BUT THAT WAS FAR FROM UNIQUE.
SOMEONE ELSE, SOME-WHERE...
WILL UNDOUBTEDLY PUT THE WORLD IN CRISIS.
SOMEONE ELSE WILL SAVE IT.
THAT'S HOW LONG THE JOURNEY WE'RE ON IS.
ALL SPIRITS.
WITHIN THAT CIRCLE, THERE'S SOMETHING WE HAVE NO MEMORY OF, BUT WE SEEK TO REFINE IT.
I THINK THAT'S WHAT THE SPIRIT PURSUES.

……
I LOVED HIM.
I ADMIRED HIM.
THAT'S WHY I COULDN'T FORGIVE HIM.
A SPIRIT THAT DOESN'T KNOW FORGIVENESS IS VENGEFUL.
VENGEANCE SNATCHES THE SPIRIT'S MOVEMENT FROM AN UPWARD SPIRAL...
AND CLOSES IT OFF IN A CIRCLE THAT GOES NOWHERE.
IT'S A FRIGHTENING POWER.
FORGIVENESS, THEN...
AFFIRMS THE STATE OF EVERYTHING.
A **RESCUING** POWER.
I BELIEVE THAT...
THIS POWER TO **FORGIVE** IS ONE PART OF THE THING...
SOUGHT BY THE SPIRIT.

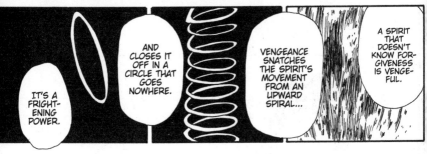

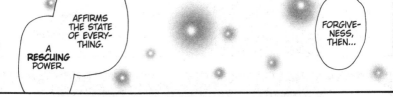

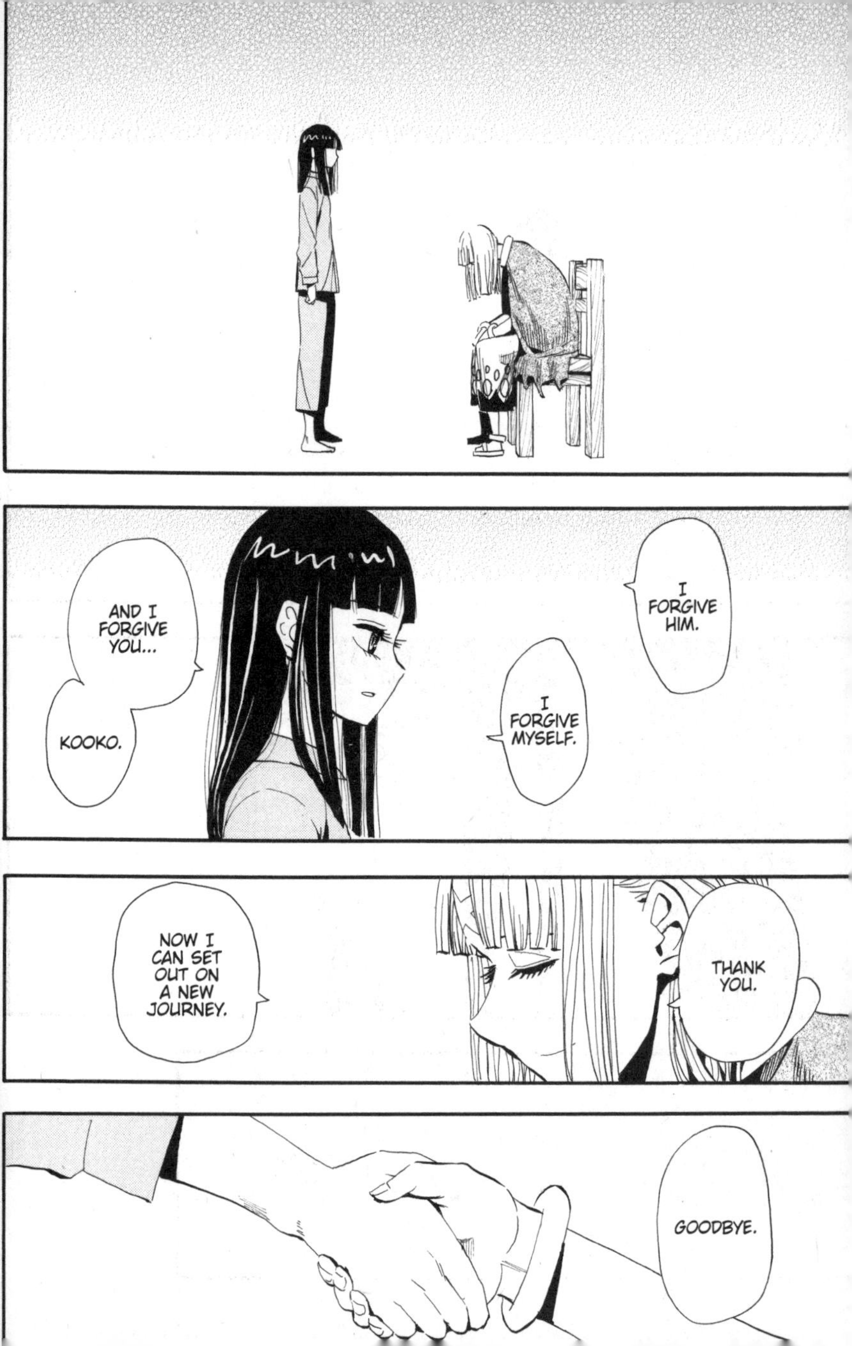
I FORGIVE HIM.
I FORGIVE MYSELF.
AND I FORGIVE YOU...
KOOKO.
THANK YOU.
NOW I CAN SET OUT ON A NEW JOURNEY.
GOODBYE.

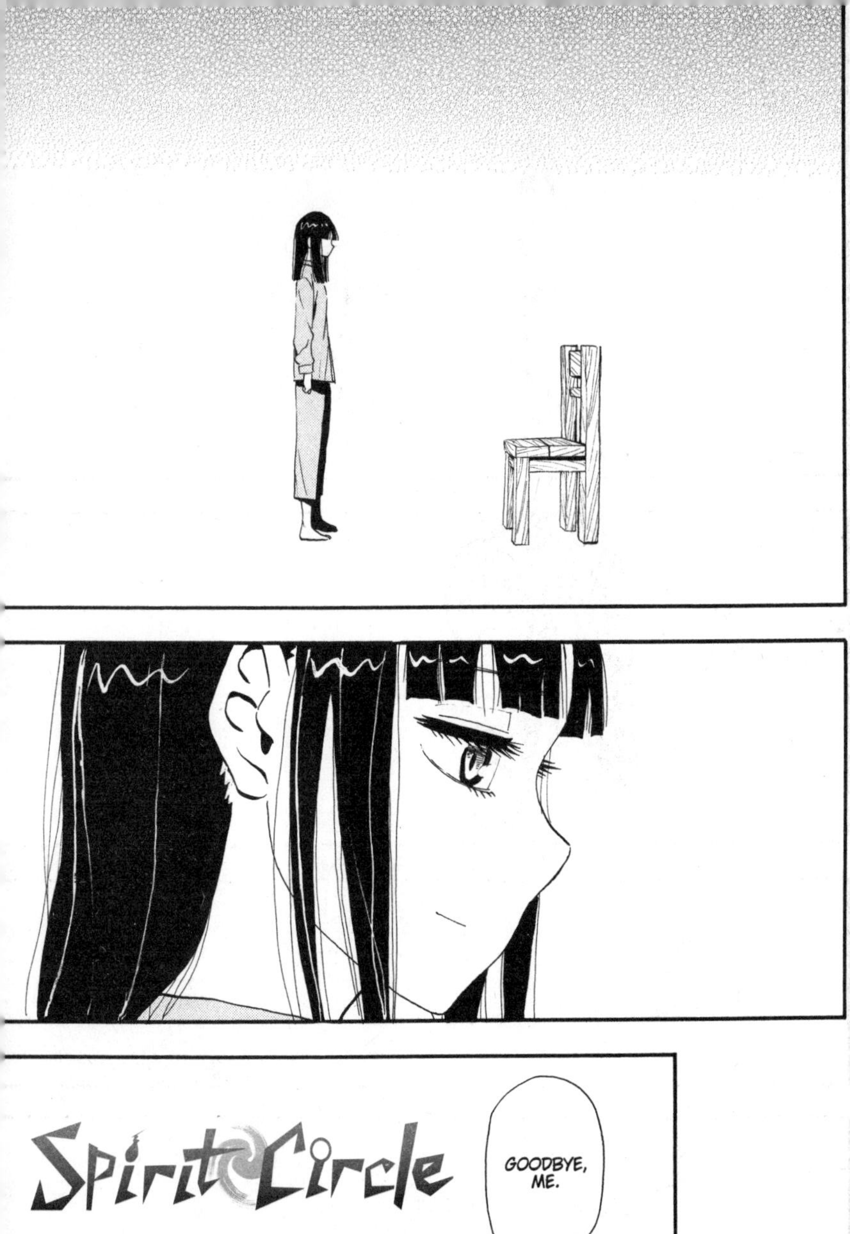
GOODBYE, ME.
Spirit Circle

The end!

Volume 6
End

Production staff
Jueru Choden
Hitoshi Usui
Akira Sagami

Title logo/Cover design
Eiichi Hagiwara (bigbody)

Supervising editor
Takehiro Sumi

AFTERWORD

Hello! This is Satoshi Mizukami. I think I may have crammed a little too much into this story, so it must have been tough to read all the way to the end. Thank you. Well done.

While I was writing my previous series, *Lucifer and the Biscuit Hammer,* I underwent something called "regressive hypnosis" out of curiosity. It's a type of hypnosis believed to draw out memories of early childhood and past lives.

What I saw was through the eyes of an old Greek man from BCE. He was the manager of a library. At one point, he realized someone was there, even though library hours were over, so he moved toward them to say something. Whoever it was quickly stood up, tripped over the desk, dropped a knife, and ran away. The old man picked up the knife and took it home. He told no one about this and kept quiet until his death.

This was all I saw. But when the hypnotist asked me about details, the answers came easily to my lips. The fact that his name was Sphinx--I couldn't remember his real name. I had an idea about who the man with the knife was. I thought it might have been his grandson. The fact that he'd gone to Egypt when he was younger and made a sphinx, and when he returned, he became famous in the area, but he himself always hated the way that work turned out. That no one around him had seen that awkward half-dog, half-cat face, so they were praising him for something he disliked. That it filled him with dissatisfaction. The fact that his son had felt pressured by his father's fame and constant scowl and left home. That the son had died in a construction accident in a distant town. That perhaps the grandson had held a grudge for this, thinking the old man had killed his father, and came to kill his own grandfather. The fact that right before the old man died, he thought it would really inconvenience his neighbors if his body wasn't found for some time.

That experience was what inspired the Flor chapter. All of *Spirit Circle* came about because I wanted to draw that.

The scene in the last chapter of *Spirit Circle*, where the past lives are shaking hands, is something I already had in my head when I was drawing *Lucifer.* This concept and the Flor chapter were the root of *Spirit Circle.*

I originally planned for it to be three or four volumes, but it just wouldn't come together. At best, I tried to narrow the focus to the story of Fuuta, the protagonist, and otherwise draw as little as I could. But my desires won out, and I wound up slowly drawing all the things that came to mind while I was working on the series. Next thing I knew, we were at Volume 6.

I was trying to avoid taking up too much space on your bookshelves. What do you think about it being six books? It's a bit of a bother, isn't it? If so, I apologize.

I let my guard down, and now this afterword is so long.

• At first, I was planning to just list the characters' lives, but I couldn't get the right structure for that. Right before the magazine serialization started, I thought up the characters Fuuta and Kouko, and the overall story structure finally clicked.

• Right up until the middle of the serialization, I couldn't decide on the precise details of Fortuna's life. My editor and I would rack our brains at meetings every month--"What exactly did this guy do?"

• I thought about all kinds of details for the Lafalle chapter (the chapter in the future), but I didn't get the chance to reveal them in the work. (Like the fact that there was no currency, and pretty much all work was done for the honor of it.)

• The reason I became so interested in spiritual matters was because of an article I saw while surfing adult sites, called "How to Deliberately Dream Dirty." That led me to lucid dreaming and out-of-body experiences.

I'd like to write about all of these and so many other things, but it doesn't look like it'll all fit into the space I have, so I'd like to finish here--especially since this is threatening to turn more into a list of excuses than an afterword.

Now then, I've read some arguments both for and against the final chapter. And while this may be tooting my own horn, I do like this manga that I've drawn. How about you? I'd be very glad if you enjoyed it.

If there are people out there who weren't satisfied and feel strongly that stories should be a certain way, please do create something of your own. Some people have gone pro like that--no, really! And when you create something you're satisfied with, I'd love to see it.

All right, everyone. Take care.

And scene.

April 4, 2016

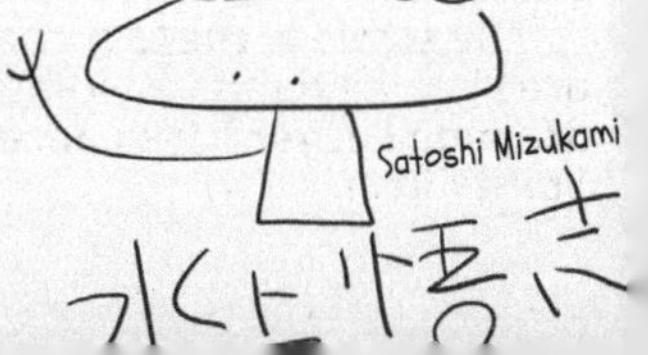
Satoshi Mizukami

Spirit Circle

SEVEN SEAS ENTERT

Spirit Circle VOL.6

story and art by SATOSHI MIZUKAMI

TRANSLATION
Jocelyne Allen

ADAPTATION
Ysabet Reinhardt MacFarlane

LETTERING AND LAYOUT
Lys Blakeslee
Rachel J. Pierce

COVER DESIGN
Nicky Lim

PROOFREADER
Shanti Whitesides
Danielle King

ASSISTANT EDITOR
J.P. Sullivan

PRODUCTION ASSISTANT
CK Russell

PRODUCTION MANAGER
Lissa Pattillo

EDITOR-IN-CHIEF
Adam Arnold

PUBLISHER
Jason DeAngelis

Originally published in Japan in 2016 by SHONENGAHOSHA Co., Ltd., Tokyo.
English translation rights arranged through TOHAN CORPORATION, Tokyo.

ISBN: 978-1-626929-86-9

Printed in Canada

First Printing: January 2019

10 9 8 7 6 5 4 3 2 1

FOLLOW US ONLINE: *www.sevenseasentertainment.com*

READIN

This book reads
If this is your fi
reading from the
take it from the
numbered diagram here. It may seem backwards at first, but you'll get the hang of it! Have fun!!

1
2
4
5
7
8
9

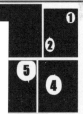

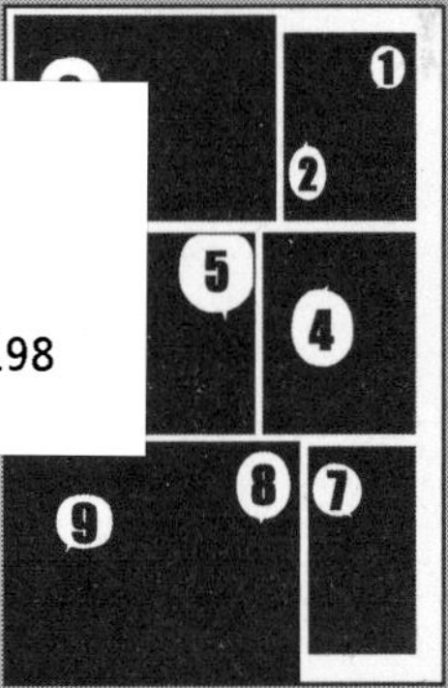